THE BOOK OF LORD SHANG

ABRIDGED EDITION

TRANSLATIONS FROM THE ASIAN CLASSICS

THE BOOK OF
LORD SHANG

Apologetics of State Power in Early China

ABRIDGED EDITION

SHANG YANG

EDITED AND TRANSLATED BY
YURI PINES

COLUMBIA UNIVERSITY PRESS
New York

Columbia University Press
Publishers Since 1893
New York   Chichester, West Sussex
cup.columbia.edu

Library of Congress Cataloging-in-Publication Data
Names: Shang, Yang, -338 B.C., author. | Pines, Yuri, editor, translator.
Title: The book of Lord Shang : apologetics of state power in early China / Shang
Yang ; edited and translated by Yuri Pines.
Other titles: Shang jun shu. English. Abridged
Description: Abridged edition. | New York : Columbia University Press, [2019] |
Series: Translations from the Asian classics | Includes bibliographical references
and index.
Identifiers: LCCN 2018041819 | ISBN 9780231179898 (pbk.)
Subjects: LCSH: Philosophy, Chinese—Early works to 1800. | Political science—
China—Early works to 1800. | China—Politics and government—To 221 B.C.—Early
works to 1800.
Classification: LCC B128.S472 E6 2019 | DDC 181/.115—dc23
LC record available at https://lccn.loc.gov/2018041819

Columbia University Press books are printed on permanent
and durable acid-free paper.
Printed in the United States of America

Cover design: Noah Arlow

CONTENTS

PREFACE TO THE ABRIDGED EDITION

This new edition of the *Book of Lord Shang* has two notable features. First, I abridged those sections that were too technical and could fit only a very few readers' interest. For instance, I have abridged the discussion that dealt with technicalities of ascertaining the dates of individual chapters. Readers who are interested in these details can consult my article in *Early China* that deals specifically with the dating of the *Book of Lord Shang* (Pines 2016a). I have also abridged many technical notes to the translation (e.g., "character X stands for character Y"), unless my choice had a major impact on the understanding of the text.

Second, this edition also underwent certain revisions and modifications. Most notably, I have improved the translation in several dozen places, in which colleagues had pointed at certain infelicities in the original translation. Moreover, I have slightly expanded the discussion of the text's reception during the Republican period (1912–1949), reflecting my new understanding of a few relevant points.

I hope that the resultant version will be both more easily accessible to the students and the general public.

Yuri Pines
December 2018

ACKNOWLEDGMENTS

I was attracted to the Book of Lord Shang right away when I encountered it (still in Russian translation) as an undergraduate student. I was fascinated back then by the book's forceful language, its originality, and its authors' blatant and provocative style, which makes reading it, in the words of A. C. Graham, a "refreshing" experience (1989, 292). Later, as a graduate student, I re-read the text (this time in Chinese) and was much impressed by the depth of some of its chapters, most notably chapter 7, "Opening the Blocked," which I consider one of the finest philosophical essays in early China. It was then that I noticed a surprising lack of interest in Shang Yang and his legacy among Western scholars and decided that sooner or later I would do my best to reintroduce this thinker to colleagues in Chinese studies and to those interested in comparative political thought. These aspirations are realized in the present book.

During the years in which I prepared this manuscript, I was given an opportunity to present my findings at a few scholarly conferences and publish them in journals and in collected volumes. I am indebted to all those colleagues, editors, and reviewers who contributed enormously to the maturation of the current manuscript. I am grateful to the journal *Early China*, which allowed incorporation in chapter 2 of the present book significant parts of my article on the dating of the *Book of Lord Shang*: "Dating a Pre-imperial Text: The Case Study of the *Book of Lord Shang*," *Early China* 39 (2016).

I am particularly indebted to colleagues and friends who read parts of the manuscript and made very useful comments, especially Paul R. Goldin, Martin Kern, Andrew Plaks, and Kai Vogelsang. Billy French painstakingly edited the penultimate version of my translation, greatly improving my English and pointing out some embarrassing inaccuracies, to which am deeply grateful. Special thanks to Ms. Amit Niv, who prepared the map on page x. Needless to say, any remaining mistakes and questionable interpretations in the final version are my sole responsibility.

In preparing this work, I was supported by the Israel Science Foundation (Grant 511/11) and by the Michael William Lipson Chair in Chinese Studies at the Hebrew University of Jerusalem. In preparing the paperback edition, I was able to revise not a few inaccuracies and infelicities in my earlier translation. I am grateful to the colleagues who helped me to improve the translation of selected passages, specifically Paul Goldin, Christoph Harbsmeier, Li Wai-yee, and Kai Vogelsang.

Last but not least: my deep thanks go to Wang Yu 王宇, who tolerated my years-long engagement with the *Book of Lord Shang*!

THE BOOK OF LORD SHANG

ABRIDGED EDITION

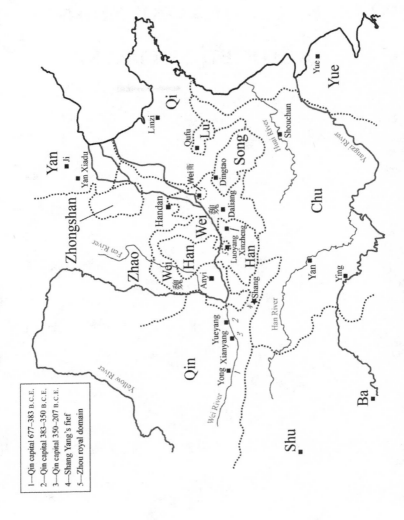

THE WARRING STATES WORLD AROUND 350 B.C.E.

1—Qin capital 677–383 B.C.E.
2—Qin capital 383–350 B.C.E.
3—Qin capital 350–207 B.C.E.
4—Shang Yang's fief
5—Zhou royal domain

Yan

Ji ■

Yan Xiadu ■

Zhongshan

Zhao

Fen River

Handan ■

Wei 魏

Wei 魏

Anyi ■

Han 韓

Qin

Yueyang ■
Yong ■ Xianyang
Wei River

Shu ■

Yellow River

Qi

Linzi ■

Qufu ■
Lu
Wei 衛 ■

Song

Dingtao ■

Daliang ■

Luoyang / Xinzheng

Han

Shang ■

Han River

Yan ■

Ba ■

Ying ■

Chu

Shouchun ■

Huai River

Yangzi River

Yue ■
Yue

PART I

INTRODUCTION

The *Book of Lord Shang* (*Shangjunshu* 商君書) is one of the most important—and least studied—texts of the formative age of Chinese philosophy and political culture, the so-called age of the Hundred Schools of Thought (fifth–third centuries B.C.E.). The book's importance is threefold. First, it is one of the foundational texts of early Chinese political thought, a rich repository of bold and novel—even if highly controversial—ideas about state-society relations, historical evolution, human nature, and the like. It is also the earliest surviving treatise of a major intellectual current of that age, the so-called Legalist School (*fa jia* 法家).[1] Second, this book is attributed to Shang Yang 商鞅 (a.k.a. Gongsun Yang 公孫鞅 or Lord of Shang 商君, d. 338 B.C.E.),[2] the singularly successful political practitioner whose reforms propelled the state of Qin 秦 to supremacy in the world of the Warring States (Zhanguo 戰國, 453–221 B.C.E.). Even though this attribution is not entirely correct because portions of the book were composed long after Shang Yang's death, the *Book of Lord Shang* remains a major testament to the ideas of Qin reformers, the architects of the future Qin Empire (221–207 B.C.E.). Third, the book's vision of empowering the state by establishing total control over its material and human resources had a lasting impact on Chinese statesmen. As the earliest work to advocate the policy of "enriching the state and strengthening the army" (*fuguo qiangbing* 富國強兵), the *Book of Lord Shang* became—despite its notoriety in the eyes of the majority of imperial literati—an important text for supporters of the state's socioeconomic and military activism throughout China's long imperial history and well into the twentieth century.

Its importance notwithstanding, the *Book of Lord Shang* remains largely outside the focus of Western Sinology. Although Shang Yang's ideas are duly discussed in most introductory-level studies,[3] in-depth analyses of the *Book of Lord Shang* are woefully lacking. The translation that Jan J. L. Duyvendak published in 1928—one of the finest Sinological productions of that time but now much outdated—remains the single English monograph dedicated to the *Book of Lord Shang* (see Duyvendak [1928] 1963). It is joined by two volumes of translated Chinese articles, and a few articles by Western scholars, yet their overall number is minuscule.[4] The situation in other major European languages is quite similar, the major exception being a brief period of interest in the *Book of Lord Shang* by Soviet Sinologists in the 1960s and 1970s.[5] As a result, recent advances in studies of the text in China and to a lesser extent in Japan have passed largely unnoticed in the West.

There are several reasons for the lack of scholarly interest in the *Book of Lord Shang*. Some are technical: the text's bad state of preservation—for example, numerous instances of textual corruption and occasional lacunae—as well as the paucity of good commentaries hinder in-depth study of its content. Ongoing doubts about the text's dating and authenticity further discourage scholars from systematically addressing its ideas. To these problems—which many other Warring States period texts share—one should add peculiar reasons for dislike of the *Book of Lord Shang* in particular. Some scholars consider it too oriented toward the practical and lacking sufficient philosophical sophistication;[6] others may be discouraged by the excessive—and somewhat grotesque—politicization of the figure of Shang Yang during the infamous anti-Confucian campaign of 1973–1975 (see chapter 4, part I); and yet others probably share the imperial literati's distaste for a text that gained notoriety because of its blatant assault on traditional culture and moral values. To a certain extent, Su Shi's 蘇軾 (1036–1101) millennium-old statement that "from the Han 漢 [206/202 B.C.E.–220 C.E.] onward, scholars have been ashamed to speak about Shang Yang,"[7] may reflect the attitudes of not just many traditional but also many modern scholars.

Yet now technical problems can no longer justify the neglect of the *Book of Lord Shang*. In recent decades, scholarly understanding of the text in China and to a lesser extent in Japan has advanced tremendously. Textual studies have culminated with a new critical edition by Zhang Jue (2012), which greatly facilitates scholarly engagement with the *Book of Lord Shang*; other major studies (most notably by Zheng Liangshu [1989] and Yoshinami Takashi [1992]) have brought about a much more sophisticated understanding of the text's dating and composition. In addition, a series of recent remarkable paleographic discoveries allow us to contextualize the *Book of Lord Shang* in the actual socioeconomic policies of the state of Qin, bringing about a qualitative leap in our understanding of the text's ideas (see, e.g., Tong Weimin 2013). Facing fewer technical obstacles than our predecessors, we can also liberate ourselves from the shackles of political expediency, which dominated studies of this text in the twentieth century. It is time to engage the *Book of Lord Shang* not as a foil in ideological debates pro or contra modern totalitarian or statist ideologies, but as an important monument of political thought of the Warring States period, a text that contributed considerably toward the formation of the Chinese Empire, a precious repository of insightful and innovative—even if highly controversial and at times fairly alienating—ideas. Only having understood the text on its own terms and within contemporaneous political and ideological contexts can we ask which—if any—of its ideas are relevant to our times.

My edition consists of two parts. Part I, dedicated to the study of the text, is divided into four chapters. In the first chapter, I introduce the career of the putative author of the *Book of Lord Shang*, Shang Yang, and the background of the book's formation. In the second (slightly abridged for the paperback edition), I deal with the book's textual history, composition, and dating of individual chapters. The third chapter discusses the book's major ideas, and the fourth deals with the history of its reception in imperial and modern China. In part II, I present an annotated translation of the text, including a brief introduction to each individual chapter. I hope that my study will contribute to renewed interest in the *Book of Lord Shang* among both Sinologists and scholars of political philosophy in other cultures and regions.

1

SHANG YANG AND HIS TIMES

S hang Yang, the alleged author of the *Book of Lord Shang*, is arguably the most famous and most influential statesman of the Warring States period. His biography is narrated in chapter 68 of *Records of the Historian* (*Shiji* 史記) by Sima Qian 司馬遷 (ca. 145–ca. 90 B.C.E.); other chapters provide additional details about Shang Yang's career. The biography itself is not entirely reliable: it contains many literary embellishments and the admixture of later legends; many of the stories told by Sima Qian (or by the authors of his primary sources) should be read *cum grano salis* (Yoshimoto 2000). Nonetheless, the biography is not pure fiction, either; some paleographic discoveries actually corroborate a few of its details. It can therefore be conveniently utilized to reconstruct the factual skeleton of Shang Yang's career.

AN ASPIRING OFFICIAL

Shang Yang (originally named Gongsun Yang 公孫鞅) was a scion of the ruling house of the tiny statelet of Wei 衛 located to the south of the Yellow River in today's Henan Province (hence, his occasional appellation as Wei Yang 衛鞅, or Yang of Wei). Once an important medium-size polity, his home country had deteriorated to a position of utter insignificance by the time of his birth, so that even aristocratic pedigree could not ensure him a decent career. Having realized this, Gongsun Yang departed to the neighboring state of Wei 魏 (hereafter "Wei" refers only to this larger polity unless otherwise indicated). This was a clever choice. At this time (ca. 360s B.C.E.), Wei was approaching the apex of its power. Its ruling house descended from a ministerial lineage in the state of Jin 晉, the major superpower of the preceding Springs-and-Autumns period (Chunqiu 春秋, 770–453 B.C.E.). By the middle fifth century B.C.E., the heads of the Wei lineage had become de facto (and in 403 B.C.E. de jure) independent of their mother polity. Having partitioned Jin with two other ministerial lineages—Zhao 趙 and Han 韓 (not to be confused with the later Han 漢 dynasty)—the Wei leaders positioned themselves as the true heirs to the glory of Jin and acted as the major hegemonic power in the Chinese world.

The state of Wei was an appropriate destination for an aspiring man-of-service not only because it was powerful but also because it was the most amenable to foreign advisers. Back in the times of the founding father of an independent Wei polity, Lord Wen 魏文侯 (r. 446–396 B.C.E.), Wei adopted a novel policy of welcoming experts in administrative and military affairs from whatever social background and from whatever country of origin. Soon enough, Lord Wen could boast of a stellar team of advisers. Most notable of them were Confucius's major disciple Zixia 子夏 (507–? B.C.E.), the skilled strategist Wu Qi 吳起 (d. 381 B.C.E.), and an important reformer, Li Kui 李悝 (fl. ca. 400 B.C.E.), who is often viewed as Shang Yang's precursor. These men strengthened the state of Wei and bolstered the prestige of their patron, Lord Wen, who was, after all, a usurper *strictu senso*. After Lord Wen's death, the policy of employing skillful individuals of heterogeneous backgrounds continued, gradually becoming the rule not just in the state of Wei but throughout the Chinese *oikouménē*.

If we believe an anecdote told in the *Stratagems of the Warring States* (*Zhanguo ce* 戰國策) and retold by Sima Qian, Gongsun Yang started his career in Wei as a retainer of the prime minister, Gongshu Cuo 公叔痤. On his deathbed, Gongshu Cuo asked his ruler, Lord Hui (later King Hui of Wei 魏惠王, r. 369–319 B.C.E.) either to appoint Yang prime minister or to execute him so that he would not serve a foreign country. Lord Hui did not heed either suggestion, which gave Yang the chance to respond to a job offer issued by the newly ascended Lord Xiao of Qin 秦孝公 (r. 361–338 B.C.E.). Gongsun Yang's westward relocation to Qin changed his own fate as well as that of Qin and the entire Chinese world.

The state of Qin, to which Shang Yang headed, was a less-enviable employer than Wei. Once a great power, this state had declined in the fifth century B.C.E. because of internecine conflicts between the rulers and powerful ministers. By the early fourth century B.C.E., Qin was reduced to a marginal polity with little influence on the interstate dynamics of that age. The country's resurrection started under Lord Xiao's father, Lord Xian 秦獻公 (r. 384–362 B.C.E.), who initiated reforms aimed at restoring centralized power and reinvigorating the military. Yet it was under Lord Xiao that these reforms truly matured. Upon his ascendancy, Lord Xiao issued an edict in which he emphasized the desire to restore the erstwhile glory of his ancestors and to end the age of humiliation by foreign powers; he invited foreign advisers to come and propose ways of strengthening the state and promised to award them fiefs (*Shiji* 5:202). Shang Yang was among those who responded to this call, and he was to satisfy his employer completely.

THE WORLD OF THE WARRING STATES

Before we continue with Shang Yang's career, it is time to pause and ask what challenges—and opportunities—necessitated reforms in Wei, Qin, and other contemporaneous polities. In the early fourth century B.C.E., the Chinese world stood at a crossroads. On the one hand, it faced a severe crisis that threatened the very foundations of the sociopolitical order; on the other hand, this age also offered unprecedented opportunities for innovative statesmen and thinkers. Among a variety of recipes for curing political and social ills, those offered by Shang Yang proved by far the most effective, albeit highly questionable in moral terms.

The crisis that engulfed the Chinese world from the second quarter of the first millennium B.C.E. can be defined as a progressive devolution of state power. The first to lose their authority were the nominal rulers of "All-under-Heaven" (*tianxia* 天下), the kings of the Zhou 周 dynasty (1046–256 B.C.E.). Back at the beginning of their rule, the Zhou "Sons of Heaven" (*tianzi* 天子) enfeoffed relatives and allies in strategic locations throughout their realm (Li Feng 2006). The kings initially exercised authority over the fiefs, but these fiefs gradually turned into highly autonomous entities. By the eighth century B.C.E., as the Zhou dynasty was badly battered by domestic and foreign foes, the former fiefs became independent states de facto. These states waged wars, formed alliances, annexed weaker neighbors, and paid little if any attention to the kings' nominal superiority. On the ruins of the Zhou dynastic realm, a new multistate system arose, and stabilizing this system in the absence of the effective authority of the Sons of Heaven became an arduous task.

Throughout much of the Springs-and-Autumns period, efforts were made to find a viable modus operandi for the multistate order. Initial attempts at stabilization focused on the idea of hegemony: a powerful state was expected to act under the aegis of the Son of Heaven and impose its will on smaller polities. By the late seventh century B.C.E., unilateral hegemony had failed and was replaced by competing alliances led in the north by the state of Jin 晉, the nominal protector of the house of Zhou, and in the south by the rising power of Chu 楚. At first, the two alliance leaders tried to achieve stability for their allies, yet their efforts were undermined by intense interalliance competition. A few statesmen's last-ditch attempts to attain peace in All-under-Heaven through the grand disarmament conferences of 546 and 541 B.C.E. failed miserably as well. By the late sixth century B.C.E., the simultaneous weakening of Jin and Chu and the subsequent rise of peripheral powers, especially the southeastern "semibarbarian" polities of Wu 吳 and Yue 越, marked the final collapse of efforts to salvage a viable multistate order. A centuries-long "war of all against all" ensued, eventually giving the period under discussion its ominous name: the age of the Warring States.[1]

Parallel to the disintegration of the Zhou realm, similar processes of weakening of the ruler's authority occurred in most of the regional states that comprised the Zhou *oikouménē*. By the late seventh century

B.C.E., it was the turn of regional lords to be challenged by their under-lings, heads of powerful ministerial lineages. These lineages monopo-lized top positions in the state hierarchy, turning them into their hereditary holdings. Parallel to this shift, they also appropriated land allotments, which had formerly been granted to ministers in exchange for service, and turned them into ministates in their own right under the lineage's control. The allotments' masters maintained independent administration, were in full possession of the material and human resources of the allotment, and even conducted independent military and diplomatic activities, expanding the territory of the allotment at the expense of weaker neighbors. The lords of the state continued to enjoy ritual prestige, but in terms of political, economic, and military power they were completely eclipsed by their ministers.[2]

The lack of effective authority within individual states brought about woeful turmoil. Through the sixth and fifth centuries B.C.E., dozens of regional lords were assassinated, expelled, or otherwise humiliated by their underlings; others survived only by skillfully exploiting conflicts among the ministers. Most states eventually became entangled in debilitating struggles between the lords and powerful aristocrats, among major ministerial lineages, and often among rival branches within these lineages. These struggles in turn caused repeated foreign intervention, blurring the differences between internal and external affairs and sweeping away the remnants of sociopolitical stability.

The crisis of the regional states reached its nadir in 453 B.C.E. (de jure in 403 B.C.E.), when the state of Jin—once the leading superpower—was partitioned among the three ministerial lineages of Wei, Han, and Zhao. In Qi 齊, another powerful polity, the trajectory was different: a single powerful ministerial lineage, the Chen 陳 (Tian 田), elimi-nated its rivals, usurped power, and in 386 B.C.E. replaced the seven-century-old ruling lineage, appropriating thereby the state of Qi. Other states, such as Qin and Chu, avoided ministerial usurpations but suffered repeated outbreaks of domestic turmoil. Stemming the forces of disintegration became the singularly important dictum for states-men of the age.

As it happened, the events of the fifth century B.C.E. marked a shift toward the regeneration of centralized authority. Having usurped power in their domains, the leaders of the Wei, Han, and Zhao lineages in Jin as well as the heads of the Chen lineage in Qi were determined to prevent renewed fragmentation. They instituted a series of reforms aimed at limiting ministerial power. Hereditary officeholding and the adjacent system of hereditary land allotments, the hallmarks of the aristocratic age, were discontinued and replaced with a system of flexible appointments and salaries paid primarily in grain and precious metals. Henceforth, even when allotments were granted (which in itself became a rarity), the recipient was expected to benefit economically but not to rule the allotment as an independent stronghold. More consequentially, the pool of potential candidates for officeholding increased dramatically. In marked departure from the practices of the aristocratic age, persons of relatively humble origin, members of the so-called *shi* 士 stratum, were now eligible for the highest positions of authority. The rise of *shi* marked the end of the aristocratic age and the beginning of a new era in Chinese history.[3]

Shi originally were the lowest segment of the hereditary aristocracy: minor siblings of aristocratic families, whose birthright did not entitle them to occupy high offices. Most made their living as stewards and retainers of noble lineages: specialists in ritual, military, or administrative matters. *Shi* were the major beneficiaries of the internecine conflicts that decimated aristocratic lineages. For regional lords, it was expedient to replace the unruly aristocrats with the "men-of-service" (as I occasionally call the *shi* henceforth). *Shi* could be appointed but also dismissed or moved to another position, if necessary. Being immensely weaker than their aristocratic predecessors, the *shi* ministers were in no position to challenge their lords. Thus, replacement of hereditary officeholders with men-of-service allowed the rulers to regain their authority in administrative matters, contributing to the formation of what Mark E. Lewis aptly names the "ruler-centered state" (1999a, 597). Lord Xiao of Qin's call for skilled foreign advisers to come to his state may have been prompted, among other things, by his desire to employ these men at the expense of the members of the Qin ruling lineage, who had previously occupied major ministerial positions and who had repeatedly challenged his predecessors.

Yet the replacement of aristocrats with *shi* had more far-reaching consequences than merely changing the balance of power at the top of the government apparatus. It entailed, first, a profound reconceptualization of the nature of membership in the elite, which was no longer determined by pedigree but now based on meritocratic criteria. Henceforth, one's abilities, morality, and intelligence were the primary factors determining one's position. The proliferation of meritocratic ideas prompted lively discussions about the skills that should entitle a person to enter the elite ranks (Pines 2013a); Shang Yang, as we shall see, was an active participant in these debates. Second, the decline of the hereditary aristocracy meant profound cultural change: aristocratic culture, centered on the elaborate ritual system, was no longer valid. Third, and more broadly, the very idea that precedents from the past were sufficient for the present could now be questioned. New questions could be asked, and new answers were sought. This openness to new ideas became the hallmark of the intellectual history of the Warring States period.

Aside from profound sociopolitical, cultural, and intellectual changes, new departures in economics and warfare contributed toward the extraordinary dynamism of the Warring States period. Economically, the introduction of iron utensils revolutionized agriculture, allowing higher yields, prompting the development of wastelands, bringing about demographic growth, and accelerating urbanization and the commercialization of the economy. Most notably, it allowed a heretofore unthinkable intervention by the state in the economic lives of its subjects, contributing to the formation of an "agromanagerial" polity depicted by Karl A. Wittfogel in his seminal—and hugely controversial—book *Oriental Despotism* (1957). Through a variety of negative and positive incentives—changing taxation rates, distributing iron tools and draft animals, initiating irrigation projects, and the like—the state could encourage the expansion of arable lands and an increase in agricultural yields. These new agromanagerial functions, in turn, necessitated rapid expansion in the government bureaucracy, creating new employment opportunities for the men-of-service.[4]

Simultaneously with the "iron revolution" in agriculture, another revolution occurred on the battlefields. The introduction of the crossbow and parallel developments in other military technologies prompted the replacement of aristocratic chariot-based armies with mass-infantry armies staffed by peasant conscripts. Military campaigns became longer, more devastating, and crueler; the chivalric codes of the aristocratic age were abandoned, and commanders on the field had to be concerned less with personal valor and more with the ability to maintain huge armies, provide them with adequate supplies, and coordinate their movements. At home, administrators had to learn how to mobilize the entire male population, train it, and ensure the conscripts' loyalty on the battlefield or, at a minimum, prevent them from deserting. Once again, this new situation meant expanding the state apparatus to the benefit of men-of-service.[5]

This peculiar combination of manifold crises, manifold novel departures, and manifold opportunities characteristic of the Warring States period was conducive to the development of political thought. It is not surprising, then, that the period under discussion has remained unparalleled in Chinese history in terms of its creativity, intellectual audacity, ideological diversity, and the long-term impact of the thinkers' ideas. Many dozens of eminent *shi*—respectfully called the "Masters" (*zi* 子)—sought answers to questions that would remain relevant to the Chinese world both before the imperial unification of 221 B.C.E. and in its aftermath. How can stability in the subcelestial realm in general and in individual states in particular be ensured? How can smooth relations at the top of the government apparatus be maintained? How can officials at the center and in local administration be prevented from abusing their ever-increasing power? How can the loyalty and obedience of generals be retained without curbing their initiative and autonomy of command? How can the people be made to fight for their ruler? How can resources continue to be extracted from the populace without overburdening it and without causing emigration or, worse, rebellion? How can devoted, loyal, and skilled officials be trained? How can individuals who deserve to enter government service be identified, and what skills should they possess? These questions set the framework within which fierce intellectual debates ensued.

The immense pluralism of thought in the Warring States period—which is reflected in a common, even if somewhat misleading, designation of this era as the age of the "Hundred Schools" (*baijia* 百家)—should not obscure the fact that, aside from common questions, the competing thinkers also agreed on some of the answers. For instance, they universally endorsed the idea that the only path to universal peace and stability was the unification of "All-under-Heaven" under the aegis of a single monarch. The monarchic form of rule was another point of consensus, although the precise nature of monarchic power was hotly debated. The thinkers, moreover, broadly agreed that a meritocratic system of appointments was preferable to a pedigree-based system and that the economic concerns of the lower strata deserved the utmost solicitude, although the commoners should not be allowed to participate directly in government. These ideas were challenged only by a tiny minority of dissenters.⁶

Within this broad consensus, fierce debates ensued regarding the implementation of these common ideals. For instance, although all agreed that the entire subcelestial realm should be unified, it was not at all clear how to attain this goal, insofar as most thinkers—before Shang Yang—rejected a purely military solution. Another issue of disagreement was the role of morality in politics. Confucius 孔子 (551–479 B.C.E.), the earliest known *shi* master, advocated a regime in which officials would be morally cultivated persons and the ruler himself would undergo moral self-cultivation. Mozi 墨子 (ca. 460–390 B.C.E.) proposed a more radical vision: morality should be imposed on all members of society from above through a combination of the ruler's example (the supreme monarch was supposed to be "the worthiest and the most able" [*xian ke* 賢可] person "under Heaven") and coercion by the state apparatus. In distinction, the authors of a hugely influential text, the *Laozi* 老子 (ca. fourth century B.C.E.), argued that good order would be achieved not through promulgation of moralizing discourse but through the sage ruler's internalization and emulation of the norms of the ineffable cosmic Way (Dao 道). As we shall see, Shang Yang's writings resemble the *Laozi* in dissociating political praxis from moralizing discourse, but he did it in an incomparably more radical—some will say more appalling—way.

Distinct visions of the ways to govern society and the state were not promulgated out of pure intellectual curiosity. Rather, proponents such as Confucius, Mozi, their numerous disciples, and, arguably, the authors and propagators of the *Laozi* were all aspiring officeholders. Their goal was to present the rulers and their top aides with attractive solutions to the state's concerns. Some failed miserably in their expectations (neither Confucius nor Mozi succeeded in making an impressive career); others—such as some of Confucius's disciples—were more successful. Yet none of the thinkers throughout the Warring States period was as successful in his quest for power and influence as Shang Yang. Understanding Shang Yang's actual achievements and his policies is essential for properly understanding the message of "his" book.

A QIN REFORMER

An anecdote in *Records of the Historian* tells of Shang Yang starting his career in Qin with four interviews. The first three were unsuccessful because he tried to convince Lord Xiao to follow long-term policies of empowerment ("the Way of Thearchs" and "The Way of Monarchs," and "the Way of Hegemons"); only when he spoke of "the arts of strengthening the state" was he heeded. This story is almost certainly the historian's invention: I doubt that after three unsuccessful interviews the ruler would have had time to listen to Shang Yang again. Yet the next piece of information in the biography is more reliable: in 359 B.C.E., Shang Yang overpowered his conservative opponents in court debates (recorded in chapter 1 of the *Book of Lord Shang*) and henceforth was heeded. He was appointed to the position of left *shuzhang* 左庶長, chief minister, and launched his first series of reforms.

The *Records of the Historian* indicates that there were two major stages to the reforms. In 359 B.C.E., after winning the court debates, Shang Yang took the following steps:

He ordered the people to be grouped in squads of five and ten, and supervise each other, bearing mutually binding legal responsibility. Those who failed to report villainy would be cut in two at the waist. Those who reported villains would be rewarded equally to those who cut off enemy's heads. Those who concealed villains would be penalized equally to those who surrendered to the enemy.

Families with two or more adult males who did not separate households would have their taxes doubled. Those with military merit would receive ranks proportionally. Those engaged in private feuds would be penalized according to the gravity [of the offense]. Those who concentrated their energy on the basic occupations, those who farmed and wove and contributed a lot of grain and silk would be exempted from corvée labor. Those engaged in profiting from secondary occupations, and those who were poor because of their laziness, would all become government slaves. Members of the ruling lineage who had no military merit would not be listed in the rosters [of nobility]. [Shang Yang] clarified degrees of ranks and status of the noble and the base; each were allocated fields and houses, slaves and clothes according to their rank. Those with merits would be glorious and prosperous, while those without merit, even if rich, would not be permitted to show off [their wealth]. (*Shiji* 68:2230; modifying the translation from Watson 1993, 92–93)

Nine years later, parallel to relocating the capital to Xianyang 咸陽, Shang Yang launched another set of reforms:

An order was issued to prohibit cohabitation of father and sons, elder and younger brothers in the same room. He gathered small cantons and settlements to create counties, in which the magistrate and his assistant were established: altogether 31 counties. He opened up the one-thousand pace and one-hundred pace ridges among the fields, and equalized taxes and levies. He equalized measures of volume, weight, and length. (*Shiji* 68:2232, translation from Watson 1993, 94)

These two series of reforms encompass almost every important aspect of the state's life. They concern the penal code (the duty to denounce criminals); the economy (modification of tax procedures so as to encourage the formation of additional independent households, a much debated change in land allocation,[7] unification of weights and measures); the administration (reform of the regional administration); and, most notably, a major alteration to Qin's social system (discussed later in this chapter). Surely, Sima Qian bolstered Shang Yang's image as a radical and comprehensive reformer. But how reliable is this narrative? It is appropriate here to repeat an insightful warning by Mark E. Lewis against a common tendency to attribute gradual and long-term reforms to a single brilliant statesman or thinker (1999a, 603–604). The reforms in Qin, as elsewhere, emerged largely as a series of ad hoc arrangements, spanning generations, and it is clear that many of the steps attributed to Shang Yang could have either begun before his arrival at Qin or continued for decades after his death (see also Yoshimoto 2000). And yet Sima Qian's narration is not just a literary exercise. Clearly, many reforms were indeed initiated by Shang Yang, and there is abundant evidence to corroborate this point.

Some aspects of Sima Qian's story can be confirmed from paleographic materials. For instance, an inscription on one of the measures of volume manufactured under Shang Yang's unification laws clearly specifies that the reform of measures was conducted in 344 B.C.E.—a few years later than indicated by Sima Qian but fundamentally according to the parameters mentioned in the *Records of the Historian*.[8] The same inscription also confirms the correctness of Sima Qian's biography insofar as it mentions Shang Yang's new rank as *da liangzao* 大良造, to which he was promoted in 352 B.C.E. Yet more important evidence is provided by archaeology. Material data suggest a sweeping change in Qin social structure, reflected in burial sites, in the immediate aftermath of Shang Yang's reform.

The overhaul of Qin's social structure was Shang Yang's single most important step—and also the single most important topic discussed throughout the *Book of Lord Shang* (see chapter 3, part I). Until recently, our knowledge of this reform derived primarily from Han dynasty sources and from a badly damaged section of chapter 19 of the *Book of Lord Shang*. Today, this information can be augmented by paleographic sources, most notably legal texts discovered in the early Han Tomb 247 at Zhangjiashan, Jiangling 江陵張家山 (Hubei); Qin administrative and legal materials discovered in Tomb 11, Shuihudi, Yunmeng 雲夢睡虎地 (Hubei), and in a well and defense moat from the former Imperial Qin county of Qianling 遷陵, unearthed at Liye, Longshan 龍山里耶 (Hunan); and Han military documents from Tomb 5, Shangsunjiazhai, Datong County 大通縣上孫家寨 (Qinghai). Although it is likely that the system designed by Shang Yang differed from that employed in the Imperial Qin and Former Han dynasties, its essentials were probably the same. At its heart was the replacement of erstwhile aristocratic ranks with the new system of twenty (initially fewer) ranks of merit for which most males were eligible regardless of pedigree or economic status. The eight lowest ranks were distributed in exchange for military achievements, in particular the decapitation of enemy soldiers, or could be purchased by wealthy individuals in exchange for grain; successful rank holders could be incorporated into the military or civilian administration and thereafter be promoted up the social ladder.[9]

Each rank, as indicated in the extract from the *Records of the Historian* quoted earlier, granted its holder economic, social, and legal privileges, such as the right to cultivate a certain amount of land, the right to be given slaves to assist in its cultivation, as well as the right to redeem certain punishments.[10] The ranks were not fully inheritable; under normal circumstances, a man could designate one heir to his rank, but the heir received a rank one or two positions lower than his father, and the decrease was sharper for the holders of higher ranks (except for the one or two highest ones). This system therefore generated a much higher degree of social mobility than had prevailed in the aristocratic age. It effectively transformed the society from one based on pedigree, in which the individual's position was determined primarily by his or her lineage affiliation, into a much more open one in which individual merit, especially military merit, for the most part determined social position (Yates 1987; Teng 2014). Sima Qian's statement that even members of the ruling lineage could not expect ranks without adequate achievements is confirmed by the regulations regarding unranked descendants of the ruling house (*Shuihudi* [1990] 2001, 137; Hulsewé 1985, 174, D164). Upward mobility was also amazing, as indicated by the fact that even a bondservant could receive a rank of merit in exchange for military achievements (*Shuihudi* [1990] 2001, 55; Hulsewé 1985, 83, A91; see also Yates 2002, 313). Manifold data confirm that in the aftermath of Shang Yang's reforms Qin became a highly mobile society in which pedigree played only a secondary role in determining one's status.

The creation of the system of ranks of merit had far-reaching sociopolitical consequences. First, it broke the monopoly of the hereditary aristocracy on power and effectively abolished this stratum, or at the very least radically weakened it. Second, it empowered the state, which henceforth gained unprecedented control over determining an individual's social (and to a certain extent economic) status and, mutatis mutandis, over social life in general. Although it is doubtful that Qin ever attained the ideal advocated throughout the *Book of Lord Shang*—that is, the unification of the social, political, and economic hierarchies—there is no doubt it advanced considerably toward this goal. And third, the new system brought about a radical change in the composition of the elite and even its cultural outlook. This change is most clearly observable from the mortuary customs of Qin elites and subelites. After Shang Yang's reforms, there was a true mortuary revolution: for instance, bronze ritual vessels, the hallmark of aristocratic culture, disappeared almost entirely from post-350 B.C.E. Qin tombs, and new and previously unattested mortuary customs—such as the so-called catacomb burials—proliferated (Shelach and Pines 2006). This is a rare instance when material data confirm textual information neatly, and it is yet another indication of the reform's depth, comprehensiveness, and ultimate success. Actually, even if Shang Yang's entire corpus of reforms was to be reduced to the introduction of the ranks-of-merit system alone, that single reform would suffice to make him one of the most remarkable statesmen in China's long history.

A MILITARY LEADER

In addition to his career as a reformer, Shang Yang was renowned as a military leader; indeed, throughout the Warring States period and well into the Han times, this aspect of his career was no less prominent than his sociopolitical innovations.[11] Recall that his arrival in Qin coincided with the reinvigoration of Qin's armies, which scored several victories over its major neighbor and rival, the state of Wei.

Shang Yang contributed to further Qin successes. In 352 B.C.E., shortly after his promotion to the *da liangzao* rank, Shang Yang inflicted a strategic defeat on his erstwhile employer, Wei, conquering its former capital, Anyi 安邑.[12] Shang Yang scored another victory over Wei in the next year; it was due to these successes that Qin leaders felt confident enough to relocate their capital to Xianyang in 350 B.C.E. In 343 B.C.E., Qin's new position as a superpower was recognized by the Zhou Son of Heaven, who delivered to Lord Xiao a special gift of sacrificial meat (*Shiji* 5:203).

Shang Yang was apparently involved not just in domestic reforms and military affairs but also in diplomacy. A Chu bamboo slip from Tomb 1, Tianxingguan, Jiangling 江陵天星觀 (Hubei), dates one year as the "year of the visit by the Qin guest Gongsun Yang" (Hubei Sheng Jingzhou 1982, 109). We do not know when the visit took place or under what circumstances, but its importance must have been exceptional enough to merit its being the most notable event in the life of Chu in that year.[13] Perhaps this meeting was part of Shang Yang's efforts to secure the continuation of the Qin–Chu alliance, which allowed Qin to concentrate its military efforts against the state of Wei. If this guess is correct, Shang Yang succeeded in his goal, but for the leaders of Chu the alliance was a bad gamble: Qin, led by Shang Yang, started its expansion against Chu soon after defeating Wei (*Shiji* 40:1720).

Shang Yang proved his military prowess again in 341–340 B.C.E. when he seized the opportunity presented by Wei's crushing defeat at the hands of its eastern neighbor, Qi, to launch an attack on the embattled Wei from the west. The results were impressive: Wei armies were eliminated, and Prince Ang 公子卬 was captured. This success proved to be problematic for Shang Yang's reputation, though. An anecdote, recorded originally in the *Springs and Autumns of Mr. Lü* (*Lüshi chunqiu* 呂氏春秋, ca. 240 B.C.E.) and referred to briefly in the *Stratagems of the Warring States*, implies that Shang Yang attained this victory due to a dirty trick: he enticed his erstwhile friend, the Wei commander Prince Ang, to come to the Qin camp to negotiate a peaceful solution to the conflict between the two states. Once Ang arrived, however, he was ambushed and imprisoned; his leaderless army was then easily defeated.[14] This story, if true, appears to be a perfect illustration of one of the infamous maxims of the *Book of Lord Shang*: "he who in [military] affairs advances whatever the enemy is ashamed of benefits" (4.1).[15]

However, there are several reasons to doubt the story as told in the *Lüshi chunqiu* and retold by Sima Qian. First, the battle took place more than twenty years after Shang Yang had left Wei. That Shang Yang, who was then just a petty retainer of a powerful minister, would have been the prince's friend, seems implausible. Second, that a Wei prince would fall into a trap laid by Shang Yang, a mortal enemy of his state who had inflicted repeated defeats on Wei in the past, is also difficult to believe. Third, the earliest reference to Qin's victory—in a Wei chronicle, the *Bamboo Annals* (*Zhushu jinian* 竹書紀年)—does not mention the prince's imprisonment.[16] It is more likely, then, that the story of Shang Yang's trickery was invented after the fact either as part of Wei's search for an excuse for its inglorious defeat or as a way of smearing Shang Yang's name or both.

Whatever the truth about the campaign of 340 B.C.E., its results were highly significant for Shang Yang. In what appears as an outline of further Qin expansion, he was awarded an allotment of fifteen settlements in Shang 商 and Yu 於, the lands bordering the states of Chu and Wei[17] (it is only from this time that "Shang Yang" or "Lord of Shang" 商君 becomes Yang's appropriate appellation). This was an almost unimaginable award: tiny in terms of the Springs-and-Autumns period but huge in terms of the Warring States period norms. Shang Yang was now at the apex of his power—and on the verge of his tragedy.

A VICTIM

By the end of Lord Xiao's reign, Shang Yang was the most powerful statesman in the world of the Warring States. His combined position as *da liangzao shuzhang* 大良造庶長 placed him at the apex of both the pyramid of ranks of merit and the administrative apparatus.[18] According to one account, Lord Xiao even contemplated abdicating in favor of his meritorious minister, echoing the model abdication of the legendary sage king Yao 堯 in favor of his longtime aide Shun 舜.[19] Whether this abdication story has a kernel of truth is impossible to verify, but it is highly plausible that Shang Yang's exceptional power caused envy and frustration among members of the Qin ruling lineage. A moralizing account by Sima Qian tells of a wise man warning Shang Yang of his imminent downfall; yet, according to the norms of the genre, the adviser was not heeded (*Shiji* 68:2233–2235). And the downfall was near indeed. Soon after the death of his patron, Lord Xiao, Shang Yang was accused of plotting rebellion and summarily executed.

The precise reasons for Shang Yang's execution by Lord Xiao's successor, Lord (later King) Huiwen 秦惠文王 (r. 337–311 B.C.E.), are not clear. Sima Qian reports that when the future king was still a crown prince, he transgressed against the law and was due to suffer penal mutilation. The heir could not be mutilated, nor could he be pardoned: hence, the mutilation (cutting off the nose) was imposed on his tutor and his teacher, both of whom were high-ranking members of the Qin ruling lineage. This humiliating punishment appears to have aggravated the resentment against Shang Yang among the members of this lineage whom his reforms had sidelined (*Shiji* 68:2232, 2233). Now, as Lord Huiwen ascended the throne, the time of revenge had arrived.

An alternative story, told in the *Stratagems of the Warring States*, emphasizes Lord Huiwen's fear of Shang Yang's excessive power. There are discrepancies in the details here as well: Did Shang Yang try— unsuccessfully—to escape from Qin back to Wei (which reportedly refused to grant him refuge in order to avenge Prince Ang's imprisonment)? Did he plot rebellion in his domain, Shang? Trying to discover the truth among conflicting narratives is pointless. What is sure is that the life of a minister whose twenty-one years in power reshaped the state of Qin and propelled it to a position of supremacy among the Warring States ended ingloriously when he was torn apart by chariots. Even a relatively sympathetic account in the *Stratagems of the Warring States* notes that "the people of Qin did not pity" Shang Yang.[20]

It is a bitter irony of history that the only major thinkers of the Warring States period who suffered execution—Shang Yang, Han Fei 韓非 (d. 233 B.C.E.), and Li Si 李斯 (d. 208 B.C.E.)—were precisely those later identified as "Legalists," the term that stands for staunch supporters of centralized power and opponents of ministerial machinations. The irony becomes greater when we notice that a similar fate did not befall

thinkers who were renowned for a critical attitude toward power holders, such as some of the followers of Confucius, not to mention radical
iconoclasts such as the authors of the *Zhuangzi* 莊子 (ca. third century
B.C.E.). To be sure, none of the Legalist thinkers was executed because
of his ideology: each was implicated—unjustly—as a plotter or rebel. Yet
it is difficult to avoid the feeling that the atmosphere of mistrust
between the ruler and his aides, generated in these thinkers' writings,
eventually backfired. Indeed, Sima Qian considers Shang Yang's destiny
well deserved: the merciless thinker brought about his own downfall
(*Shiji* 68:2237).

Shang Yang's death did not bring about the cessation of his policies,
however, the positive results of which were visible to all. Nor do we
know much about the persecution of his immediate followers, except
for one case: a certain Shi Jiao 尸佼, who allegedly fled to Shu 蜀 (Sichuan, then not yet under Qin control) after Shang Yang's death.[21] Whatever the case, it seems reasonable to assume that a significant number
of like-minded statesmen remained in Qin after Shang Yang's execution and that they continued to contribute to the formation of the book
that bears his name.

2

THE TEXT

History, Dating, Style

History was not kind to the texts associated with the Legalist school. Of the ten works recorded in the "Legalist" section of the Han 漢 dynasty (206/202 B.C.E.–220 C.E.) imperial catalog, only two—the *Book of Lord Shang* and *Han Feizi* 韓非子—survive more or less intact; of two more—*Shēnzi* 申子, attributed to Shen Buhai 申不害 (d. 337 B.C.E.), and *Shènzi* 慎子, attributed to Shen Dao 慎到 (fl. ca. 300 B.C.E.)—only scattered fragments remain; six others ceased circulating more than a millennium ago. Although the *Book of Lord Shang* fared better than most other Legalist writings, it has come down to us badly battered by the vicissitudes of history, having suffered the loss of five out of an original twenty-nine chapters and considerable corruption in some of the remaining chapters. Serious studies of the text—such as parsing it into paragraphs and sentences (*zhangju* 章句), providing it with adequate glosses, and analyzing its dating and composition—started in earnest only in the late nineteenth century and only recently can be said to have reached a relatively advanced level. Understanding this complex background is a necessary preliminary step to accessing the text.

The paperback version of this chapter abridges parts of the largely technical discussion about the text's dating from the original hardback version. Those interested in a more detailed version of my arguments may consult Pines 2016a.

TEXTUAL HISTORY

The first references to writings associated with Shang Yang come from *Han Feizi*, authored by Han Fei, the self-declared synthesizer and improver of the ideas of his "Legalist" predecessors, Shang Yang and Shen Buhai. On one occasion, when urging the ruler to be able to alter existing norms and regulations and to dispense, when necessary, with public opinion, Han Fei says, "It is explained in the 'Internal and External' of Lord Shang."[1] The current *Book of Lord Shang* does not include a chapter titled "Internal and External" 內外; judging from the content of Han Fei's argument, he refers to what is currently the first chapter of the *Book of Lord Shang*, "Revising the Laws" ("Geng fa" 更法). Elsewhere, Han Fei cites Shang Yang directly. After explicating Shang Yang's principle of imposing heavy punishments on minor offenses, Han Fei says:

公孫鞅曰: 行刑, 重其輕者——輕者不至, 重者不來。是謂以刑去刑。
　　Gongsun Yang said: "When [the state] implements punishments, inflicts heavy [punishments] on light [offenses]: then light [offenses] will not come, and heavy [crimes] will not arrive. This is called: 'eradicating punishments with punishments.'"[2]

This statement by Gongsun Yang (i.e., Shang Yang) appears almost verbatim in two of the chapters of the *Book of Lord Shang*: chapter 4, "Eliminating the Strong" ("Qu qiang" 去強), and chapter 13, "Making Orders Strict" ("Jin ling" 靳令) (4.4 and 13.5). Possibly, then, Han Fei had access to the writings attributed to Shang Yang. Indeed, elsewhere he mentions that families within the boundaries possess "laws/methods of Shang [Yang] and Guan [Zhong]" 商管之法.[3] Judging from the context, these "laws" or "methods" (*fa* 法) refer not only to legal or administrative regulations bequeathed by these statesmen but also to the texts attributed to them—that is, the (proto-) *Book of Lord Shang* and (proto-) *Guanzi* 管子.[4] If Han Fei is right, then the *Book of Lord Shang* might have circulated broadly in the Chinese world on the eve of imperial unification.

The *Book of Lord Shang* was relatively well known throughout the Former Han dynasty 前漢 (206/202 B.C.E.–9 C.E.). Several eminent Han statesmen reportedly studied Shang Yang's teachings, and a few leading courtiers openly endorsed his ideas.[5] Sima Qian claims to have read at least two chapters of the *Book of Lord Shang*: chapter 7, "Opening the Blocked" ("Kai sai" 開塞), and chapter 3, "Agriculture and Warfare" ("Nong zhan" 農戰). The first of these chapters is mentioned also in a slightly earlier treatise, *Huainanzi* 淮南子 (ca. 140 B.C.E.).[6]

By the end of the Former Han dynasty, the first catalog of the imperial library was compiled by Liu Xiang 劉向 (79–8 B.C.E.) and his associates. The catalog mentions the book named *Lord Shang* 商君 in twenty-nine chapters in the "Legalists" subsection of the "Masters" (or "Philosophers," *zi* 子) books. Separately, the catalog lists a book named *Gongsun Yang* 公孫鞅 in twenty-seven chapters in the "Strategists" (*bing quanmou* 兵權謀) subsection of the "Military Books" section (*bing shu* 兵書). Scholars disagree as to whether *Gongsun Yang* should be considered an independent text by Shang Yang. I tend to accept the analysis by Wang Shirun 王時潤 (1879–ca. 1937), who explains the double record as a lapse by Liu Xiang: whereas Liu Xiang was in charge of collating and recording the masters' texts, Ren Hong 任宏 (fl. 30–10 B.C.E.) collated independently the military texts.[7] The final catalog, *Bielu* 別錄, and its subsequent abridgment, *Qilue* 七略, prepared by Liu Xiang's son, Liu Xin 劉歆 (46 B.C.E.–23 C.E.), contained quite a few double records of the texts collated by both scholars. Most of these double records were erased by the historian Ban Gu 班固 (32–92 C.E.), who incorporated *Qilue* in the bibliographical treatise of his work *History of the [Former] Han Dynasty* (*Hanshu* 漢書).[8] Why the double record of Shang Yang's book survived is not clear; but the similarity in the number of chapters suggests that both records refer to different versions of the same text and not to two different works.

The *Book of Lord Shang* continued to circulate in the aftermath of the Han dynasty's fall in 220 C.E.; it is recorded (under the title *Master Shang* 商子 or, alternately, *Book of Lord Shang*) in the imperial catalogs of the Sui 隋 (581–618) and Tang 唐 (618–907) dynasties; both mention the text as comprising five scrolls (*juan* 卷) and do not refer to the number of chapters (*pian* 篇).[9] Under the Tang, the *Book of Lord Shang* was still relatively well known; sections of it were incorporated by Wei Zheng 魏徵 (580–643) in *Essentials of Orderly Rule from Multiple Books* (*Qunshu zhiyao* 群書治要, 631), and references to it appear in *Comprehensive Institutions* (*Tong dian* 通典) by Du You 杜佑 (735–812).[10] However, by the time of the Song dynasty 宋 (960–1279) we have first indications of textual corruption in the *Book of Lord Shang*. Zheng Qiao 鄭樵 (1104–1162) mentions in the bibliographic section of *Comprehensive Treatises* (*Tong zhi* 通志) that three of the twenty-nine chapters mentioned in the Han catalog are lost; a similar statement is made in the *Bibliographic Treatise from the Jun Studio* (*Jun zhai dushu zhi* 郡齋讀書志) by Chao Gongwu 晁公武 (1105–1180).[11] By the end of the Song dynasty, one more chapter is reported to have been lost, and by the end of the Yuan dynasty 元 (1271–1368) another had followed.[12] In the early Ming dynasty 明 (1368–1644), two versions of the text existed, one with twenty-five and another with twenty-four chapters, but it was only the latter, shorter version that continued in circulation.[13] All currently available recensions miss chapters 16 and 21 of the twenty-six-chapter Song version. Of the three chapters that were lost between the Han and the Song dynasties, only one fragment survived in Wei Zheng's compilation.[14]

The loss of chapters is only the most visible aspect of the text's deterioration over the centuries. To this problem, one should add many specific instances of textual corruption within the surviving chapters. This corruption is most obvious in the chapters that deal with military matters (especially chapters 10–11, of which only fragments remain intact) and specific administrative and military regulations, such as chapter 19. It seems that early scribes and later literati who were in charge of reproducing the text were less acquainted with matters peculiar to the book's immediate military and administrative context, which resulted in several lacunae, misplaced slips, miswritten characters or, later, printing errors and the like.

Aside from direct corruption, the *Book of Lord Shang* suffered from centuries of neglect by the imperial literati, which resulted in minimal editorial efforts on their part. The book was never divided into paragraphs and sentences (*zhangju* 章句); it had almost no annotations (only a few glosses by anonymous commentators are found in a single early recension);[15] and we know of no serious scholarly work on it prior to the end of the eighteenth century. This neglect made the text notoriously difficult for later readers and may explain why they often eschewed it, preferring to learn about Shang Yang's legacy from the much-better-preserved "Biography of Shang Yang" in the *Records of the Historian*.

The earliest surviving editions of the *Book of Lord Shang* date from the mid-sixteenth century.[16] One was published by Fan Qin 范欽 (1506–1585), the founder of the Tianyige 天一閣 library. Another one, a roughly contemporary annotated edition prepared by Feng Qin 馮覲 in 1559, exists now only in a recension prepared in 1626 by Feng's grandson Feng Zhi 馮贄. Four other editions from the late sixteenth and early seventeenth century survive. Yet all of them are superseded by the first known critical edition of the text prepared by the great Qing 清 (1644–1912) man of letters Yan Wanli 嚴萬里, better known by his later name, Yan Kejun 嚴可均 (1762–1843).[17] Yan had in his possession a recension of the *Book of Lord Shang* dating back to the Yuan dynasty; he collated it with Fan Qin's edition and another lost Ming recension from the Qin Silin's 秦四麟 (fl. 1590) private library and published a new text in 1793. Later, Yan (now under the name of Yan Kejun) prepared a second improved edition (1811), but it was his first edition that became more popular, being republished in 1876 by Zhejiang Publishing House as part of the compilation *Twenty-Two Masters* 二十二子. This later version—which corrected some of Yan's printing errors but unfortunately made a few new ones—became the foundation for most subsequent publications of the *Book of Lord Shang* throughout the twentieth century.[18]

Several other critical editions of the text appeared in the nineteenth century. The collation by Sun Xingyan 孫星衍 (1753–1818) and Sun Fengyi 孫馮翼 (fl. 1800) that was published in 1803 prompted Yan Wanli (now under the name of Yan Kejun) to prepare a second improved edition of the text in 1811. These publications, in addition to another critical edition by Qian Xizuo 錢熙祚 that was published in 1839, generated renewed interest in the *Book of Lord Shang*. By the late nineteenth century, the book had benefited from efforts of such eminent scholars as Sun Xingyan, Yu Yue 俞樾 (1821–1907), and Sun Yirang 孫詒讓

(1848–1908), whose glosses became indispensible for all subsequent publications of the text through the twentieth century and beyond.[19] Their efforts in turn influenced many new annotated editions published through the Republican period (1912–1949). Of these editions, the most notable are those by Wang Shirun (1915, which served as the basic text for Jan Duyvendak's English translation [(1928) 1963]), Zhu Shizhe 朱師轍 (1921, revised in 1948, with the revision reprinted in 1956 and serving as the basic text for Leonard Perelomov's Russian translation [1968, 1993]), and Jiang Lihong 蔣禮鴻 (prepared in 1944 but not published until 1986 and then republished in 1996 and later), which eventually became the standard version in the mainland, being incorporated into *New Edition of the Masters Collection* (*Xinbian zhuzi jicheng* 新編諸子集成). Other editions, such as those by Yin Tongyang 尹桐陽 (1918) and Jian Shu 簡書 (1931), although less accurate, have also contributed to the improved understanding of the text.[20]

After the establishment of the People's Republic of China in 1949, textual work on the *Book of Lord Shang* slowed, but it accelerated all of a sudden in the early 1970s in the context of the anti-Confucian campaign (see chapter 4, part I). Many publications on Shang Yang and the *Book of Lord Shang* appeared then, but most have little, if any, scholarly value. One stands apart, though: *The Book of Lord Shang, Commented and Translated* (商君書注譯, 1974) by Gao Heng 高亨 (1900–1986). Gao, who studied the *Book of Lord Shang* long before the Cultural Revolution (1966–1976), managed to avoid blatant politicization in his study and presented a balanced and academically solid work that by far surpassed that of his predecessors. The only significant defect of his publication is the use of simplified characters, which makes his edition less appropriate for a critical study of the text.

In recent decades, many editions of the *Book of Lord Shang* have been published, but few merit mention; scholars in most cases simply reproduced earlier recensions and Gao Heng's translation into colloquial Chinese (*baihua* 白話). The major exceptions to this rule are several publications by Zhang Jue 張覺 (1993, 2006), who became deeply engaged in studying the *Book of Lord Shang* in the early 1990s. His efforts culminated in a new critical edition in 2012, which fully benefited from modern library facilities and which by far supersedes anything published on the *Book of Lord Shang* heretofore. Zhang Jue consulted ten different recensions from the Ming and Qing period and, according to his testimony, "selected the best" of each without exclusively following any of them. His work records all cases of textual discrepancies among various recensions, collects most of the earlier commentaries, and thus is immensely helpful for researchers. Moreover, it contains a rich apparatus of auxiliary materials, including detailed introductions to each of the extant early recensions of the *Book of Lord Shang*.

Needless to say, my research benefited enormously from Zhang Jue's efforts, and in the translation given here I normally follow his edition unless indicated otherwise. It should be noted, however, that even this excellent edition suffers from several flaws. Zhang Jue's parsing of the text and his attempts to divide it into paragraphs and sentences are not always convincing. Some of his personal glosses are of lower quality than could have been expected; and his marked lack of interest in recent studies is self-defeating. Zhang neither incorporates insights from excavated materials nor appears to be interested in them in general. Moreover, his repeated attacks on Gao Heng result in the rejection of many sensible suggestions made by Gao and sometimes in the glossing over of Gao's views. These negative aspects notwithstanding, Zhang's work remains an impressive scholarly achievement to which I am immensely indebted.

DEBATES OVER THE TEXT'S DATING

Because of the lackluster interest in the *Book of Lord Shang* on the part of imperial literati, there were very few discussions of its dating throughout the imperial period.[21] Traditional scholars focused—if at all—not on the text's dates but on its authenticity: that is, whether it was composed by Shang Yang or not. The first known instances of questioning Shang Yang's authorship date from the Southern Song dynasty 南宋 (1127–1279). Zhou Duanchao 周端朝 (1172–1234) noticed that the book refers to "a lot of later affairs" 多附會後事 and contains "redundant and excessive words" 汎濫淫辭.[22] He concluded that the book was inadequate as an introduction to Shang Yang's ideas; instead, one would be better off reading the biography in the *Records of the Historian*. Huang Zhen 黃震 (1213–1280) also noticed the low literary quality of the text and claimed that the book is too "disordered" 煩亂 to have been produced by a "gifted law official" such as Shang Yang: "its authenticity is doubtful and cannot be verified" 真偽殆未可知 (*Huangshi richao* 55:30). These comments did not inspire further studies of the text.

It was only under the Qing dynasty that more substantial claims were made about the book's authenticity. Some scholars, such as Ma Su 馬驌 (1621–1673) and Wang Zhong 汪中 (1745–1794), noticed that chapter 15, "Attracting the People" ("Lai min" 徠民), was obviously written long after Shang Yang's death.[23] The compilers of the great imperial encyclopedic project *Complete Books in the Four Treasuries* (*Siku quanshu* 四庫全書) opined, in turn, that the entire *Book of Lord Shang* is late because the first chapter uses the posthumous title "Lord Xiao of Qin." If Shang Yang was executed immediately after the lord's death, when could he have prepared the book?[24] These claims laid the ground for modern scholars' doubt regarding the book's authenticity.

During the Republican period, interest in the authenticity of early texts in general and of the *Book of Lord Shang* in particular intensified, and the topic was addressed, even if briefly, by almost every eminent scholar of that age. The dominant tendency then was to point out obvious or perceived anachronisms in the text (i.e., its references to events that happened after Shang Yang's execution) and to dismiss the book in its entirety as a later forgery, unworthy of further study. In the heyday of the atmosphere of "doubting antiquity" (*yigu* 疑古), a cavalier attitude toward many early texts, including the *Book of Lord Shang*, prevailed. Although a notable minority of scholars were engaged in detailed study of the book, they were clearly outnumbered by those who—echoing Hu Shi 胡適 (1891–1962)—considered Shang Yang an important reformer but not a thinker and surely not an author of the *Book of Lord Shang*.[25]

The dismissive attitude toward the *Book of Lord Shang* displayed in the majority of Republican period studies reflected several common methodological problems. First, scholars were quite often eager to trumpet the discovery of yet another "anachronism," which, however, under closer scrutiny cannot be accepted as evidence for the book's belatedness. For instance, the fact that chapter 1, "Revising the Laws," refers to Lord Xiao of Qin by his posthumous appellation does not necessarily suggest that the chapter was penned after Lord Xiao's death; the ruler's name could have been updated by later editors or transmitters of the text. Similarly, a close similarity of chapter 13 of the *Book of Lord Shang* to chapter 53, "Chi ling" 飭令, of the *Han Feizi* does not presuppose, pace Qian Mu 錢穆 (1895–1990), Fu Sinian 傅斯年 (1896–1950), and others, that the former is later than the latter;[26] actually, the opposite is much more probable (see Pines 2016a, 171; Mozawa 1991). But even when there are obvious anachronisms in the *Book of Lord Shang* (they are undeniable), does this mean that the entire book or just a few chapters were composed long after Shang Yang's death? This simple question somehow escaped many of the grand masters of the Republican period, even though the fallacy of their methodology was pointed out quite early, for instance by Chen Qitian 陳啓天 (1893–1984) (Chen Qitian 1935, 113–121).

The Republican period legacy of dismissing the *Book of Lord Shang* remained influential in the West up to the end of the twentieth century, resulting in a minuscule number of studies of the *Book of Lord Shang* there.[27] In China and Japan, however, it ceded to a much more sophisticated approach. The dominant scholarly opinion nowadays is that the *Book of Lord Shang*—like many other preimperial texts—came into existence after a long period of accretion during which chapters or paragraphs were added, altered, and possibly edited out.[28] With this understanding in mind, scholars are no longer engaged in the methodologically untenable attempt to date the entire book as a single entity but rather try to date its individual chapters and determine their authorship. The roots of this approach are discernible already in the Republican period itself (e.g., Chen Qitian 1935; Rong Zhaozu 1937), and the approach was later endorsed by Gao Heng (1974, 6–12). Yet it was only with Zheng Liangshu's magnum opus (1989) that the concept of accretion can be said to have been fully absorbed into the study of the *Book of Lord Shang*.

Zheng Liangshu presents an insightful—albeit at times overtly speculative—theory of the formation of the *Book of Lord Shang*. He reads the *Book of Lord Shang* as a testimony to the evolution of "Shang Yang's school" (*Shang Yang xuepai* 商鞅學派). Zheng's highly detailed study outlines what he considers traces of ideological evolution among Shang Yang's followers as reflected in changing emphases in different chapters of the treatise. Zheng's study was almost immediately followed by another magnum opus by Yoshinami Takashi (1992), who proposed an alternative scenario of the book's formation. Notably, both scholars assert that the vast majority of the chapters were produced after Shang Yang's death, although they differ with regard to certain details.

In recent years, attempts to date individual chapters of the *Book of Lord Shang* and to assert their authorship continue. The current tendency, reflecting the general mood of "trusting antiquity" (*xin gu* 信古) that is now prominent among mainland scholars, is to assert that most of the chapters were penned by Shang Yang, with only a few added after his death. The most radical representative of this trend is Zhang Jue (2012, echoing his earlier studies), who considers only chapter 15 ("Attracting the People") as spurious and regards all the rest as authentic. Other scholars who address the dating question (Zhang Linxiang 2008; Tong Weimin 2013) are less radical, but in general the dates they propose for most of the chapters are markedly earlier than the dates put forward by Zheng Liangshu and Yoshinami Takashi.

In general, I think that the accretion hypothesis proposed by Zheng Liangshu, Yoshinami Takashi, and other scholars can advance our knowledge of the *Book of Lord Shang* if we avoid certain methodological pitfalls embedded in its simplistic utilization. To begin with, recall that most of the currently extant Warring States period texts bear the imprint of at least four contributors: the original author; his disciples and followers; later editors, such as Liu Xiang and his associates; and manifold copyists and transmitters, especially those who under the Han dynasty transcribed the pre-Qin texts into a "modern" Han script (Allan 2015, 23–24). The degree of intervention by editors, copyists, and transmitters in the text's content is debatable, but at least in certain cases it may be considerable, ranking from a new arrangement of the text to excision of supposedly "duplicate" or "spurious" chapters and paragraphs, to substitution of barely legible or allegedly "wrong" characters with new ones, to—most annoyingly—the addition of new textual segments. In a few cases, later editors identify themselves and their rearrangements (see, e.g., Sato Masayuki 2003, 30–32, regarding the *Xunzi* and Goldin 2011a, 39, regarding the *Mengzi*); but most of them remain silent, as in the case of the *Book of Lord Shang*. This silence does not rule out, however, the possibility that later editors and transmitters tampered with the text's content.

Nor should we treat every chapter a priori as an organic unit to be analyzed in the context of the text's accretion. Actually, chapters differ considerably in their nature. Some were produced as separate essays and circulated independently for a considerable period of time before being put together with other essays to form the "book" that we have.[29] These "organic" chapters have a distinct style and normally are well organized with an identifiable beginning and conclusion; in the case of the *Book of Lord Shang*, many of these chapters might have originated from Shang Yang's and his followers' court memorials (see, e.g., chapters 6, 9, 15, 17, 23, 24, and 25). Yet in other cases a chapter is just a patchwork prepared by later editors from independent paragraphs (*zhang* 章) associated with a putative author. Chapters 13 and 18 of the *Book of Lord Shang* may well represent this "composite" type. It makes perfect sense to try to date the organic chapters but surely not the composite ones.

It is with these understandings in mind that I proceed now to present my hypothesis about the dating of some of the book's chapters. I try to avoid inevitably speculative attempts to date every single chapter or to guess who its author was. Yet I believe we have enough data to determine with relative precision the dating of at least some of the book's chapters and to propose tentative dating for many more. At the current stage of our knowledge, any definitive answer regarding the process of the book's accretion is impossible, but even a partial answer will advance us considerably toward better understanding the nature and the content of the *Book of Lord Shang*.

THE TEXT'S DATING: A TENTATIVE RECONSTRUCTION

The next section of my discussion is abridged from the original edition (my detailed arguments are presented also in Pines 2016a). To summarize my approach: I tried to establish several criteria according to which individual chapters of the text could be dated. I gave more weight to "internal" criteria (e.g., historical information contained in the chapter, its language, and, whenever relevant, interrelations among the text's chapters) than to "external" criteria (e.g., references or citations of the text elsewhere).[30] To be sure, not every chapter can be dated with any precision: for instance, my criteria cannot be used to date "composite" chapters (those that were assembled from smaller textual units, such as chapter 18, "Charting the Policies" ["Hua ce" 畫策]). Uncertainties aside, the results appear to be satisfactory: we can offer tentative dates for more than half of the text's chapters.

Without entering too many technical details (for which see Pines 2016a), I shall summarize here my findings. First, insofar as many chapters discuss the ways to unify All-under-Heaven, but not a single one (with the possible exception of chapter 26, "Fixing Divisions" ["Ding fen" 定分]) evinces any knowledge of the eventual imperial unification of 221 B.C.E., it is plausible that most or all the chapters were composed before the establishment of the Qin Empire. Second, the vocabulary and occasional references to the economic and military situation during the time of their composition indicate that most of the book's chapters were produced in the fourth century B.C.E. (the major exceptions are chapters 26 and 15, "Attracting the People"). Third, I concur with Zheng Liangshu's assertion that the *Book of Lord Shang* (or at least significant parts thereof) reflects intellectual developments within the so-called "Shang Yang's school."[31] The evolution of the authors' ideas is particularly notable in the case of chapter 4, "Eliminating the Strong," and its commentaries; chapter 20, "Weakening the People"; and chapter 5, "Explaining the People" ("Shuo min" 說民). Both commentaries moderate the provocative language of chapter 4 and try to make some of its appalling messages less alienating (see Pines 2012a). Less explicit but no less interesting cases of intellectual development among Shang Yang's followers are chapters 6, "Calculating the Land" ("Suan di" 算地), and chapter 15, "Attracting the People:" the latter modifies some of the fundamental policy proposals outlined in the former (Yoshinami 1985). For further details of my arguments, see the introductions to individual chapters in part II of this book.

My findings suggest that the composition of the *Book of Lord Shang* was a lengthy process that spanned well over a century. The earliest dateable chapters—such as 12, "Military Defense" ("Bing shou" 兵守) and 2, "Orders to Cultivate Wastelands" ("Ken ling" 墾令)—were probably produced at the early stage of Shang Yang's career (i.e., in the 360s or early 350s B.C.E.). Other chapters that may come from Shang Yang's lifetime and quite possibly from an early stage of his career are 3, "Agriculture and Warfare," and 4. Chapters 6 and 7, the ideological centerpieces of the entire book, were probably produced later but in all likelihood still during Shang Yang's lifetime or shortly thereafter. The military chapters 10 and 11 as well as chapter 19 definitely come from the fourth century B.C.E., as is suggested by their unawareness of the use of cavalry.[32] Chapters 13, 20, and 5 (all of which are related to chapter 4) were surely composed sometime after chapter 4, but we have no clear dates of composition. Chapters 17, "Rewards and Punishments" ("Shang xing" 賞刑), and 9, "Implementing Laws" ("Cuo fa" 錯法), could not have been written before the end of the fourth century B.C.E. The last two chapters in the book (in terms of their date of composition) are 15 and 26, which postdate Shang Yang's life by a century or even more. For several chapters (14, 23, 24, 25) I failed to discover unequivocal indicators of the date of their composition. My tentative results, summarized in table 2.1, are the working hypothesis that underlies my discussion of the ideology of the *Book of Lord Shang* in chapter 3.

THE BOOK'S STYLE AND ITS COMPOSITION

The *Book of Lord Shang* is not a literary masterpiece. In terms of style, the sophistication of its arguments, and its literary richness, it fares badly in comparison with texts by many other preimperial masters, most notably with the ideologically close *Han Feizi* (for which see Goldin 2013, 11). This is especially true of its early chapters, whose language is dull and which are devoid of such literary embellishments as metaphors, parables, and the like. The authors generally eschew discussions of the recent past; the former paragons are mentioned only en passant; and even historical anecdotes, a ubiquitous means of presenting one's

TABLE 2.1 Dating of the Chapters in the *Book of Lord Shang*

Chapter	Dating	Comments
1. Revising the Laws (更法)	pre-300 B.C.E.?	May be based on authentic records of the start of Shang Yang's career in Qin
2. Orders to Cultivate Wastelands (墾令)	pre-350 B.C.E.	Probably from the earliest stages of Shang Yang's reforms in Qin
3. Agriculture and Warfare (農戰)	pre-350 B.C.E.?	Earliness suggested by the verbal usage of the term *wang* and by a relatively unpolished style
4. Eliminating the Strong (去強)	pre-350 B.C.E.?	Earliness suggested by the verbal usage of the term *wang* and by a relatively unpolished style; the chapter is designed as Shang Yang's "canon"
5. Explaining the People (說民)	350–300 B.C.E.?	Exegesis on chapter 4
6. Calculating the Land (算地)	350–330 B.C.E.?	Philosophically mature; economic data come from considerably earlier than 309 B.C.E.
7. Opening the Blocked (開塞)	350–330 B.C.E.?	Philosophically mature; related to chapter 6; earliness suggested by the verbal usage of the term *wang*
8. Speaking of the One (壹言)	350–330 B.C.E.?	Too short to determine but is very close in content to chapters 6 and 7, the major points of which it summarizes
9. Implementing Laws (錯法)	post-306 B.C.E.	Mentions Qin strongman Wu Huo (d. 306 B.C.E.)
10. Methods of War (戰法)	360–300 B.C.E.	Unawareness of cavalry suggests pre-300 B.C.E. date
11. Establishing the Roots (立本)	360–300 B.C.E.	Unawareness of cavalry suggests pre-300 B.C.E. date
12. Military Defense (兵守)	pre-360 B.C.E.?	Geographical and military information relates it to the state of Wei, prior to Shang Yang's arrival to Qin

TABLE 2.1 *(continued)*

Chapter	Dating	Comments
13. Making Orders Strict (靳令)	?	A composite chapter, related or derivative of chapter 4
14. Cultivation of Authority (修權)	?	The first to discuss administrative affairs; sounds more accommodating toward ideological opponents than earlier chapters
15. Attracting the People (徠民)	255–235 B.C.E.	Dating based on the chapter's historical data
17. Rewards and Punishments (賞刑)	post-325 B.C.E.	Uses the term *wang* as the ruler's appellation
18. Charting the Policies (畫策)	?	A composite chapter, dating impossible
19. Within the Borders (境內)	350–300 B.C.E.?	Reflects early stages of Qin's "ranks of merit" system but possibly penned after 325 B.C.E.
20. Weakening the People (弱民)	350–300 B.C.E.?	Exegesis of chapter 4; section 20.11 is unrelated to the rest of the chapter and seems to have been composed much later
22. External and Internal (外內)	350–330 B.C.E.?	Relative earliness suggested by the verbal usage of the term *wang*
23. Rulers and Ministers (君臣)	?	No clear indicators
24. Interdicting and Encouraging (禁使)	?	Sophisticated style and peculiar content (focus on administration) may suggest a late date of composition, but this supposition is currently unverifiable
25. Attention to Law (慎法)	?	Sophisticated administrative thought may indicate relative lateness, but this supposition is currently unverifiable
26. Fixing Divisions (定分)	ca. 230 B.C.E.?	Reflects administrative realities from the eve of imperial unification

argument in the vast majority of preimperial philosophical texts (Schaberg 2011), are all but absent. The authors' individual voices are rarely heard, and we know next to nothing of their aspirations or frustrations. Although the text is bitterly polemical, the opponents remain nameless, as is the case in most other texts from the first half of the Warring States period.[33] The style of many chapters resembles, even if superficially, the style of the *Laozi*, as William Baxter summarizes it: "it is entirely free of narration, in the sense that its statements are general and not anchored to any particular persons, times, or places. There is no indication of who is speaking, no direct reference to historical events. This contrasts strikingly with Confucian discourse" (1998, 240).

Baxter's observations are applicable to the vast majority of the *Book of Lord Shang*'s chapters. They, too, are free of narration; the statements are not anchored to particular persons, times, or places; the authors remain nameless; and historical events are referred to only in a couple of demonstrably late chapters (e.g., 15, 17). The book's style is plain and straightforward. The authors seek neither religious nor metaphysical justifications for their proposals; philosophical digressions in the text are few and far between (although when they do occur, they are highly insightful, as discussed in the next chapter). This ostensible simplicity is most appropriate for a book that repeatedly derides "argumentativeness and cleverness" (3.4, 3.5, 4.3, 5.1, 25.4).

The last point is essential for understanding the book's style. As in many other preimperial texts, in the *Book of Lord Shang* the peculiar literary form is intrinsically linked to the text's message. It is appropriate here to quote an insightful observation by Joachim Gentz and Dirk Meyer:

> In early Chinese texts, the literary form can relate to the argument of the text in various ways. Sometimes the literary form itself serves as an argument. . . . In other cases, literary forms serve as illustrative bodies that mirror the basic argumentative approach. The ways in which the ambiguous interlocked parallelisms in the *Laozi*, the playful and floating style in the *Zhuangzi*, the simple and clear sentences in the *Shangjun shu* [*Book of Lord Shang*], the natural

metaphors in the *Mengzi*, or the artificial constructions in the *Xunzi* reflect aspects of their respective argumentations may serve as examples. (Gentz and Meyer 2015, 13)

This observation singularly befits the *Book of Lord Shang*, especially its early chapters, which indeed are characterized by "simple and clear sentences." Take, for instance, chapter 4, which may have been conceived from its inception as Shang Yang's "canon" (see the introduction to that chapter on pp. 129–131). The chapter brings minimalism and straightforwardness to their extremes. It consists of short and energetic sentences; everything—including grammatical particles—is sacrificed for the sake of brevity (even the ubiquitous particle *ye* 也 is present only once). The text's messages are clarified in an almost sloganlike fashion; one may dislike them, but one cannot miss them. A correct policy will make the state strong (*qiang* 強) and turn its leader into the True Monarch (*wang* 王); a wrong choice will cause the state's collapse (*wang* 亡). These are one's policy choices: take it or leave it.

The style of chapter 4 is reflective, to a certain extent, of the bulk of the *Book of Lord Shang*. For instance, most of the chapters similarly (even if less radically) reduce the usage of particles (the so-called empty words, *xuci* 虛詞) to an absolute minimum, as is appropriate for a text that deals with "substantial" (*shi* 實) matters. Not all "empty words" are excluded, though. Some are hugely popular with the authors, in particular words that create an impression of logicality and the absolute correctness of their proposals. One of their favorite terms is *bi* 必 (surely, inevitably): it recurs no fewer than 186 times in the *Book of Lord Shang* (in comparison, in the much longer *Mengzi* this particle is used 100 times).[34] Even more popular are illative particles meaning "hence" or "therefore," such as *gu* 故 (252 times), *shigu* 是故 (15 times), and *shiyi* 是以 (16 times), and especially a related term for indicating the policy's outcome, *ze* 則, "then" (more than 500 times).[35] The preponderance of illative particles suggests a logical inference even when in fact there is none. Gentz's observation that in the *Sunzi* "the illative *gu* 故 . . . [is] used in high frequency throughout the text, often without strong logical implications and rather as 'false illative conjunction'" (2015, 125), is fully applicable to the *Book of Lord Shang* as well. Perhaps the authors hoped that the more they used this illative, the more convincing their arguments would appear to the readers.

Another interesting feature of the *Book of Lord Shang* is the number of chapters—no fewer than seven—that use the first-person pronoun *chen* 臣, literally meaning "I, your subject/your minister." It is conceivable that these chapters derived from court memorials submitted by Shang Yang and his successors to Qin rulers. It may be significant, though, that the editors who collected these memorials preferred to retain *chen* rather than a common first-person pronoun such as *wu* 吾. Perhaps they were hinting that an appropriate mode of intellectual activity is that directed exclusively from a minister toward the ruler rather than being targeted to fellow intellectuals. However, it is clear that by circulating these memorials, the editors did hope to engage a much broader audience than the ruler alone. Despite its pronounced derision of "argumentativeness and cleverness" and of men-of-service engaged in matters of "broad learning" (2.14, 3.6), the book as a whole is fully engaged in polemics with members of the educated elite in general.

Speaking of the book's editors, we may notice their sophistication, as reflected in the book's composition. Although we have no idea when the disparate essays associated with Shang Yang became a coherent "book" that began to be circulated as an organic whole, there are indications that the book's editors carefully preplanned the arrangement of the chapters. This preplanning is most easily noticeable in the book's being framed by the only two chapters that mention Gongsun Yang (i.e., Shang Yang) by name. In both chapters (1 and 26), Shang Yang is engaged in discussions with Lord Xiao: in the first, he advises the lord to dispense with the past and to revise (*geng* 更) the laws; in the last, he explains, conversely, how the laws should be fixed (*ding* 定) and promulgated. This framing creates a full cycle from change to stability, from a small but aspiring territorial state in the first chapter to an empire in the making (All-under-Heaven) in the last one. Clearly, this arrangement is not accidental: the two chapters were conceived as a framework of the entire book.

Yet careful arrangement is observable not just in these two chapters. Chapter 2, "Orders to Cultivate Wastelands," directly follows chapter 1, which ends with Lord Xiao's issuing of precisely this order. Chapter 3, "Agriculture and Warfare," the longest in the book, focuses on the singularly important topic of turning the population into farmers and fighters. Chapter 4, "Eliminating the Strong," as noted earlier, might have been conceived from its inception as the summa of Shang Yang's wisdom. It is followed by the exegetical chapter 5 (with the first half of this exegesis oddly becoming chapter 20). Then follow two interlinked chapters (6 and 7), which are the most sophisticated intellectually and provide the philosophical rationale for the entire book. The next chapter, 8, "Speaking of the One" ("Yi yan" 壹言) is a brief summary of previous points. Although it is likely that the quasi-chronological order of these chapters is accidental, the arrangement here and throughout the text is not. The editors in all likelihood wanted to present a systematic introduction to Shang Yang's thought and then to show its evolution, including the exploration of military theories (chapters 10–12) and administrative ideas (chapters 24–26). There are some mishaps (e.g., placing chapter 20 at its current position rather than immediately after chapter 4 and placing the military-related chapter 19 in a later part of the text), but traces of careful editing are still visible overall. Whoever was in charge of compiling the book, he was well acquainted with the ideas of "Shang Yang's school" and sought efficient ways to introduce these ideas to the readers.

3

THE IDEOLOGY OF THE TOTAL STATE

One of the best-known texts for the study of Chinese intellectual history is the essay "The Essentials of the Six Schools" 六家之要指 by Sima Qian's father, the historian Sima Tan 司馬談 (d. 110 B.C.E.). In this essay, Sima Tan depicts the Legalist school as follows:

> The Legalists are strict and have little kindness.... [They] neither distinguish between kin and stranger, nor differentiate between noble and base: everything is determined by the law [or standard, *fa*]. Thus they abolish the kindness of treating one's kin as kin and honoring the honorable. It is a one-time policy that could not be constantly applied.... But as for honoring rulers and derogating subjects, and clearly distinguishing offices so that no one can overstep [his responsibilities]—none of the Hundred Schools could amend this. (*Shiji* 130:3289–3291; for other translations, see Smith 2003, 141, and Goldin 2011b, 89)

Being the earliest text to classify the Warring States period thought according to the "Six Schools" label, Sima Tan's account became singularly influential throughout the imperial era and well into our days (Smith 2003). The depiction of the Legalists as committed to the supremacy of law (or standard), on the one hand, and to maintaining clear distinctions between the ruler and the subject and among the officials, on the other, fueled subsequent (mis)perceptions of the

"Legalist school" for centuries to come (Goldin 2011b). This depiction is particularly misleading with regard to Shang Yang's legacy. The elder Sima glossed over the thinker's major idea—namely, the creation of a powerful state that would direct the populace to the mutually supporting goals of agriculture and warfare. In this chapter, I want to abandon the Sima family prism and focus on the *Book of Lord Shang* as the primary source for Shang Yang's thought.[1] I try to demonstrate that, rather than being a champion of the "rule of law," as Shang Yang is perceived in China well into our days (e.g., Wu Baoping and Lin Cunguang 2015), he was primarily an architect of the idea of a total state and one of the earliest proponents of radical social engineering in human history.

IDEOLOGICAL FOUNDATIONS: HISTORY, HUMAN NATURE, AND THE STATE

The *Book of Lord Shang* is a highly polemical treatise. Its authors repeatedly criticize their manifold opponents, such as the "knowledgeable and clever" advisers who mislead the ruler or the traditional-minded scholars whose moralizing discourse hinders resolute political action. This polemical spirit is not accidental. Shang Yang's program was a novel departure in his time, and his reforms met with a plethora of skeptical and overtly opposing voices, some of which are recorded in the first chapter of the book itself. In the face of this opposition, the authors of the *Book of Lord Shang* had to provide ideological justifications for their proposed departures from well-established practices. These justifications constitute the philosophical rationale for Shang Yang's policies.

The most powerful argument in favor of political reforms promulgated throughout the *Book of Lord Shang* is the dictum to adjust the sociopolitical system to changing circumstances. The first and arguably the best-known chapter of the book, "Revising the Laws," focuses precisely on this point. During an alleged discussion in front of Lord Xiao of Qin, Shang Yang (then still named Gongsun Yang 公孫鞅, a newcomer to the court of Qin) rebuffed his conservative opponents, who claimed that "one who imitates antiquity does not err":

Former generations did not adopt the same teaching: So which antiquity should one imitate? Thearchs and Monarchs did not repeat one
another: So which rituals should one conform to? Fuxi and Shennong
taught but did not punish; the Yellow Thearch, Yao, and Shun punished but did not implicate [the criminals'] families; and Kings Wen
and Wu[2] both established laws appropriate to the times and regulated rituals according to their undertakings. Rituals and laws are
fixed according to the times; regulations and orders are all expedient; weapons, armor, utensils, and equipment, all are used according to their utility. Hence, I say: there is no single way to order the
generation; to benefit the state, one need not imitate antiquity. (1.4)

This statement encapsulates the essentials of Shang Yang's message.
Antiquity and its paragons are not disparaged, but their model was
appropriate for their time only and cannot be followed today. Simply
put, there can be no unified model of the past. The lesson to be learned
from the paragons' successes—if there is one—is to be flexible and adap-
tive. This idea permeates the *Book of Lord Shang*: the ruler should never
confine himself to established patterns but rather do whatever is expedient. Responding to "the times" and modifying one's methods of rule
constitute the book's major recipe for political success.

The idea of "changing with the times" was not controversial in itself;
rather, as Martin Kern argues, it was shared by the majority of preimperial and early imperial thinkers (2000, 170–174). What distinguishes
Shang Yang from these thinkers, though, is his philosophy of history,
most notably the idea of historical evolution. This idea is pronounced
with utmost clarity in those sections of the *Book of Lord Shang* that
explore the origins of the state, and it is to these sections that I turn
now. Let us focus here on a single narrative, arguably the most sophisticated, presented in chapter 7, "Opening the Blocked." This chapter
starts with the following statement:

When Heaven and Earth were formed, the people were born. At that
time, the people knew their mothers but not their fathers; their way
was one of attachment to relatives and of selfishness. Attachment
to relatives results in particularity; selfishness results in malignity.
The people multiplied, and as they were engaged in particularity and

malignity, there was turmoil. At that time, the people began seeking victories and forcefully seizing [each other's property]. (7.1)

From the first phrases we can see the distinctiveness of Shang Yang's approach. The majority of preimperial narratives of state formation depicted primeval society as plagued by intrinsic turmoil; in distinction, a minority view, evident in some chapters of the *Zhuangzi* 莊子, considered the prepolitical age as an era of harmony and peace.[3] "Opening the Blocked" combines both approaches: turmoil is not intrinsic to a stateless society; rather, it evolves gradually because of population pressure. The idea of primeval harmony is even more clearly pronounced in chapter 18, "Charting the Policies," which explains that when "the people were few, but trees and animals plenty," there were no reasons for social conflict; there were "neither punishments nor regulations, yet there was order" (18.1).[4] Yet, as "Opening the Blocked" explains, when "the people multiplied," the intrinsic selfishness of human beings began endangering social order. As the weaknesses of stateless society became evident, it had to be reformed:

Seeking victories results in struggles; forceful seizure results in quarrels. When there are quarrels but no proper [norms], no one attains his natural life span. Therefore, the worthies established impartiality and propriety and instituted selflessness; the people began rejoicing in benevolence. At that time, attachment to relatives declined, and elevation of the worthy was established. (7.1)

The promiscuous (or matriarchal?) kin-based order, which fostered selfishness, proved inadequate in coping with population pressure and its resulting struggles; hence, unidentified "worthies" (*xianzhe* 賢者) intervened, replacing that order with the incipient stratified society based on "elevation of the worthy." It was at this stage that morality was first taught to the populace, apparently calming the struggles and the forceful mutual seizure of property of the earlier age. We witness, then, profound social, ideological, and political change. However, morality and social stratification alone could not resolve the fundamental problem of human selfishness, which, after a new cycle of population increase, became equally damaging to a new social order:

In general, the benevolent are devoted to the love of benefit, whereas
the worthy view overcoming one another as the [proper] Way. The
people multiplied yet lacked regulations; for a long time they
viewed overcoming one another as the [proper] Way, and hence
there again was turmoil. Therefore, the sages took responsibility.
They created distinctions among lands, property, men, and women.
When distinctions were fixed but regulations were still lacking,
this was unacceptable; hence, they established prohibitions.
When prohibitions were established but none supervised [their
implementation], this was unacceptable; hence they established
officials. When officials were instituted but not unified, this was
unacceptable; hence, they established the ruler. When the ruler
was established, the elevation of the worthy declined, and the
esteem of nobility was established. (7.1)

This narrative of the state formation differs markedly from that of
other known texts.[5] The state was created not as a singular act of the
sages, but as a result of a lengthy process of increasing political complexity and social change. Society evolves from an egalitarian, promiscuous, kin-based order to an incipient stratified order and then to a
mature political organization based on property distinctions, prohibitions, and officials. This process is crowned with the establishment of
a ruler, and it is only then that we can speak of a fully formed state.
This is an extraordinarily sophisticated and dynamic model.

The chapter's authors avoid excessive eulogizing of the state. From
their point of view, it is conceivable that during a lengthy prestate
period there were no rulers, yet this situation was not necessarily
unmanageable back then. However, once population pressure had generated social tensions, overall adjustment of the political system became
necessary, and the formation of the state became inevitable. Although
moral education could, for a certain period of time, moderate the
intrinsic selfishness of human beings, it could not fundamentally alter
it, especially when demographic growth brought about increased contention. Competition among worthies became as unmanageable as the
earlier contention among ordinary individuals. The narrative implies
that morality simply became a veneer for the pursuit of selfish

struggles. Therefore, only through the formation of an effective political system could the sages preserve order, and their way was not that of eradicating selfishness but of preventing it from damaging social life. This prevention was accomplished not through education but primarily through effective implementation of laws, regulations, and prohibitions—that is, precisely what the *Book of Lord Shang* consistently considers the best remedy for social turmoil. The chapter summarizes:

> In antiquity, the people resided together and dwelled herdlike in turmoil; hence, they were in need of superiors. So All-under-Heaven is happy having superiors and considers this orderly rule. Now, if you have a sovereign but no laws, it is as harmful as having no sovereign; if you have laws but are unable to overcome [those] who wreak havoc, it is as if you have no laws. Although All-under-Heaven have no peace without a ruler, they delight in flouting his laws: hence, the entire generation is in a state of confusion. Yet to benefit the people of All-under-Heaven nothing is better than orderly rule; and in orderly rule nothing is more secure than establishing the ruler. The Way of establishing the ruler is nowhere broader than in relying on laws; in the task of relying on laws, nothing is more urgent than eradicating villainy; the root of eradicating villainy is nowhere deeper than in making punishments stern. Hence, the True Monarch prohibits through rewards and encourages through punishments; he pursues transgressions and not goodness; he relies on punishments to eradicate punishments. (7.6)

The sophistication of Shang Yang's political thought is presented here at its best. First, ever since the demise of primeval harmony, society cannot function without a clearly pronounced hierarchical order headed by a ruler. Second, the ruler is a necessary but insufficient precondition of social order: he must rely on the legal system and especially on stern punishments, which will cause his rule to be really effective. Third, although in principle the people "are happy" to be guarded by the ruler, they are intrinsically inclined to flout the laws; hence, unless they are overawed by stern punishments, they will damage the very order on which their peace and prosperity depends.

The ruler-centered political system is a social must, but it has to be actively protected from members of society whose selfishness and narrow-mindedness lead them to repeated transgressions. This is the rationale of Shang Yang's political model.

In the last part of this chapter, I turn back to the idea of historical evolution in the *Book of Lord Shang* as allowing a future change in the current state structure, but before we get to that point, let us explore the second pillar of Shang Yang's ideology: his belief in the fundamental conflict between the general interests of the human collective and the selfish interests of individuals. The text explains: "The people's disposition is to be ruled well; but their activities bring about turmoil" (5.4). That is, human beings are objectively in need of orderly rule, but their actions undermine sociopolitical stability. Why is this so? It is because of the intrinsic "selfishness" (*si* 私) of any single individual. Whereas the state and the ruler represent "commonality" (*gong* 公),[6] individuals are driven by selfish interests only and cannot be expected to abandon them. It is the task of the ideal political system envisioned by Shang Yang to maintain the contradiction between selfish and common needs in a way so as to benefit the latter.

How will this blessed situation be achieved? Here Shang Yang comes up with a brilliant solution. It is precisely individuals' selfishness and their covetous inborn nature (*xing* 性) that can be utilized not to jeopardize but rather to strengthen political order. "The people follow after benefit as water flows downward: it has no preference among the four directions. The people do only whatever brings them benefit, and the benefit is granted by superiors." (23.3). What is needed then is just to direct the people to pursue personal benefits in ways that will serve common needs. The authors explain how to achieve this goal in chapter 6, "Calculating the Land":

> The nature of the people is to seek food when they are hungry, to seek respite when they are belabored, to seek joy when they are embittered, to seek glory when they are humiliated: this is the people's disposition. In seeking benefit, the people lose the standard of ritual;[7] in seeking a name (repute), they lose the constant of their nature.[8] How can I demonstrate this? Now, criminals violate the

prohibitions of rulers and superiors above and lose the ritual of subjects and sons below; hence, their name is dishonored and their
body endangered, but they still do not stop: this is because of benefit. In the generations of old, there were men of service (*shi*) who did
not have enough clothes to warm their skin or enough food to fill
their bowels. They exerted their four limbs and injured their five
internal organs above, but they behaved ever more broad-heartedly.
This was not the constant of their nature, yet they did: this was
because of the name. Hence, it is said: wherever the name and benefit meet, the people will go in this direction. (6.4)

This discussion is one of the earliest systematic—and, unfortunately,
most frequently neglected—analyses of human nature in Chinese history.[9] Two major factors influencing human behavior are the quest for
riches and the desire for a name (*ming* 名, referring not only to repute
but also more generally to high social status, which can be bequeathed
to posterity; see Pines forthcoming B). The first causes them to transgress against moral and legal norms; the second even transcends their
quest for life and causes them to endanger themselves. These two
desires, which "stop only when their coffin is sealed" (17.4), are the people's basic disposition (*qing* 情). This disposition is not to be altered but
to be properly understood and then manipulated: "When a law is established without investigating the people's disposition, it will not succeed" (8.3). The text explains:

Farming is what the people consider bitter; war is what the people
consider dangerous. Yet they brave what they consider bitter and
perform what they consider dangerous because of the calculation [of
a name and benefit]. Thus, in [ordinary] life, the people calculate
benefits; [facing] death, they think of a (good) name. One cannot but
investigate whence the name and benefit come. When benefits come
from land, the people fully utilize their strength; when the name
comes from war, the people are ready to die. (6.5)

To direct the population to the "bitter" and "dangerous" pursuits that
benefit the state—namely, agriculture and warfare—one should

establish a combination of positive and negative incentives that will do so. The entire sociopolitical system advocated by Shang Yang can be seen as the realization of this recommendation.

TILLERS AND SOLDIERS: SOCIAL ENGINEERING

Chapter 7 of the *Book of Lord Shang*, discussed in the previous section, contains the following statement:

> King Wu seized [power] by rebellion but valued compliance; he fought for All-under-Heaven but elevated yielding; he seized [the world] by force but held it by righteousness.[10] Nowadays, strong states engage in conquests and annexations, and the weak are committed to forceful defense. Above, they do not reach the times of Yu [Shun] and Xia; below, they do not embrace [the ways of Kings] Tang and Wu.[11] [The ways of] Tang and Wu are blocked; hence, every state of ten thousand chariots is engaged in war, and every state of one thousand chariots is engaged in defense. These ways have been blocked for a long time, but contemporary rulers are unable to discard them; hence, the Three Dynasties lack the fourth. (7.3)

Establishing the "fourth" dynasty—namely, unifying "All-under-Heaven"—was a common desideratum of competing thinkers of the Warring States period, yet fierce debates revolved around the proper ways to attain this goal (Pines 2000b; 2012b, 11–43). For Shang Yang, the answer is clear. To succeed, the ruler should liberate himself from the desire to emulate the paragons of the past, who were able to apply simultaneously martial and civilian means of rule, because doing what they did is simply no longer possible. In the age of ubiquitous war, one should commit oneself to strengthening the army and being ready to wage lasting war until all enemies are subjugated. And because this army needs provisions, agriculture should be encouraged to ensure adequate supplies. Proper policies will bring about the situation of "a rich state and a strong army" (*fuguo qiangbing* 富國彊兵), a stock phrase whose earliest usage is documented precisely in the *Book of Lord Shang* (8.2) (see also Graziani forthcoming).

How to enrich and empower the state is specified in the opening phrases of one of the programmatic chapters, "Speaking of the One," chapter 8:

> Whenever a state is established, one must understand regulations and measures, be cautious in governance and law, be diligent in [pursuing] the state's commitments, and consolidate essential occupations. When regulations and measures are timely, the customs of the state can be transformed, and the people will follow regulations. When governance and law are clear, there are no deviations among officials. When the state is committed to the One, the people can be used. When essential occupations are consolidated, the people are glad to farm and enjoy war. Thus, when the sage establishes laws and transforms customs, he causes the people from morning to dusk to engage in farming: this must be investigated. (8.1)

This statement can serve as a convenient introduction to Shang Yang's political program. The fundamentals of the state can be combined into two groups: the first deals with the administrative system (regulations and laws), while the second focuses on the "state's pursuits" and "essential occupations"—namely, agriculture and warfare. I start my discussion with the latter issue because turning the unwilling population into diligent farmers and valiant soldiers is the single most pronounced concern of the *Book of Lord Shang* and may well be considered the singularly spectacular achievement of Shang Yang's reforms.

The text is remarkably candid about the means by which the people can be manipulated to follow the pursuits desired by the ruler. Chapter 9, "Implementing Laws," clarifies:

> Human beings have likes and dislikes; hence, the people can be ruled. The ruler must investigate likes and dislikes. Likes and dislikes are the root of rewards and penalties. The disposition of the people is to like ranks and emoluments and to dislike punishments and penalties. The ruler sets up the two in order to guide the people's will and to establish whatever he desires. When ranks come only after the people have fully used their force, when rewards come only after

their merits are established, when the ruler is able to let his people trust these [two] as [unequivocally] as they visualize the sun and moon—then the army has no rivals. (9.3)

The people can be manipulated to do whatever the ruler considers necessary through a combination of positive and negative incentives. The latter are immediately identifiable with Shang Yang's promulgation of harsh punishments and are often deemed the essence of Shang Yang's program, but, actually, the text more frequently emphasizes positive incentives—ranks and emoluments—as essential to attract the people to the unpleasant tasks of tilling and making war. Chapter 23, "Ruler and Ministers," further explains:

> The people can be induced to till and fight, can be induced to become itinerant servants, and can be induced to study: it all depends on how superiors[12] grant them [ranks and emoluments]. If superiors grant these in exchange for merit and toil, the people go to war; if they grant them for [studying] the *Poems* and *Documents*, the people study. (23.3)

The recommendation, which is repeated throughout the book (e.g., section 3.1), appears quite simple: grant ranks and offices exclusively to those involved in agriculture and warfare and deny those ranks and offices to talkative advisers, whose activities are singled out in the text as particularly detrimental. Ranks and offices become the primary means of social engineering. Careful implementation of the system of ranks of merit (which, remember, was the hallmark of Shang Yang's reforms) will profoundly reshape the people's behavior. Henceforth, to satisfy their material and social aspirations, the people will have to engage in agriculture and warfare alone. Yet making ranks an efficient means of social engineering is possible only when these ranks determine the social and economic life of the populace in its totality. This in turn requires preventing any alternative means of enrichment and empowerment. This topic recurs throughout most of the chapters, and it is summarized most clearly in chapter 18, "Charting the Policies," which states:

Those who do not work but eat, who do not fight but attain glory, who have no rank but are respected, who have no emolument but are rich, who have no office but lead—these are called "villains" (18.6).

Behind this short and energetic statement one can discern Shang Yang's bold idea: to prevent those outside the system of ranks from possessing political, social, and economic power. The state will exclusively grant this power; it is up to the government to decide who will enjoy food, glory, respect, riches, and leadership. Those whom the text identifies as "villains" are actually remnants of autonomous social and economic elites, who, in the authors' eyes, have no right to exist. Whether Shang Yang's reforms succeeded in eliminating these elites is debatable, but it is appropriate to mention here that the currently available Qin paleographic sources give no indications of their later existence.[13] This means that the ranks granted by the state became the exclusive, or at the very least the primary, means of enhancing one's status. This system turned the ranks into a powerful tool to encourage the people to engage in those occupations deemed essential by the state.

MAKING THE PEOPLE FIGHT

Ranks and rewards were particularly important in the military field. As is well known, Qin, like its eastern and southern peers, had by Shang Yang's time witnessed a momentous transformation from aristocratic chariot-based armies to mass-infantry armies staffed by peasant conscripts, in which chariots (and later cavalry) played an auxiliary role (Lewis 1990, 54–67; Yang Kuan 1998, 303–317).[14] Among the major problems of the new armies were training and disciplining the conscripts and making them fight valiantly, and dealing with these problems is one of the pivotal topics in the *Book of Lord Shang*. The authors' solution is unequivocal: only when the state turns military exploits into the major (or only) avenue of status enhancement will the people readily sacrifice themselves. Therefore, "the way of using soldiers is to commit oneself to unifying rewards" (6.1). "Ranks and emoluments are the essence of the army" (9.1). Elsewhere, the authors explain their point in full:

> When the sage rules the state, he unifies rewards, unifies punishments, and unifies teaching. When rewards are unified, the army has no rivals. . . . What is called "unifying rewards" means that benefits, emoluments, official position, and rank uniformly derive from military [attainments] and that there are no other ways to dispense them. Therefore, the knowledgeable and the ignorant, the noble and the base, the courageous and cowardly, the worthy and unworthy— all fully utilize their innermost wisdom and fully exhaust the power of their limbs, going forth to die in the service of their superiors. The bravos and the worthies from All-under-Heaven will follow [the ruler] just as water flows downward. Hence, his troops will have no rivals, and his orders will be implemented throughout All-under-Heaven. (17.1–2)

This statement reduces military affairs to the single problem of the soldiers' motivation to fight, and this problem is reduced in turn to the policy of rewarding meritorious soldiers and officers by enhancing their socioeconomic status. How this idea was implemented is clear from chapter 19, "Within the Borders." The chapter reflects a persistent preoccupation with the quotas of severed heads and the correlation between meeting these quotas and the soldier's rank. It explains:

> After the battle, when [severed] heads are exposed, they are checked for three days; if the general has no doubts, he delivers ranks of merit to soldiers and officers. As for delivering ranks of merit: if this was not done after [the heads] were hung for three days, the four sub-commandants of the county should be dismissed, and the county's assistant magistrate and commandant should be fined. He who is able to attain one head of an armored soldier should be promoted one rank; his field should be increased by one *qing*,[15] his house plot should be increased by nine *mu*. For every rank, he is granted the right to one retainer, and then he is allowed to become a military or civilian official. (19.6)

This section, like all of chapter 19, reflects how much Shang Yang's reforms militarized society and bureaucratized the military. The social impact of military service is clear from the fact that military distinction, specifically the beheading of enemy combatants, serves as a primary means of advancing up the social ladder. Being granted a rank is not a hollow honor; rather, it entitles the owner to manifold social and economic benefits and eventually the right to join officialdom. Elsewhere, the chapter specifies the rank holders' further legal and sumptuary privileges (19.7, 19.8). It also explains that the officers' promotion was based not on individual valor but on the success of their unit. It clarifies the quota of severed heads for a battle in the open field (two thousand heads) and for the conquering of a besieged fortress (eight thousand heads) (19.5). It further discusses appropriate rewards for different types of rank-and-file soldiers and commanders. Clearly, rank mattered a great deal, and it conceivably was indeed the singularly important motivating force that encouraged soldiers to fight.

Speaking of the bureaucratization of the army, we can note that one of the military commanders' primary tasks was to determine appropriate rewards for each combatant. Look, for instance, at head count, discussed earlier. Exhibiting severed heads and checking them for three days were presumably done not only out of humanitarian concern for innocent people being slaughtered but also to prevent the inflation of ranks: after all, the compensation for success on the battlefield was too expensive to be dispensed lightly. Granting the reward was performed jointly by military and civilian authorities (presumably, the general had to report to the county authorities, who then had the duty to reward the soldiers), which suggests minimization of distinctions between the military and the civilian hierarchy. The administrators' failure to reward deserving soldiers was severely punished; this is yet another indication of the overall importance of military rewards in Qin's social life.

One of the most interesting depictions of the fully bureaucratized war is the discussion of siege warfare in chapter 19. At the beginning of the siege,

the state minister of works examines the breadth and the width of the wall. The state commandant divides *xiao* and *tu* soldiers for every square foot and orders [them] to attack. He fixes the time and says: "Those who are the first to succeed will be considered the best of the vanguard; those who are the last will be censured as the worst of the rear; those who are twice censured will be dismissed." (19.9)

Then, after the sappers have dug tunnels beneath the enemy's walls, the battle starts:

The State Commandant divides areas [for attack] and assaults them with the troops of the central army. The general creates a wooden platform and observes the operation together with the Chief Supervisor and General (or Royal?) Inspector. Those who are the first to break into [the fortress] are designated the best of the vanguard; those who are the last to enter are designated the worst of the rear. As for the sappers, their ranks are fully filled by volunteers; if there are not enough volunteers, they are supplemented with those who want promotions. (19.9)

This account is fascinating. War is perceived as primarily a bureaucratic procedure, with officers (from both military and civilian arms of the government) meticulously assigning duties to every unit and then assessing the soldiers' performance. The general, sitting on the observation platform, appears more concerned with calculating rewards and punishments than with managing the purely military aspects of the assault. This account may create the impression of a mechanistic view of warfare, but that is the wrong interpretation. The crack troops—identified here tentatively as "sappers"—are volunteers, who apparently are willing to brave death in exchange for higher rewards than those distributed to average soldiers. If the identification of the sappers as volunteers is correct, then it can testify to the success of Shang Yang's reforms: at least some Qin soldiers were indeed ready to brave death in exchange for a handsome reward. And, as in other parts of the book, there are no spiritual incentives for the warriors: killing and being killed are just a routine experience in advancing up the social ladder.

Granting ranks of merit to successful soldiers was arguably Shang Yang's greatest invention, and its overall success in reshaping Qin's social system and in reinvigorating its armies is undeniable. Yet rewards were not the only means employed by the state under Shang Yang's aegis to facilitate military exploits. No less important was the system of negative incentives—namely, resolute and inevitable punishments of deserters from the battlefield. The text clarifies:

> When the people are brave, war ends in victory; when the people are not brave, war ends in defeat. He who is able to unify the people in war, his people are brave; he who is unable to unify the people in war, his people are not brave. . . . When you enter a state and observe its governance, you know that he whose people are usable is powerful. How can I know that the people are usable? When the people look at war as a hungry wolf looks at meat, the people are usable.
>
> As for war: it is something the people hate. He who is able to make the people delight in war is the [True] Monarch. Among the people of a powerful state, fathers send off their sons, elder brothers send off their younger brothers, wives send off their husbands, and all say: "Do not come back without achievements!" They also say: "If you violate the [military] law and disobey orders, you will die, and I shall die. Under the canton's control,[16] there is no place to flee from the army ranks, and migrants can find no refuge."
>
> To order the army ranks: link them into five-men squads, distinguish them with badges, and bind them with orders. Then there will be no place to flee, and defeat will never ensue. Thus, the multitudes of the three armies will follow the orders as [water] flows [downward], and even facing death they will not turn back. (18.3)

The discussion here becomes much more sophisticated. Rewards—even if handsome—are insufficient to create a powerful army; what matter no less are strict military discipline and the rule of terror against deserters and other breakers of orders. The inevitability of punishment—an inevitability attained in part thanks to the complete registration of the population, which makes escaping government control extremely difficult (see more on this subject later in this chapter)—is the guarantee of compliance. Then, the combination of positive and negative incentives brings about a profound internalization of military values—that is, the militarization of culture. Soldiers will fight to the death not out of an abstract commitment to the ruler and the state; even though they may even continue to hate war, they will know that war is their only chance not just to survive but also to benefit.

Later in this chapter, I turn to the militarization of culture and the issue of indoctrination in the *Book of Lord Shang*; here, suffice it to say that these means were intended to play an important but still pronouncedly auxiliary role in fostering the martial spirit of Qin conscripts. Overall, the conscripts were to be encouraged primarily through the combination of rewards and punishments. Manipulating these two handles remained the essential point in Shang Yang's social engineering, aimed at turning the populace into tillers and soldiers.

FILLING THE GRANARIES

Let us turn now to the second handle of becoming the True Monarch: agriculture. The *Book of Lord Shang* emphasizes the similarity between agriculture and warfare, which are often jointly called "the One" (*yi* 壹). Full granaries are the precondition for military victory, and diligent tilling, just like military valor, should be encouraged primarily through granting ranks. For instance, the canonical chapter 4, "Eliminating the Strong," summarizes:

> When [the state] raises an army and launches an attack, then ranks and responsibilities are granted based on military [exploits], and it will surely be victorious. When it restrains the army and [pursues] farming, then ranks and responsibilities are granted based on grain [production], and the state will become rich. (4.11)

This statement suggests that producing high yields of grain could generate a reward on a par with decapitating enemies, and it is quite possible that Shang Yang indeed envisioned such a system at the start of his reforms. Yet even if this were so, the system was never actualized: granting ranks in exchange for high yields remained an ad hoc arrangement that was never fully developed, unlike the system of rewarding military exploits (Korolkov 2010, 101–103). However, one can read this passage differently: there would be no fixed correspondence between a particular yield and a particular rank, but, rather, the rank would be purchasable exclusively in exchange for grain. Indeed, the *Book of Lord Shang* mentions elsewhere, "Hence, when the people are rich and cannot be used, let the people use provisions to attain ranks; ranks will surely [be bestowed] according to one's efforts; then the farmers will not be indolent" (20.3). Ranks would not follow yields automatically, but the farmer would have the chance to translate his newly accumulated grain surplus into enhanced social status.

We do know that in the state of Qin ranks could indeed be purchased, which can be proved, for instance, with some scattered evidence from the Liye 里耶 slips.[17] But how the system worked and how it was related—if at all—to the recommendations of the *Book of Lord Shang* are more difficult to say. In principle, selling rank in exchange for grain alone would bring about multiple social and economic benefits. First, it would encourage agricultural production. Second, it would restrict the socially undesirable extreme enrichment of a few individuals: "When [the people] are rich, reduce this by [selling] ranks: then they will not be excessive" (8.2). Third, the system would allow siphoning off some subjects' wealth, thereby increasing the state's profit margins. Fourth, it would increase the price of grain, alleviating the authors' fears that when "basic commodities [i.e., grain] are cheap," the farmers would be discouraged from engaging in agriculture (4.9; cf. 22.2). The problem with all of these assessments is that neither the text itself nor other currently available materials clarify how the system worked.

Although the nature of positive incentives to grain producers in the *Book of Lord Shang* remains vague, the second handle—that is, negative incentives to all those not engaged in agricultural production—is abundantly clear. Chapter 22, "External and Internal" ("Wai nei" 外內), specifies:

If you can cause merchants and peddlers and crafty and tricky people not to prosper, then even if you do not want to enrich the state, you will not but attain that. Hence, it is said: "He who wants the farmers to enrich his state makes food within the borders expensive.

He must impose multiple taxes on those who do not farm and heavy levies on profits from the markets." Then the people will have to work in the fields. Those who do not work in the fields will have to exchange [their products] for food; when food is expensive, those who work in the fields benefit.[18] When working in the fields brings benefit, then those who engage in it are many. When food is expensive, and purchasing it is not profitable, and in addition [it] is heavily taxed, then the people will have to cast away [the occupations of] merchants and peddlers and crafty and tricky people and engage in profiting from the soil. Thus, the people's strength is fully committed to the soil alone. (22.2)

The discussion encapsulates the recommendations in the *Book of Lord Shang*, which are detailed in chapter 2, "Orders to Cultivate Wastelands," and elsewhere. A series of discriminatory measures against merchants and artisans should discourage the people from engaging in these professions; thus, they will have no choice but to shift toward agriculture. As Roel Sterckx (2015) has noted, this advocacy of clear antimerchant policies distinguishes the *Book of Lord Shang* from other preimperial texts (see also Ōchi Shigeaki 1993, 182–188). The reasons for this assault on merchants and artisans are both economic and social. Economically, by discouraging nonagricultural pursuits, the state would be able to direct the population toward farming, increasing thereby agricultural production. Socially, weakening the merchants would further serve the goal of eliminating independent economic and social elites, as discussed earlier.

Careful reading of the chapters on agricultural policies (2, 6, 15) of the *Book of Lord Shang* suggests an evolution in the authors' economic outlook and in Qin's actual policies. The earliest, chapter 2, appears the least sophisticated. According to this chapter, the goal of increased land cultivation should be achieved primarily (if not exclusively) by actively discouraging nonagricultural pursuits: merchants, elite and subelite members, and their dependents should be discriminated against so as to direct them toward farming. In chapter 6, a more balanced view is promoted: what matters is not just the size of cultivated territories but also the maintenance of a proper ratio between the people and the land; hence, "when the people exceed the land, devote yourself to opening up [new lands]; when the land exceeds the people, engage in attracting [immigrants]" (6.1). Chapter 6 pays more attention to the need to employ positive incentives to encourage the people to farm, while simultaneously preserving the recommendation to discriminate against merchants, artisans, and unruly men of service. The last (in terms of its date of composition) chapter that deals with agriculture, 15, "Attracting the People," focuses exclusively on attracting immigrants. This chapter offers a variety of preferential policies that would have been inconceivable for the authors of early chapters: immigrants should be relieved of military service and even allowed ten-year-long free exploitation of "mountains, hills, and swamps" (15.3). It seems that the book's authors as well as Qin policy makers in general gradually learned that coercive means are insufficient for agricultural advancement and that lenient policies may be more expedient in the long term.

This increased sophistication aside, one cannot but notice how simplistic the overall economic outlook of the *Book of Lord Shang* appears in comparison with actual Qin policies. The authors' dramatic dislike of merchants—who should be humiliated, suppressed, and squeezed out of their profits—demonstrates their insufficient understanding of the positive aspects of a market economy. Their view of artisans as exclusively engaged in parasitic "skillful arts" (*jiyi* 技藝) (3.2, 3.3) is similarly odd: the authors seem to be unaware of—or unwilling to acknowledge—the artisans' huge contribution to the Qin economy (Barbieri-Low 2007). Yet what is truly perplexing is the text's silence on the manifold aspects of Qin's agromanagerial economy, which are fully elucidated in the unearthed Qin documents from Shuihudi, Liye, and elsewhere. Such topics as the production and distribution of iron tools to the peasants, policies of tax incentives to new cultivators, maintenance of government fields (*gong tian* 公田), employment of convicts, mining, hydraulic works, and the like—all the aspects of Qin's economy that allowed this state to attain its superpower status—are glossed over (see more on this issue in Pines forthcoming A). It is possible that this negligence reflects a relatively underdeveloped stage of the Qin economy at the time of the book's composition.[19] Alternatively, it may reflect the peculiar nature of the *Book of Lord Shang*, which was designed as a polemical treatise rather than as a comprehensive blueprint for social and political development (a topic that I address later in this chapter). Here, suffice it to say that the authors of the *Book of Lord Shang* reduce the ultimate solution of the problem of "a rich state and a strong army" to a single issue: creating a sociopolitical structure that would direct the entire population to tilling and fighting and would allow no other avenue of enhancing one's social, economic, or political status. The authors summarize:

> Hence, my teaching causes those among the people who seek benefits to gain them nowhere else but in tilling and those who want to avoid harm to escape nowhere but to war. Within the borders, everyone among the people first devotes himself to tilling and warfare and only then obtains whatever pleases him. Hence, though the territory is small, grain is plenty, and though the people are few, the army is powerful. He who is able to implement these two within the borders will accomplish the way of Hegemon and Monarch. (25.5)

EMPOWERING THE STATE: LAW, CENSUS, BUREAUCRACY

One of the (in)famous controversial dictums in the *Book of Lord Shang* states, "When the people are weak, the state is strong; when the people are strong, the state is weak. Hence, the state that possesses the Way devotes itself to weakening the people" (20.1). Elsewhere, the text specifies:

> In the past, those who were able to regulate All-under-Heaven first had to regulate their own people; those who were able to overcome the enemy had first to overcome their own people. The root of overcoming the people is controlling the people as the metalworker controls metal and the potter clay. When the roots are not firm, the people will be like flying birds and running animals: Who will then be able to regulate them? The root of the people is law. Hence, those

who excel at orderly rule block the people with law; then [a good] name and lands can be attained. (18.2)

These outspoken statements clarify one of the premises of the text: the persistent conflict between society ("the people") and the state. The people's intrinsic selfishness constantly endangers social order, and to safeguard this order, the ruler should resolutely rein in his subjects, which, in turn, requires empowering the state vis-à-vis society.

The primary means of controlling the population, as outlined in the quotation from section 18.2, is law (*fa* 法). *Fa* is a multifaceted term in early Chinese texts in general and in the *Book of Lord Shang* in particular,[20] but whenever it is used in the context of controlling the people, it refers primarily to punitive laws. The *Book of Lord Shang* is notorious for advocating heavy punishments for even petty offenses. For example:

> When penalties are heavy and rewards are light, then superiors love the people, and the people are [ready] to die for their superiors. . . . [In the state of the True] Monarch, for every nine punishments there is one reward; in a powerful state, for every seven punishments there are three rewards; in a due-to-be-dismembered state, for every five punishments there are five rewards. (4.4)

However, this system is neither arbitrary nor senselessly cruel. The authors repeatedly clarify that the goal of their harshness is to over-awe the people, thereby eliminating transgressions and ultimately bringing about a reduction in the use of punishments. For instance, chapter 17, "Rewards and Punishments," clarifies:

> The prohibitions of the former kings, such as [carrying out] executions, cutting off feet, or branding the face, were imposed not because they sought to harm the people but only to prohibit villainy and to stop transgressions. Hence, to prohibit villainy and stop transgressions nothing is better than making punishments heavy. When punishments are heavy and [criminals] are inevitably captured, then the people dare not try [to break the law]. Hence, there are no

penalized people in the state. When there are no penalized people in the state, it is said: "Clear punishments eliminate executions." (17.3)

Executing and mutilating criminals are justified not only as efficient means of ensuring the people's compliance with the state's requirements but also as ways to make punishments redundant. This is also the goal of the regulations that encourage mutual denunciation by family members and colleagues, which the text advocates elsewhere (17.3). "Eradicating punishments through punishments" is a recurring theme not only in the *Book of Lord Shang* (discussed more fully later in this chapter) but also more broadly in early Chinese legal thought in general, associated even with a canonical text such as the chapter "Da Yu mo" 大禹謨 of the *Canon of Documents* (see more in Sanft 2017). In the *Book of Lord Shang*, it serves as a primary justification for harsh laws. Another, less frequently noticed justification is that the laws are not arbitrary. Rather, they should be fundamentally accepted by the people: hence, the text advocates establishing laws only after taking careful account of the people's disposition:

> Hence, in ruling the state, the sage establishes laws after observing customs and then attains orderly rule; he inspects the roots of the state's affairs and then acts appropriately. Without the observation of current customs and without the inspection of the roots of the state, laws can be established, but the people will be in turmoil; undertakings will be numerous, but achievements few. This is what I, your minister, call "to err." (6.9)

Why should laws be established only after observing the people's customs? The authors explain that such observation is a precondition for the full internalization of the laws and the resulting full compliance. In a surprising statement, the text advocates taking public opinion into consideration as a sine qua non for successful law making:

> This is the orderly rule of the state: when [affairs] are determined by a household, you will become the Monarch; when [affairs are]

determined by officials, you will be strong; when [they are] determined by the ruler [himself], you will be weak. . . . If criminals are invariably denounced, then the people will make decisions in their hearts. When superiors issue orders and the people know to respond, when utensils take shape in the household and are utilized by officials,[21] then affairs are determined by a household. Hence, [in the state of] the True Monarch, punishments and rewards are determined by the people's hearts; the use of the utensils is determined at the household level. . . . The well-ordered state values decisions made below. . . . In the state that possesses the Way, orderly rule is attained without heeding the ruler, and the people have no need to follow officials. (5.9)

This curious passage, which, as Mark E. Lewis has noted, "[when] read out of context sounds like an appeal for democracy or anarchy" (1990, 93), testifies that Shang Yang, despite his pronounced disregard of the people, was aware of the importance of public opinion even in an overtly authoritarian political system. Of course, discerning "the people's hearts" does not mean blindly following public opinion. Rather, the authors envision a dialectic relation between the laws and the people. Laws should be based on an understanding of the people's disposition (i.e., their intrinsic quest for rewards and fear of punishments) and should accord with their customs. Then, strict enforcement of the laws will cause the people not just to comply with but also to internalize the laws, making the laws fully efficient.[22]

It is in this context that we can understand the text's repeated advocacy of "clarity" (*ming* 明) in the laws. Actually, the last chapter in the book (26, "Fixing Divisions") focuses primarily on the dissemination of legal knowledge among the populace, which is considered a precondition for full compliance with the laws. We know that at least some of the chapter's recommendations were put into practice by Imperial Qin bureaucrats and that legal knowledge among the populace at large was impressive indeed (Korolkov 2011; Sanft 2014a, 140–142). Importantly, legal knowledge was required not only to prevent transgressions but also to protect the people from bureaucratic abuse: "When the officials clearly know that the people understand the laws and ordinances, they dare not treat the people but in accord with the law, and the people will dare not violate the law and disobey the law officials" (26.4).

Law serves as a primary means of control over the population, but there are other, less-harsh, but no less efficient means. Of these, universal registration figures prominently. The text recommends: "Within the four borders, the authorities should possess [records of] the names of all men and women, recording those who are born and erasing those who have died" (19.1). Registration is a necessary means not only for efficient taxation and mobilization of the conscripts but also for general surveillance. The statement that "under the canton's control, there is no place to flee from the army ranks, and migrants can find no refuge" (18.3) presupposes full registration of the population, which makes either deserting from military ranks or migrating from one's village difficult.[23] The *Book of Lord Shang* repeatedly insists that the population's movements should be closely monitored: "Do not let the people shift locations on their own initiative" (2.12).

Registration of the population might have been invented long before Shang Yang recommended it, yet the *Book of Lord Shang* appears to advocate radically expanding the registered data and turning registration into a means of economic and not just political control:

> A strong state should know thirteen numbers within its borders: the number of granaries and residents; the number of adult men and women; the number of the old or infirm; the number of officials and men of service; the number of those who obtain emoluments by talking; the number of beneficial people;[24] the number of horses, oxen, hay, and straw. If one wants to strengthen one's state but does not know these thirteen numbers, then even if the state's soil is advantageous and residents are numerous, it will be increasingly weakened to the point of dismemberment. (4.10)

This statement envisages the establishment of comprehensive control over economic life. Although currently available Qin population registries and related materials do not allow an unequivocal conclusion as to whether the authorities knew all the details about their subjects, there is no doubt, as suggested earlier, that they moved in this direction.[25] Making everything "legible," "rational," and "knowable," which James C. Scott identifies as a fundamental vector of the development of the European modern state (1998, 2), stands at the background of the measures advocated in the *Book of Lord Shang* and implemented by Qin bureaucrats.[26]

The meticulous registration of the population and of its wealth as well as the effective implementation of laws in general would not be possible without an elaborate administrative mechanism. But, somewhat oddly, we have no clear elucidation of the functioning of this mechanism in the *Book of Lord Shang*. This functioning is mentioned only en passant—for instance, when the procedure of rewarding meritorious soldiers is discussed. The text refers elsewhere to close surveillance of the population by the canton (*xiang* 鄉, a subcounty unit) authorities (18.3), recommends establishing uniform administrative patterns throughout "the hundred counties" (2.6, 2.14, 2.16), and so forth, but none of these references amounts to a detailed discussion of the administrative system. The only significant exception is chapter 26, the latest chapter (in terms of its date of composition), which provides a detailed account about the system of law officials and of disseminating legal knowledge below. This chapter indicates that fully developed administrative thought was a late development within "Shang Yang's school."

This muted discussion of administrative arrangements, which parallels the similar muted discussion of the state's agromanagerial role discussed earlier, may be explained in two ways. One possibility is that the text simply reflects the realities of the fourth century B.C.E., of which we know little and which may differ considerably from the realities of the late-third-century B.C.E. state and empire of Qin, from which most currently available paleographic documents derive. It is technically possible that Qin in Shang Yang's time was still a relatively unsophisticated polity, which matured only a century or so after the start of reforms. However, I doubt the validity of this explanation. It is more likely that in order to understand why certain topics are given prominence in the *Book of Lord Shang* but others are glossed over, we should consider the nature of the text.

Recall that the *Book of Lord Shang* is primarily a polemical treatise, aimed at convincing the authors' patrons and, possibly, their opponents of the advantages of the policies that it proposes. Naturally, the text focuses on particularly controversial topics, such as granting ranks of merit exclusively to diligent tillers and valiant soldiers rather than to, say, the progeny of the elite. When the issue was not controversial, it may not have required a systematic discussion. The bureaucratization of society and the increasing economic activism of the state apparatus were common vectors of development among the competing Warring States, although it is conceivable that in Qin this development was faster and more profound than elsewhere (Yang Kuan 1998, 188–277; Lewis 1999a). Insofar as these issues did not generate heated debates, they may have not merited detailed discussion in the *Book of Lord Shang*.

RULER, MINISTERS, AND OFFICEHOLDERS

As noted in chapter 1, part I, Shang Yang is often associated with Shen Buhai, Han Fei, and, less frequently, Shen Dao as members of the same school: the Legalists.[27] There are indeed many similarities among the texts attributed to these thinkers, but the differences are no less pronounced, at least in terms of the texts' emphases. The *Book of Lord Shang* is concerned primarily with empowering the state vis-à-vis society, whereas the *Han Feizi* and the surviving fragments of Shen Buhai's (and to a lesser extent Shen Dao's) writings focus primarily on ruler–minister relations and administrative issues in general. The latter issues are much less emphasized in the *Book of Lord Shang*. Although the text does address such problems as bureaucratic abuse of power, corruption and dereliction of duties by officials, and the possibility that officials might subvert the ruler's power, it does so infrequently and mostly in chapters that apparently belong to its later layer. In early chapters, we do find remarks about "wicked officials" 邪官 who exploit the populace (2.1, 2.16) and the dictum that "when governance is large, the state is small" (4.2), which possibly implies awareness of the maladies generated by an excessively large bureaucratic apparatus, but these issues are never discussed at length. Among the later chapters, only one, chapter 24, "Interdicting and Encouraging," focuses on the problem of

bureaucratic corruption. This chapter includes an unusually perceptive remark about the inherent weaknesses of bureaucratic rule:

> Nowadays, [the ruler] relies on many officials and numerous clerks;
> to monitor them he establishes assistants and supervisors. Assistants
> are installed and supervisors are established to prohibit [officials]
> from pursuing [personal] profit; yet assistants and supervisors also
> seek profit, so how will they be able to prohibit each other? (24.2)

This appears to be a rare insight concerning the administrative system's fundamental inability to monitor itself in the long term. But how
can this problem be solved? The suggested solution is to rely exclusively
on impersonal "power of authority" (*shi* 勢) and to employ proper
"methods" (*shù* 數) of rule. The text does not explain, however, how
exactly these methods will solve the perennial problem of "Quis custodiet ipsos custodes?" (Who will guard the guardians?). Overall, this
topic remains at the margin of the book's discussions.

What does matter to the authors—and what establishes clear parallels between the *Book of Lord Shang* and the *Han Feizi*, among other
works—is the text's insistence on the advantage of impersonal administrative methods over individual decision making by the ruler and his
aides. These methods can be referred to as *shù* 數, "methods," or *shù*
術, "techniques," but they are most commonly called *fa* 法, in this context better translated as "standards." This is the second most important meaning of the term *fa* in the *Book of Lord Shang* (cf. Yang Soon-ja
2010). Relying on *fa* means employment of uniform standards of promotion and demotion and of conferring ranks and offices. An alternative to this system is the habitual bestowal of ranks, offices, and positions of power on the ruler's personal favorites. The latter method, as
the authors repeatedly warn, will have negative consequences:

> In ruling the state, if you discard the power of authority and rely on
> the persuaders' talk, then you personally will be cultivated but will
> have meager achievements. Thus, when you employ the *shi*[28] engaged
> in the *Poems*, the *Documents*, and persuaders' talk, the people will
> wander and disregard their ruler; if you employ reclusive *shi*, the

people will be estranged and reject their superiors; if you employ brave *shi*, the people will be quarrelsome and disregard the prohibitions; if you make use of the *shi* who are skillful artisans, the people will be volatile and easily migrate; when the *shi* who are merchants and peddlers are at ease and yet reap benefits, then the people follow their lead and question their superiors. Hence, when these five types of people are employed by the state, the fields are covered by weeds, and the army is weak. (6.6)

The five types of *shi* enumerated in this passage have one thing in common: none is engaged in agriculture and warfare. Promoting these men is tantamount to abandoning the essential means of encouraging the people to till and fight; the authors equate such promotion with abandoning the ruler's power of authority. Yet this passage actually does not discuss the danger of capricious promotions to the ruler's personal position; rather, these promotions are targeted because of their negative impact on the system of the ranks of merit. If talkative *shi* are promoted, farmers and soldiers will seek alternative routes of advancement and abandon their fundamental occupations. This topic is reiterated in other identifiably early chapters, such as chapter 3, "Agriculture and Warfare." In later chapters, the emphasis changes: by disregarding impartial norms of promotion, the ruler will directly impair his authority. For instance, the authors of chapter 25, "Attention to Law," explain to the ruler why the common discourse of "elevating the worthy" may be detrimental to his power:

Elevation of the worthy is what the world calls "orderly rule": that is why orderly rule is in turmoil. What the world calls a "worthy" is one who is defined as upright; but those who define him as good and upright are his clique. When you hear his words, you consider him able; when you ask his partisans, they approve it. Hence, one is ennobled before one has any merits; one is punished before one has committed a crime. . . .

These men who form cliques do not wait for me to accomplish their affairs. When the ruler promotes one of their associates, the people turn [their] back on the sovereign and incline toward private connections. If the people turn [their] back on the sovereign and incline toward private connections, then the ruler is weak, whereas the ministers are powerful. (25.1–2)

Here the danger of partial promotions based on the vague and hence unreliable definition of worthiness (cf. Pines 2013a) is connected with consolidation of ministerial cliques or partisan associations (*dang* 黨), which will bring about the most negative result, that is, "weak ruler and powerful ministers" (compare to Ōchi Shigeaki 1993, 188–193). This argument strongly resembles that given in such texts as *Guanzi* and *Han Feizi*,[29] and it is quite possible—albeit unverifiable—that it reflects a later development within "Shang Yang's school."

These passages can be seen as indirect criticism of the sovereign for deviating from proper administrative norms, but in general the *Book of Lord Shang* only infrequently addresses problems concerning the ruler's functioning. The text often laments the ineptitude of "the rulers of our age," but it does not discuss how to improve their quality or how to place an adequate ruler on the throne. Somewhat exceptionally for Warring States period texts, the *Book of Lord Shang* also largely eschews discussions about the advantages or disadvantages of delegating power to meritorious aides.[30] Nor does the text discuss the ruler's personality: the impersonal system of rule should ideally accommodate any sovereign.[31] Only very rarely do the authors put forward recommendations for how to improve the ruler's conduct. This issue is addressed directly only in chapter 14, "Cultivation of Authority:"

When the common and the private are clearly separated, petty men do not envy the worthy, and the unworthy are not jealous of the meritorious. Hence, when Yao and Shun were established in All-under-Heaven, this was not in order to benefit privately from All-under-Heaven—they were established for the sake of All-under-Heaven. They selected the worthy, elevated the able, and transmitted [power] to them not because of alienation between father and son and intimacy with strangers, but because the Way of order and disorder was clear to them.[32] Hence, the Three Kings treated their relatives righteously,[33] and the Five Hegemons used law to rectify regional lords—all this was not in order to benefit privately from All-under-Heaven. They ruled All-under-Heaven for the sake of All-under-Heaven. Hence, they earned their [great] name and attained merit; All-under-Heaven was fond of their rule, and no one was able to harm them. But now all rulers and ministers of [this] calamitous age act in a petty way, monopolizing the benefits of a single state and appropriating the authority of their office so as to benefit their private [interests]. This is the reason by which the state is endangered. Hence, the interrelationship between the common and the private is the root of survival or ruin. (14.4)

This passage differs in certain details from the rest of the *Book of Lord Shang*. The distinction is most visible in such features as the positive reference to the Yao and Shun abdication legend, the endorsement of "elevating the worthy" discourse, and, most fundamentally, the vehement attack on the rulers' (and not just the ministers') selfishness. These peculiarities notwithstanding, the passage—and the chapter—do belong to the general ideological framework of the *Book of Lord Shang*. The call for the ruler to rein in his selfish desires is more overt in this passage than elsewhere in the text, but the topic itself is hinted at, even if not engaged directly, in other chapters. Insofar as the ruler represents the polity's common interests (*gong* 公), it is only natural to call upon him to abide by impersonal norms and regulations, to avoid following his personal (*si* 私) whims, and thereby to fulfill his responsibility toward the subjects.

UNIFYING THE TEACHING AND
MODIFYING CUSTOMS

In the twentieth century, not a few scholars dubbed Legalists in general and Shang Yang in particular "totalitarians" (see, for example, Creel 1953, 135–158; Rubin 1976, 55–88; Fu Zhengyuan 1996). Some of the aspects of Shang Yang's ideals depicted in this chapter—a powerful state that overwhelms society, rigid control over the populace, centralization, harsh laws, the state's radical intervention in socioeconomic life, and the like—lend support to this characterization. Yet before we adopt this designation, let us ask whether the *Book of Lord Shang* also advocates the state's control over the intellectual realm, a kind of control that should be a sine qua non for a true totalitarian polity.

The answer to this question is not simple. On the one hand, the book clearly advocates intervention in the realm of thought and culture. For instance, chapter 3 states:

> *Poems, Documents*, rites, music, goodness, self-cultivation, benevolence, uprightness, argumentativeness, cleverness: when the state has these ten, superiors cannot induce [the people] to [engage in] defense and fighting. If the state is ruled according to these ten, then if the enemy arrives, it will surely be dismembered, and even if the enemy does not arrive, the state will surely be impoverished. If the state eradicates these ten, then the enemy will not dare arrive, and even if he arrives, he will surely be repelled; when an army is raised and sent on a campaign, it will surely seize [the enemy's land]; whereas if the army is restrained and does not attack, the state will surely be rich. (3.5)

This attack on traditional culture and on moral values recurs in several other chapters of the *Book of Lord Shang* (4.3, 13.4) and epitomizes what I have dubbed elsewhere (Pines 2012a) an "alienating rhetoric." These statements can be read as a call for a radical cultural overhaul, akin to that orchestrated by Shang Yang in the social realm. Yet a more careful look reveals that this attack on traditional culture focuses not so much on its content but on its bearers, the talkative men-of-service whom the authors identify with the state's perennial weakness:

> Nowadays, all the rulers of our age are worried that their states are endangered and their soldiers are weak, so they strive to heed the persuaders. Persuaders form legions; they multiply words and adorn sayings but are of no real use. The sovereign is fond of their arguments and does not seek their substance. The persuaders are satisfied; the roads are full of skillful talkers, and from generation to generation they go on and multiply. The people see that this is

the way to reach kings, lords, and grandees, and all learn from them. They form cliques and associations, debate state affairs, and come in profusion. Lower people are fond of them; grandees like them. Therefore, among the people few are engaged in agriculture, whereas "peripatetic eaters"[34] are plenty; as they are plenty, the farmers are indolent; as the farmers are indolent, the land becomes wasteland.

If learning becomes habitual, the people turn their backs on farming: they follow talkers and persuaders, speak grand words, and [engage in] false debates. They turn their backs on farming and travel to get food, trying to exceed each other in words. Hence, the people abandon their superiors, and those who do not behave as subjects become more and more numerous. This is the teaching that impoverishes the state and weakens the army. If the state makes use of the people according to their words, then the people do not take care of farming. It is only the clear-sighted ruler who knows that being fond of words will neither strengthen the army nor expand the territory. Only the sage in ruling the country engages in the One [i.e., agriculture and warfare]; he consolidates [efforts] on agriculture, and that is all. (3.10)

This passage specifies accusations against traveling persuaders. What matters is not so much the content of their speeches but rather their negative impact on the people's mores: they distract the people from substantial occupations and cause them to engage in hollow talk and needless learning, which will inevitably ruin the state's economic and military strength. The problem, then, is not so much with traditional culture and clever argumentation per se, but with the manipulation of them by traveling persuaders, whose success at the ruler's courts undermines the text's major recommendation: to link one's position exclusively to merit in farming and making war.

The authors' dislike of "turning learning into habit" is related to another important point in their ideology: the valorization of simplicity (*pu* 樸) and even of ignorance (*yu* 愚), which are considered essential both for making peasants fully committed to farming and for facilitating government control over its subjects. Chapter 2, "Orders to Cultivate Wastelands," clarifies that should elite members be prohibited from engaging in argumentation and learning, the prohibition will immensely improve the people's mores:

> If peasants neither hear about extraordinary things nor observe different methods, then knowledgeable peasants will have no way to depart from their original occupation, and ignorant peasants will not become knowledgeable or fond of learning. If ignorant peasants do not become knowledgeable or fond of learning, they will strenuously devote themselves to agriculture. If knowledgeable peasants have no way to depart from their original occupation, then wastelands will surely be cultivated. (2.14)

The cultivation of wastelands is closely associated with the preservation of the farmers' ignorance. Elsewhere, the blessed result of this ignorance or simplicity is political: "when [the people] are committed to farming, they are simple; when they are simple, they fear orders" (6.3). Both economically and politically, education is harmful: it distracts the people from their diligent work and diminishes their submissiveness. One is immediately reminded of a dictum given in the *Laozi*: "Empty their [the people's] heart and fill their belly, weaken their will and strengthen their bones."[35] The parallels between the two texts become even more pronounced when we consider that both valorize the people's "simplicity." The latter term is rarely used in a positive context outside these two texts, and never does it recur so frequently as in the *Book of Lord Shang*.[36]

That said, the text does speak—even if infrequently—of "teaching" (or "indoctrination," *jiao* 教) as a positive goal. Does this mean brainwashing the people with the ideology approved by the authors? Not necessarily. A careful look at the usage of the term *jiao* in the *Book of Lord Shang* shows that it does not imply fundamental transformation of the people—for example, overcoming their intrinsic egoism. Rather, the people should understand where their benefit lies and whence the danger comes, as a result of which they will comply with the state's demands out of sheer self-interest. We have observed the importance of this internalization in encouraging the soldiers to go to war, and it is in this context that the term *jiao* appears most prominently. It is explained in full in chapter 17, "Rewards and Punishments:"

> What is called "unification of teaching" is that none of these—the broadly educated, the argumentative, the knowledgeable, the trustworthy, the honest, those skilled at ritual and music, those who cultivate their conduct, those who establish cliques, or those who are appointed due to their reputation or [after] having requested an audience—will be allowed to become rich and noble, to criticize punishments, or to establish their private opinions independently and submit them to superiors. . . . Even if one is sagacious and knowledgeable, crafty and glib-tongued, generous or simple, he should not be able to seek benefits from superiors unless he has merit. Thus, the gates of riches and nobility are exclusively in the field of war. He who is able to [distinguish himself at] war will pass through the gates of riches and nobility; he who is stubborn and tenacious will meet with constant punishments and will not be pardoned.
>
> Therefore, fathers and elder brothers, minor brothers, acquaintances, relatives by marriage, and colleagues all say: "What we should be devoted to is only war and that is all." Hence, the able-bodied are devoted to war, the elderly and infirm are devoted to defense; the dead have nothing to regret; the living are ever more devoted and encouraged. This is what I, your minister, call the "unification of teaching."
>
> The people's desire for riches and nobility stops only when their coffin is sealed. And [entering] the gates of riches and nobility must be through military [service]. Therefore, when they hear about war, the people congratulate each other; whenever they move or rest, drink or eat, they sing and chant only about war. This is why I, your minister, say: "Clarifying teaching is like arriving at no teaching." (17.4)

This passage is fascinating. If it did not belong to the humorless *Book of Lord Shang*, I would suggest that its usage of the term *jiao* (teaching), with its unmistakable association with Confucian discourse, is ironic.[37] From the first phrases, the authors dissociate this term from any kind of educational activity, which they perceive as actually detrimental to *jiao*. What is called "unification of teaching" here refers to a recurring topic in the *Book of Lord Shang*: strict adherence to the system of the exclusive distribution of ranks and honor through military service. When this system functions, it causes the people to internalize the notion that the only way to satisfy their desires for riches and glory is to engage in war; hence, war, which elsewhere in the book is frankly associated with what the people hate (18.3), becomes the focus of the people's aspirations. We have encountered the same war-oriented mentality in passage 18.3, quoted earlier. There, too, the adoration of war comes purely from egoistic motives: first, war is the only way to enhance one's status; and, second, fighting is also the only way to avoid a deserter's due punishment. When the inevitability and desirability of war are internalized, the people no longer need to be encouraged to go to the front: they will eagerly volunteer to do it!

It is important to notice here that, fundamentally, the *Book of Lord Shang* does not envision any more sophisticated military indoctrination. Any person knowledgeable of the history of mass armies in the Western Hemisphere may be perplexed: Why did the authors not promote any positive means of encouraging the people's commitment to war? Why do we never encounter in this text (or any other) the adoration of the martial spirit akin, for example, to the Romans' maxim "Dulce et decorum est pro patria mori" (It is sweet and glorious to die for the fatherland); the dehumanization of the enemy; the identification of martiality with masculinity; the presentation of war as the only way to ensure the people's security; or any other device employed worldwide to encourage men to fight? The answer perhaps has to do with the authors' fundamental mistrust of any education and indoctrination. Rather than being brainwashed to sacrifice themselves for the state out of some abstract commitment, the people should be directed to do so according to their intrinsic and immutable selfishness. Fighting to the death in order to attain rank or just to avoid the inevitable punishment inflicted on deserters and their kin is preferable to fighting for the sake of some chimera. Instead of cheating the people with hollow ideological constructs, the authors prefer to clarify substantial gains and losses from engagement in war or evading it, respectively, and then let the people's basic "disposition" direct them to the ends desired by the state.

In the final reckoning, the Book of Lord Shang does not propose an ideological superstructure that should bind the people together or that should somehow influence their actions. Indoctrination is envisioned primarily as a negative action, which should prevent the corrosive impact of moralizing discourse from distracting the people from agriculture and warfare. The authors, however, do not put forward any alternative set of messages to replace this discourse. Similarly, whenever they talk of "teaching" or of "transforming" (hua 化) and unifying the people's customs,[38] they do not imply any active dissemination of ideas or ideals among the populace. A perfect state should manipulate its subjects exclusively through the combination of rewards and punishments: clearly outlined rules that explicate personal gains and losses for compliance or transgression. Any ideological incentives then become redundant. Thus, the text's lack of interest in brainwashing makes it insufficiently "totalitarian."

EPILOGUE: IMMORAL MEANS AND MORAL ENDS

The final question I want to address here is the issue of Shang Yang's perceived amorality. A. C. Graham's designation of Legalism as an "amoral science of statecraft" is well known.[39] But is that designation justified? Let me go one step further and ask: Should we place Shang Yang's ideal state in which farming and waging war are the sole means of enhancing one's status—a state devoid of the pleasures of traditional culture, a state haunted by harsh laws and regulated by hyperactive bureaucracy—squarely among the anti-utopias?

Many scholars answer affirmatively (e.g., Lévi 2005, 38–42; Zhang Linxiang 2006). Yet before we follow them, let us look closely at the text's self-perception. As noted earlier in this chapter, the Book of Lord Shang does contain a few chapters that abound in controversial attacks on traditional culture and morality, and these statements squarely confirm the image of this book not just as "amoral" but also as immoral (or "antihumanistic" [Huang Shaomei 2010]). Yet, as I have demonstrated elsewhere, these "alienating" chapters do not represent the ideology of the *Book of Lord Shang* as a whole (Pines 2012a). Most other chapters justify the oppressive measures advocated by the authors as a necessary means toward attaining laudable moral ends. As shown earlier in this chapter, harsh punishments are presented as a way to eradicate the very need for punishments. It is time now to see whether similar arguments apply to other morally problematic prescriptions of the *Book of Lord Shang*.

To answer this question properly, we should turn back to the dialectical view of history presented in chapter 7, discussed earlier. The chapter, we recall, argues that moral means of ruling the populace were appropriate to the bygone times of a small and unsophisticated population, yet these means are no longer adequate. But what does the chapter say about the future? What will happen after the ruler heeds the authors' recommendations and becomes a True Monarch—that is, after he unifies the entire subcelestial realm and forms "the fourth dynasty?" Will the dialectic of history outlined in the chapter's narrative of state formation apply to the future, allowing the discontinuation of oppressive measures?

The answer to the latter question is yes, I think. Although the *Book of Lord Shang* is concerned primarily with the present rather than with the future, some of its statements suggest that the authors do envision a more relaxed situation once their program is fully implemented. For instance, chapter 18 summarizes its own brief narrative of state formation in the past and its relevance to the present: "Therefore, in order to eradicate war with war, even waging war is permissible; to eradicate murder with murder, even murdering is permissible; to eradicate punishments with punishments, even making punishments heavy is permissible" (18.1). The same idea is echoed in chapter 4: "Punishments give birth to force; force gives birth to strength; strength gives birth to awesomeness; awesomeness gives birth to kindness: kindness is borne of force" (4.8).

These and parallel statements—for example, the promise in chapter 7 that merciless punishments will eventually restore "the utmost virtue" in All-under-Heaven (7.5)—exemplify the dialectical spirit of the *Book of Lord Shang*. The harsh means that are currently inevitable actually serve moral ends: when the goal of subjugating domestic and foreign rivals is attained, peace and tranquility will be possible. This peace through unifying All-under-Heaven, remember, was the common desideratum of the vast majority of preimperial thinkers. The question was how to implement the goal of subjugating rivals: and to this question Shang Yang and his followers provide a harsh but ultimately convincing answer. Rather than trying to attain moral ends through moral means—as advocated by Mengzi 孟子 (ca. 380–304), among others[40]—the authors of the *Book of Lord Shang* promulgate an alternative vision: violence and oppression are the necessary evil en route to universal good.

It is tempting to compare Shang Yang's view with that of another famous dialectician, Mao Zedong 毛澤東 (1893–1976), one of the very few leaders in Chinese history under whose aegis the *Book of Lord Shang* regained respectable status (as discussed in the next chapter).[41] In his famous speech "On the People's Democratic Dictatorship" (June 30, 1949), Mao explained how the dialectic of the coercive state would cause it to wither away in the future:

> "Don't you want to abolish state power?" Yes, we do, but not right now; we cannot do it yet. Why? Because imperialism still exists, because domestic reaction still exists, because classes still exist in our country. Our present task is to strengthen the people's state apparatus—mainly the people's army, the people's police and the people's courts—in order to consolidate national defense and protect the people's interests. Given this condition, China can develop steadily, under the leadership of the working class and the Communist Party, from an agricultural into an industrial country and from a new-democratic into a socialist and communist society, can abolish classes and realize the Great Harmony (*da tong* 大同). (Mao Zedong 1975, 4:418)[42]

The resemblance between Mao Zedong's and Shang Yang's historical perspective is obvious. At the current stage of history, both argue, coercion and war are necessary and inevitable. In the future, they may—and probably should—disappear. Mao ends with the promise of utopia, *da tong* 大同 (translated in the quoted passage as "Great Harmony" but more appropriately rendered "Great Uniformity"). This ideal, outlined in the chapter "Action of Rites" ("Li yun" 禮運) in the *Records of the Rites* (*Liji* 禮記), became the epitome of stateless utopia for Chinese thinkers and statesmen for millennia to come (Pines 2012b, 143–144). At the time of the composition of the *Book of Lord Shang*, this utopia still did not exist, but utopian motifs are clearly discernible in the book nonetheless. For instance, the last chapter, "Fixing Divisions," ends with the following statement:

> Hence, when the sages are established in All-under-Heaven, and nobody suffers capital punishment, it is not because they have abolished capital punishment. Rather, the laws are clear and easily understandable, and law officials and clerks are established as teachers to direct [the people] to understand [the law]. The myriad people all understand what should be avoided and what should be pursued. They should avoid disaster and pursue good fortune: all will thereby govern themselves. (26.6)

This depiction of a perfect administrative mechanism that brings about "self-governance" (*zi zhi* 自治) of the people once again resembles Mao's dialectic vision of the dictatorship as a stage toward the state's withering. The *Book of Lord Shang* puts forward elsewhere even stronger statements in favor of the ultimate victory of morality. Although chapter 13, "Making Orders Strict," contains one of the harshest assaults on traditional moral values, it also has the following surprising finale:

> The sage ruler understands the essentials of things. Hence, in ordering the people, he possesses the most essential; thus, he firmly holds the rewards and punishments to support the One. . . . The sage ruler, in ordering others, should first attain their hearts; hence, he is able to employ force. Force gives birth to strength; strength gives birth to awesomeness; awesomeness gives birth to virtue; virtue

is born of force. The sage ruler alone possesses it; hence, he is able to implement benevolence and righteousness in All-under-Heaven. (13.6)

Whether this section belongs to the original chapter or was added later (Pines 2012a, 101) is of minor importance to us here. What is important is that the passage is consistent with the ideas expressed elsewhere in the *Book of Lord Shang* and is clearly reflective of if not the book's earliest message, then at least the evolution of its ideology in the process of its formation. It does not deny the importance of coercion, and it rejects application of moral means of rule under the current conditions of bitter competition among rival states, but it also clearly promises a future of "benevolence and righteousness" under the future sage's rule. This finale gives us a hint of a barely noticed utopian strand in the *Book of Lord Shang*.

We may now summarize the issue of an ideal state in the *Book of Lord Shang*. It seems to me appropriate to speak of two ideals or perhaps of two stages of a single ideal. On the most immediate level, the book promises to create a rich and powerful state, the residents of which will be uniformly and unequivocally committed to farming and waging war. The state will establish total control over the populace so as to prevent evildoing, on the one hand, and to fully utilize human and material resources, on the other. This state will turn into a formidable war machine that will smash its rivals and ultimately unify All-under-Heaven. Then, a new stage may begin. This future stage is never discussed in full in the text, but from a few scattered references to it, we may assume that this new political entity will no longer need to resort to either war or punishments. It probably will resemble the utopian state depicted in the self-congratulatory stele inscriptions of the First Emperor (秦始皇, r. 221–210 B.C.E.), who promised that "warfare will never rise again" and boasted of the universal compliance and tranquility supposedly attained under his sagacious rule.[43]

The First Emperor, the sixth-generation descendant of Shang Yang's employer, Lord Xiao of Qin, was the one who brought Shang Yang's designs to full realization. However, for Shang Yang's legacy, this success proved to be a Pyrrhic victory. Henceforth, his image was forever linked to that of the Qin dynasty, which, after the astounding success of its unification, ended with an even more astounding failure, smashed by an unprecedented popular uprising. Shang Yang's success was no longer self-evident, and negative aspects of his legacy could be highlighted to turn him into an odious figure of whom "scholars are ashamed to speak."[44]

4

THE TEXT'S RECEPTION AND IMPACT

S hang Yang was already a highly controversial figure during
his lifetime, and controversies continued to accompany his
assessment by posterity.[1] On the one hand, his undeniable
achievement in empowering Qin made him a hero for those who sought
to emulate his success in attaining "a rich state and a strong army."
Moreover, the cruelty of his destiny—being executed by the state that
he had served faithfully for more than two decades—also aroused a certain degree of sympathy among members of the educated elite, allowing him to join a pantheon of martyrs whose merit could not save them
from persecution.[2] On the other hand, Shang Yang's perceived immorality, his constant derision of fellow intellectuals, his overt disdain
of traditional culture and of moralizing discourse—all generated
huge enmity, which neither the positive outcomes of his policies nor
his personal tragedy could alleviate. In the long term, this enmity prevailed, turning Shang Yang into one of the most maligned statesmen
in Chinese history, one "who was vilified for two millennia, particularly in recent times."[3]

In the first centuries after Shang Yang's death, there was a relatively
balanced view of this reformer and of his ideas. Although full and
enthusiastic endorsement of his legacy is limited primarily to the single case of his self-proclaimed follower and improver, Han Fei,[4] many
other discussions of Shang Yang at the time do admit his merits. The
account of Shang Yang's career in the *Stratagems of the Warring States* can

serve as an example of recognition of this statesman's achievements even by his critics.[5] Other critics of Shang Yang—such as Xunzi, the Han statesman Jia Yi 賈誼 (200–168 B.C.E.), and even Sima Qian—also readily acknowledge the positive outcomes of at least some of his policies.[6] This recognition does not alleviate enmity toward him—as mentioned earlier, Sima Qian, for instance, considers the statesman's cruel fate well deserved (*Shiji* 68:2237)—but at least it contributes toward a balanced view of the Qin reformer.

Balanced assessments aside, already in the Warring States period we can hear voices of deep hatred toward Shang Yang. Mengzi 孟子 (ca. 380–304 B.C.E.) never mentions Shang Yang by name, but his invective against warmongers, for whom he considers death an insufficient punishment, and his derision of those engaged in wasteland cultivation are clearly directed if not against Shang Yang personally, then against like-minded statesmen.[7] More notably, the authors of *Lüshi chunqiu*, the major compendium composed on the eve of imperial unification in the state of Qin, gloss over Shang Yang's achievements altogether, never refer to his legacy, and mention him only once in a chapter ominously named "Unrighteous" ("Wu yi" 無義).[8] That this clear anti–Shang Yang stance is adopted by the authors of the text written in Qin to serve the soon-to-be-established empire, the text purportedly prepared as the summa of the intellectual achievements of the Warring States period, is revealing. Scholars from the entire Chinese world, who gathered in Qin to provide its ruler with a blueprint for the future empire, differed on many points but were united in their pride as intellectuals without whose endorsement no ruler would succeed in unifying All-under-Heaven.[9] Shang Yang, who derided this stratum of "peripatetic eaters" (3.10), was equally hated by them, and they preferred to dismiss his merits and emphasize his immorality instead. The same attitude is discernible in another multiauthored compilation prepared in the early decades of the Han dynasty, the *Huainanzi*.[10]

Just like *Lüshi chunqiu*, which was aimed to serve the would-be First Emperor of Qin, the *Huainanzi* was composed as a possible blueprint for the newly ascended Emperor Wu of the Han dynasty 漢武帝 (r. 141–87 B.C.E.) (Vankeerberghen 2001). Yet Emperor Wu rejected the *Huainanzi*'s call for a relaxed laissez-faire mode of rule and adopted a policy of territorial expansion and socioeconomic activism, which closely resembled that of the First Emperor. This quest for the enrichment and empowerment of the state could have made Emperor Wu a natural admirer of the *Book of Lord Shang*. This did not happen, though. Despite the close resemblance of his policies to those of Qin, Emperor Wu opted to distance himself declaratively from the Qin model and to endorse, however superficially, the Confucian classics as the major source of ideological legitimacy. It was at the very beginning of his reign that one of his top advisers, Prime Minister Wei Wan 衛綰, proposed never again to employ followers of the allegedly immoral thinkers: "Shen [Buhai], Shang [Yang], Han Fei, and [the Warring States period diplomats] Su Qin 蘇秦 and Zhang Yi 張儀" (*Hanshu* 6:156). This recommendation was approved, and although its impact remained limited in the short term, it did indicate a turning point in the court's attitude toward Shang Yang and other "Legalists." Even when the Legalists' legacy was endorsed de facto, the court preferred to distance itself from their names. On a symbolic level, Shang Yang, much like the Qin dynasty and the First Emperor, became a liability, not an asset.[11]

The process of Shang Yang's marginalization and his subsequent demonization spanned a few generations. At the time of Emperor Wu, Shang Yang was still respected by some men of letters, such as Dongfang Shuo 東方朔 (*Hanshu* 65:2864), and his legacy was openly embraced by some of the architects of Emperor Wu's policies, most notably the renowned economic activist Sang Hongyang 桑弘羊 (152–80 B.C.E.). During the 81 B.C.E. court debates over the government's economic, military, and personnel policies (known as the Salt and Iron Debates; for their content, see *Yantielun* 鹽鐵論), Sang Hongyang eulogized Shang Yang as a model meritorious statesman. Yet Sang met with vehement criticism from the group of Confucian literati, who used the debates to attack the government's policies and to call for a complete overhaul of the ruling personnel. For the literati, Shang Yang was responsible not for Qin's success but for its ultimate failure: "Shang Yang made heavy punishments and stern laws into Qin's foundation: hence, Qin was lost after two generations."[12] Despite the obvious fallacy of the literati's statement (after all, Shang Yang's policies ensured the lasting success of the state of Qin for six generations before the First Emperor rather than its speedy collapse after unification), their approach outlined the future change in attitude toward Shang Yang: no longer a successful, even if morally dubious, statesman but a symbol of cruelty per se, a person without any achievements to speak of.

The Salt and Iron Debates were one of the peaks in a long drama that evolved from the time of Emperor Wu on: the struggle over the future course of the Chinese Empire. In the wake of the first century B.C.E., the activist Qin (or, more precisely, the Warring States) model was gradually sidelined and replaced with a more relaxed system that downplayed military and economic activism and was accommodative rather than distortive of the elites' interests.[13] For moderates, Shang Yang, much like the First Emperor of Qin, was a major foe. He was blamed henceforth not just for his real flaws, such as excessively harsh laws, but also for a variety of imagined misdeeds, such as the introduction of private landownership and the resultant impoverishment of peasant households.[14] Vehement anti–Shang Yang propaganda influenced even those thinkers who retained a positive view of his achievements: henceforth, any endorsement of his legacy would be conditional at best. For instance, in a text composed near the end of the Former Han by either the editor of the *Book of Lord Shang*, Liu Xiang, or his son, Liu Xin, a high evaluation of Shang Yang is immediately overshadowed by harsh criticism.[15] The text starts with praise:

> Lord Shang in his entire life never had a second thought: he committed himself fully to the common [good] and did not look after his private [interests]. Internally, he caused the people to follow the tasks of tilling and weaving vigorously, so as to enrich the state; externally, he boosted rewards for fighters and attackers so as to encourage the military men. His laws and ordinances were invariably implemented; inside, he did not flatter the noble and the [ruler's] favorites; outside, he was not unfair toward strangers and those coming from afar.[16] Therefore, his orders were implemented and prohibitions enforced: once the laws were issued, villainy stopped. This does not differ from what the *Documents* call "without deviating, without forming cliques,"[17] or what the *Poems* call "the Way of Zhou is like a whetstone and is straight like an arrow,"[18] or the encouragement of fighters in

Sima's Methods [of War], or Zhou Houji's stimulation of farming.[19] Thereby Qin annexed the regional lords. Hence, Sun Qing [i.e., Xunzi] said: "[Qin] is victorious for four generations not because of luck but because of [proper] methods."[20] (*Shiji* 68:2238)

This is a very rare panegyric of Shang Yang: not only are his merits fully recognized, but his impartiality is also compared to those of the ancient paragons, and his encouragement of tilling and fighting is equated with the policies of model statesmen of the past. Yet this flattering depiction of his attainments is immediately moderated by the insistence that his treachery, immorality, and harshness diminished his success, making him unequal to eminent statesmen of the past, such as Guan Zhong 管仲 (d. 645 B.C.E.), the architect of Qi hegemony in the mid-seventh century B.C.E.. Then the text turns to an outright attack on Shang Yang:

> Now, Wei Yang [Shang Yang] internally employed the punishments of knife and saw,[21] externally deepened executions by battleaxes; one who overstepped by six feet was penalized, one who threw ashes on the road was mutilated. One day he observed the Wei River and ordered drowning[22] seven hundred prisoners there, turning the Wei River water crimson. The cries and tears moved Heaven and Earth, those who resented or hated him piled up like a mountain: [so that when he was persecuted by Qin,] he had no place to escape and find cover, nowhere to return to and be protected. His body was torn apart by the chariots, his family executed, and nobody of his surname left: this is because he departed far from those who assist Hegemons and Monarchs. (*Shiji* 68:2238)

The crimes of Shang Yang here accrue to an extent unseen in earlier texts: he is presented as a real monster, a sadistic adherent of the rule "of knife and saw," someone who alienated everybody under Heaven. This harsh depiction severely qualifies the earlier exposition of his achievements; and although the text ends on the more accommodative note that, despite his brutality, Shang Yang did not deserve to be executed by King Huiwen,[23] the damage to Shang Yang's image is undeniable. Thus, in contrast to the views expressed by Han Fei and Sang Hongyang, it seems that by the end of the Former Han unequivocal admiration of Shang Yang was no longer possible. It is not surprising that it was shortly after the end of the Former Han that a frustrated man of letters, Feng Yan 馮衍, created an ode in which he called on "burn[ing] the laws and techniques of Shang Yang" (*Hou Hanshu* 28B:994). Shang Yang was rapidly losing legitimacy within the intellectual community.

The early years of the Latter Han dynasty (25–220) mark another rarely noticed watershed in future views of Shang Yang. It was then that the empire's rulers discontinued universal military service, which was the hallmark of the Warring States period legacy in general and of Shang Yang's reforms in particular (Lewis 2000). Henceforth, few if any statesmen could appreciate Shang Yang's success in turning unwilling peasant conscripts into valiant soldiers. Thus, even among those who continued to admire his achievement in enriching the state and strengthening the army, few understood the essential aspects of his legacy. This also perhaps explains the gradual decline in interest in the *Book of Lord Shang* in subsequent generations (see also chapter 2, part I).

As time passed, the negative stereotype of Shang Yang became deeply entrenched in the minds of imperial literati. To be sure, positive comments on the *Book of Lord Shang* and on Shang Yang personally did not disappear altogether from imperial political discourse. Especially in times of military, political, or economic crisis, statesmen looking for ways to re-empower their state were ready to turn to him. Thus, Liu Bei 劉備, the founder of the Shu-Han 蜀漢 state (221–263) in the aftermath of the collapse of the Han dynasty, recommended the *Book of Lord Shang* as a must-read to his heir (*Sanguo zhi* 32:891). Later, an important institutional thinker, Du You 杜佑 (735–812), who sought ways to strengthen the weakening Tang dynasty, similarly hailed Shang Yang's contribution to the state's empowerment (*Tong dian* 13:3). In the Northern Song dynasty, Shang Yang merited a laudatory short poem by the major reformer Wang Anshi 王安石 (1021–1086) and, somewhat surprisingly, approving remarks even from Wang's archrival, the renowned historian Sima Guang 司馬光 (1019–1086).[24] Yet these and similar voices remained a distinct minority.[25] The overwhelming view of Shang Yang by imperial men of letters was as negative as the view of him held by the literati participants in the Salt and Iron Debates.

The Song dynasty marks a further decline in Shang Yang's image. With the proliferation of the Neo-Confucian moralizing discourse, the idea of an assertive and powerful state associated with Shang Yang became even less popular than before. In the late imperial centuries, Shang Yang was mentioned, if at all, almost exclusively in a negative context as a cruel and immoral statesman, not as a model to be emulated. Even reformers of the late imperial period, such as Zhang Juzheng 張居正 (1525–1582), who is often dubbed a "Legalist" (Miller 2009), eschewed invoking Shang Yang as a possible source of inspiration.[26] Overall, the late imperial period is marked by a mixture of enmity and indifference toward Shang Yang and the *Book of Lord Shang*. Even when Yan Wanli published a critical edition of this book in 1793 (see chapter 2, part I), the text appeared to be more attractive from a philological than a political point of view.

Yet within a century the attitude toward the *Book of Lord Shang* and toward Shang Yang's legacy started changing. The ailing Qing dynasty faced a series of military and economic debacles. In the aftermath of the Opium Wars (1840–1860), China lost its status as an aspiring universal polity and entered the age of nation-states, with unmistakable parallels to the Warring States era. Facing assault from foreign powers and worsening domestic turmoil, imperial intellectuals started to look for ways to strengthen the state. The old problem of how to maximize the utilization of economic and human resources so as to attain the status of "a rich state and a strong army" was popular again, and with that popularity Shang Yang's legacy was rediscovered, even if somewhat belatedly.

The earliest thinker to notice Shang Yang's potential importance for China's current affairs was a radical nationalist, Zhang Binglin 章炳麟 (a.k.a. Zhang Taiyan 章太炎, 1869–1936). In an essay titled "Shang Yang," published in 1900, Zhang lamented the two-millennia-long slandering of this gifted thinker and statesman. He dubbed Shang Yang a "political thinker" (*zhengzhijia* 政治家),[27] a new term in that age of rapid introduction of Western ideas. According to Zhang Binglin, Shang Yang by no means denigrated the people: his laws were designed to protect the commoners' interests, and he had not turned to democracy only because the people of Qin were too primitive at that time. Twisting the laws so as to empower the ruler and weaken the people was not the fault of Shang Yang, but rather of Han sycophants, such as Xiao He 蕭何 (d. 193 B.C.E.), Gongsun Hong 公孫弘 (200–121 B.C.E.), and Dong Zhongshu 董仲舒 (ca. 195–115 B.C.E.). Zhang conceded moral flaws in Shang Yang's thought, most notably his rejection of filial piety, but he hailed his ability to revitalize Qin and summed up by noting that Shang Yang's attainments unequivocally outweigh his flaws.[28] Although Zhang's work *Forceful Book* (*Qiu shu* 訄書), which included an essay on Shang Yang, did not enjoy broad circulation at the time of its publication, it is important as the earliest example of a shift in interest in Shang Yang from the philological to the political realm and the first attempt to discuss this thinker from a point of view informed by modern political theories.

Almost immediately after Zhang Binglin's publication, a new and more powerful defense of Shang Yang came from the camp of Zhang's major intellectual rival, the eminent late Qing reformer Kang Youwei 康有爲 (1859–1927), notably from Kang's major associates, Mai Menghua 麥夢華 (1874–1915) and Liang Qichao 梁啓超 (1873–1929). Kang himself sought inspiration for his radical reforms in a reinterpreted Confucian legacy, but in the aftermath of the collapse of reforms in 1898 his associates turned to extra-Confucian sources of inspiration.[29] Mai Menghua's *Critical Biography of Lord Shang* (*Shang jun pingzhuan* 商君 評傳), published in 1903, became a milestone in the studies of Shang Yang's legacy. In distinction from Zhang Binglin, whose analysis of Shang Yang's ideas was based primarily on Sima Qian's "Biography of Lord Shang," Mai Menghua offered a radically novel analysis of the *Book of Lord Shang* in the context of its relation to modern Western political thought. Mai pointed out that Shang Yang's ideas were related to those of imperialism, nationalism, statism (*guojiazhuyi* 國家主義), and historical evolution. Shang Yang's promulgation of legal officials was tantamount to the endorsement of an independent judiciary, and his ideas of the law's transparency and of the equality of all in front of the law had clear parallels in Western thought and practices as well. Mai was not oblivious of the intellectual and moral weaknesses of some of Shang Yang's proposals, but his overall evaluation of this thinker was extraordinarily high: Shang Yang was China's Bismarck and China's Lycurgus.[30]

Mai Menghua's essay had greatly influenced Liang Qichao, arguably China's single most influential intellectual at the dawn of the twentieth century. Liang's publications, the most notable of which is *On the History of the Development of Legal Theory in China* (*Zhongguo falixue fada shi lun* 中國法理學發達史論, 1906), had promulgated the image of Shang Yang as a proponent of the rule of law (*fa zhi* 法治)—that is, the promoter of a progressive Western idea that was lacking in Confucian China. Liang Qichao had also hailed Shang Yang as one of China's six greatest statesmen.[31] Given the exceptional impact of Liang on the intellectual life of his time, the proliferation of positive views of Shang Yang since the first decade of the twentieth century comes as no surprise. Shang Yang became henceforth the country's long-forgotten and now rediscovered intellectual asset.

The resurrection of interest in Shang Yang can be demonstrated from manifold parameters. For instance, Shang Yang's thought became a topic to be taught in some of the "New Schools" established as part of the late Qing educational reforms, as well as in newly established universities (Zhu Shizhe 1948 [1956], 1). Numerous annotated editions of the *Book of Lord Shang* were published, some of which were penned by important officials and politicians.[32] In the introduction to these new editions, the authors hailed Shang Yang as the promoter of the idea of "a rich state and a strong army"—that is, precisely those things that the young Chinese Republic lacked most.[33] Others, like Hu Hanmin 胡漢民 (1879–1936), one of the most eminent leaders of the Guomindang 國民黨 (Kuomintang, Party of the Nation), who wrote a preface to a new edition of the *Book of Lord Shang* published by Jian Shu, lauded Shang Yang's perceptive analysis of laws as an essential social necessity and the thinker's insistence on the laws' transparency (Hu Hanmin [1931] 1975). Notably, however, the widespread positive view of Shang Yang did not yield many in-depth studies of the *Book of Lord Shang*. Perhaps due to the widespread view of the text as spurious (see chapter 2 above), discussants preferred to analyze Shang Yang's views primarily on the basis of his biography in the *Records of the Historian*. The major exception was a highly innovative study of the *Book of Lord Shang* published by Chen Qitian (1935), but it was largely ignored, possibly because of Chen's negative political image in the eyes of both pro-Guomindang and pro-Communist scholars.[34]

Whereas most Republican-era discussants focused either on the statism of Shang Yang or on his legal philosophy, others were more inspired by his and his fellow "Legalists'" vehement anticonservatism. Thus, even a leading liberal thinker, Hu Shi 胡適 (1891–1962), was willing to forgive the Legalists their notorious oppressiveness and endorse what is usually considered the major Legalist-inspired atrocity—namely, the book burning initiated by Legalist thinker Li Si 李斯 and mandated by the First Emperor in 213 B.C.E.:[35]

> Political dictatorship is surely frightening, but the dictatorship of adoring the past is even more frightening. . . . After two thousand years, fed up with two millennia of "narrating the past to harm the present and adorning empty words to harm the substance," we cannot but admit that Han Fei and Li Si were the greatest statesmen in Chinese history. Although we cannot completely endorse their methods, we should never let their brave spirit of opposing those who "do not make the present into their teacher but learn from the past" fall into oblivion: it deserves our utmost admiration! (Hu Shi [1930] 1998, 6:480–481)

Hu Shi's willingness to endorse the Qin biblioclasm is revealing. The association of Legalism with historical progress turned the supposed suppression of conservative opposition from a despotic act into a glorious step toward the liberation of the mind. However, not all Republican-period scholars shared Hu Shi's enthusiasm. For many, Legalists in general and Shang Yang in particular remained associated with dictatorship and oppression, which they detested under the Guomindang regime. For instance, the leading leftist historian Guo Moruo 郭沫若 (1892–1978) remained staunchly anti-Legalist and anti-Shang Yang (see Guo Moruo [1945] 2008). This complex legacy explains a certain ambiguity in attitudes toward Shang Yang in the early years of the subsequent Mao Zedong era (1949–1976). He was neither vilified nor excessively endorsed, and his legacy was not the focus of studies of early Chinese thought.[36]

This ambiguity ceased abruptly in the early 1970s. Mao Zedong's Great Proletarian Cultural Revolution, launched in 1966, with its vehement assault on China's cultural traditions in general and on Confucianism in particular, was in itself conducive of a positive reassessment of the radical iconoclast of the past, Shang Yang. His fortunes further improved when the ailing Chairman Mao, facing the need to define his own place in China's history, assessed himself as "Marx plus the First Emperor"—that is, the possessor of supreme intellectual and supreme political authority. Mao's approval of the First Emperor (which was not made public but was known in political and academic circles) meant that the First Emperor's intellectual associates, the Legalists in general and Shang Yang in particular, could now be fully endorsed. The radical wing of the Communist Party leadership, the so-called Gang of Four led by Mao's wife, Jiang Qing 江青, used this association to launch the infamous anti-Confucian campaign in 1973–1975.[37]

The complexity of the anti-Confucian campaign and its political and ideological background cannot be addressed here in full; my focus is only on the figure of Shang Yang. His popularity surged all of a sudden. Dozens of "small groups" (xiaozu 小組) of students, workers, and other representatives of the "revolutionary masses" were involved in reassessing and promoting his legacy, as were eminent scholars, who had to endorse him unequivocally in their publications. Shang Yang was lionized as a great "progressive" thinker who had fought against the "reactionary classes."[38] Attempts were even made to position him and his fellow Legalists as direct predecessors of "Mao Zedong's Thought" (Liu Zehua 2012). The campaign itself was short and inconsequential, but it demonstrated how the legacy of a thinker twenty-three centuries old could all of a sudden become relevant in our times.

In the aftermath of the artificial outburst of enthusiasm toward Shang Yang's thought, interest in this thinker receded, and his legacy was thoroughly depoliticized. Studies of the *Book of Lord Shang* returned to departments of early Chinese history and philosophy, and scholars who are engaged in such studies now focus overwhelmingly on the past rather than on the present.[39] The dichotomous Maoist view of intrinsic antagonism between Shang Yang and Confucius, or between Legalism and Confucianism, gave way to a more nuanced approach that highlights the common ground among the competing "schools of thought" rather than their contradictions.[40] Yet despite this apparent harmonizing view of the Warring States period legacy, the renewed prejudices against the Legalists in general and against Shang Yang in particular are palpable. In distinction from other preimperial intellectual currents, neither Legalism nor Shang Yang has merited establishment of a scholarly association (*xue hui* 學會) in China; relatively few students focus on Shang Yang and the *Book of Lord Shang* in their master's and doctoral studies; and the number of Shang Yang–related publications in Chinese remains small in comparison to the number for other thinkers, even though it is incomparably larger than in Western languages. Oddly, Shang Yang is glossed over—albeit infrequently—even in some of Chinese studies of native political thought (for instance, Chen Hongtai 2013).

The emotions that accompanied debates over Shang Yang in the past to a certain extent receded, yet they did not disappear entirely. In some of the publications both in China (mainland and Taiwan) and outside it, we still find strong endorsement or rejection of Shang Yang. Critics emphasize the intrinsic oppressiveness of Shang Yang's political theory and deny that it has any moral ideals. For instance, Jean Lévi opines that for Shang Yang even the creation of the unified empire was not an entirely satisfactory goal; rather, much like the leaders of conflicting superpowers in George Orwell's anti-utopian novel *1984*, he had to perpetuate fears of an imagined enemy in order to maintain his reign of terror (2005, 40–41). Huang Shaomei ominously titled her recent monograph *A Study of Shang Yang's Antihumanistic Outlook* (*Shang Yang fanrenwenguan yanjiu* 商鞅反人文觀研究, 2010). And Zhang Linxiang concludes that Shang Yang's "ideal society is just a society in which the cessation of punishments and the putting off of arms result exclusively from the people's total submission to the tyranny and abuses of the dictatorship; although stable and unified, this society is merciless and unrelenting" (2006, 88). Zhang further emphasizes:

Based on Shang Yang's theories, the state of Qin established a military state organization, which was able to use stern laws so as to direct the people to agriculture and warfare, to comprehensively mobilize the state's power so as to engage in unprecedented wars of expansion and annexation and to eradicate the rival six states. It is true that putting an end to prolonged military turmoil and attaining unification reflected the general course of social development and accorded the people's expectations. Yet the fact that unification was attained by Qin and not by another state and that it was attained in this and not in an alternative manner means the victory of savagery over civilization. It is a hugely unfortunate event in the history of our nation. (2006, 88)[41]

The last phrase of this summary is revealing: even nowadays Shang Yang's legacy may still be viewed through the prism of political expediency, and his success is lamented by those who would like to see China a more liberal country. Yet not everybody shares this gloomy view of Shang Yang and his legacy. Many overtly laudatory accounts of him come from the margins of the academic community,[42] but some leading scholars share highly positive evaluations of this thinker. For them, not just his political attainments matter but also his ultimate goals, which they consider to be utterly moral. This approach is represented, for instance, in Zeng Zhenyu's laudation of Shang Yang's moral aims:

There are certain commonalities between Confucius and Shang Yang. They differ only in the means via which they propose the advancement of an ideal society based on morality. For Confucius, the means are ethical education and consequent transformation of the populace. Shang Yang, in distinction, believes that only after reliance on heavy punishments will humans be able to advance on to the new stage of a society ruled by morality. In the depth of his heart, Shang Yang was still an ethical thinker. (2003, 117)

Scholarly divergences are amplified in a variety of blogs and online publications that have proliferated in recent years, overshadowing scholarly production. Some of these alternate types of publication denigrate the *Book of Lord Shang* as the "blackest book" in Chinese history, whereas others strongly defend Shang Yang and hail his achievements.[43] The abundance of contradicting assessments reflects the fact that there is no clearly pronounced Communist Party line pro or contra Shang Yang. As Confucius rapidly regains position as China's ultimate symbol, his perceived foe, Shang Yang, can no longer be effusively lauded by the state and party establishment, but nor does he deserve outright denigration. In the accommodative atmosphere of recent decades, most premodern statesmen and thinkers are viewed positively or at the very least not stigmatized.

Insofar as current (2016) policy makers focus on Shang Yang, they overwhelmingly do it within the context of his alleged insistence on the "rule of law." Lively debates occur between those who consider Shang Yang's legal ideas as coterminous with the Occidental concept of the rule of law (e.g., Wu Baoping and Lin Cunguang [2015]) and those who dismiss this connection as just a superficial resemblance (e.g., Cheng Liaoyuan [2011]). Scholarly debates aside, some of Shang Yang's observations—for example, about the importance of the full enforceability of laws—appear highly relevant to China's policy makers. Not incidentally, the would-be general secretary of the Communist Party of China, Xi Jinping 習近平 (b. 1953), cited one of the *Book of Lord Shang*'s maxims—namely, that "every state has laws, but there is no law to make laws inevitably implementable" (18.4)—in his speech in 2007.[44] This maxim predictably became one of the most frequently cited phrases in debates over the rule of law after that and especially in the aftermath of Xi Jinping's ascendancy to the top party and state positions in 2012–2013. This fact alone buttresses the ongoing relevance of the *Book of Lord Shang*.

Beyond catchphrases, Shang Yang's potential political relevance could be even greater insofar as his cherished goal—"a rich state and a strong army"—remains one of the fundamental desiderata of China's political establishment. Indeed, "rich and strong" (*fuqiang* 富強)—conveniently glossed as "rich state and strong people" rather than "strong army"[45]—is the first of the twelve slogans endorsed at the Eighteenth Congress of the Communist Party of China in 2012 as a "core socialist value" and has been promoted widely in China ever since. However, the party is careful to avoid direct association of this "core value" with Shang Yang. Evidently, his controversial background is not conducive to explicit endorsement of his legacy in the twenty-first century. More substantially, because China does not appear to be in need of turning its people into tillers and soldiers, Shang Yang's ideas are less relevant to its current course.

This observation brings me to a final question: What is the value of studying Shang Yang's thought currently? That his ideas are hugely important for scholars of early Chinese history is self-evident and does not need further discussion here. But what can scholars of comparative political thought learn from him? To paraphrase Brian Van Norden (1996, 226), should the Book of Lord Shang remain just of high "notional" interest (i.e., to expand our horizons but not to influence our lives), or can it become a "real" option (i.e., that the modern audience can learn something useful from)?[46] An almost intuitive answer makes the former choice. After all, few, if any, of us would seriously contemplate living under Shang Yang's regime of a total state that directs everybody to agriculture and warfare through rewards and punishments, a state that declares its will to weaken and overpower its people and to diminish spiritual culture to the love of war. Nor can a reader forget a variety of appalling statements in the Book of Lord Shang; even though these statements do not necessarily constitute the text's bottom line, they are alienating enough to discourage full engagement with Shang Yang's legacy.

Yet even if the ideas of the Book of Lord Shang are irrelevant to most of us, they may still be applicable under certain circumstances. Let us recall the sad situation of failed states or those that dangerously approximate this definition: states torn apart by tribal, confessional, or political conflicts; states unable to consolidate their population and mobilize it to any common task; malfunctioning states that suffer from persistent turmoil and are threatened externally. For these polities, the advice to embrace democracy and human rights sounds as morally lofty and, alas, as irrelevant as Mengzi's dictum to unify All-under-Heaven through "benevolence and righteousness" at the heyday of the Warring States era. Alternatively, Shang Yang's simple and effective recipes—to outline the primary goals of the polity and direct the entire population to fulfill these goals, to establish clear and uniform criteria for individual socioeconomic advancement, and to combine harshness with fairness—may appear quite appealing. Simplistic as it is, Shang Yang's thought, which proved effective in turning one failed state (Qin) into a regional superpower, may be applicable elsewhere. Yet one should be immediately reminded of Sima Tan's insight, quoted in chapter 3 above: Shang Yang's is "a one-time policy that could not be constantly applied."

PART II

THE *BOOK OF LORD SHANG*

NOTES ON TRANSLATION

This translation of the *Book of Lord Shang* is based primarily on Zhang Jue's collated text published in 2012. I have routinely consulted two other editions of the text by Gao Heng (1974) and Jiang Lihong (1996, composed in 1944). For a few specific problems, I consulted the edition by Zhu Shizhe ([1948] 1956) and the edition by Jian Shu ([1931] 1975).

The division of chapters into paragraphs (*zhang* 章) is mine: in most cases, it follows Zhang Jue's suggestions, but in a few cases I disagree with Zhang.

Whenever I refer to notes by earlier scholars—such as Yu Yue 俞樾 (1821–1907), Sun Yirang 孫詒讓 (1848–1908), Tao Hongqing 陶鴻慶 (1859–1918), Yu Chang 于鬯 (1862–1919), Wang Shirun 王時潤 (1879–ca. 1937), Yin Tongyang 尹桐陽 (1882–1950), Zhu Shizhe 朱師轍 (1878–1969), and Jian Shu 簡書 (1886–1937)—I normally do so according to Zhang Jue's edition because the latter is currently the best available.[1] Only in the cases of notes by Gao Heng and Jiang Lihong do I refer specifically to their editions, which are equally accessible.

In translating key terms of the text, I wanted to preserve wherever possible a single English translation for each term. At times, this approach did not work, though. For instance, the singularly important term *fa* 法 usually refers to laws, specifically punitive laws (see, for example, chapter 26), but it can also be used in the broader meanings of "standards" (as in chapter 14), "methods" (as in chapter 10), or, as a verb, "to imitate" or "to model" oneself after somebody (as in chapter 1). In this case, artificial uniformity in translation would impair the reader's understanding of the text.

As mentioned in chapter 2, part I, the *Book of Lord Shang* is characterized by minimalism, simplicity, and straightforwardness, which makes the book (or at least some of its chapters, such as 2, 4, and 19) literally inferior in comparison to other early Chinese texts. In translating these chapters, I tried to avoid excessive adornment of the text. Whenever possible, I preferred to limit interventions in the original's style to the absolute minimum, mostly by adding necessary terms in square brackets but also by avoiding wordiness. This leaves not a few sentences sounding enigmatic, yet I prefer to explain these enigmas in the notes rather than to admix my interpretations directly into the translation. In a few cases, I felt it necessary to add a short explanation of a term in the text itself, putting it in parentheses. In figure brackets, I add material that is missing from the text but the restoration of which was proposed by other scholars on the basis of parallel passages in the *Book of Lord Shang*. When I am not sure about whether the proposed addition belongs to the text or not, or when I suspect that a current sentence is a later interpolation, I place it in double figure brackets.

For the paperback edition I abridged a few technical notes (e.g., "character X stands for character Y"), unless my choice had a major impact on the understanding of the text.

1

REVISING THE LAWS (更法)

Chapter 1 is by far the best-known part of the *Book of Lord Shang*. This renown derives primarily from its incorporation almost verbatim into Shang Yang's biography in the *Records of the Historian*.[1] The chapter is framed in a form of court debates in front of Lord Xiao of Qin, held, according to the *Records of the Historian*, in 359 B.C.E. Lord Xiao is willing to endorse sweeping reforms but hesitates because of possible opposition from conservative public opinion. Gongsun Yang (i.e., Shang Yang), then still a newcomer at the court of Qin, resolutely supports the lord and defeats his conservative opponents. The chapter provides the rationale for Shang Yang's eventual departure from the established patterns of rule: the times are changing, and sociopolitical regulations (laws and rituals) are about to change as well. The chapter also introduces Shang Yang's view of the people in a nutshell: they are too stupid to have their opinions taken into consideration, but their well-being is the ultimate goal of the new policies ("One cannot deliberate the beginnings with the people but can rejoice with them once the matter is accomplished" [1.2]). The chapter positions Shang Yang as an innovative thinker, unbound by tradition and the intellectual inertia of previous ages. It is highly appropriate that it opens the entire *Book of Lord Shang*.

Many readers have noticed the similarity between the debates depicted in the opening chapter of the *Book of Lord Shang* and a section of the *Stratagems of the Warring States* (*Zhanguo ce*), which depicts similar

deliberations at the court of the state of Zhao 趙 around 307 B.C.E.
Although opinions differ about which of the two texts is earlier, I believe
that the priority of the *Book of Lord Shang* can be taken for granted.
Meticulous textual and contextual analyses by Zheng Liangshu (1989,
9–19) and Tong Weimin (2013, 73–77) strongly support the idea that
chapter 1 of the *Book of Lord Shang* inspired the *Stratagems* anecdote
rather than vice versa.

* * *

1.1: Lord Xiao was debating his plans. Three grandees—Gongsun Yang,
Gan Long, and Du Zhi[2]—were in attendance on the ruler. They considered the changes in the affairs of the [current] age, discussed the basis
of rectifying laws, and sought after the way of employing the people.

* * *

1.2: The ruler said:

"To not neglect the altars of soil and grain[3] when succeeding the
throne: this is the Way of the ruler. To implement laws and to commit oneself to enlightening the sovereign and the superior: this is
the [proper] conduct of the minister. Now, I want to change the laws
so as to attain orderly rule, to revise rituals so as to instruct the
hundred clans.[4] Yet I am afraid that All-under-Heaven will criticize
my [actions]."

Gongsun Yang said:

"I, your minister, have heard: 'One who hesitates in action accomplishes nothing; one who hesitates in undertakings achieves nothing.' You, my lord, should concentrate your thoughts on changing the
laws: pay no attention to the criticism of All-under-Heaven. Moreover, he whose actions rise above the rest will be disapproved by his
generation; he whose thinking is exceptionally perceptive will certainly be ridiculed by the people. The saying goes: 'The ignorant are in
the dark even about things that have been accomplished; the wise grasp
[the matter] in the bud.' One cannot deliberate the beginnings with
the people but can rejoice with them once the matter is accomplished.

The *Methods of Guo Yan* says:[5] 'He who discusses superb virtue does not conform to the common [opinion]; he who accomplishes great achievement does not consult with the multitudes.' [The purpose of] the law is to care for the people; [the purpose of] ritual is to benefit undertakings. Hence, whenever it is possible to strengthen his state, the sage does not emulate the past; whenever it is possible to benefit the people, he does not follow rituals."

Lord Xiao said: "Excellent!"

* * *

1.3: Gan Long said:

"This is not right. I, your minister, have heard: 'The sage instructs without altering the people's [habits]; the wise attains orderly rule without changing the laws.' He who bases himself on the people being as they are and instructs them will succeed without effort. Rely on laws to attain proper rule: then the officials will be well versed [in the law], and the people will be at peace. Now, if you change the laws, if you do not follow Qin's precedents, and if you revise the rituals to instruct the people, then I, your minister, am afraid that All-under-Heaven will criticize you, my lord. I hope you will thoroughly examine this."

Gongsun Yang said:

"Your words, sir, are the words of the common people of our age. An ordinary man is at peace with whatever he has become accustomed to; a scholar is immersed in whatever he has heard about. These two can occupy an office and preserve the law, but you cannot discuss whatever is beyond the [existing] laws with them. The [founders of the] Three Dynasties did not use the same rituals but still became monarchs; the Five Hegemons did not employ the same laws but still became hegemons.[6] Hence, the wise [man] creates laws, whereas the ignorant is restricted by them; the worthy revises rituals, whereas the unworthy is bound by them. A man who is bound by rituals is not worth talking to on [important] undertakings; a man who is restricted by laws is not worth debating changes with. My lord: do not hesitate!"

* * *

1.4: Du Zhi said:

"I, your minister, have heard: 'If benefit does not increase hundred-fold, one should not modify the law; if achievements do not increase tenfold, one should not alter [ritual] vessels.' I, your minister, [have also] heard: 'One who imitates antiquity will never err; one who conforms to rituals will never do wrong.' Please, my lord, consider this!"

Gongsun Yang said:

"Former generations did not adopt the same teaching: So which antiquity should one imitate? Thearchs and Monarchs did not repeat one another: So which rituals should one conform to? Fuxi and Shennong taught but did not punish; the Yellow Thearch, Yao, and Shun punished but did not implicate [the criminals'] families;[7] and Kings Wen and Wu[8] both established laws appropriate to the times and regulated rituals according to their undertakings. Rituals and laws are fixed according to the times; regulations and orders are all expedient; weapons, armor, utensils, and equipment, all are used according to their utility. Hence, I say: there is no single way to order the generation; to benefit the state, one need not imitate antiquity. [Kings] Tang and Wu rose to become monarchs without imitating antiquity; Yin [Shang] and Xia dynasties were destroyed not because they altered rituals. Therefore, he who turns his back to antiquity should not be necessarily criticized; he who follows rituals does not necessarily deserve much approval. My lord, do not hesitate!"

* * *

1.5: Lord Xiao said: "Excellent! I have heard that in impoverished alleys people consider many things strange, while petty scholars argue a lot. What the ignorant laughs at, the wise is sad about; what the madman is joyous at, the worthy is worried about. To be bound by what the generation criticizes is not something I will hesitate about." Lord Xiao thereupon issued orders to cultivate wastelands.[9]

2

ORDERS TO CULTIVATE
WASTELANDS (墾令)

The second chapter of the *Book of Lord Shang* is sometimes viewed as related to the government ordinances that Lord Xiao of Qin allegedly issued to encourage cultivation of wastelands (Barbieri-Low and Yates 2015, 72). In my eyes, this interpretation is inaccurate. What we have in the chapter are not legal texts but rather twenty short recommendations about how to push the population toward farming. Each briefly introduces the desired policies, summarizes their social effects, and concludes with the uniform desideratum "then wastelands will surely be cultivated" (則草必墾矣). It is arguably the dullest and least-sophisticated chapter in the entire book. It is also probably among the earliest.

There is no visible logic in the internal organization of the twenty items, and their reasoning about the effects of the proposed actions is at times difficult to follow. Some of the policies are aimed at improving the lot of the peasants: for example, preventing exploitation by "wicked officials" (2.1, 2.16) or "fix[ing] taxes according to estimates of grain yield" (2.2), which indeed became the norm in the state of Qin (Korolkov 2010, 142–169). Yet the authors' primary emphasis is on directing the people to agricultural work by reducing the attractiveness of alternative occupations. Three groups figure prominently in the text as targets for discrimination. The first are members of the high elite, nobles and officials, whose lavish lifestyle (2.4, 2.6, 2.7) and social advancement due to "broad learning" (2.14) spoil the people's mores and distract them from agriculture. Moreover, members of the elite protect their dependents, who thereby escape agricultural labor. These dependents—composed of a variety of members of the lower elite and subelite—are the second group targeted by Shang Yang. The text repeatedly attacks "drifting people," those who "rely on their mouths to eat," "those who are treacherous, impetuous, fond of private connections, and have no faith in agriculture," "those who hate agriculture, who are indolent, and who have insatiable desires," "narrow-minded and short-tempered people," "ruthless people," "lazy and indolent people," "wasteful people," and the like (2.4, 2.7, 2.8, 2.11, 2.13, 2.16, 2.20). By restricting their ability to enjoy elite patronage for their living, the state will direct these people toward agricultural production. The third group against whom the offensive should be launched are merchants. They should be squeezed of their profits, humiliated, and discriminated against so as to make their occupation singularly unattractive (2.5, 2.6, 2.10, 2.15, 2.17, 2.19).

There are many indications that chapter 2 was written at a very early stage of Shang Yang's career. The chapter reflects the situation of an aristocratic system that was current in the state of Qin prior to Shang Yang's reforms. For instance, it remains conspicuously silent about ranks of merit. Instead, when it refers to elite members, it cautions against the power of hereditary nobles (*dafu* 大夫) (2.14) and of the heads of noble lineages (*jia zhang* 家長) (2.7), i.e., groups that disappeared from Qin's social landscape in the aftermath of Shang Yang's reforms and are never mentioned again in the *Book of Lord Shang*. Elsewhere, the chapter warns against exemptions from taxation and labor services granted to minor sons of the nobles and to the merchants' servicemen (2.13, 2.18), which again hints at the situation in pre-reform Qin society.

Aside from these and other indicators that connect this chapter with the pre-reform situation in the state of Qin (Pines 2016a, 163–164), there are also meaningful silences that likewise suggest an early date of composition. In particular, one is perplexed by the authors' lack of concern with any positive measures to encourage peasants to invest in opening up new fields. The chapter does not mention such incentives as distributing tools or draft animals to the farmers willing to develop wastelands or granting them temporary relief from taxes or conscription, nor does it address hydraulic works or any other proactive measures by the state authorities aimed at supporting land reclamation. In distinction from later chapters (such as 6 and 15), chapter 2 never raises the possibility of attracting immigrants. This contrasts markedly with Qin's actual economic policies (for which see, e.g., Pines with others 2014, 19–24) and suggests that the chapter was composed before Qin's agromanagerial economy matured. The authors' inability to devise positive means of encouraging intensive agricultural work turns the chapter's recurrent mantra "then wastelands will surely be cultivated" into a somewhat simplistic and unconvincing recommendation. Nonetheless, the chapter is a valuable glimpse into the mindset of Shang Yang and like-minded reformers at the outset of reforms. It is also a precious testimony to the socioeconomic conditions in the state of Qin at the time. For instance, the authors' fear that "learning" will distract farmers from tilling (2.4) indicates that it was possible back then for a "knowledgeable peasant" (2.14) to change his social status due to superior education and suggests a relatively early arrival of the age of social mobility in the state of Qin.

* * *

2.1: In governing do not procrastinate: then wicked officials will not be able to profit privately from the people, the hundred officials will not delay each other in performing their tasks, and peasants will have extra time.[1] If wicked officials do not profit privately from the people, then the peasants will not be impoverished. If the peasants are not impoverished and have extra time, then wastelands will surely be cultivated.

* * *

2.2: Fix taxes according to estimates of grain yield; then taxation will be uniform, and the people below will be equalized.[2] If taxation is uniform, it will be trusted; if it is trusted, officials[3] will not dare behave wickedly. If the people are equalized, they will be cautious; if they are cautious, they will dislike change. If taxation is uniform, officials dare not behave wickedly, and the people are cautious and dislike change, then above[4] they will not reject their superiors, while in the middle they will not be embittered toward officials. If above they do not reject their superiors, while in the middle they are not embittered toward officials, then able-bodied people will be strenuous in agriculture and will not change [their ways], while minors will tirelessly study [their example]. If minors tirelessly study [the example of adults], then wastelands will surely be cultivated.

* * *

2.3: Do not fix ranks, responsibilities, or offices according to foreign powers:[5] then the people will not esteem learning and will also not despise agriculture. If the people do not esteem learning, they will be ignorant; if they are ignorant, they will have no external ties; if they have no external ties, the state will be at peace and will not be endangered. If the people do not despise agriculture, they will exert themselves in agriculture and not be careless. If the state is at peace and is not endangered, while [the people] exert themselves in agriculture and are not careless, then wastelands will surely be cultivated.

* * *

2.4: If emoluments are bountiful and taxes abundant, then too many people rely on their mouths to eat,[6] and agriculture is devastated. So impose [on rich households] levies according to the number of mouths in their households and double their conscript obligations.[7] Then deviant, floating, and idle people will have nothing to rely upon for sustenance; if they have nothing to rely upon for sustenance, they will have to be engaged in agriculture, and should they be engaged in agriculture, then wastelands will surely be cultivated.[8]

* * *

2.5: Allow neither merchants to buy grain nor peasants to sell grain. If peasants cannot sell grain, then indolent peasants will strenuously exert themselves.[9] If the merchants cannot buy grain, then in the years of abundant harvests they will not be overjoyed; if in the years of abundant harvests they will not be overjoyed, then in the years of famine they will not make copious profit.[10] If there is no copious profit, the merchants become fearful; when fearful, they will want to become peasants. If indolent peasants strenuously exert themselves, and merchants want to become peasants, then wastelands will surely be cultivated.

* * *

2.6: If the sounds [of music] and [fine] clothes do not pervade the hundred counties, then the people will neither look at [fine clothes] while at work nor listen to [the sounds of music] while at rest. If while at rest they do not listen to [the sounds of music], their mood (*qi* 氣) will not become licentious; if while at work they do not look [at fine clothes], their minds will surely be one. If their minds are one and their mood is not licentious, then wastelands will surely be cultivated.

* * *

2.7: Do not allow the use of hired labor; then the heads of the noble lineages will not be able to engage in construction and renovation, favored sons will not eat indolently, indolent people will not be lazy,[11] and hirelings will have no means of sustenance. Then they[12] will have to become peasants. If heads of the noble lineages are not able to engage in construction and renovation, there will be no damage to agricultural activities. If favored sons and indolent people are not lazy, then old fields will not become wasteland. If there is no damage to agricultural activities and peasants are even more engaged in agriculture, then wastelands will surely be cultivated.

* * *

2.8: Abolish hostels for travelers: then those who are treacherous, impetuous, fond of private connections, and have no faith in agriculture will have nowhere to go. When the people who stay at the hostels for travelers have no means of sustenance, they will surely turn to agriculture; if they turn to agriculture, then wastelands will surely be cultivated.

* * *

2.9: Unify [control over] mountains and marshes: then those who hate agriculture, who are indolent, and who have insatiable desires will have no means of sustenance.[13] If they have no means of sustenance, they will surely turn to agriculture; if they turn to agriculture, then wastelands will surely be cultivated.

* * *

2.10: Raise the prices of wine and meat by placing heavy levies on them, increasing them to ten times the original cost.[14] Then merchants and peddlers will be few, peasants will not be able to get excessively drunk, and the great ministers will not overeat in a wasteful manner. If merchants and peddlers are few, superiors will not waste grain; if the people are not able to get excessively drunk, the peasants will not be idle; if the great ministers are not wasteful, there will be no delay in the state's affairs and the sovereign will not err in his undertakings. If superiors do not waste grain and the people are not idle at agriculture, then wastelands will surely be cultivated.

* * *

2.11: Double the punishments and bind the criminals through [the system of] mutual responsibility; then narrow-minded and short-tempered people will not fight, ruthless people will not contend, lazy and indolent people will not drift, wasteful people will not appear, and evil people will not cheat. If these five types of people do not exist within the borders, then wastelands will surely be cultivated.

* * *

2.12: Do not allow the people to shift locations on their own initiative; then ignorant people[15] and those who disrupt agriculture will have nothing to rely upon for sustenance and will have to engage in agriculture. If the minds of ignorant and impetuous people are one, the peasants will surely be tranquil. If the peasants are tranquil and ignorant, then wastelands will surely be cultivated.

* * *

2.13: Issue a comprehensive order to conscript minor sons,[16] employ each according to his task,[17] and enhance the conditions for their exemption.[18] Let them obtain their provisions from the officials in charge of food rations, who would regulate [the amount provided].[19] If minor sons are unable to avoid corvée service or to attain high official positions, they will not drift into the service of other people.[20] Then they will have to engage in agriculture. If they engage in agriculture, then wastelands will surely be cultivated.

* * *

2.14: Great ministers and nobles of the state's capital[21] should not be allowed to engage in affairs of broad erudition, sophisticated argumentation, or drifting and settling.[22] Do not allow them to drift and settle among the hundred counties, so that peasants will neither hear about extraordinary things nor observe different methods.[23] If peasants neither hear about extraordinary things nor observe different methods, then knowledgeable peasants will have no way to depart from their original occupation, and ignorant peasants will not become knowledgeable or fond of learning. If ignorant peasants do not become knowledgeable or fond of learning, they will strenuously devote themselves to agriculture. If knowledgeable peasants have no way to depart from their original occupation, then wastelands will surely be cultivated.

* * *

2.15: Issue orders to bar females from the army's markets.[24] Order the merchants (in these markets) to prepare armor and weapons for themselves; let them watch when the army rises. Also, order that no one transfer grain privately to the army's markets. Then evil stratagems will have no place from which to arise, those who illicitly transport grain will not hoard it privately,[25] and lazy and indolent people will not drift to the army's markets. There will be no place to sell stolen grain, and the suppliers of grain will have no private [benefits]. If lazy and indolent people do not drift to the army's markets, then the peasants will not be licentious, and the state's grain will not be wasted; then wastelands will surely be cultivated.

* * *

2.16: Let the hundred counties be governed by the same pattern: then those who follow deviant [officials] will not be able to alter regulations, and those who commit transgressions and are dismissed will not be able to cover up for those who had promoted them.[26] If transgressions and promotions are not covered up, there will be no wicked men among the officials. If the deviant [official] does not embellish [his deeds] and a replacement does not alter [regulations], then official entourages will be small, and the people will not be exhausted. If there are no wicked [men] among the officials, the people will not drift;[27] if the people do not drift, their occupations will not be undermined. If official entourages are small, levies will not become troublesome. If the people are not exhausted, peasants will have more time. If peasants have more time, levies are not troublesome, and occupations are not undermined, then wastelands will surely be cultivated.

* * *

2.17: Make tolls at the passes and the markets heavy; then peasants will hate the merchants, and the merchants in their hearts will cast doubt upon [their own] indolence. If peasants hate the merchants, and the merchants doubt [their own] indolence, then wastelands will surely be cultivated.

* * *

2.18: Conscript the merchants according to the number of members of their households. Order servants, grooms, runners, and pages all to be named [for corvée service]; then peasants will be at ease, whereas the merchants will be overworked.[28] If the peasants are at ease, good fields will not become wastelands; if merchants are overworked, then the rites of sending gifts back and forth will not spread over the hundred counties.[29] Then the peasants will not starve, and one's conduct will be without embellishments.[30] If the peasants do not starve and one's conduct is without embellishments, the people will be strenuous in public works and will not neglect their private affairs. Then the peasants' undertakings will surely be successful. If the peasants' undertakings are surely successful, then wastelands will surely be cultivated.

* * *

2.19: Do not allow those who transport grain to rent carts or rent out their carts on return. The weight loaded on carts and oxen should be registered. Then transport back and forth will be swift, and occupation [in transportation] will not undermine agriculture. If this occupation does not undermine agriculture, then wastelands will surely be cultivated.

* * *

2.20: Do not let [convicted] criminals request food from clerks; this way villainous people will remain without a master.[31] If the villainous people are without a master, then villainy will not be encouraged; if villainy is not encouraged, then villainous people will have no one to depend on. If villainous people have no one to depend on, peasant [work] will not be undermined; when peasant [work] is not undermined, then wastelands will surely be cultivated.

3

AGRICULTURE AND WARFARE (農戰)

Chapter 3 is the longest in the *Book of Lord Shang*, as is appropriate to one titled "Agriculture and Warfare." Indeed, the central message of the entire book points to agriculture as the singularly appropriate way of enriching the state and warfare as the only effective way of overpowering rivals and attaining security and peace. The chapter repeatedly reiterates this message (3.1, 3.6, 3.7). Moreover, it emphasizes how closely these two pursuits are linked: this linkage is reflected in their designation as "the One" (*yi* 壹). Agriculture provides material resources that enable the state to wage war; war expands the territory under state control and allows further agricultural enrichment. The chapter promises that the ruler who is able to unify the population in pursuing the One will become the True Monarch—that is, the unifier of All-under-Heaven (3.4, 3.7).

Its title notwithstanding, chapter 3 does not address practical issues concerning agricultural and military activities. Rather, its focus is on how to make tilling and fighting singularly attractive from a social point of view. The solution is simple: ranks and offices should be allocated exclusively to diligent tillers and valiant soldiers (3.2), whereas those involved in intellectual pursuits, commerce, and artisanship should be prevented from advancing up the social ladder. This recommendation encapsulates the new social system based on the ranks of merit that became the hallmark of Shang Yang's reforms (see chapters 1 and 3 in part I).

Among the three groups of unproductive populations who should be prevented from attaining office and rank, intellectuals figure most prominently. Those who study the *Canons of Poems* and *Documents*, those who advance through glib talk and argumentativeness, peripatetic men-of-service who enjoy the patronage of "external powers" (i.e., foreign states), and those who sell and buy promotions: all arouse the author's (or authors') ire. Intellectual pursuits—in particular engagement in the *Poems* and *Documents* and in moralizing discourse—are the true malady of the state: their success distracts the people from tilling and fighting (3.5). The intellectuals are "caterpillars" (3.6) who corrupt the officials' conduct above and the people's mores below; they weaken the state economically, militarily, administratively, and ultimately politically by encouraging dissent from below (3.10). They are the greatest threat to the state's power.

The authors' repeated appeals to the ruler to get rid of "traveling persuaders" (i.e., scholars who move from one court to another in search of better employment) and those engaged in learning indicate that by the time of the chapter's composition (presumably at a relatively early stage of Shang Yang's reforms), the power of the educated elite at the court of Qin was still considerable. The chapter serves as a testimony to the uphill battle faced by Shang Yang and his associates in their struggle to reshape Qin society and create a new sociopolitical system.

* * *

3.1: The means whereby the sovereign encourages the people are offices and ranks; the means by which the state prospers are agriculture and warfare. Today the people seek offices and ranks, yet they are attainable not through agriculture and warfare but through crafty words and empty ways: this is called "to exhaust the people."[1] He who exhausts his people, his state will surely lack strength; he who lacks strength, his state will surely be dismembered.

* * *

3.2: He who excels at ruling the state teaches the people to engage exclusively in the One (i.e., agriculture and warfare) in order to attain offices and ranks. Hence, {those who are not engaged in the One}[2] will have neither offices nor ranks. When the state eliminates [superfluous] talk, the people will be simple; if they are simple, they will not be licentious. If the people see that the benefits above come from a single opening,[3] they will engage in the One. If they engage in the One, the people will not recklessly demand [riches]. If the people do not make reckless demands, they will have abundant force; when force is abundant, the state will be strong. Yet nowadays all the people within the borders say: "One can escape from agriculture and war and still get offices and ranks." Therefore, the powerful and eminent are able to change their occupation: they diligently study *Poems* and *Documents* and then follow foreign powers. At best, they attain renown, and at the least they are able to seek after offices and emoluments.[4] As for the petty and insignificant: they become merchants and peddlers, engage in skillful arts, and all escape agriculture and warfare. In such a situation, the state is endangered. If the people consider this a [proper] teaching,[5] the state will be dismembered.

* * *

3.3: He who excels at ruling the state does not neglect agriculture, even if his granaries are full; he does not indulge in talk, even if the state is large and the population is plentiful: then the people will be simple and are [committed to] the One. If the people are simple and are [committed to] the One, then offices and ranks cannot be obtained through glibness; if they cannot be obtained through glibness, then treachery will not arise; if treachery does not arise, then the sovereign is not deluded. Yet nowadays the people within the borders and those who hold offices and ranks see that in the court one can obtain offices and ranks through glib talk and argumentativeness; hence, one cannot implement constant [norms] for offices and ranks. Therefore, when entering [the court], they prevaricate in front of the sovereign, while when retreating they think of their private [interests]. As [they think] how to fulfill their private [interests], they peddle influence to the underlings.[6] Lying to the sovereign and thinking of private [interests] are not beneficial to the state, but they do so because of ranks and emoluments. Peddling influence to the underlings is inappropriate for a loyal minister, but they do so to seek wealth.[7]

Therefore, lower officials who hope to be promoted all say: "If I have enough wealth, then I can make the superior official do what I want." They [also] say: "If I seek promotion without using wealth, it is like using a cat as bait for the rat: surely it is hopeless. If I seek promotion through earnestly serving the superior, it is like using a severed rope to straighten a crooked tree: it is even more hopeless. If through these two means I cannot get promotion, then how can I avoid pressing the people below to get their wealth in order to serve my superior and thereby request promotion?!" The hundred clans say: "I diligently farm to fill the ruler's granaries first and then use the remnants to feed my parents; I fight selflessly for my superiors so as to attain glory for the ruler and peace for my state. Yet the granaries are empty, the ruler is debased, my house is poverty-stricken: So is not it better to seek office?!" The relatives intermingle and think about the matter even more intensively. The powerful and eminent diligently study *Poems* and *Documents* and then follow foreign powers; the petty and insignificant become merchants and peddlers, engage in skillful arts, and all thereby escape agriculture and warfare. If the people consider this a [proper] teaching, how can one avoid farmers becoming ever fewer and soldiers ever weaker?

* * *

3.4: He who excels at ruling the state, his methods of appointing officials[8] are clear; hence, he does not entrust the matter to knowledge and deliberations. The superiors are engaged in the One; hence, the people do not recklessly demand [riches]. Therefore, the force of the state is consolidated.[9] A state with consolidated force is strong; the state that is fond of talk will be dismembered. Hence, it is said: when one thousand people are engaged in agriculture and warfare, yet there is a single man among them engaged in *Poems*, *Documents*, argumentativeness, and cleverness, one thousand people will all become remiss in agriculture and warfare. When one hundred people are engaged in agriculture and warfare, yet there is a single man among them engaged in skillful arts, one hundred people will all become remiss in agriculture and warfare. The state relies on agriculture and warfare for its security; the sovereign relies on agriculture and warfare to be respected. So if the people are not [engaged in] agriculture and warfare, it is because the ruler is fond of words and has lost the constant [norms in appointing] officials.[10] When there are constant [norms in appointing] officials, the state is well governed; when there is commitment to the One, the state is rich; when the state is rich and well governed, this is the Way of the Monarch.[11] Hence, it is said: the Way of the Monarch is not external[12]—be personally engaged in the One and that is all.

* * *

3.5: Now, if the ruler appoints [the people] only after considering their talents, abilities, knowledge, and cleverness, then the knowledgeable and the clever will observe the sovereign's likes and dislikes and how he employs officials to manage affairs so as to conform to the sovereign's mind. Therefore, [the appointment of] officials will lack constant [norms], the state will be in turmoil and not engaged in the One, and argumentative persuaders will not [be reined in by] the law. In this case, how can the people's pursuits not be numerous; how can land not be laid waste?

Poems, Documents, rites, music, goodness, self-cultivation, benevolence, uprightness, argumentativeness, cleverness: when the state has these ten, superiors cannot induce [the people] to [engage in] defense and fighting.[13] If the state is ruled according to these ten, then if the enemy arrives, it will surely be dismembered, and [even] if the enemy does not arrive, the state will surely be impoverished. If the state eradicates these ten, then the enemy will not dare arrive, and even if he arrives, he will surely be repelled; when an army is raised and sent on a campaign, it will surely seize [the enemy's land]; whereas if the army is restrained and does not attack, the state will surely be rich. When the state is fond of force, it attacks with what is difficult [to resist]; he who attacks with what is difficult [to resist] will surely prosper. [When the state is] fond of argumentation, it attacks with what is easy [to resist]; he who attacks with what is easy [to resist] will surely be endangered.

* * *

3.6: Thus, whereas the sage and the clear-sighted ruler cannot fully grasp the myriad things, they understand the essentials of the myriad things. Hence, in ruling the state, they investigate the essentials and that is all. [Yet] today many of those who rule the state have no understanding of the essentials. At court, when they talk about orderly rule, they are incessantly engaged in contradicting each other. Therefore, the ruler is benighted by doctrines, officials are confused by words, the people are remiss in agriculture. Hence, all the people within the borders are transformed: they grow fond of argumentation and enjoy learning; they become merchants and peddlers, engage in skillful arts, and escape agriculture and warfare. If this is so, [the state's demise] is not far away. When [such] a state has [military] undertakings, then its students hate the law, its merchants are fond of transformations, and its skillful artisans are useless: hence, this state is easy to defeat. After all, when few are engaged in agriculture, yet "peripatetic eaters"[14] are plenty, this state will be impoverished and endangered.

Now: various sorts of caterpillars are born in spring and die in autumn, but once they appear, the people lack food for several years. And now: when a single person tills, but one hundred are eating what he produces, it is much worse than all the caterpillars! Hence, even if in every rural canton[15] there is a bundle of *Poems* and *Documents*, and in every household one scroll, it is still of no use for orderly rule. It is not the technique to reverse [poverty and danger]. Therefore, the former kings reversed them through agriculture and warfare. Thus, it is said: "He [in whose state] one hundred people farm and a single one lives from their work will be the [True] Monarch; he [in whose state] ten people farm and a single one lives from their work will be strong; he in whose state half of the people farm and another half lives from their work is endangered." Hence, he who rules the state well wants the people to farm. If the state is not engaged in farming, then it cannot be self-reliant in power struggles with other regional lords: it is because the strength of its multitudes is insufficient. Thus, regional lords exploit its weaknesses and rely on its deterioration; the country is invaded and dismembered, yet none is inspired [to rescue it]: by then it is already too late.

* * *

3.7: The sage knows the essentials of ordering the state; hence, he causes the people to direct their mind toward farming. If the mind turns toward farming, the people are simple and can be rectified; if they are ignorant, they can be easily employed; if they are reliable, they can be used in defense and fighting.[16] When [committed to] the One, they are rarely deceitful and place great weight on their dwelling; when [committed to] the One, they can be motivated by rewards and punishments; when [committed to] the One, they can be used abroad.[17] After all, the people are close to their superiors and sacrifice themselves for the regulations just because from morning to dusk they are engaged in agriculture. And the people cannot be used whenever they see that talkative peripatetic men-of-service who serve the ruler can attain respect, that merchants and peddlers can enrich their households, and that those engaged in skillful arts can fill their mouths. If the people see how these three enjoy convenience and benefits, they will surely avoid farming; if they avoid farming, the people will treat their dwellings lightly; if they treat dwellings lightly, they surely will not engage in defense or fighting for the sake of their superiors.

In general, he who rules the state well is worried that the people will disperse and cannot be consolidated; hence, the sage engages in the One so as to consolidate them. If the state engages in the One for one year, it will be strong for ten years; if it engages in the One for ten years, it will be strong for one hundred years; if it engages in the One for one hundred years, it will be strong for a thousand years; he who is strong for a thousand years will become the [True] Monarch.[18]

* * *

3.8: The ruler maintains rewards and punishments so as to assist the teaching of the One; hence, his teaching can attain constancy, and governance can yield accomplishments. [Yet] the [True] Monarch attains the utmost essentials of orderly rule over the people; hence, he does not rely on rewards, yet the people are intimate with their superiors; he does not rely on ranks and emoluments, yet the people follow their occupations; he does not rely on punishments and penalties, yet the people will give up their life to him.[19]

* * *

3.9: When the state is imperiled and the sovereign is worried, persuaders form legions: but they are of no use for assuaging the perils. After all, the state is imperiled and the sovereign is worried because of [rivalry] with powerful enemies and great states. The ruler can neither subdue a strong enemy nor defeat a great state; hence, he maintains defensive preparations, investigates the lay of the land, and consolidates the people's force so as to prepare himself for external engagements. Only thus can troubles be eradicated and the Monarchy realized. Hence, a clear-sighted ruler cultivates his governance and engages in the One. He eradicates whatever is useless and puts an end to the people's engagement in superficial learning and in excessive occupations. He unifies them in farming: then the state can be enriched and the people's force can be consolidated.

* * *

3.10: Nowadays all the rulers of our age are worried that their states are endangered and their soldiers are weak, so they strive to heed the persuaders. Persuaders form legions; they multiply words and adorn sayings but are of no real use. The sovereign is fond of their arguments and does not seek their substance. The persuaders are satisfied; the roads are full of skillful talkers, and from generation to generation they go on and multiply. The people see that this is the way to reach kings, lords, and grandees, and all learn from them. They form cliques and associations, debate state affairs, and come in profusion. Lower people are fond of them; grandees like them. Therefore, among the people few are engaged in agriculture, whereas "peripatetic eaters" are plenty; as they are plenty, the farmers are indolent; as the farmers are indolent, the land becomes wasteland.

If learning becomes habitual, the people turn their backs on farming: they follow talkers and persuaders, speak grand words, and [engage in] false debates. They turn their backs on farming and travel to get food, trying to exceed each other in words. Hence, the people abandon their superiors, and those who do not behave as subjects become more and more numerous. This is the teaching that impoverishes the state and weakens the army. If the state makes use of the people according to their words, then the people do not take care of farming. It is only the clear-sighted ruler who knows that being fond of words will neither strengthen the army nor expand the territory. Only the sage in ruling the country engages in the One (i.e., agriculture and warfare); he consolidates [efforts] on agriculture, and that is all.

4

ELIMINATING THE STRONG

with 20. Weakening the People

and 5. Explaining the People

C hapter 4 occupies a special place in the *Book of Lord Shang*. First, in terms of its thematic scope, it presents a synopsis of almost all the topics covered in the rest of the book. Social, economic, military, and cultural policies; legal principles; views of the people's political role; elements of administrative thought—all are mentioned, even if briefly, in this chapter (the only meaningful silences are about ruler–minister relations and about running the state apparatus). Second, in terms of style, it uses short and energetic sentences, some almost sloganlike; everything—including grammatical particles—is sacrificed for the sake of brevity (even the ubiquitous particle *ye* 也 is present only once). This laconism not only complicates our understanding of the text at times but also creates a peculiar "take it or leave it" effect: policies are proclaimed, but the rationale for the proposed course of action is rarely if ever provided. Third, this is the only chapter in the entire treatise to merit a detailed, line-by-line internal exegesis. This exegesis is provided in two chapters: 20 and 5. The relation between the three chapters was first noticed by Meng Jifu (1942), whose analysis is now widely accepted by the scholarly community. It seems that chapter 4 was conceived as a canonical text, probably a summa of Shang Yang's wisdom that deserved special commentarial treatment.[1]

Chapter 4 is also exceptional in the *Book of Lord Shang* in terms of its notoriety. It is the richest depository of appalling statements, which

epitomize what I have termed elsewhere the book's "alienating rhetoric" (Pines 2012a). The chapter derides fundamental moral norms and
repositories of traditional culture—such as "rites and music, *Poems* and
Documents, goodness and self-cultivation, filiality and fraternal obligations" (4.3); calls for the creation of a regime in which "villains . . .
rule [the] good" (4.3); and advocates military victory by performing
"whatever the enemy is ashamed of" (4.1). These provocative pronouncements may have contributed to the negative image of the *Book
of Lord Shang* for millennia to come. Chapters 20 and 5, in distinction,
tend to moderate this harsh message by presenting explanations for
such statements: for instance, "villains" are not really "villains" but
just law-abiding people (5.2); in war, shameful acts are not encouraged
(20.4); and traditional moral values are derided not as such but because
they generate moral laxity, which will bring about the state's weakness
and its ultimate collapse (5.1). It is likely, then, that the exegetical chapters reflect an attempt by Shang Yang's followers to moderate, even if
not necessarily to reject, his initial harshness.

Some issues in the relationship between chapter 4 and the two exegetical chapters remain unresolved. Why was the exegesis divided in
two chapters? Why did the editors of the text place chapter 20, which
comments on the first part of chapter 4, in a different *juan* of the *Book
of Lord Shang*? Why did four out of the last five sections of chapter 4
remain without a commentary in either chapter 20 or chapter 5? How
should we understand a few discrepancies between the source text and
its citations in the exegesis? Are they the result of textual corruption
or of the exegetes' deliberate efforts to modify the original text? How
are chapters 4, 5, and 20 related to chapter 13, which closely parallels
significant parts of chapter 4? There are no clear answers to any of
these questions. In any case, to highlight the proximity of chapters 4,
20, and 5, I have decided to translate them together, re-creating what
may have been designed from the beginning as a line-by-line exegesis
of chapter 4.[2] For the reader's convenience, in translating exegetical
sections in chapters 20 and 5, I have highlighted in bold those sentences
that are directly quoted from chapter 4. The last section of chapter 20
(20.11) has been made an appendix to the three chapters because this

section is unrelated to chapter 4 and was possibly misplaced into chapter 20 (see the discussion in the separate introduction to the appendix).

* * *

4.1. One who eliminates the strong with strength is weak; one who eliminates the strong with weakness is strong.[3] When the state engages in goodness, there will surely be many villains. When a rich state is ruled as if poor, it is called multiplying riches; he who multiplies riches is strong. When a poor state is ruled as if rich, it is called multiplying poverty; he who multiplies poverty is weak. He whose army performs whatever the enemy dares not perform is strong; he who in [military] affairs advances whatever the enemy is ashamed of benefits. The sovereign values multiple changes; the state values minimal changes.[4] When the state has few things, it will be dismembered; when the state has many things, it will be strong.[5] When a thousand-chariot state[6] preserves one thousand things, it will be dismembered.[7] When [its] warfare is ordered and the army is [ready to be] used, this is called "strong." When [the people] are chaotic at war and the army is indolent, the state will be dismembered.

> 20.1: When the people are weak, the state is strong; when the people are strong, the state is weak.[8] Hence, the state that possesses the Way devotes itself to weakening the people. {When the people are weak, they are simple; when they are strong, they are excessive.}[9] When they are simple, they are strong; when they are excessive, they are weak; when they are simple,[10] they are regulated; when they are excessive, they are inclined to overstep [regulations]. When they are weak, they can be employed; when they are inclined to overstep [regulations], they are strong.[11] Hence, it is said: **"One who eliminates the strong with strength is weak; one who eliminates the strong with weakness is strong."**
>
> 20.2: As for the people, if [the ruler] is good to them, then they are close [to him];[12] if they benefit from being used, they are

harmonious; if they are usable, they can be appointed; if they are harmonious, they fully dedicate themselves; when they are appointed, they enrich themselves through government [service].[13] When superiors abandon the standards and rely on those whom the people consider **good, there are many villains.**

20.3: When the people are poor, they strenuously seek wealth; when they strenuously seek wealth, they become excessive; when they are excessive, then there are parasites. Hence, when the people are rich and cannot be used, let the people use provisions to attain [ranks]; [ranks] will surely [be bestowed] according to one's efforts;[14] then the farmers will not be indolent. When the farmers are not indolent, the six parasites will have no sprouts. Hence, **the state is rich,** and the **people** are **well ordered; this is "multiplying strength."**[15]

20.4: As for the army: it is easy to weaken it and difficult to strengthen it. When the people enjoy their life, are peaceful and at ease, it is difficult to make them risk their lives in time of danger. When it is easy to do so, the [state] is strong. When one is ashamed of [military] affairs, villainy multiplies. When rewards are few,[16] you will not lose. When numerous villains are stopped, the enemy loses. It is surely beneficial—the army will attain utmost power and awesomeness. When in [military] affairs one is ashamed of nothing, it is beneficial to use the army. He who resides for a long time in the position of benefit and power will surely become the True Monarch. Hence, **"he whose army performs whatever the enemy dares not perform is strong; he who in [military] affairs advances whatever the enemy is ashamed of benefits."**[17]

20.5: When there are standards, the people are at peace with hierarchy; when the sovereign makes changes, he employs the able and attains the suitable; when the state preserves peace,[18] while the sovereign holds power, it is beneficial. Therefore, **"the sovereign values multiple changes; the state values minimal changes."**

20.6: When benefits come from a single opening, the state has plenty of things; when they come from ten openings, the state has few things.[19] He who preserves a single [opening will attain] orderly rule; he who preserves ten [openings will attain] turmoil. Orderly rule means strength; turmoil means weakness; when one is strong, things will come; when one is weak, things will leave. **Hence, "the state that is able** to bring **things is strong; when it** makes **things** leave, it is weak."[20]

20.7: When the people are debased, they value ranks; when they are weak, they respect officials; when they are poor, they take rewards seriously. When one rules the people by punishments, they enjoy being used; when one makes the people fight by rewards, they regard death lightly. Hence: **"When [the state's] warfare is ordered and the army is [ready to be] used, this is called 'strong.'"**

When the people have private [avenues of] glory, they disdain the ranking system and despise officials; when they are rich, they treat rewards lightly. If one regulates the people's shame and humiliation through punishments, then when war comes, they go to war. When the people are afraid to die, their affairs are **chaotic**, and yet they [still are obliged go to] war, they will then be **indolent** in **military** service and agriculture, and **the state** will be weak.[21]

4.2: Farmers, merchants, and officials are the three constant functions in the state. The three functions give birth to six parasitic affairs: "end-of-year," "food," "beauty," "likes," "aspirations," "conduct." When the six take root,[22] [the state] will surely be dismembered. The root of the three functions is in the three kinds of people; the root of the six [parasitic] affairs is in one Man.[23] [The state] that is ordered by standards is strong; that which is ordered by administrative measures will be dismembered.[24] When officials who rule according to constant [patterns] order [their affairs] well, they should be promoted.[25] When governance is large, the state is small; when governance is small, the state is large.[26] When you strengthen them [the people], you aggravate dismemberment; when you weaken them, you increase strength. Hence, he who attacks the strong with strength will collapse; he who attacks the strong with weakness will become the [True] Monarch.[27]

When a strong state is not engaged in warfare, poison infiltrates its intestines; rites, music, and parasitic affairs are born; [the state] will surely be dismembered. When the state wages war, poison infiltrates the enemy; it lacks rites, music, and parasitic affairs; [the state] will

surely be strong. When promotion is based on one's toil and appointment on one's merit, that is called "strength"; when parasitic affairs
are born, dismemberment is certain. When there are few farmers and
many merchants, then the nobles are poor, the merchants are poor, and
the farmers are poor; the three functions are poor, and the state will
surely be dismembered.[28]

20.8: **"Farmers, merchants, and officials: these three are the constant functions in the state."** Farmers open up lands, merchants
bring products, officials order the people. **"Three functions give
birth to six parasitic affairs that are: 'end-of-year,' 'food,' 'beauty,'
'likes,' 'aspirations,' 'conduct.' When the six take root, [the state]
will surely be dismembered."** When farmers have extra food, they
lavishly feast at the end of the year. When merchants have excessive
profits due to [the customers'] like of beauty, this harms [production
of] utensils. When officials are put in place but are not made use of,
they have the distress of "aspirations" and "conduct." When the six
parasites become a custom, the army will surely be defeated.

20.9: When laws are crooked, rule is disordered. When the good
are appointed, there is much talk. When order is attained through
multiple [routes], the state is disordered.[29] When there is much
talk, the army is weak. When laws are clear, governance is moderate; when one relies on force, talk is quelled. When governance is
moderate, the state is well ordered. When talk is quelled, the
army is strong. Hence: **"when governance is large, the state is
small; when governance is small, the state is large."**

20.10: When the government does whatever the people detest, the
people are weak; when the government does whatever the people
delight in, the people are strong. When the people are weak, the
state is strong; when the people are strong, the state is weak. When
the government does whatever the people delight in, the people are
strong; when the people are strong and are further empowered, the
army's weakness multiplies. When the government does whatever
the people detest, the people are weak; when the people are weak
and are weakened further, the army's strength is multiplied. Hence,
employing the strong multiplies weakness; [employing] the weak
multiplies strength and turns one into the [True] Monarch. He who

rules the strong by strength is weak; his weakness is preserved; he who rules the weak by weakness is strong; the strong are eliminated.[30] When the strong are preserved, [the ruler] is weak; when the strong are eliminated, [the ruler becomes] Monarch. Hence: **"he who gov-erns the strong with strength, [his state] will be dismembered; he who** governs **the strong with weakness** is the [True] **Monarch."**[31]

4.3: When the state has rites and music, *Poems* and *Documents*, goodness and self-cultivation, filiality and fraternal obligations,[32] uprightness and argumentativeness—when it has these ten, superiors cannot cause [the people] to fight, and [the state] will surely be dismembered to the point of final collapse. When the state lacks these ten, superiors can cause [the people] to fight, and [the state] will surely prosper to the point of [its ruler] becoming [the True] Monarch. When the state employs good people to rule villains, it will suffer turmoil to the point of dismemberment; when the state employs villains to rule good peo-ple, it will be ruled well to the point of empowerment. If the state rules through *Poems*, *Documents*, rites, music, filiality, fraternal obligations, goodness, and argumentativeness, then when the enemy arrives, the state will be dismembered; and even if the enemy does not arrive, it will be impoverished. When one does not rule through these eight, then the enemy dares not arrive; and even if he arrives, he will be repelled; and when an army is raised in invasion, it will be able to seize [the enemy's territory] and, after seizing it, will surely be able to hold it; whereas when one restrains the army and does not attack, [the state] will surely be rich. When the state is fond of force, it is called "attacking with what is difficult [to resist]." When the state is fond of talk, it is called "attacking with what is easy [to resist]." When the state attacks with what is difficult [to resist], it raises [an army] once and receives tenfold gains; when it attacks with what is easy [to resist], it dispatches [an army] ten times and loses one hundred.[33]

5.1: Argumentativeness and cleverness are the assistants of turmoil; rites and music are symptoms of excessiveness and indolence; kind-ness and benevolence are the mother of transgression; appointment based on reputation[34] is the rat[35] of villainy. When turmoil has assistants, it is actualized; when excessiveness and indolence have symptoms, they are practiced; when transgression has a mother, it is born; when villainy has a rat, it cannot be stopped. When the eight come together, the people overcome the government; when there are none of the eight, the government overcomes the people. When the people overcome the government, the state is weak; when the government overcomes the people, the army is strong. Hence, **"when the state has these** eight, **the superiors cannot cause [the people] to** put up defense and **fight, and it will surely be dismembered to the point of collapse; when the state has none of** the eight, **superiors can cause [the people] to** put up defense and **fight, and the state will surely prosper to the point of [its ruler] becoming [the True] Monarch."**

5.2: When the good are employed, the people are attached to their relatives; when villains are employed, the people are attached to regulations. Those who are harmonious and cover up for each other are "good"; those who are separate and regulate each other are "villains." When the "good" are commended, transgressions are concealed; when "villains" are appointed, crimes are punished. When transgressions are concealed, the people overcome the law; when crimes are punished, the law overcomes the people. When the people overcome the law, the state is in turmoil; when the law overcomes the people, the army is strong. Hence, it is said: **"When the state employs good people to rule villains, it will suffer turmoil to the point of dismemberment; when the state employs villains to rule good people, it will be ruled well to the point of empowerment."**

5.3: **When the state attacks with what is difficult [to resist], it raises [an army] once and receives tenfold gains; when it attacks with what is easy [to resist], it raises [an army] ten times and loses one hundred. When the state is fond of force, it is called "attacking with what is difficult [to resist]." When the state is fond of talk, it is called "attacking with what is easy [to resist]."** For the people, it is easy to engage in talk and is difficult to be usable. When the state's laws encourage the people to make what is difficult for them, the army employs what is difficult for the people, and the state attacks with force, it raises [an army] once and receives tenfold gains. When the state's laws encourage the people to make what is easy for them, the army employs what is easy[36] for the people, and the state attacks with talk, it raises [an army] ten times and loses one hundred.

4.4: When penalties are heavy and rewards are light, then superiors love the people, and the people are [ready] to die for their superiors. When rewards are heavy and penalties are light, then superiors do not love the people, and the people are not [ready] to die for their superiors. When a thriving state implements penalties, the people benefit and fear [superiors]; when it implements rewards, the people benefit and love [superiors].[37] When [the state] implements punishments, [it should] inflict heavy [punishments] on light [offenses] {{and light on heavy [crimes]}}: then light [offenses] will not arise, and heavy [crimes] will not come.[38] When the state lacks strength yet implements knowledge-able and skillful [policies], it will surely collapse.[39]

Use punishments to handle cowards: they will surely become brave. Use rewards to handle the brave: they will [be ready to] die. When cowards are brave, and the brave are [ready] to die, the state will have no rivals, and it will be strong; the strong will surely become the [True] Monarch. Use punishments to make the poor become rich; use rewards to make the rich become poor.[40] When a well-ordered state can cause the poor to become rich and the rich to become poor, then it will have abundant force; he who has abundant force will become the Monarch. [In the state of the True] Monarch, for every nine punishments there is one reward; in a strong state, for every seven punishments there are three rewards; in a due-to-be-dismembered state, for every five punishments there are five rewards.

5.4: When penalties are heavy, ranks are respected; when rewards are light, punishments inspire awe.[41] When ranks are respected, superiors love the people; when punishments inspire awe, the people are [ready to] die for their superiors. Hence, **"when a thriving state implements penalties, the people benefit"**; when it employs rewards, the superiors are revered. When the law is detailed, punishments are overflowing; when the law is simple, punishments are moderate. The people can be both ordered and in turmoil:[42] if you order them when they are in turmoil, there is even more turmoil. Hence, order them when they are ordered, and orderly rule will come; order them when they are in turmoil, and turmoil will come. The people's disposition is to be ruled well, but their activities bring about turmoil. Hence, **"when [the state] implements punishments, [it should] inflict heavy [punishments] on light [offenses]: light [offenses] will not arise, and heavy [crimes] will have no chance of arriving."** This is what is called "ordering them when they are ordered." If in implementing punishments you punish heavily [only the] heavy [crimes] and lightly the light ones, then light [offenses] will not be stopped, and heavy [ones] will have no chance to be stopped either. This is what is called "ordering them when they are in turmoil." Hence, when light [offenses are punished] heavily, then punishments are eliminated, affairs are accomplished, and the state is strong; when heavy [crimes are punished] heavily and light [offenses are punished] lightly, then punishments arrive, and [troublesome] affairs are born: the state will be dismembered.

5.5: When the people are courageous, reward them with what they desire; when they are cowardly, eradicate[43] this with what they detest. Hence, when cowards are encouraged with punishments, they become brave; when the brave are encouraged with rewards, they are [ready to] die. **"When cowards are brave, and the brave are [ready] to die, the state will have no rivals, and** [its ruler] **will surely become the Monarch."**

5.6: When the people are poor, they are weak; when they are rich, they are excessive; when they are excessive, there are parasitic [affairs]; when there are parasitic [affairs], [the state] is weak.[44] Hence, **when they [the people] are poor,** increase their [wealth] **by punishments, and they will become rich; when they are rich,** diminish [their wealth] by **rewards, and they will become poor.** [To] raise up an ordered state, value **causing the poor to become rich and the rich to become poor.** When the poor become rich, and the rich poor, the state is strong. When the three functions[45] are without parasitic [affairs], the state is strong; and when for a long time they are without parasitic [affairs], [the ruler] will surely become the Monarch.

5.7: **Punishments give birth to force; force gives birth to strength; strength gives birth to awesomeness; awesomeness gives birth to** virtue; virtue **is born of punishments.**[46] Hence, when punishments are plentiful, rewards are heavy; when rewards are minuscule, punishments are heavy. The people have things they desire and things they detest; they desire the six excesses and detest the four difficulties.[47] When they follow the six excesses, the state is weakened; when they implement the four difficulties, the army is strong. Hence, the True Monarch punishes nine times and rewards once. When he punishes nine times, the six excesses are stopped; when he rewards once, the four difficulties are implemented. When the six excesses are stopped, there are no villains in the state; when the four difficulties are implemented, the army has no rival.

4.5: If the state engages in the One for one year, it will be strong for ten years; if it engages in the One for ten years, it will be strong for one hundred years; if it engages in the One for one hundred years, it will be strong for a thousand years; he who is strong for a thousand years is the [True] Monarch.[48] Awesomeness is what allows one to take over ten, what allows voice to take over substance. Hence, he who is able to inspire awe will become the Monarch.[49] [The state] that is able to give birth [to force] but not to reduce [it] is called a "self-attacking state"; it will surely be dismembered. [The state] that is able to give birth [to force] and to reduce [it] is called an "enemy-attacking state"; it surely will be strong.[50] Hence, attack the [parasitic affairs], attack the [people's] force, attack the enemy.[51] If you are able to do two of these and discard only one, you will be strong; if you are able to do all three of these, you will be awe-inspiring and will surely become the [True] Monarch.[52]

5.8: The people's desires are myriad, but benefit comes from a single [opening]. If the people are not engaged in the One, they will not be able to satisfy their desires; hence, [have them] engage in the One. When they are engaged in the One, their force is consolidated; when their force is consolidated, they are strong; when they are strong and are used, their strength multiplies. Hence, "[the state] **that is able to give birth to force and to reduce it is called an "enemy-attacking state"; it surely will be strong."** When you block the private ways [through which the people hoped to] fulfill their aspirations, and open a single gate [through which and only through which they will] attain whatever they desire, this causes the people first to engage in whatever they detest[53] and only then to attain whatever they desire; hence, the force is abundant. When the force is abundant but is not used, then their aspirations are (not?) exhausted;[54] when their aspirations are (not?) exhausted, they have private [interests]; when they have private [interests], [the state] is weak. Hence, "[the state] **that is able to give birth to force but not to reduce it is called a 'self-attacking state;' it will surely be dismembered."** Hence, it is said: the state of the True Monarch does not store up force, and its households do not hoard grain. The state does not store up force [because] the inferiors can be used; the households do not hoard grain [because] superiors accumulate it.[55]

4.6: When decisions are made by every tenth hamlet, the state is weak; when they are made by every ninth (fifth?)[56] hamlet, the state is strong. He who orders [affairs] by the daytime is the Monarch; he who orders [affairs] by night is strong; he who orders [affairs] by the next day, [his state] will be dismembered.

5.9: This is the orderly rule of the state: when [affairs] are determined by a household, you will become the Monarch; when [they are] determined by officials, you will be strong; when [they are] determined by the ruler [himself], you will be weak. [Punish] heavily for light [offenses], [thereby] eliminating punishments; let the officials [adhere to] constant [methods]; then there will be orderly rule. Restrict punishments and bind [the people] through mutual surveillance. [Promises of] rewards should not be broken. If criminals are invariably denounced, then the people will make decisions in their hearts. When superiors issue orders and the people know to respond, when utensils take shape in the household and are utilized by officials,[57] then affairs are determined by a household. Hence, [in the state of] the True Monarch, punishments and rewards are determined by the people's hearts; the use of the utensils is determined at the household level.

When orderly rule is clear, [the people are] uniform; when it is dim, they differ. When they are uniform, [policies] can be implemented; when [the people] differ, [policies] are stopped. When they are implemented, there is orderly rule; when they are stopped, there is turmoil. When there is orderly rule, decisions are made by a household; when there is turmoil, they are made by the ruler. The well-ordered state values decisions made below. Hence, [the state] in which **decisions are made by every tenth hamlet is weak**; [the state] in which decisions **are made by every** fifth **hamlet is strong**.

When decisions are made by the household, one has extra [time]; hence, it is said: **"he who orders [affairs] by the daytime is the Monarch."** When officials make decisions, [the time] is not sufficient: hence, it is said: **"he who orders [affairs] by night is strong."** When the ruler himself makes decisions, there is turmoil; hence, it is said: **"he who orders [affairs] by the next day, [his state] will be dismembered."** In the state that possesses the Way, orderly rule is attained without heeding the ruler, and the people have no need to follow officials.

4.7: In registering the number of the people, record the living and erase the dead. When the people do not abscond from [producing] grain,[58] fields will not be covered by wild grasses. Then the state is rich. He whose state is rich is strong.

* * *

4.8: When one eradicates punishments through punishments, the state is ordered; when one brings punishments through punishments, the state is disordered. Hence, it is said: "when in implementing punishments you [punish] heavily for light [offenses], punishments are eradicated, affairs are accomplished, and the state is strong; when you [punish] heavily for heavy [offenses] and lightly for light [ones], punishments are brought in, [more] affairs are born, and the state is dismembered." Punishments give birth to force; force gives birth to strength; strength gives birth to awesomeness; awesomeness gives birth to kindness: kindness is borne of force.[59] One puts forward force to accomplish valiant fighting; fighting is used to accomplish clever stratagems.

* * *

4.9: When grain is born, gold is dead; when gold is born, grain is dead.[60] When basic commodities are cheap, yet producers are many while consumers are few, then farmers will face difficulties, and deceitful [undertakings] will be encouraged; the army will be weak, and the state will surely be dismembered to the point of final collapse.[61] When a *liang* (ounce) of gold is born within the borders, twelve *shi* (piculs) of grain are dead outside the borders.[62] When twelve *shi* of grain are born within the borders, one *liang* of gold is dead outside the borders. When the state is fond of giving birth to gold within the borders, then both gold and grain are dead, both granaries and treasury are empty.[63] When the state is fond of giving birth to grain within the borders, then both gold and grain are born, both granaries and treasury are full, and the state is strong.

* * *

4.10: A strong state should know thirteen numbers within its borders: the number of granaries and residents;[64] the number of adult men and women; the number of the old and infirm; the number of officials and men-of-service; the number of those who obtain emoluments by talking; the number of beneficial people;[65] the number of horses, oxen, hay, and straw. If one wants to strengthen one's state but does not know these thirteen numbers, then even if the state's soil is advantageous and residents are numerous, it will be increasingly weakened to the point of dismemberment.

* * *

4.11: The state in which there are no resentful people is called a strong state. When [the state] raises an army and launches an attack, then ranks and responsibilities are granted based on military [exploits], and it will surely be victorious. When it restrains the army and [pursues] farming, then ranks and responsibilities are granted based on grain [production], and the state will become rich. He who raises an army and defeats the enemy, who restrains his army and enriches his state, is the [True] Monarch.

APPENDIX: ADDENDUM TO CHAPTER 20

The last segment of chapter 20 neither is related to the exegesis of chapter 4 nor shares the stylistic characteristics of the rest of chapter 20. It is likely that it was misplaced in this chapter from another text. The first sentences of this segment overlap with a segment of chapter 9, and the last section appears as a belated (and historically inaccurate) abridgment of a discussion borrowed from the *Xunzi*. Judging from the historical information in this segment, it clearly could not have been produced before the mid–third century B.C.E. Its extensive reference to recent history resembles chapter 15 of the *Book of Lord Shang* (again, one of the latest in the treatise), which may reflect a common trend of late Warring States period thinkers (as exemplified in many chapters of, for example, *Xunzi*, *Han Feizi*, and *Lüshi chunqiu*) to resort to history in order to demonstrate the correctness of their arguments.

* * *

20.11: When a clear-sighted ruler employs his ministers, their utilization should be related to their merits, and rewards should reflect the full exertion of their labor. When the sovereign lets his people trust this as [they trust] the sun and moon, he will have no rivals. Now, Li Lou could see an autumn hair from the distance of one hundred paces but could not exchange his eyes with others; Wu Huo could lift the weight of one thousand *jun* but could not exchange his superior strength with others. The worthiness of the sage is his disposition, but it cannot be lent to others.[66] Now, all the power holders of our age want to be supremely sagacious, [yet the realization of this goal] is in what is called upholding standards. Rejecting standards yet trying to attain orderly rule is like carrying heavy luggage along a distant road without horses or oxen or crossing a great river without boat or oars.

Now, multitudes of subjects and a strong army are the assets of thearchs and monarchs, yet if one does not utilize clear standards to preserve them, this means placing oneself next door to danger and ruin. Hence, when the clear-sighted ruler examines the standards, among the people within the borders no one has a deviant and excessive heart, all the drifting and resident men-of-service are pressed into battle lines, and the myriad people are fully committed to tilling and fighting.

How do I know that this is so? The people of Chu are swift in arranging ranks and fast like the whirlwind; their steel produced at Wan[67] and iron spears are sharp as wasps and scorpions; their armor made of shark skin and rhinoceros hides is as hard as metal and stone. The Yangzi and the Han River serve as their moats; the Ru and the Ying rivers serve as their boundaries; they are protected by the Deng Forest and are surrounded by Fangcheng.[68] Yet when the Qin army arrived, Yan and Ying were overturned like a withered tree; Tang Mie died at Chuisha, Zhuang Qiao started [rebellion] from within, and Chu was divided into five.[69] It is not that its territories were not vast, [its] soldiers numerous, or [its] armor, weapons, and resources lacking. It is because it lacked standards that it was neither victorious in fighting nor steadfast in defense. {{It abandoned scales and weights and tried to estimate what is heavy and what is light.}}[70]

6

CALCULATING THE LAND (算地)

C hapter 6 is the second longest in the *Book of Lord Shang* and, arguably, the richest intellectually. The chapter addresses a broad variety of issues concerning economic, social, administrative, and legal policies, and it is careful to explain their underlying rationale. It elucidates the norms of land utilization, addresses the causes of the population's geographic mobility and the ways to reduce it, and explores fundamental issues of human nature. The latter discussion makes chapter 6 one of the philosophical centerpieces of the entire book. The *Book of Lord Shang*'s discussion of human nature may be an important—and unjustifiably neglected—contribution to the later discourse on this topic (this point is highlighted in Xiao Yang 2006 and Sato Masayuki 2013a, 2013b).

Three points are central to the chapter. First, economically speaking, the ruler's primary goal should be to maintain a proper balance between population and cultivated lands. Hence, in marked distinction to chapter 2, this chapter states that opening up new lands is not a singularly acceptable policy: at times, the focus should rather shift to attracting immigrants (6.1, 6.2). Second, the entire spectrum of socioeconomic policies should be based on understanding the essentials of human nature. Insofar as all humans are motivated by the simultaneous quest for riches and a good name (*ming* 名, referring here both to repute and to social status), the ruler should maintain a system in which material and social benefits are distributed exclusively in exchange for engaging in farming and warfare (6.4, 6.5). This means—as recommended in chapter 3—blocking the ways to social and economic advancement for all those who are not engaged in these two primary occupations, be they men-of-service (*shi*), artisans, or merchants (6.6). The authors furthermore recommend—in an echo of chapter 4 and in anticipation of chapter 7—to make full use of negative incentives against evildoers, meaning employment of harsh punishments to deter villainy (6.10). Third, socioeconomic and military policies should be designed to prevent the people from emigrating; this means making land rather than one's "body" (i.e., individual skills) the chief repository of a person's "capital" (6.6, 6.8). The combination of these policies will critically empower the state in its competition with its neighbors.

The philosophical sophistication and refined style of chapter 6 may be indicative of its belonging to a later layer of the book than, say, chapters 2, 3, and 4. Yet the chapter cannot have come too late: its mention of the usage of a small *mu* 畝 of 100 paces' length and its dissatisfaction with that usage (6.2) are indicative of its being penned during the process of Qin's move from using a small *mu* to a larger, 240-pace-long *mu*. Because we know from the Qin *Statute on Land* unearthed from Tomb 50 at Haojiaping, Qingchuan 青川郝家坪 (Sichuan), that by 309 B.C.E. the large *mu* was the standard measurement of agricultural fields (Hulsewé 1985, 211–212; Korolkov 2010, 76–90), it is clear that the chapter was composed much earlier, either during Shang Yang's lifetime or shortly thereafter.

* * *

6.1: In general, the trouble of the rulers of our age is that when using the army, they do not assess [its] strength, and when managing grass and weeds, they do not measure the land. Thus, if the land is narrow but the people are numerous, this means that the people exceed the land; if the land is extensive but the people are few, this means that the land exceeds the people. When the people exceed the land, commit yourself to opening up [new lands]; when the land exceeds the people, engage in attracting [immigrants]. When one opens up, [lands] can be multiplied.[1] When the people exceed the land, achievements of the state are few, and the army is weak; when the land exceeds the people, the resources of mountains and marshlands are not utilized. Casting away Heaven's resources and following the people's indulgence means that the rulers of our generation are committed to erroneous [policies]; yet superiors and inferiors are engaged in these [behaviors]. Thus, even if the people are plentiful, the army is weak; even if the land is vast, strength is minuscule.

* * *

6.2: Hence, in ruling the state and making use of[2] the land, the correct standard of the former kings was: mountains and forests occupy one-tenth; swamps and marshlands occupy one-tenth; valleys, dales, and running rivers occupy one-tenth; towns, settlements, paths, and roads occupy {one}-tenth; {infertile fields occupy two-tenths, fertile fields occupy} four-{tenths}.[2] Hence, when ruling the state, apportion the fields by calculating proportions [as follows]:[3]

The territory of five hundred small *mu* is enough to provide for one serviceman: [yet] this means that the land is not properly utilized. A territory of one hundred *li* squared can provide for ten thousand soldiers, [yet] the number is [still] small.[4] Cultivated fields should suffice to feed the people; towns, settlements, and roads should suffice to settle the people; mountains, forests, marshes, swamps, valleys, and dales should suffice to provide benefits; marshes, swamps, dikes, and dams should suffice to accumulate [water].[5] Hence, when an army is dispatched, provisions are ample, and resources are abundant; when the army is at rest, the people are working, and the accumulated [surplus] suffices for a long time. This is what is called the standard of utilizing territory and being ready for battle.

* * *

6.3: The rulers of our generation possess the territory of several thousand *li* squared, but their provisions do not suffice to prepare for battle or fill the granaries, and their army is comparable to that of their neighbors. I, your subject,[6] therefore worry about this on behalf of the rulers of our generation. After all, when the territory is large but is not cultivated, it is as if you have no territory; when the people are numerous but are not used, it is as if you have no people. Hence, the method of ruling the state is to commit oneself to developing wastelands; the way of using soldiers is to commit oneself to unifying rewards.[7] When external private profits are blocked, the people are committed to farming; when they are committed to farming, they are simple; when they are simple, they fear orders. When private rewards are forbidden below, the people concentrate their force on [fighting] the enemy; when they concentrate on [fighting] the enemy, [the army] is victorious. How do I know that? The people's disposition is that when they are simple, they generate labor and take their strength lightly; when they are impoverished, they generate knowledge and weigh benefits. When they take their strength lightly, they are not fearful of death and are glad to be used [in the army]; when they weigh benefits, they are fearful of punishments and are at ease with bitter [toil]. When they are at ease with bitter [toil], the strength [that is, potential] of the soil is fully utilized; when they are glad to be used, the strength of the army is fully utilized.

* * *

6.4: The ability of the well-governed state to fully utilize its land resources and to cause the people to die [for its sake] is due to the name (repute) and benefit that it brings [to the people]. The nature of the people is to seek food when they are hungry, to seek respite when they are belabored, to seek joy when they are embittered, to seek glory when they are humiliated: this is the people's disposition. In seeking benefit, the people lose the standard of ritual;[8] in seeking a name, they lose the constant of their nature.[9] How can I demonstrate this? Now, criminals violate the prohibitions of rulers and superiors above and lose the ritual of subjects and sons below;[10] hence, their name is dishonored and their body endangered, but they still do not stop: this is because of benefit. In the generations of old, there were men-of-service (shi) who did not have enough clothes to warm their skin or enough food to fill their bowels. They exerted their four limbs and injured their five internal organs above, but they behaved ever more broad-heartedly. This was not the constant of their nature, yet they did: this was because of the name. Hence, it is said: wherever the name and benefit meet, the people will go in this direction.

* * *

6.5: When the sovereign holds the handles of a (good) name and benefit and is able to bring together the name [only] to the meritorious, this is the method [of proper rule].[11] The sage examines [the nature of] authority to operate the handles; he examines the method to direct the people. The method is the technique employed by the ministers and the sovereign; it is the essential [matter] of the state. Hence, it never happened that a ten-thousand-chariot [state] lost its method and was not endangered or that ministers and the ruler lost the techniques and there was no turmoil. In our generation, the ruler wants to open up land and order the people, and yet he does not examine the method; the ministers want to fully perform their affairs and yet do not establish the techniques; hence, in the state there are disobedient people, and the ruler has ministers who do not heed orders.

Thus, in ruling his state, the sage causes the people to follow farming at home and to plan for war abroad. Farming is what the people consider bitter; war is what the people consider dangerous. Yet they brave what they consider bitter and perform what they consider dangerous because of the calculation [of a name and benefit]. Thus, in [ordinary] life, the people calculate benefits; [facing] death, they think of a (good) name. One cannot but investigate whence the name and benefit come. When benefits come from land, the people fully utilize their strength; when the name comes from war, the people are ready to die. When at home you direct the people to fully utilize their strength, grass does not cover wastelands; when abroad you cause the people to be ready to die, you will overcome the enemy. When the enemy is overcome and grass does not cover wastelands, then without moving you will acquire the merit of being rich and strong.[12]

* * *

6.6: But now things are different. The rulers of our age are devoted exclusively to matters that are of no urgency to the state. They behave as if they are Yao or Shun, but their merits do not compare with those of Tang and Wu:[13] this is the fault of power holders. I, your subject, would like to discuss their errors:

In ruling the state, if you discard the power of authority and rely on the persuaders' talk, then you personally will be cultivated but will have meager achievements. Thus, when you employ the *shi*[14] engaged in *Poems*, *Documents*, and persuaders' talk, the people will wander and disregard their ruler; if you employ reclusive *shi*, the people will be estranged and reject their superiors; if you employ brave *shi*, the people will be quarrelsome and disregard the prohibitions; if you make use of the *shi* who are skillful artisans, the people will be volatile and easily migrate; when the *shi* who are merchants and peddlers are at ease and yet reap benefits, then the people follow their lead and question their superiors. Hence, when these five types of people are employed by the state, the fields are covered by weeds, and the army is weak.

The capital of persuading *shi* is their mouth; the capital of reclusive *shi* is their mind; the capital of brave *shi* is their [fighting] spirit; the capital of skillful artisan *shi* is their hands; the capital of merchant and peddler *shi* is their bodies. Hence, for them, All-under-Heaven is just one home, and they move across it with their bodies as their capital. The people's capital is accumulated in their bodies, and they can empower themselves anywhere abroad;[15] carrying their accumulated capital, they flock to any place as if to their home: even for Yao and Shun it would be difficult [to make this situation orderly]. Hence, [kings] Tang and Wu prohibited it; thereby they established their achievements and accomplished [a good] name.

* * *

6.7: The sage is not able to rely on what the world considers easy so as to overcome what is considered difficult; rather, he must rely on what is considered difficult to overcome what is considered easy. Hence, when the people are ignorant, they can be overcome by knowledge; when the generation is knowledgeable, they can be overcome by force. When the people[16] are ignorant, they treat their force as easy, while treating sophistication as difficult; when the generation is sophisticated, they treat knowledge as easy, while treating force as difficult. Hence, Shennong taught plowing and became the king of All-under-Heaven: [the people] accepted him as teacher due to his knowledge.[17] Tang and Wu devoted themselves to force and attacked [their enemies]: the regional lords submitted to their power.[18] Nowadays, the generation is sophisticated, and the people are indulgent, which is modeled after the times of Tang and Wu. Yet [the rulers] perform the activities of Shennong, thereby damaging the prohibitions [appropriate to our] age; hence, the country of one thousand chariots is confused and disordered.[19] To be further devoted to this [behavior] means to err.

* * *

6.8: The nature of the people is such that when measuring, they take what is longer; when weighing, they take what is heavier; when using scales, they seek profits. The clear-sighted ruler carefully observes these three [behaviors]; only then can he establish orderly rule in the state and attain the people's abilities. There are only a few things that the state demands of the people but many ways through which the people can avoid these demands. [What the state demands is,] at home, to direct the people to agriculture [and], abroad, to focus the people on waging war. Hence, in ruling the state, the sage multiplies prohibitions to stop the pretentious[20] and relies on force to eradicate deceitfulness. When the two are used simultaneously, then the people within the borders [focus on] the One; when they are [focused on] the One, they engage in agriculture; when they engage in agriculture, they are simple; when [they are] simple, they are at peace in their dwellings and hate going abroad. Hence, the sage, in ruling the state, causes the people's capital to be stored in the soil and causes them to be endangered anywhere abroad. When capital is {accumulated}[21] in the soil, they are simple; when they are endangered abroad, they are suspicious. When the people are simple within [the state] and are suspicious abroad, they will exert themselves in agriculture and be victorious in war. When the people exert themselves in agriculture, their capital is accumulated;

when they are victorious in war, their neighbors are endangered. When capital is accumulated, it cannot be carried off while running away; when the neighbors are endangered, the [people] have no home [abroad] to which they can flock. Without capital, without a home to flock to, and endangered abroad: even a crazy man will not do it (will not leave his country).

* * *

6.9: Hence, in ruling the state, the sage establishes laws after observing customs and then attains orderly rule; he inspects the roots of the state's affairs and then acts appropriately. Without the observation of current customs and without the inspection of the roots of the state, laws can be established, but the people will be in turmoil; undertakings will be numerous, but achievements few. This is what I, your subject, call "to err."

* * *

6.10: So punishments are used to prohibit evil, and rewards are to support prohibitions. Disgrace, humiliation, toil, and bitterness are what the people detest; prominence, glory, leisure, and joy are what the people are devoted to. Hence, when the punishments in the state are not detested, whereas ranks and emoluments are insufficient to cause devotion—this is the omen of a ruined state. Thus, when those penalized can escape and have their punishment revoked, petty men are depraved and licentious and do not consider punishments bitter; then they behave haughtily toward their superiors and seek benefit. When the gates of prominence and glory are not unified, then noble men serve the powerful to accomplish their name.[22] When the petty men do not avoid prohibitions, punishments multiply; when the noble men do not follow orders, penalties are imposed. When punishments multiply and penalties are imposed, the state has many villains. In this case, the rich will be unable to preserve their wealth, and the poor will be unable to engage in their occupation; the fields will be covered with seeds, and the state will be impoverished. When the fields are covered with seeds, deceit is born among the people; when the state is impoverished, the superiors lack [the means to grant] rewards.

Hence, when the sage exercises orderly rule, convicts have no position in the state, and felons hold no office. When convicts are ranked [together with noble men], noble men disregard their position. When {felons}[23] wear brocade and eat meat, petty men hope [to gain] similar benefits. When the noble men disregard their position, they are ashamed to claim merits; when petty men hope to reap benefits, they are proud of[24] their depravity. So punishments and penalties are to stop the villains; offices and ranks are to encourage [gaining] merits. Now, if the state has ranks, but the people are ashamed of them, or when it establishes punishments, but the people are fond of them, this means that the techniques and the methods are in deep trouble.

* * *

6.11: Hence, when the noble man holds authority,[25] he establishes techniques of rule by rectifying [everything]; he establishes offices and makes rank esteemed so as to correspond [to office]; he investigates one's labor, elevates the meritorious, and then makes the appointments. Then superior and inferior are balanced. When superior and inferior are balanced, then ministers are able to fully commit their strength, and the sovereign is able to monopolize the handles of authority.

7

OPENING THE BLOCKED (開塞)

C hapter 7 is the second ideological centerpiece of the *Book of Lord Shang*. As such, it is closely related to chapter 6, "Calculating the Land," which is even directly cited in section 7.2. Yet whereas chapter 6 justifies the author's proposal of a novel sociopolitical system in terms of its correspondence to human nature, the emphasis in chapter 7 shifts to the concept of historical change. In the first section, the authors present a story of the evolution of human society from an egalitarian, promiscuous, kin-based order in which "the people knew their mothers but not their fathers" to an incipient stratified society ruled by the "worthies" and then to a well-functioning bureaucratic state. This is arguably the single most sophisticated model of the genesis of the state in the entire corpus of traditional Chinese texts (see Pines and Shelach 2005), and it allows the authors to promulgate their major idea: "When the affairs of the world change, one should implement a different Way" (7.1). Everything—from social arrangements to kinship structures to moral values—can and should be altered once the objective conditions, such as population pressure and the resultant scarcity of resources, necessitate this change.

The authors conclude that benevolence and rule by virtue were applicable in the past but are no longer relevant. The knowledgeable and crafty people of the current generation can be ruled effectively only if they are overawed by the state's superior force. Stern punishments are the only way to prevent the people from committing crimes and to preserve sociopolitical order. Similarly, military prowess is the only way for survival in the age of the competing Warring States. Should the rulers understand this and heed the author's advice, they will restore order to the state internally and empower it externally to the point of reunifying "All-under-Heaven" and establishing "the fourth" dynasty (7.3). Notably, in this future, perfectly ordered state there will be no need to impose punishments because the people will be overawed and not dare to transgress the law. Hence, the authors end with optimistic promises: "by killing and punishing, I return to virtue" (7.5), and "rel[iance] on punishments [will] eradicate punishments" (7.6).

* * *

7.1: When Heaven and Earth were formed, the people were born. At that time, the people knew their mothers but not their fathers; their way was one of attachment to relatives and of selfishness. Attachment to relatives results in particularity; selfishness results in malignity. The people multiplied, and as they were engaged in particularity and malignity, there was turmoil. At that time, the people began seeking victories and forcefully seizing [each other's property].[1] Seeking victories results in struggles; forceful seizure results in quarrels.[2] When there are quarrels but no proper [norms], no one attains his natural life span. Therefore, the worthies established impartiality and propriety and instituted selflessness; the people began rejoicing in benevolence. At that time, attachment to relatives declined, and elevation of the worthy was established.

In general, the benevolent are devoted to the love of benefit,[3] whereas the worthy view overcoming one another as the [proper] Way.[4] The people multiplied yet lacked regulations; for a long time they viewed overcoming one another as the [proper] Way, and hence there again was turmoil. Therefore, the sages took responsibility. They created distinctions among lands, property, men, and women. When distinctions were fixed but regulations were still lacking, this was unacceptable; hence, they established prohibitions. When prohibitions were established but none supervised [their implementation], this was unacceptable; hence, they established officials. When officials were instituted but not unified, this was unacceptable; hence, they established the ruler. When the ruler was established, the elevation of the worthy declined, and the esteem of nobility was established.

Thus, in the early ages, [the people] were attached to relatives and were devoted to themselves; in the middle ages, they elevated the worthy and rejoiced in benevolence; in the recent age, they esteem nobility and respect officials. When they elevated the worthy, they used the Way to overcome each other; but the establishment of the ruler caused the worthies to become useless. Being attached to relatives, they considered selfishness as the Way; but the establishment of impartiality and propriety caused selfishness no longer to be practiced. In these three cases, it is not that their affairs are opposite; it is that the Way of the people is base and what they value changes. When the affairs of the world change, one should implement a different Way.

* * *

7.2: Hence, it is said: "The Way of the Monarch has its rope." The Way of the Monarch is one end; the Way of the Minister is another end— their direction is different, but the rope is one.[5] Therefore, it is said: "When the people are ignorant, one can become monarch through knowledge; when the generation is knowledgeable, one can become monarch through force."[6] When the people are ignorant, they have extra force, but their knowledge is insufficient; when the generation is knowledgeable, they are extra crafty, but their force is insufficient. The nature[7] of the people is that when they lack knowledge, they study; when their force is exhausted, they submit. Hence, Shennong taught how to plow and became Monarch: [the people] accepted him as teacher due to his knowledge.[8] [Kings] Tang and Wu[9] devoted themselves to force and attacked regional lords: [the people] submitted to their power. So, when the people are ignorant, then, lacking knowledge, they ask questions; when the generation is knowledgeable, then, lacking extra strength, they submit. Hence, he who rules All-under-Heaven through knowledge[10] discards punishments, whereas he who forcefully attacks regional lords brushes aside virtue.

* * *

7.3: The sage does not model himself after the past, nor does he follow the present.[11] When you model yourself after the past, you lag behind the times; when you follow the present, you are blocked by [others'] power. The Zhou did not model themselves after the Shang; the Xia did not model themselves after Yu [Shun].[12] Configurations of power under the Three Dynasties were all different, but each ruled [All-under-Heaven]. Hence, there is a way to become Monarch, but there are different patterns of being attached to it. King Wu seized [power] by rebellion but valued compliance; he fought for All-under-Heaven but elevated yielding; he seized [the world] by force but held it by righteousness.[13] Nowadays, strong states engage in conquests and annexations, whereas the weak are committed to forceful defense. Above, they do not reach the times of Yu [Shun] and Xia; below, they do not embrace [the ways of Kings] Tang and Wu.[14] [The ways of] Tang and Wu are blocked; hence, every state of ten thousand chariots is engaged in [offensive] war, and every state of one thousand chariots is engaged in defense. These ways have been blocked for a long time, but contemporary rulers are unable to discard them; hence, the Three Dynasties lack the fourth. Only the clear-sighted ruler is able to heed this.

* * *

7.4: Now, let me submit [my views] to clarify these points. In the past, the people were simple and generous; nowadays, the people are crafty and deceitful. Hence, those who imitate the past prioritize virtue as precaution [against transgressions], whereas those who order[15] [things] according to the present advance punishments and turn them into law—that is why the common folk are confused. In our generation, establishing whatever the people like and dismissing whatever they detest is called "righteousness," whereas establishing whatever the people detest and eliminating whatever they like is called "unrighteousness." Yet the name and the substance of these two should be exchanged:[16] one must investigate this. When you establish what the people like, they will ultimately be hurt by what they detest; but when you establish what the people detest, they will peacefully reside in doing what they like.[17] How do I know this? When the people worry, they become thoughtful; when they are thoughtful, they generate [proper] measures. When the people are happy, they are licentious; when they are licentious, they give birth to laxity. Hence, if you order them through punishments, the people are overawed; when they are overawed, there is no depravity; when there is no depravity, the people reside in peace, doing what they like. If you instruct them through righteousness, the people indulge themselves; when the people indulge, there is turmoil; when there is turmoil, the people will be hurt by what they detest. What I call "punishments"[18] is the root of righteousness, whereas what our generation calls righteousness is the way of violence. Hence, if you order the people through what they detest, they will surely end in what they like; if you do it through what they like, they will surely be defeated by what they detest.

* * *

7.5: In the well-ordered state, there are many punishments and few rewards.[19] Hence, [in the state of] the True Monarch there are nine punishments and one reward, whereas in the due-to-be-dismembered state there are nine rewards and one punishment. Now, there are major and minor transgressions: hence, there are heavy and light punishments. There is small and great goodness: hence, there are abundant and minimal rewards. These two are commonly employed in our generation. Yet when you punish the crime only after it has been committed, you cannot eradicate depravity; when you reward whatever the people consider righteous, you cannot stop transgressions. When punishments cannot eradicate depravity and rewards cannot stop transgressions, turmoil is inevitable. Hence, the True Monarch inflicts punishments on about-to-be-committed transgressions: then major wickedness will not be born. He rewards [those who] inform about the depraved: then [even] minor transgressions are not lost. When, in ordering the people, you can prevent depravity from being born and minor transgressions from being lost, the state is well ordered. When the state is well ordered, you are powerful. When a single state implements this, it will be the only one to be ruled well within its boundaries. When two states implement this, the soldiers receive temporary respite.[20] When All-under-Heaven implements this, the utmost virtue is restored. Thus, by killing and punishing, I return to virtue, whereas [what is called] righteousness corresponds to violence.

* * *

7.6: In antiquity, the people resided together and dwelled herdlike in turmoil; hence, they were in need of superiors. So All-under-Heaven is happy having superiors and considers this orderly rule. Now, if you have a sovereign but no laws, it is as harmful as having no sovereign; if you have laws but are unable to overcome [those] who wreak havoc, it is as if you have no laws. Although All-under-Heaven have no peace without a ruler, they delight in flouting his laws: hence, the entire generation is in a state of confusion. Yet to benefit the people of All-under-Heaven nothing is better than orderly rule, and in orderly rule nothing is more secure than establishing the ruler. The Way of establishing the ruler is nowhere broader than in relying on laws; in the task of relying on laws, nothing is more urgent than eradicating depravity; the root of eradicating depravity is nowhere deeper than in making punishments stern. Hence, the True Monarch prohibits through rewards and encourages through punishments; he pursues transgressions and not goodness; he relies on punishments to eradicate punishments.

8

SPEAKING OF THE ONE (壹言)

C hapter 8 briefly summarizes the major ideas of earlier chapters. Its main message is that proper employment of rewards and punishments will direct the people exclusively to agriculture and warfare; any deviation from this system is highly unwelcome. The chapter reiterates the need to prevent those who remain outside the state-mandated hierarchy of power from ascending social ladder (8.1). It furthermore (8.3) echoes section 7.3 in calling upon the ruler neither to model his rule after the past nor to follow present conventions. The laws should reflect the people's customs (8.3; cf. 6.9). It is the ruler's personal responsibility to understand these principles and to implement them (8.3).

Chapter 8 also emphasizes the importance of political flexibility and constant adaptation to changing circumstances. The ruler should be able both to "consolidate" the people's force into agriculture and warfare and to "spend" that force through selling ranks of honor and directing the people to war. Otherwise, excessive wealth and power may be concentrated in the hands of individuals, which is highly undesirable (8.2). Overall, political and intellectual dynamism are the chapter's hallmark.

* * *

8.1: Whenever a state is established, one must understand regulations and measures, be cautious in governance and law, be diligent in [pursuing] the state's commitments, and consolidate essential occupations. When regulations and measures are timely, the customs of the state can be transformed,[1] and the people will follow regulations. When governance and law are clear, there are no deviations among officials. When the state is committed to the One, the people can be used. When essential occupations are consolidated, the people are glad to farm and enjoy war. Thus, when the sage establishes laws and transforms customs, he causes the people from morning to dusk to engage in farming: this must be investigated.

After all, the people participate in [military and agricultural] undertakings and die for the sake of regulations because the superiors are clear in establishing glorious names and doling out rewards and penalties. When merits are determined without using argumentative persuasion and without [going through] private gates,[2] then the people are glad to farm and enjoy war. When they see that men-of-service who respect agriculture and war are elevated, while the people engaged in persuasive talk and skillful arts are demoted, and traveling scholars are disdained,[3] the people will devote themselves to the One. Their households will surely be rich, and they will be prominent in the state. The superiors open common [routes] of benefit, block private gates, and thereby attract the people's force. Toiling for private [interests] does not bring prominence in the state; private gates are not [used] to make requests of the rulers. In this case, meritorious subjects are encouraged: the superior's orders are implemented, and land covered by wild grass is opened up; the deviant people are stopped, and depravity has no sprouts. He who in ruling the state is able to consolidate the people's force and make the people engage in the One will be strong; the state [that lets its dwellers] engage in the root and prohibits branch [occupations][4] will be rich.

* * *

8.2: When the sage rules the state, he is able to consolidate force and to spend force.[5] When regulations and measures are clear, the people's force is consolidated; if it is consolidated but is not transformed,[6] it cannot be put into practice; if it is put into practice, but [the state is] not rich, turmoil is born. Hence, he who rules the state well consolidates force to attain a rich state and a strong army;[7] he spends force to engage the enemy and encourage farming. When one opens but does not block, knowledge increases;[8] when it increases, but [the enemy] is not attacked, there is depravity. When one blocks and does not open, the people are confused; when [they are] confused and are not used, they have extra force; when there is extra force, but [the enemy] is not attacked, there are villainous parasites. Hence, consolidate force by engaging in the One; spend force by attacking the enemy.

He who rules the state well values that the people [focus on the] One. When the people [focus on the] One, they are simple; when [they are] simple, they farm; when they farm, they can easily be made diligent; when they are diligent, they are rich. When they are rich, reduce this by [selling] ranks: then they will not be excessive. When they are excessive, reduce this with punishments, and they will commit themselves to farming. Hence, he who is able to consolidate force but is unable to use it will surely [bring about] turmoil; he who is able to spend force but is unable to consolidate it will surely perish. Hence, the clear-sighted ruler knows to adjust the two of these, and his state is powerful; he who does not know to adjust the two of these—his state will be dismembered.

* * *

8.3: When the people are not well ordered, it is the ruler who leads them downward. When the laws are not clear, it is the ruler who prolongs turmoil. Hence, the clear-sighted ruler neither leads [the people] downward nor prolongs turmoil. He holds power and establishes himself; he promulgates laws, and [the state] is well ordered. Thereby he seizes the villainous above, and the officials do not negate [him]; he determines rewards and punishments, and the utensils and utilitarian [vessels] have their measures. If so, the regulations of the state are clear, and the people's force is fully [utilized], elevations and ranks are respected, and all kinds of people are employed [appropriately].

All the rulers of our age want to order the people, yet they just help [the people] to create turmoil. It is not that rulers enjoy creating turmoil; it is just that they are happy with the past and do not inquire into our times. Thus, above they model themselves after the past and are blocked by it; below they follow the present[9] and do not change with the times. Moreover, they neither understand the changes in the customs of our age nor investigate the people's conditions. Hence, they multiply rewards, thereby bringing about punishments; they make punishments light and thereby eliminate rewards. So superiors establish punishments, but the people do not submit; rewards are exhausted, but villains only increase in number.

Hence, in dealing with the relations between the people and their superiors, put punishments first and let rewards follow. Thus, when the sage rules his state, he neither models himself after antiquity nor follows the present. He relies on what [is appropriate] to his age and thereby attains order; he evaluates customs and makes them into law.[10] Thus, when a law is established without investigating the people's disposition, it will not succeed, whereas when orderly rule is implemented in accordance to what is appropriate to our times, [inferiors] will not object. Hence, the rule of the sage is to be diligent in his actions, to investigate his tasks, and to focus on the One—that is all.

9

IMPLEMENTING LAWS (錯法)

C hapter 9 is yet another short chapter that resembles chapter 8 in terms of its focus. The authors argue that the proper implementation of rewards and punishments and the reliance on impersonal methods of control are essential means of maintaining social and political order. Echoing chapter 6, the authors remind the reader that the people's "disposition" (qing 情) is to be attracted by ranks and emoluments and to dislike punishments and penalties (9.3). Bestowing and inflicting these things on the basis of clear and unequivocal standards will help the ruler to direct the population to agriculture and warfare. The only exceptional point in the chapter is the promise that he who possesses the Way will be able to prosper even in a tiny territory of one square li (9.2). This idealistic (one is almost tempted to say "Mengzi-like") promise clearly stands at odds with the book's constant advocacy of large and powerful states as singularly viable.

Chapter 9 probably belongs to a later stratum of the Book of Lord Shang because its last sentences mention a Qin strongman, Wu Huo 烏獲 (d. 306 B.C.E.), who lived long after Shang Yang's death. The same textual segment recurs also in chapter 20.11, where, however, it was clearly misplaced from elsewhere. It is more likely that the segment did belong to the original text of chapter 9, and, if so, the chapter's date of composition could not be earlier than around 300 B.C.E.

* * *

9.1: I, your subject, have heard: in the past, clear-sighted rulers implemented laws, and there were no deviations among the people; they undertook [military] activities, yet the [required] materials forged themselves;[1] they bestowed rewards, and the army was strong. These three are the roots of orderly rule. Now, "implementing laws so that there are no deviations among the people" [works] because the laws are clear and benefit the people. "Undertaking activities and having the materials forge themselves" [work] because merits are clearly distinguished. When merits are clearly distinguished, the people fully utilize their strength; when the people fully utilize their strength, materials forge themselves. "Bestowing rewards and having the army strong" refers to ranks and emoluments. Ranks and emoluments are the essence of the army. Hence, when the ruler bestows ranks and emoluments, the way [they are distributed] should be clear. When the way is clear, the state daily grows stronger; when the way is obscure, the state daily approaches dismemberment. Hence, directing [the people] with ranks and emoluments is the crux of surviving or perishing.

It is not that a dismembered state and a due-to-perish sovereign lack ranks and emoluments; it is that the way of bestowing them is wrong. The Three Monarchs and Five Hegemons directed [their subjects] by nothing more than ranks and emoluments, yet their merits exceeded myriadfold those [of current rulers]:[2] it is because they were clear in directing [the people]. Therefore, when a clear-sighted ruler employs his subjects, their utilization should be related to their labor, and rewards should be granted according to their merits. When [relations between] merits and rewards are clear, the people strive to acquire merits. If the state is ruled such that the people fully utilize their strength in striving to acquire merits, the army will surely be strong.

* * *

9.2: When [the people] of the same rank can enslave each other, it is because of [the difference] between poverty and wealth. When [states] of the same substance can annex each other, it is because of [the difference] between weakness and strength. Among territorial rulers,

some are strong, and some are weak: this is because of [the differ-
ence] between order and turmoil. If you possess the Way, a territory
of one *li* is enough to preserve yourself and to attract men-of-service
and ordinary people; if it contains a market with a well, merchandise
can be assembled.[3] When you have land, you should not talk of poverty; when you have people, you should not talk of weakness. When
the land is truly utilized, one should not worry about lacking
resources; when the people are truly used, one should not be afraid of
the strong and violent. When your virtue is clear and the teachings
are implemented, then you can cause the people's possessions to
become your asset. Hence, a clear-sighted sovereign utilizes not just
his own possessions and employs not just his own people.[4]

* * *

9.3: What the clear-sighted monarch values is [bestowing] ranks for
substantial [attainments]. Ranks should be [bestowed] for substantial
[attainments] and made honorable and illustrious. If they are not honorable, the people will not be anxious to be arrayed according to their
positions; if they are not illustrious, the people will not serve for the
sake of ranks. If ranks are easy to attain, the people will not value superior ranks. When positions, ranks, emoluments, and rewards do not
come from this [the ruler's] gate, the people will not be [ready] to die
when striving for position.

Human beings[5] have likes and dislikes; hence, the people can be
ruled. The ruler must investigate likes and dislikes. Likes and dislikes
are the root of rewards and penalties. The disposition of the people is
to like ranks and emoluments and to dislike punishments and penalties. The ruler sets up the two in order to guide the people's will and to
establish whatever he desires. When ranks come only after the people
have fully used their force, when rewards come only after their merits
are established, when the ruler is able to let his people trust these [two]
as [unequivocally] as they visualize the sun and moon—then the army
has no rivals.

* * *

9.4: When the ruler bestows ranks but the army remains weak, when he confers emoluments but the state remains poor, when laws are established but [governance] remains disordered—these three are the worry of the state. Hence, if the ruler advances flatterers and those who request audiences yet degrades the meritorious and strong, then even if ranks are bestowed, the army remains weak. If the people can get benefits and emoluments without having to risk their lives in the face of difficulty, then emoluments are issued, but the state remains poor. If laws lack measures and methods but undertakings every day become even more superfluous, then even after laws are established, governance remains disordered.

Hence, when the clear-sighted ruler employs his people, he lets each of them fully utilize his strength and thus estimates his merits; when merits are established, wealth and nobility follow, and there is no private kindness.[6] Thus, educational transformation is accomplished.[7] If so, then ministers are loyal, the ruler is clear-sighted, orderly rule is manifest, and the army is strong. Hence, in general the rule of the clear-sighted ruler relies on force and not on kindness; hence, he does not worry and is not belabored yet can establish achievements.

* * *

9.5: When measures and methods have been established, laws can be put in order. Therefore, the ruler cannot but be very cautious about himself.[8] After all, Li Zhu was able to see an autumn hair from the distance of one hundred paces but could not exchange his eyes with others;[9] Wu Huo was able to raise the weight of one thousand *jun* but could not exchange his superior strength with others.[10] The sage can preserve his nature but cannot exchange it with others. Nonetheless, achievements can be attained: this is what is called the law.[11]

10

METHODS OF WAR (戰法)

The three military chapters of the *Book of Lord Shang*, 10–12, were badly damaged in the process of transmission: their combined length is equal to that of an average, regular chapter. This problem notwithstanding, these chapters present in a relatively systematic way the authors' major ideas about the interrelation between the military and the political spheres and about waging war. Scholars sometimes treat the three chapters as being authored by the same person or at the same time, but this may not be the case. The first two chapters bear a strong resemblance to the rest of the *Book of Lord Shang* in terms of their ideas and their vocabulary, and both clearly analyze war through the prism of the overall political and economical prowess of the state: "The root of the [proper] method of war is invariably in [adequate] government" (10.1; cf. 11.1, 11.2).

Chapter 12, "Military Defense," is different in nature: it evidently was composed outside the state of Qin, and it is concerned—uncharacteristically for the *Book of Lord Shang*—exclusively with defensive warfare. It starts with enumerating the difficulties faced by a state that has to combat enemies on the four frontiers; this state has to compensate for its strategic vulnerability with the ability to utilize its human resources fully. The situation of the state surrounded by equally powerful enemies on four sides and its comparison with another state that backs the sea (presumably Qi 齊) strongly indicate that the chapter was written in the state of Wei 魏, where Shang Yang's career started. If this assessment is correct, chapter 12 is one of the earliest datable military treatises of the Warring States period. It may serve also as the earliest testimony of the practice of the population's total mobilization for defensive warfare. Through mobilizing not just men but also women, the elderly, and the infirm (12.3), and by making them "ready to die" (12.2), the defenders could withstand the assault of a sizable enemy's army. It should be noted, however, that the discussion of actual functions of the defenders under the siege remains rudimentary in comparison to similar discussions in other works—for example, chapters of the *Mozi* dedicated to the defense of fortresses (*Mozi chengshou*; see the discussion in Yates 1979, 583–585).

Another notable feature of the military chapters is an unmistakable similarity between chapter 10, "Methods of War," and the *Sunzi* 孫子. Such topoi as the need to assess the relative advantages and disadvantages of the enemy and of one's own side (10.3), the military leader's prescience (10.3; cf. Galvany 2015), the importance of preserving the soldiers' and commanders' calmness of spirit (10.4), and the need to be flexible on the battlefield and adapt one's tactics to the enemy's situation (10.2–10.4) are all common ideas in the *Sunzi*. So is the notion of prearranging victory in the ancestral temple (10.5)—that is, through strategic planning. The only significant difference between the two texts is the role of the commander. In the *Sunzi*, the commander is the singularly important figure in ensuring the army's success. In contrast, chapter 10 in the *Book of Lord Shang* relegates the commander to a position clearly secondary to that of the ruler: "If the decisions are based on calculations made in the ancestral temple, then one will win under a worthy commander and also under an inferior commander" (10.5). By reducing the commander's role (but still assigning him responsibility for military failures, 10.6), the authors skillfully avoid the pitfall of the *Sunzi* and of many other military texts, which by lionizing the general turn him into a potential rival of the ruler as the locus of authority (see more in Lewis 1990, 97–135). In the *Book of Lord Shang*, the ruler's superiority over the general remains unquestionable.

* * *

10.1: In general, the root of the [proper] method of war is invariably in [adequate] government. When [the government] is victorious, the people do not contend; when they do not contend, they have no selfish thoughts and are thinking only of their superiors. Hence, the government of the True Monarch causes the people to be fearful when feuding in their settlements and to be brave when fighting the enemy. When the people are used to forcefully attack danger, they consider death a light matter.

* * *

10.2: When you observe the enemy and it looks as if they flee without stopping, let them go. Thus, the *Methods of War* [states]: "When you win in a grand battle, follow the fleeing [enemy] no farther than ten *li*; when you win in a small battle, follow the fleeing no farther than five *li*."

* * *

10.3: When you raise an army, assess the enemy. If your government is not equal to his, do not fight him; if your provisions are not equal to his, do not engage him in a protracted [campaign]; when the enemy's forces are numerous, do not attack; when he is exhausted and is not equal to you, strike him without hesitation. Hence, it is said: prudence is the greatest law of the military. Evaluate the enemy; investigate whose forces are more numerous—then it will be possible to predict victory and defeat.

* * *

10.4: The soldiers of the True Monarch are neither boastful in victory nor resentful in defeat. To remain not boastful after victory is due to clarity of techniques; to remain not resentful after defeat is due to understanding what was inadequate.

* * *

10.5: When the soldiers' strengths and weaknesses are comparable,[1] then, if the commander is worthy, one will win; if the commander is inferior, one will lose. If the decisions are based on calculations made in the ancestral temple,[2] then one will win under a worthy commander and also under an inferior commander. He whose government relies for a long time on victorious techniques will surely be powerful enough to become the [True] Monarch. If the people are submissive and heed their superiors, then the state is rich and the army victorious; he who implements this for long[3] will surely become the [True] Monarch.

* * *

10.6: His [the commander's] mistakes: facing no enemy, he penetrates deeply, leaving behind narrow passes and fortifications that can cut off his retreat. His people are exhausted and suffer from hunger and thirst, while the route of retreat is full of danger: this is the way of defeat. Hence, the commander should lead his people [as] he mounts a good horse: he cannot but be balanced.

11

ESTABLISHING THE ROOTS (立本)

11.1: In general, when one employs an army, there are three stages to victory. If the army had still not been raised, laws should be enforced; when laws are enforced, they become customs; [when they become customs],[1] equipment is ready. These three should be implemented within the borders, and only then can the army be dispatched on a mission. In implementing these three, there are two powers: the first is called "when the law is supported, it is implemented"; the second is called "when employment [of the law] means inevitable seizure [of a culprit], then the law had been established."[2] Thus, when [the ruler] relies on his multitudes, it is called a "straw roof"; when he relies on those who embellish his preparations, it is called "being crafty"; when he relies on the reputation of his ministers, this is called "deception." He who relies on one of those three, his soldiers will be captured. Hence, it is said: "The strong [state] should resolutely direct [the people's] mind to fighting; when they [are committed] to fighting, they fully [utilize] their strength; when they fully [utilize] their strength, then everything is ready [for war]." Hence, [the ruler] will have no rivals within the seas.

* * *

11.2: When orderly rule is implemented, resources are accumulated; when resources are accumulated, rewards can be bountiful. When rewards are unified, ranks are respected; when ranks are respected, rewards can bring benefit. Hence, it is said: the army is born of orderly rule but differs [from it (?)]; customs are born from the law and are completely modified; superior power is rooted in one's heart and is adorned by proper preparedness of power.[3] When these three are properly ordered, strength can be established. Hence, the strong must be ruled well, and the well ruled will surely be strong; the rich must be ruled well, and the well ruled will surely be rich; the strong must be rich, and the rich will surely be strong. Thus, it is said: "There is a three-fold way of being strong and well ruled"; here I discuss its roots.

12

MILITARY DEFENSE (兵守)

12.1: The state that has to fight on four fronts values defensive warfare; the state that borders the sea values offensive warfare. If the state that has to fight on four fronts is fond of raising troops to repel the four neighbors, it will be imperiled. The four neighbors raise one army [each] for just one campaign, but you have to raise four armies [to repel them]; hence, you are called the imperiled state. If the state that has to fight on four fronts is unable to utilize a ten-thousand-families settlement to repel a ten-thousand-strong army, this state is imperiled. Hence, it is said: "The state that has to fight on four fronts should commit itself to defensive warfare."

* * *

12.2: In protecting a walled settlement, it is best to use the force of the going-to-die people to fight the force of the going-to-live invader.[1] When razing the walls, [an invader faces] the strength of the going-to-die people. If the invader does not level the walls, he has nowhere to enter; this is called "fighting the force of the going-to-live invader with the force of the going-to-die people." When the walls are completely leveled so that the invader has a place to enter, then the invader is exhausted, whereas the people within [the walls] will surely be rested.[2] Fighting the exhausted with the force of those who are rested is called "fighting the force of the going-to-die invader with the force of the going-to-live people."[3] Everyone says: "The trouble of besieging a city is that all are ready to die for the city."[4] These three are not the trouble of insufficient [forces] but the error of the commander.[5]

* * *

12.3: The way of defending a fortress is by accumulating power. When there is an invader, put military registers in order and divide the multitudes of the three armies according to the number of the invader's observation chariots. The three armies are: first, the army of adult men; second, the army of adult women; third, the army of the elderly and the infirm:[6] these are called "the three armies." For the army of adult men: issue ample provisions and sharp weapons and array them to await the enemy. For the army of adult women: issue ample provisions and baskets to carry earth and array them to await orders. When the invaders arrive, have them create earthen obstructions and dig traps; have them release the bridges[7] and destroy the houses [in the countryside]; have them transfer whatever is transferrable [into the fortress] and burn the rest so that the invader will get nothing to support his assault. For the army of the elderly and the infirm: have them pasture oxen, horses, sheep, and pigs. Feed them with whatever is edible of grass and trees so as to save provisions for adult men and women.

You must be cautious to prevent contact between the three armies. If the adult men come into contact with the army of adult women, then the men will value the women; the treacherous people will use contact for their intrigues, and the state will perish. They [the men and women] will be pleased to stay together and be fearful of fighting early; hence, the brave people will not fight. If the adult men and women come into contact with the army of the elderly and the infirm, then the elderly will cause the adults to be sad, and the infirm will cause the strong to be sorrowful; with sadness and sorrow in their hearts, the brave people will become anxious, and the meek people will not fight. Hence, it is said: "You must be cautious to prevent contact between the three armies." This is the way of accumulating power.

13

MAKING ORDERS STRICT (靳令)

Chapter 13 closely echoes and at times reproduces verbatim sections of chapter 4. It is also very close to chapter 53, "Chi ling" 飭令, of the *Han Feizi*. Zheng Liangshu has thoroughly discussed the relations between the three (1989, 82–103), and I largely accept his analysis, according to which chapter 4 is anterior to chapter 13, which, in turn, is anterior to the *Han Feizi* version. Chapter 13 may well be an alternative version of chapter 4, but it is briefer than the latter, especially insofar as administrative and economic issues are concerned. The organization of chapter 13 is somewhat haphazard. For instance, it employs the term *six parasites* several times in sections 13.2 and 13.3, but the term is not explained until section 13.4. Another odd feature is the last section (13.6), which hails the sage ruler's ability "to implement benevolence and righteousness in All-under-Heaven." How is this statement related to the derisive view of "benevolence and righteousness" as one of the "six parasites" in section 13.4? It is possible that the final section was added or modified at a later stage of the chapter's transmission. Alternatively, it is possible that the distinction being made in the two appearances of the same term in both passages (13.4 versus 13.6) is between fraudulent and real "benevolence and righteousness": the former is mere moralizing discourse, which the *Book of Lord Shang* consistently views as detrimental to the state's prowess; the latter is the reality of perfect order and peace that will be attained after merciless punishments and resolute warfare eliminate domestic and external foes. In any case, this final passage moderates the harshness of chapter 13 and turns it into an example of a more accommodative rhetoric in the *Book of Lord Shang* (Pines 2012a).

* * *

13.1: When orders are strict, there is no procrastination in governing; when laws are fair, there are no depraved officials. When laws have been fixed, one should not harm them with talk about "goodness." When the meritorious are appointed, the people talk little; when the "good" are appointed, the people talk a lot.[1] In implementing orderly rule, decisions [should be made at] the countryside level: when decisions are made by every fifth hamlet, [the ruler] will be the [True] Monarch; when they are made by every tenth hamlet, [the state] will be strong; when ruling is done the next day, [the state] will be dismembered.[2] Rule through punishments; make war through rewards.

Pursue transgressions, not goodness. Thus, after the law has been established, if it is not modified, the eminent people will have to change their plans; when their plans are changed, the punishments will stop.[3] Nobles and commoners are employed differently; the ranks of the hundred officials are respected; lavish emoluments are issued according to their [the recipients'] merits.[4] Then there are neither villainous people in the capital nor villainous markets in regional capitals.[5] When things are superfluous and the multitudes are engaged in branch [occupations], farmers are lax, and villains are victorious, then the state will surely be dismembered.

When the people have extra provisions, let them receive offices and ranks in exchange for grain. When office and rank reflect [the people's] hard [toil], farmers are not indolent.

When a four-inch pipe has no bottom, it surely cannot be filled; when office is received, rank bestowed, and emolument issued not according to one's merit, then this is "having no bottom."

* * *

13.2: When a poor state engages in war, poison infiltrates its enemy; it has no six parasites and will surely be powerful. When a rich state makes no war, carelessness is born in its intestines; it has the six parasites and will surely be weakened.[6]

When the state grants office and bestows rank according to merits, this is called letting strategic knowledge and military valor prosper. When strategic knowledge and military valor prosper, this state will be without rivals. When the state grants office and bestows rank according to merit, its governance is moderate, and [superfluous] talk is reduced: this is what is called "to eliminate law with law, to eliminate talk with talk."[7] When the state grants office and bestows rank according to the six parasites, then its governance is toilsome, and talk is born; this is what is called "to summon law with law, to summon talk with talk." This means that the ruler will devote himself to doctrines and talk, and the officials will be in turmoil trying to order the deviant. Deviant subjects will fulfill their aspirations, and the meritorious will retreat daily—this is called "losing."

[The state] that preserves ten is in turmoil; that which preserves one is well ordered.[8] When the law is fixed, those who are fond of employing the six parasites perish.

* * *

13.3: When the people opt to comprehensively engage in agriculture, the state is rich; when the six parasites are not employed, all of the soldiers and the people are inspired [to fight and till] and are glad to be used by the sovereign. When the people within the borders compete to attain glory, no one will be disgraced. Second to that is when they are motivated by rewards and are obstructed by penalties. Worse is when the people hate it [agriculture and warfare], worry about it, and are ashamed of it. When they beautify their appearance, obtain[9] food through talk, contact superiors so as to avoid farming and fighting, contact foreign [powers] so as to attain [positions],[10] then the state is endangered. When there are people who die of cold and hunger but do not go to war for the sake of benefit and emoluments, these are the customs of the due-to-be-ruined state.

* * *

13.4: The six parasites: rites and music, *Poems* and *Documents*, self-cultivation and goodness, filiality and fraternal duties, sincerity and trustworthiness, integrity and uprightness, benevolence and righteousness, rejection of the military, and being ashamed of waging war. When the state has these twelve,[11] the superiors are unable to direct the people to agriculture and warfare, and the state will surely be impoverished to the point of dismemberment. When the twelve assemble together, this is called "the ruler's governance is unable to overcome his ministers and the officials' governance is unable to overcome their people." This is called "the six parasites overcoming government." When the twelve take root,[12] [the state] will surely be dismembered.[13]

Hence, the prosperous state does not use the twelve; thus, this state has abundant strength, and no one under Heaven can oppose it. When its army is dispatched, it will be able to seize [the enemy's territory] and, after seizing it, will surely be able to hold it; whereas when one restrains the army and does not attack, [the state] will surely be rich. As for its court officials: they are neither slandered when they have few [attainments] nor derided when they have many.[14] One receives office and rank only after his merit is investigated; even if he is an eloquent speaker, he cannot be advanced at the expense of others. This is called "ordering through [proper] methods."

When the state attacks forcefully, it dispatches [an army] once and receives tenfold gains; when it attacks by talk, it dispatches [an army] ten times and loses one hundred. When the state is fond of force, it is called "attacking with what is difficult [to resist]." When the state is fond of talk, it is called "attacking with what is easy [to resist]."[15]

* * *

13.5: When punishments are heavy and rewards are few, [this means that] the superiors love the people, and the people are [ready] to die for their superiors. When rewards are heavy but punishments are light, [this means that] the superiors do not love the people, and the people are not [ready] to die for their superiors.[16]

When benefits come from a single opening, the state will be without rivals; when benefits come from two openings, the state will half benefit; when benefits come from ten openings, such a state cannot be protected.[17] Making punishments heavy clarifies the great regulations; if these are not clarified, this is because of the six parasites. When the six parasites come together, then the people cannot be used. Hence, the prosperous state implements penalties, and the people are close [to their rulers]; it implements rewards, and the people benefit. When penalties are implemented, inflict heavy [punishments] on light [offenses], then light [offenses] will not come, and heavy [ones] will not arrive.[18] That is what is called "eradicating punishments with punishments": punishments are eradicated and undertakings are accomplished. When crimes are heavy but punishments light, this brings punishments and gives birth to [troublesome] undertakings. This is what is called "to bring punishments with punishments"—such a state will surely be dismembered.

* * *

13.6: The sage ruler understands the essentials of things. Hence, in ordering the people, he possesses the most essential; thus, he firmly holds the rewards and punishments to support the One. {Benevolent is he whose heart is affluent.}[19] The sage ruler, in ordering others, should first attain their hearts; hence, he is able to employ force. Force gives birth to strength; strength gives birth to awesomeness; awesomeness gives birth to virtue; virtue is born of force. The sage ruler alone possesses it; hence, he is able to implement benevolence and righteousness in All-under-Heaven.

14

CULTIVATION OF AUTHORITY (修權)

C hapter 14 is the first chapter in the *Book of Lord Shang* to shift emphasis decisively from the state's relation with the people to a narrower focus on maintaining the ruling apparatus itself. The chapter's opening paragraph proclaims the pivotal role of standards (or laws, *fa* 法), trustworthiness (*xin* 信), and authority (*quan* 權) in governing the state and further emphasizes that authority—namely, the power of decision making—should remain exclusively in the ruler's hands and not be shared with the ministers (14.1). This emphasis promises an engaging discussion, but this promise is only partly realized throughout the rest of the chapter. Most of the chapter revolves around a topic raised in earlier chapters: the importance of impartial standards in the promotion of officials. These standards represent the "common" (*gong* 公) good as opposed to private (*si* 私) interests and "private deliberations" (14.2). Interestingly, private interests that may damage the common cause are not only those of the ministers but also those of the rulers: "All rulers and ministers of [this] calamitous age act in a petty way, monopolizing the benefits of a single state and appropriating the authority of their office so as to benefit their private [interests]. This is the reason why the state is endangered" (14.4).

There are no clear indications of the chapter's date, but its tone more clearly accommodates the mainstream discourse of the Warring States period. In contrast to the rest of the book (with a possible exception of

18.5), this chapter unequivocally endorses the idea of "elevat[ing]" "the worthy" (14.4), laments maltreatment of "loyal ministers" (14.2), and, most exceptionally, hails the impartiality of the legendary paragons, Yao 堯 and Shun 舜, hinting approvingly at their willingness to yield the throne to meritorious ministers (14.4). Whoever the chapter's author is, it is clear that he wanted to bridge the gap between himself and his ideological opponents rather than to alienate them, as we witness in many earlier chapters.

* * *

14.1: The state is ordered through three [things]: the first is standards,[1] the second is trustworthiness, the third is authority. Standards are what the ruler and ministers jointly uphold; trustworthiness is what the ruler and ministers jointly establish; authority is what the ruler exclusively regulates. When the sovereign loses what he should preserve, he is endangered; when the ruler and the ministers cast away standards and rely on their private [views], turmoil will surely ensue. Hence, when standards are established, divisions are clarified,[2] and when standards are not violated for private reasons, then there is orderly rule. When authority and regulations are decided exclusively by the ruler,[3] [he inspires] awe; when the people trust his rewards, success is accomplished; and when they trust his punishments, wickedness has no starting point.

Only a clear-sighted sovereign cares for his authority, takes trustworthiness seriously, and does not damage law through his private [interests]. Thus, when superiors talk much of kindness but are unable to make rewards viable, inferiors cannot be used; when severe orders are repeatedly promulgated but punishments are not inflicted, the people treat lethal [punishment] with contempt. In general, rewards are civilian [means]; punishments are military [means]; civilian and military [means] are the essentials of the law.[4] Hence, the clear-sighted sovereign is cautious with regard to the law. The clear-sighted sovereign is called "clear-sighted" because nothing is concealed from him; he is called "scrutinizing" because he cannot be deceived. Thus, his rewards are bountiful and trustworthy, his punishments heavy and inevitable;

[in rewarding] he does not overlook strangers, and [in punishing] he does not avoid relatives and intimates. Thus, the ministers cannot conceal anything from the sovereign, and inferiors cannot deceive superiors.

* * *

14.2: Rulers of our age frequently cast away standards and rely on private deliberations: this is why their states are in turmoil. The former kings set up scales and weights, established feet and inches, and we have used them until now as standards because they clarify distinctions. So if one discards scales and weights yet tries to determine weight or casts away feet and inches yet judges length, then even if one excels at scrutinizing, merchants will not accept [his judgment], considering it to lack in certainty. Standards are the scale and weight of the state: therefore, all those who turn their backs on standards and measures and rely instead on private deliberations do not understand that these things are of [the same] category.

Only Yao was able to discuss one's wisdom, ability, worthiness, or unworthiness without resorting to standards; yet the world does not consist only of the likes of Yao. Therefore, the former kings knew that they could not rely on their own deliberations and private appointments; hence, they established standards and clarified divisions so that those who were within the norms were rewarded, and those who damaged the common [interests] were prosecuted. The standards of rewards and prosecutions did not lose their appropriateness; hence, the people did not struggle. If one does not use ranks and appointments to benefit intimates and kin, hard-working ministers are not resentful. If one does not use punishments and penalties to obstruct strangers and outsiders, inferiors are close to superiors.

Thus, when appointment to office and the bestowal of rank are not done according to one's labor, loyal ministers are not promoted; when granting rewards and delivering emoluments are not in accord with one's merit, fighting men are not used.

* * *

14.3: In general, when ministers serve the ruler, they do it through what the ruler is fond of. When the ruler is fond of standards, ministers serve him according to standards; when the ruler is fond of talk, then ministers serve him through talk. When the ruler is fond of standards, then upright men-of-service stand before him; when the ruler is fond of talk, he is surrounded by slandering or flattering officials.

* * *

14.4: When the common and the private are clearly separated, petty men do not envy the worthy, and the unworthy are not jealous of the meritorious. Hence, when Yao and Shun were established in All-under-Heaven, this was not in order to benefit privately from All-under-Heaven—they were established for the sake of All-under-Heaven.[5] They selected the worthy, elevated the able, and transmitted [power] to them not because of alienation between father and son and intimacy with strangers, but because the Way of order and disorder was clear to them.[6] Hence, the Three Kings treated their relatives righteously,[7] and the Five Hegemons used law to rectify regional lords—all this was not in order to benefit privately from All-under-Heaven. They ruled All-under-Heaven for the sake of All-under-Heaven. Hence, they earned their [great] name and attained merit; All-under-Heaven was fond of their rule, and no one was able to harm them. But now all rulers and ministers of [this] calamitous age act in a petty way, monopolizing the benefits of a single state and appropriating the authority of their office so as to benefit their private [interests]. This is the reason why the state is endangered. Hence, the interrelationship between the common and the private is the root of survival or ruin.

* * *

14.5: When one casts away standards and measures and is fond of private deliberations, then villainous ministers peddle influence to arrange emoluments,[8] while the underlings of ranked officials[9] obscure [the situation] below and plunder the people. There is a saying: "When there are plenty of woodworms, the wood will be broken; when a fissure is large, the wall collapses." Thus, when great ministers compete for private [interests] and disregard their people, then inferiors are estranged from superiors; when inferiors are estranged from superiors, this is the fissure in the state. When the underlings of ranked officials obscure [the situation] below so as to plunder the people, these are the woodworms of the people. So, few states under Heaven can have fissures and woodworms and avoid being ruined. Therefore, the clear-sighted ruler relies on standards and eliminates private [deliberations]: then the state suffers from neither fissures nor woodworms.

15

ATTRACTING THE PEOPLE (徠民)

C hapter 15 is one of the latest in the *Book of Lord Shang* and is one of the most easily datable texts in the entire corpus of pre-Qin philosophical literature. Judging from the events it mentions (e.g., the Changping 長平 campaign of 262–260 B.C.E.) as well as from what it *does not* mention—that is, Qin's unstoppable expansion from the early 230s B.C.E. (15.4)—it was most likely produced in between these dates. As such, it provides an important testimony to economic, social, and administrative problems in both Qin and its neighboring polities (primarily Wei 魏 and Han 韓) during this period.

The chapter's authors try to resolve a paradox: why Qin, despite successive victories over its eastern neighbors, especially Wei, Han, and Zhao 趙, has not been able to finally overpower these states. This question became particularly acute in the aftermath of the Changping campaign, arguably the largest military encounter of the Warring States period. The two most powerful states of their age, Qin and Zhao, committed most of their human and material resources to what was supposed to become their decisive battle in the hilly terrain of southern Shanxi. After two years of standoff in fortified camps, Qin lured Zhao forces to launch an attack, which ended in disaster for Zhao. The Zhao troops were cut in two; subsequently, their lines of supply were cut off, and the starved Zhao forces had to surrender. Triumphant, Qin general Bai Qi 白起 (d. 257 B.C.E.) ordered the massacre of the surrendering Zhao soldiers; more than four hundred thousand were reportedly killed. Zhao faced imminent annihilation, but Qin was too depleted of human and material resources to launch an effective follow-up campaign. Indeed, its assault on the Zhao capital of Handan 邯鄲 in 259–257 B.C.E. ended in defeat, and the goal of final subjugation of All-under-Heaven appeared as elusive as ever (Yang Kuan 1998, 412–419). It is against this backdrop that the chapter's authors propose their idea: to overpower its adversaries, Qin should first improve the demographic balance with its rivals.

The chapter depicts a peculiar situation in which Qin suffers from underpopulation and is unable to fully utilize its land resources. It is likely that this peculiar land-to-man ratio came as a result of the rapid expansion of fertile land in the territories under Qin control in the aftermath of major hydraulic projects initiated by Qin engineers both in Sichuan (Li Bing's 李冰 famous taming of the Min River 岷江) and in the Wei River basin (Zheng Guo's 鄭國 project) in the mid–third century B.C.E.[1] The chapter contrasts Qin—with its abundant land resources and insufficient labor force—with the neighboring rival states, Wei and Han, both in the central reaches of the Yellow River, which suffered from overpopulation to the degree that "more than half of [their people] have to dwell in caves dug along the river and pond banks" (15.2). This situation allowed Qin to attract settlers from the east.

The authors present several recommendations to facilitate immigration. The immigrants should be "exempted from taxes for three generations and should not be liable for military service," in addition to being allowed free exploitation of "mountains, hills, and swamps for ten years" (15.3). This lenient treatment of immigrants contrasts sharply with the insistence in earlier chapters, such as chapter 6, on turning every subject into tiller *and* soldier.[2] Yet attracting immigrants as purely agricultural laborers appears doubly advantageous. On the one hand, their high yields could compensate the country for the loss of income from military conscripts who were distracted from agricultural work during the prolonged campaigns of the late Warring States period (Miyake Kiyoshi 2015). On the other hand, the commanders could be relieved of employing foreign-born soldiers, whose loyalty to the state of Qin was doubtful. Although it is not clear whether the system of attracting immigrants worked precisely in the way envisioned in this chapter, in general it seems to have been sufficiently successful: archaeological evidence suggests a mass influx of migrants from the East and South to the state of Qin during the generations immediately prior to the imperial unification (Teng Mingyu 2003, 2014; Chen Li 2009). To what extent this immigration facilitated the final Qin campaigns of conquest starting in the late 230s B.C.E. is a matter for further research.

* * *

15.1: In a territory of one hundred *li* squared, mountains and hills occupy one-tenth; swamps and marshlands occupy one-tenth; valleys, dales, and running rivers occupy one-tenth; towns, settlements, paths, and roads occupy one-tenth; infertile fields occupy two-tenths, fertile fields occupy four-tenths. Thus, fifty thousand laborers can be fed.[3] Its mountains and hills, swamps and marshlands, valleys and dales can provide its resources; settlements, paths, and roads suffice to settle its people. This is the former kings' correct standard for ordering the land and apportioning the people.

* * *

15.2: Now the territory of Qin is five times one thousand *li* squared, yet its arable lands are just two-tenths, and the number of fields does not reach one million.[4] It cannot fully utilize the products and treasures of its swamps and marshlands, valleys and dales, famous mountains, and great rivers: this means that the people are not sufficient for its land.

Qin's neighbors are the Three Jin; those with whom it wants to fight are Han and Wei.[5] Their lands are narrow, but the people are numerous; hence, their houses are placed close to each other and packed together. Their people, whose yields are meager and who quest for breathing space, lack a name above and fields or houses below.[6] They have to rely on evildoing and engaging in secondary occupations to make a living; more than half of them have to dwell in caves dug along the river and pond banks.[7] Evidently, their territory is not enough to provide for their people's livelihood, perhaps even to a larger extent than Qin's people are not enough to fully utilize its territory. When we consider the people's disposition, what they desire are fields and dwellings: this is what Jin really does not possess and what Qin certainly has in surplus. If in this situation the people [of Jin] do not face westward,[8] it is because Qin's men-of-service are worried, and the people are embittered.

In the humble opinion of your servant, Your Majesty's officials err in their judgment. The reason for their inability to seize[9] the people of the Three Jin is that they are too stingy in [bestowing] rank and take tax exemptions too seriously. Their argument is: "The people of the Three Jin are weak because they engage in pleasures and consider tax exemptions and rank a trivial matter. The reason for Qin's strength is that its people engage in bitter [toil] and consider tax exemptions and rank a serious matter. Now, if we increase rank [bestowals] and prolong tax exemptions, we shall cast away what makes Qin strong and engage in what makes the Three Jin weak." This is the argument of Your Majesty's officials, which is why they take rank too seriously and are too stingy in tax exemptions. In the humble opinion of your subject, this is wrong.

After all, the reason why we let the people [suffer from] bitter [toil] and strengthen the army is to enable us to attack the enemy and to attain whatever we desire. The *Methods of War* says: "When the enemy is weak, our army is strong." This means that we should not lose whatever facilitates our attacks, while the enemy loses whatever facilitates its defense. Now, the Three Jin have been unable to overcome Qin for four generations already.[10] From the time of King Xiang of Wei, they have never been victorious on the open field; and when their fortresses are besieged, they are sure to be routed. One cannot count how many times the Three Jin were defeated by Qin in small and large battles. And if despite this they still are not subdued, this is because Qin is able to occupy their territory but is unable to seize their people.

* * *

15.3: Now Your Majesty should manifest your numinous grace: those men-of-service who come from the regional lords and submit to your justice[11] should now be exempted from taxes for three generations and should not be liable for military service. Within the borders of Qin, levies should not be imposed on [profits from] mountains, hills, and swamps for ten years. Record it among the ordinances: it will suffice to attract a million [immigrant] laborers. Above I said: "When we consider the people's disposition, then what they desire are fields and dwellings: this is what Jin really does not possess and what Qin certainly has in surplus. If in this situation the people [of Jin] do not face westward, it is because Qin's men-of-service are worried, and the people are embittered." Now, when you let them benefit from fields and dwellings and exempt them from taxes for three generations, this is precisely to give them what they desire and to let them avoid what they detest. In this situation, all the people from east of the Mountain[12] shall turn westward. Thus, their [Qin officials'] words are wrong.[13] After all, to fill in broad wastelands, to extract Heavenly treasures, to let a million [immigrants] engage in the fundamental [occupation, viz., farming]: the benefits [of this situation] are abundant—is it merely "not to lose whatever facilitates our attacks"?

* * *

15.4: Moreover: What worries Qin is that when it raises armies and attacks [the enemy], the state will be impoverished, whereas when it resides in peace, focusing on agriculture, the enemy will gain a respite. Therefore, Your Majesty cannot attain both [military success and wealth] at the same time. Hence, although [Qin] has been victorious for three (four?) generations,[14] All-under-Heaven has not submitted. Now, let the old Qin [people] engage the enemy, and let the new people[15] deal with the fundamental [occupation]: then even if the army remains outside the borders for a hundred days, not a moment of seasonal work is lost within the borders. This is the desired result of attaining both: [being] rich and strong.

What I, your subject, call "the military" does not refer to complete mobilization and universal conscription. What I mean is that within the borders you are able to provide enough for the army, its soldiers, chariots, and cavalry.[16] Let the old Qin people serve in the army and the new people provide fodder and provisions. As for those states in All-under-Heaven that are not submissive: Your Majesty should "in spring encircle their farmlands, in summer eat their provisions, in autumn seize whatever they have reaped, in winter expose their stores."[17] Use the "Great Martial" to shake their foundations; use the "Broad Civilian" to pacify their descendants.[18] If Your Majesty implements this, then in ten years the regional lords will remain without the migrant population.[19] Why then should Your Majesty be too stingy in [bestowing] rank and take tax exemptions too seriously?

* * *

15.5: After the victory over the Zhou army[20] and the victory of the army at Hua[yang],[21] Qin cut off the [enemy's] heads and advanced eastward. Yet although it was already clear that eastward [advancement] was profitless, the officials considered it a great achievement because it inflicted damage on the enemy. Now, to use lands covered by grass and reeds so as to attract the people of the Three Jin and let them engage in agriculture is likewise damaging to the enemy. It is of the same substance as military victory; and, moreover, Qin gets these [migrants] to engage in grain production: this is reverting to the implementation of the "double-win" stratagem! Besides, how many people did Qin lose in the victory over the Zhou army, the Hua[yang] victory, and the Changping victory?[22] How many of the people who followed the invading army[23] were unable to engage in the fundamental [occupation]? In your subject's humble opinion, these cannot be counted. If one of Your Majesty's ministers were able to weaken Jin and strengthen Qin with half of these expenses, with results similar to that of the three victories, Your Majesty would surely reward him. Now, what I, your subject, am suggesting is that without the people spending one day of corvée, and without officials spending more than several [strings of] cash, we shall be able to weaken Jin and strengthen Qin more than even after the three victories. Yet Your Majesty still considers this unacceptable: this is what I, your stupid subject, cannot understand.

* * *

15.6: In Qi there was a man named Dongguo Chang who had many desires and wanted to have ten thousand [units] of gold. His retainer asked to be given some support [if Dongguo had the money], but [Dongguo] refused, saying, "I want to use the money to seek a fief." His retainer was angry and left him for [the state of] Song, saying, "He is too stingy with what he doesn't even have. Would it not be better to make a promise first to the one whom he already has?" Now, Jin has its people, but Qin is too stingy with tax exemptions: it is simply being stingy with what we don't even have while losing what we do have. How is it different from Dongguo Chang, who was stingy with what he didn't have and thereby lost his retainer?

Besides, in antiquity there were Yao and Shun, who responded to the times and were praised; in the middle ages there were [Kings] Tang and Wu—when they ascended the throne, the people submitted.[24] These three kings[25] are praised by myriad generations, who consider them sage monarchs; yet their way nonetheless could not be applied thereafter. Now, by making tax exemptions for three generations, you can completely absorb the people of the Three Jin. Does this not mean that Your Majesty establishes a reputation for worthiness in the current generation and lets future generations be of use to Your Majesty? Yet one who is not a sage should not speak, and heeding the sage is difficult.[26]

16

ESSENTIALS OF PUNISHMENTS (刑約)

This chapter was lost more than five hundred years ago.

17

REWARDS AND PUNISHMENTS (賞刑)

Chapter 17 differs from the rest of the *Book of Lord Shang* in terms of its composition and style. First, it is the best-organized chapter in the entire book. It comprises an opening statement, three extensive paragraphs that elucidate this statement, and then a brief summary. Second, it is the only chapter to provide extensive historical discussions about the paragon rulers of the past. The genre of historical anecdote, most vividly represented in section 17.3, was a common means through which thinkers of the Warring States period presented their views (see Schaberg 2011; van Els and Queen 2017). In the *Book of Lord Shang*, this genre is almost entirely absent (even brief references to former paragons are highly uncommon). Chapter 17 is a notable exception. Third, this chapter is distinctive in its utopian overtones, especially the idealized depiction of Kings Tang and Wu, who allegedly attained the state of blessed non-action in the aftermath of their victories (17.2). This idyllic depiction of the paragons' rule as well as an unusual stress on the importance of lavish rewards as coequal in importance to harsh punishments (17.1, 17.2) make this chapter sound less harsh than most of the *Book of Lord Shang*.

This said, the distinctive Shang Yang–related outlook is fully present in the chapter, particularly in its repeated emphasis on the need to direct the entire population to war through the combination of rewards, punishments, and indoctrination (or "teaching," *jiao* 教). The latter point is particularly interesting: no other chapter focuses on "teaching" as seriously as chapter 17 does. Yet "teaching" does not mean intensive brainwashing; rather, the fact that "the gates of riches and nobility are exclusively in the field of war" suffices to intoxicate the population to the extent that "when they hear about war, the people congratulate each other; whenever they move or rest, drink or eat, they sing and chant only about war" (17.4).

Chapter 17 is also important as one of the clearest expositions of the authors' legal philosophy. First, it clarifies the principle of equality before the law or, in its own words, "imposing punishments without regard for one's status. From chief ministers, chancellors, and generals down to nobles and commoners, whoever disobeys the king's orders, violates the state's prohibitions, or wreaks havoc on the regulations of one's superior should be executed without pardon" (17.3). One should be immediately reminded that the Qin system was that of equal legal responsibility but not necessarily equal punishments: one's rank brought about certain legal privileges, especially the right to remit mutilating punishments (see section 19.7 and the discussion of the Qin legal principles in Hulsewé 1985, 7–8). Second, the chapter specifies incentives for informers to denounce colleagues and superiors under the system of "mutual responsib[ility]" (17.3). Third, the authors reiterate the need for harsh punishments as the best deterrent against transgressions (17.3).

Chapter 17 belongs to a later layer of the book: its reference to "royal law" (17.3) strongly suggests composition after 325 B.C.E., i.e., the date when King Huiwen of Qin 秦惠文王 (r. 337–311 B.C.E.) adopted the royal title. If so, the chapter may be indicative of one line of ideological development within "Shang Yang's school": argumentative sophistication, readiness to borrow ideas and terms from rival intellectual currents, but also full preservation of the fundamental messages of earlier chapters.

* * *

17.1: When the sage rules the state, he unifies rewards, unifies punishments, and unifies teaching. When rewards are unified, the army has no rivals. When punishments are unified, orders are implemented. When teaching is unified, inferiors heed superiors. Thus, clarifying rewards eliminates waste, clarifying punishments eliminates executions, clarifying teaching eliminates alterations: then the people know how to commit themselves to the people's tasks, and the state has no divergent customs.[1] Clarifying rewards is like arriving at no rewards; clarifying punishments is like arriving at no punishments; clarifying teaching is like arriving at no teaching.[2]

* * *

17.2: What is called "unifying rewards" means that benefits, emoluments, official position, and rank uniformly derive from military [attainments] and that there are no other ways to dispense them. Therefore, the knowledgeable and the ignorant, the noble and the base, the courageous and the cowardly, the worthy and unworthy—all fully utilize their innermost wisdom and fully exhaust the power of their limbs, going forth to die in the service of their superiors. The bravos and the worthies from All-under-Heaven will follow him [the ruler] just as water flows downward. Hence, his troops will have no rivals, and his orders will be implemented throughout All-under-Heaven. Ten-thousand-chariot states will dare not repel his troops on the battlefield; one-thousand-chariot states will dare not protect their walled cities. If a ten-thousand-chariot state will try to repel his troops on the battlefield, then in the battle he will overturn their army; if a one-thousand-chariot state will protect its walled cities, then in an assault he will raze its walls. If in a battle he surely overturns the rival's army, and in an assault he surely razes the rival's walls, then he will possess all the walled cities and subdue all [the regional lords], summoning them [to his state].[3] Then, even if he were to bestow lavish grants and rewards, will there ever be any wasteful expenses?

In the past, Tang was enfeoffed at Zanmao, King Wen was enfeoffed at Qizhou, [and their land was] one hundred *li* squared.[4] Tang fought Jie at the fields of Mingtiao; King Wu fought Zhòu amid Mu Fields: they defeated the nine armies [of their enemies].[5] At the end, they apportioned the lands and enfeoffed regional lords, and the soldiers who participated in the fight were granted registered hamlets.[6] [War] chariots were put to rest and not mounted, horses were released to the south of Mount Hua, and oxen were released at the [Hong]nong Marshes;[7] they were released until their old age and not reassembled [for war]—such were the rewards of Tang and Wu! Hence, it is said: "Should the grain of Zanmao and Qizhou be used to reward all the people under Heaven, everybody would receive just one *sheng*;[8] should the money of Zanmao and Qizhou be used to reward the people under Heaven, everybody would receive just one coin." Hence, it is said: "The rulers of one hundred *li* squared were able to enfeoff their ministers because they increased the original [territory]." How were they able to grant registered hamlets to the soldiers who participated in the fight and to increase the rewards so that generosity extended to horses and oxen? [It is because] they excelled at utilizing the resources of All-under-Heaven to reward the people of All-under-Heaven. Hence, it is said: "Clarifying rewards eliminates waste."

When Tang and Wu exterminated Jie and Zhòu, no evildoers remained within the seas; All-under-Heaven was greatly stabilized. They built the five granaries, stored the five [sorts] of arms, put military affairs to rest, and implemented civilian teaching; they carried shields and halberds reversed, official tables were stored in girdles, and they created music to manifest their virtue. At that time, rewards and emoluments were not implemented, but the people were self-ordered. Hence, it is said: "Clarifying rewards is like arriving at no rewards."

* * *

17.3: What is called unifying punishments means imposing punishments without regard for one's status. From chief ministers, chancellors, and generals down to nobles and commoners, whoever disobeys the king's orders, violates the state's prohibitions, or wreaks havoc on the regulations of one's superior should be executed without pardon. If he had merits before but failed thereafter, this should not reduce the punishment. When one was good previously but transgressed thereafter, this should not diminish the law. When loyal ministers and filial sons transgress, their cases should be decided according to the rules.

When an official whose task is to safeguard the law does not implement the royal law, he should be executed without pardon, and the punishments should extend to the three degrees of his family members.[9] When his colleagues know of [his crime] and denounce it to the superiors, they avoid punishment; and, whether noble or base, they inherit their superior's office, rank, fields, and emoluments. Hence, it is said: "When punishments are heavy and criminals are mutually responsible, the people dare not try [to break the law]. When the people dare not try, there are no punishments." Hence, the prohibitions of the former kings, such as [carrying out] executions, cutting off feet, or branding the face, were imposed not because they sought to harm the people but only to prohibit depravity and to stop transgressions. So, to prohibit depravity and to stop transgressions nothing is better than to make punishments heavy. When punishments are heavy and [criminals] are inevitably captured, then the people dare not try [to break the law]. Hence, there are no penalized people in the state. When there are no penalized people in the state, it is said: "Clarifying punishments [means] no executions."

Lord Wen of Jin wanted to clarify punishments so as to become closer to the hundred clans.[10] He thereupon gathered the nobles of the regional lords at the Shiqian Palace. Dian Jie was the last to arrive, and the officer[11] asked how to deal with his crime. The lord answered: "Execute him!" The officer then broke Dian Jie's spine as an example [to the army]. The Jin soldiers were terrified. They discussed the matter, saying, "Dian Jie was the [lord's] favorite,[12] but [his spine] was broken to set an example. So what would happen to ourselves?" [Lord Wen] then raised an army to invade Cao and Wulu and overrun the walls of Zheng;[13] he [caused] Wei to deploy its field divisions eastward and overcame the Jing [Chu] army at Chengpu.[14] The soldiers of the three armies stopped [firmly] as if their feet were cut off and moved [rapidly] like flowing water. The soldiers of the three armies dared not violate the prohibitions. Hence, Lord Wen merely borrowed the way of light and heavy from Dian Jie's spine, and the state of Jin became well ordered.

In the past, Dan, the Duke of Zhou, killed Guanshu and expelled Huoshu, saying, "They violated prohibitions."[15] The multitudes under

Heaven all said: "He did not depart [from appropriate punishments] in dealing with his younger brothers, so how much less will he for strangers?" Hence, All-under-Heaven know that when the knife and the saw[16] are employed at court, all within the seas will be properly ruled. Therefore, it is said: "Clarifying punishments is like arriving at no punishments."

* * *

17.4: What is called "unification of teaching" is that none of these—the broadly educated, the argumentative, the knowledgeable, the trustworthy, the honest, those skilled at ritual and music, those who cultivate their conduct, those who establish cliques, or those who are appointed due to their reputation or [after] having requested an audience[17]—will be allowed to become rich and noble, to criticize punishments, or to establish their private opinions independently and submit them to superiors. The solid will be broken; the sharp will be blunted.[18] Even if one is sagacious and knowledgeable, crafty and glib-tongued, generous or simple, he should not be able to seek benefits from superiors unless he has merit. Thus, the gates of riches and nobility are exclusively in the field of war. He who is able to [distinguish himself at] war will pass through the gates of riches and nobility; he who is stubborn and tenacious will meet with constant punishments and will not be pardoned.

Therefore, fathers and elder brothers, minor brothers, acquaintances, relatives by marriage, and colleagues[19] all say: "What we should be devoted to is only war and that is all." Hence, the able-bodied are devoted to war, the elderly and infirm are devoted to defense; the dead have nothing to regret; the living are ever more devoted and encouraged. This is what I, your minister, call the "unification of teaching."

The people's desire for riches and nobility stops only when their coffin is sealed. And [entering] the gates of riches and nobility must be through military [service]. Therefore, when they hear about war, the people congratulate each other; whenever they move or rest, drink or eat, they sing and chant only about war. This is why I, your minister, say: "Clarifying teaching is like arriving at no teaching."

* * *

17.5: These are what I, your minister, call the "three teachings." The sage cannot comprehensively understand the essentials of all the myriad things. Hence, in ordering the state, he focuses on the essential to deal with the myriad things. Thus, his teachings are few but attainments are many. The sage's [way of] ordering the state is easy to understand but difficult to implement. Thus, the sage does not necessarily add [anything to the existing norms], and the ordinary ruler does not necessarily cast [the existing norms] away. When killing the people it is not considered evil and rewarding them, it is not considered benevolent, it is because the law of the state is clear. The sage grants offices and bestows ranks according to merit; hence, the worthy do not worry. The sage is not lenient toward transgressions, nor does he pardon crimes: hence, depravity does not arise. The sage, in ordering the state, investigates the One, and that is all.[20]

18

CHARTING THE POLICIES (畫策)

C hapter 18 is a large and heterogeneous chapter, individual sections of which are not directly related to each other. Its primary focus is on the overarching importance of law, but it contains many additional departures, some of which are fairly interesting. For instance, ensuring the law's efficacy requires not just the combination of heavy punishments and inevitable apprehension of the culprits (18.4) but also—uncharacteristically for most of the *Book of Lord Shang* (except chapter 14)—the appointment of worthy ministers who will facilitate the dissemination of law among the populace (18.5). Chapter 18 is also peculiar in its rejection of the importance of rewards, which are considered narrowly as rewarding normative behavior: "It is unacceptable to reward the good; it is like rewarding those who do not steal" (18.4). Oddly, the idea of rewards for meritorious tillers and fighters escapes the authors' attention.

Chapter 18 starts by exploring the issue of the genesis of the state, which was addressed more systematically in chapter 7. The narrative in chapter 18 is less theoretically sophisticated and more directly related to the legendary past. Its goal is to reiterate the importance of changing with the times, yet its difference from chapter 7 is a clearer assertion that primeval society enjoyed a pleasant and tranquil life: "men plowed to obtain food, women wove to obtain clothing; he [Shennong] used neither punishments nor regulations, yet there was order" (18.1). This primeval idyll is more akin to the one depicted in the

Zhuangzi (29:778 ["Robber Zhi"]), and it contrasts with the negative view of a stateless society found elsewhere in the *Book of Lord Shang* (23.1). Yet the authors of 18.1, much like those of 7.1, acknowledge that the primeval tranquility was unsustainable in the long term. This view suits their major message: every historical era requires a full-scale modification of political methods.

Chapter 18 is very blatant in its emphasis on the people being the major threat to the ruler's power: "those who were able to overcome the enemy had first to overcome their own people" (18.2). The major difficulty in dealing with the people is making them fight because war "is something the people hate" (18.3). In marked distinction from chapter 17, chapter 18 emphasizes that the people will go to war not for the sake of rank and emoluments but only out of fear of the inevitable punishment that befalls deserters.

Another notable feature of chapter 18 is the philosophical sophistication of its final sections. This sophistication is represented not only in the authors' persistent attempts to define and redefine common terms of political and ethical discourse, from "clear-sightedness" and "strength" (18.7) to "righteousness" (18.8), but also in the introduction of new concepts, such as "the principle of what is inevitably so" (*biran zhi li* 必然之理) (18.8). Actually, the very use of the term *li* 理 (principle or pattern), one of the key terms of late Warring States period philosophical discourse (Deng Guoguang 2011; Sato Masayuki 2013b, 177–235), is an exceptional feature of chapter 18: of the four times the term appears in the *Book of Lord Shang*, three are in a single passage in this chapter (18.8). The use of this term may indicate a relatively late date of composition for at least the last section of chapter 18, but the evidence is far from decisive.

* * *

18.1: Formerly, in the age of Hao Ying, the people cut trees and slaughtered animals [for food]; the people were few, whereas trees and animals plenty. In the age of the Human Thearch[1] the people consumed neither fawns nor eggs; officials had no servants to support them, and at death they could not obtain outer coffins. Undertakings [of Hao Ying and the Human Thearch] were not the same, but they all were Monarchs: this is because the times were different. In the age of Shennong, men plowed to obtain food, women wove to obtain clothing; he used neither punishments nor regulations, yet there was order; armor and weapons were not set up, but [Shennong] became a Monarch.[2]

After Shennong, the strong overpowered the weak, the many lorded over the few. Hence, the Yellow Thearch[3] created the duties of rulers and ministers and of superiors and inferiors, rituals of fathers and sons and of elder and younger brothers, and harmony between husband and wife and between spouses. At home, he applied knife and saw,[4] abroad he used armored soldiers: this was because times changed. Looking at it from this angle, it is not that Shennong was superior to the Yellow Thearch; it is just that his name is honored because he conformed to his times. Therefore, in order to eradicate war with war, even waging war is permissible; to eradicate murder with murder, even murdering is permissible; to eradicate punishments with punishments, even making punishments heavy is permissible.

* * *

18.2: In the past, those who were able to regulate All-under-Heaven first had to regulate their own people; those who were able to overcome the enemy had first to overcome their own people. The root of overcoming the people is controlling the people as the metalworker controls metal and the potter clay. When the roots are not firm, the people will be like flying birds and running animals: Who will then be able to regulate them? The root of the people is law. Hence, those who excel at orderly rule block the people with law; then a [good] name and lands can be attained.

* * *

18.3: When the name is honored and territories are extensive to the point that you become the Monarch, why is that? {It is because of victory in war.}[5] When the name is disdained and the territory is dismembered to the point of perishing, why is that? It is because of defeat in war. From ancient times until today, it has never happened that one became Monarch without victories or perished without defeats. When the people are brave, war ends in victory; when the people are not brave, war ends in defeat. He who is able to unify the people in war, his people are brave; he who is unable to unify the people in war, his people are not brave. The sage monarchs observed that monarchy is attainable through the military; hence, they demanded that the entire state participate in the military. When you enter a state and observe its governance, you know that he whose people are usable is powerful. How can I know that the people are usable? When the people look at war as a hungry wolf looks at meat, the people are usable.

As for war: it is something the people hate. He who is able to make the people delight in war is the [True] Monarch. Among the people of a powerful state, fathers send off their sons, elder brothers send off their younger brothers, wives send off their husbands, and all say: "Do not come back without achievements!" They also say: "If you violate the [military] law and disobey orders, you will die, and I shall die. Under the canton's control,[6] there is no place to flee from the army ranks, and migrants[7] can find no refuge."

To order the army ranks: link them into five-man squads, distinguish them with badges, and bind them with orders. Then there will be no place to flee, and defeat will never ensue. Thus, the multitudes of the three armies will follow orders as [water] flows [downward], and even facing death they will not turn back.

* * *

18.4: The state is in turmoil neither because its laws are in turmoil nor because the laws are useless. Every state has laws, but there is no law to make laws inevitably implementable.[8] Every state has laws that prohibit villainy and wickedness and punish robbers and bandits, but there is no law that makes the villainous and wicked, the robbers and the bandits inevitably be apprehended. Capital punishments are inflicted on the villainous and wicked, on robbers and bandits, but villainy, wickedness, robbery, and banditry do not stop: this is because [perpetrators] are not inevitably apprehended. When they are inevitably apprehended, and still there is villainy, wickedness, robbery, and banditry, it is because punishments are light. When punishments are light, not all are prosecuted; yet when all are inevitably apprehended, there are many punishments.[9]

Hence, he who is good at governance punishes the bad and does not reward the good. In such a case, there are no punishments, and the people are good. When there are no punishments and the people are good, this is because punishments are heavy. When punishments are heavy, the people dare not break [the law]. Hence, there are no punishments, and none among the people transgresses: then the entire state is good. Hence, the good are not rewarded, yet the people are good. It is unacceptable to reward the good; it is like rewarding those who do not steal.[10]

Hence, he who attains good order makes [Robber] Zhi trustworthy, and how much more Boyi![11] He who is unable to attain good order makes Boyi suspicious, and how much more Zhi! When the power [of the ruler] makes it impossible to behave wickedly, even Zhi becomes trustworthy; when the power allows one to behave wickedly, then even Boyi is made suspect.

* * *

18.5: Some states multiply orderly rule; others multiply turmoil. When the clear-sighted sovereign is above, he exclusively elevates the worthy; hence, management of the laws is in the hands of the worthy.[12] When management of the laws is in the hands of the worthy, then the laws are [disseminated] below, and the unworthy dare not transgress: this is called "to multiply orderly rule." When a ruler above is not clear-sighted, he exclusively elevates the unworthy; the state lacks clear laws, and the unworthy dare to transgress: this is called "to multiply turmoil."[13]

In the army, some multiply strength, some multiply weakness. When the people firmly want to fight in war and also have no choice but to fight, this is called "to multiply strength." When the people resolutely do not want to fight and also are able to escape fighting, this is called "to multiply weakness."

* * *

18.6: The clear-sighted sovereign does not enrich and ennoble his ministers excessively. What is called "riches" does not refer to grain, rice, pearls, and jade; what is called "nobility" does not refer to ranks, positions, offices, and duties. [When the ruler] discards laws and creates private ranks and emoluments, [this is what I refer to as] "riches and nobility."[14]

The sovereign does not exceed others in his virtuous conduct; he does not exceed others in knowledge; nor does he surpass others in courage and strength. Nonetheless, even the sagacious and the knowledgeable from among the people dare not plot against you;[15] the courageous and the strong dare not kill you; the multitudes dare not overpower their sovereign. Although the people are numbered in myriads, once hefty rewards are publicized, the people dare not contend; once heavy penalties are implemented, the people dare not resent: this [is the proper implementation of] the law.

The state is disordered when the people have too much private justice; the army is weak when the people have too much private courage. Thus, the due-to-be-dismembered state has multiple ways through which ranks and emoluments can be obtained; the customs[16] of the due-to-perish state are to disdain ranks and to think lightly of emoluments. Those who do not work but eat, who do not fight but attain glory, who have no rank but are respected, who have no emolument but are rich, who have no office but lead—these are called "villains."

* * *

18.7: "A well-ruling sovereign has no loyal ministers, a kind father has no filial sons": this means that they do not resort to good words but supervise [ministers and sons] according to the law and correct them through orders. [Thus,] no one can either transgress or join others in transgressing.

"He who is wealthy" has plenty of income and few expenditures. When there are regulations for garments and food, when food and drinks are measured, then expenditures are few. When women's affairs are fully maintained within [the household] and men's affairs are fully maintained outside, income is plentiful.

"He who is clear-sighted" sees everything, so that the ministers dare not behave villainously and the hundred clans dare not transgress. Hence, the ruler rests on a comfortable bed and listens to the sounds of silk and bamboo [musical instruments], while All-under-Heaven is well ordered.[17] What is called "clear-sighted" means causing the people to be unable not to perform [what is required].

"He who is strong" overpowers All-under-Heaven. Overpowering All-under-Heaven is due to combining [its] strength.[18] Therefore, the courageous and strong dare not act violently; the sage and the knowledgeable dare not cheat and seek employment due to empty [reputation].[19] He unites the multitudes of All-under-Heaven: hence none dares not but to perform whatever [the powerful ruler] likes or avoid whatever [the ruler] detests. "He who is strong" lets the courageous and powerful to be unable not to serve him. If his desires are satisfied, All-under-Heaven assists him; if they are not satisfied, All-under-Heaven [is still] fond of him.[20] He who relies on All-under-Heaven, All-under-Heaven abandons him; he who relies on himself will attain All-under-Heaven. He who attains All-under-Heaven is the one who is first able to attain himself; he who overpowers a strong enemy is the one who is first able to overpower himself.[21]

* * *

18.8: The sage understands the principle of what is inevitably so and the power of timely, inevitable action. Hence, he implements the government that will inevitably bring orderly rule; he fights using the people who are inevitably courageous; he issues orders that will inevitably be heeded. Hence, when his army is dispatched, it has no rivals; when his orders are issued, All-under-Heaven submits and follows him. A yellow crane, once it rises, flies for one thousand *li* because it is equipped with what makes it inevitably fly. The thoroughbreds Lili and Juju cover one thousand *li* a day because they have the power that makes them inevitably run. Tigers, leopards, bears, and brown bears are unmatched in their ferocity because they possess the principle of inevitable victory. The sage observes the fundamentals of government and understands the principle of what is inevitably so: hence, he can regulate the people as if regulating the [flow of] water from high to low or regulating the [shift of] fire from wet to dry.

Hence, it is said: "The benevolent can behave benevolently toward others but cannot cause them to behave benevolently; the righteous can love others but cannot cause others to be loving."[22] From this I know that benevolence and righteousness are insufficient to rule All-under-Heaven. The sage possesses the nature of being inevitably trusted and also possesses the method of making All-under-Heaven trust him.

What is called "righteousness" is when ministers are loyal and sons filial, there are rites between the young and the old, and distinctions between men and women. Yet this is not [real] righteousness. When the hungry cannot get food improperly, when the dying cannot get life improperly: this is the constancy of the law. Sage kings did not esteem "righteousness" but esteemed the law: laws must be clear; orders must be implemented—and that is all.

19

WITHIN THE BORDERS (境内)

C hapter 19 is a singularly important testimony to the functioning of Shang Yang's system of military merits. The
chapter is largely technical and devoid of the polemical
zeal of most other parts of the *Book of Lord Shang*. It suffers from severe
textual corruption; only through the efforts of late-imperial commentators such as Yu Yue and Sun Yirang as well as of modern scholars,
most notably Li Ling (1991), did it become fully legible again. It is often
suggested that the chapter reflects an earlier layer of the book (see, e.g.,
Zheng Liangshu 1989, 20–23; Tong Weimin 2013, 190–199), but this is
debatable. The chapter's dating is particularly contentious because of
a single character that qualifies the term *yushi* 御史 (inspector) in section 19.9: most recensions have the qualifier *wang* 王 (royal), which
means that the chapter could not have been composed before 325 B.C.E.
(the year when King Huiwen of Qin assumed the royal title), yet the
highly authoritative recension by Yan Wanli has *zheng* 正 (in this context meaning "general") and not *wang*, which then allows an earlier dating. Yet even if the chapter were composed after 325 B.C.E., it could
not have been produced much later insofar as its depiction of the Qin
system of ranks of merits lacks the top four ranks (19.5). It is likely that
the chapter was penned before the finalization of the Qin ledger of
ranks as we know it from the Han sources.[1]

The chapter is indicative of the overall militarization of society
in the aftermath of Shang Yang's reforms. One's social, political,

economical, and legal status and even one's sumptuary privileges are to be determined exclusively by one's achievements on the battlefield (19.2, 19.5, 19.7. 19.8). At the same time, the army becomes strongly bureaucratized: the soldiers' performances are regularized, their tasks are clearly defined, and the criteria for promotion and demotion, most notably the number of severed enemy heads, are of utmost importance (19.3–19.5). Elaborate rules guide the performance not just of soldiers and officers but of the higher officials as well. The latter must check the number and the identity of the severed heads and then speedily deliver the deserved rank, or they will be penalized (19.6). Granting the reward is performed jointly by military and civilian authorities (19.6), which suggests a minimization of distinctions between the military and civilian hierarchy.

The final section (19.9) presents a fascinating account of siege warfare as primarily a bureaucratic procedure. The officers (from both the military and the civilian arms of the government) meticulously assign duties to every unit and then assess their performance. The commander, sitting on the observation platform, appears more concerned with calculating rewards and punishments than with managing the purely military aspects of the assault. This profound bureaucratization of the army may create the impression of a mechanistic view of warfare, but this is not the case. The crack troops—identified here tentatively as "sappers"—are staffed by volunteers, who apparently are willing to brave death in exchange for higher rewards than those distributed to average soldiers. Yet even in their case there are no spiritual incentives: killing and being killed are just a routine procedure in advancing up the social ladder. The chapter overall provides an exceptionally useful glimpse into the functioning of the Qin military under Shang Yang.

* * *

19.1: Within the four borders, the authorities should possess [records of] the names of all men and women, recording those who are born and erasing those who have died.

* * *

19.2: Holders of rank can request from those unranked that they act as their retainers;[2] for every rank, one can request one retainer.[3] When [the rank holders] are not on military service, the retainers serve their ranked superiors[4] for six days a month; when the [rank holders] are on military service, [retainers] follow and provide for their needs.[5]

* * *

19.3: Military ranks of the first rank and lower, down to unranked inferiors, are called *xiao*, *tu*, and *cao*: they are outside the common rank system.[6] Those of the second rank and upward to *bugeng* (fourth rank) are called soldiers.[7] In battle, five men are organized into a squad and are registered accordingly. When one squad member flees, the other four members are reduced [in rank]; if they are able to attain the head of one [enemy], the reduction is revoked.[8] For every fifty men there is a platoon leader; for every hundred men, a centurion. In battle, centurions and platoon leaders are not allowed to cut off heads [individually]; when [the battalion (?)] gets thirty-three heads and more, they have fulfilled the quota, and the platoon leaders and centurions are granted one rank.[9]

* * *

19.4: A commander of five hundred [bushel] rank[10] [is guarded by] fifty men with short combat weapons.[11] A commander of two five-hundred-rank commanders is a chief general; he [is guarded by] by one hundred short-weapon bearers. A one-thousand-bushel magistrate[12] has one hundred men with short combat weapons. An eight-hundred-bushel magistrate has eighty men with short combat weapons. A seven-hundred-bushel magistrate has seventy men with short combat weapons. A six-hundred-bushel magistrate has sixty men with short combat weapons. An [enfeoffed commandery (?)] commandant[13] has one thousand men with short combat weapons. The generalissimo[14] has four thousand men with short combat weapons. When during the battle [a commander] is killed,[15] his short-weapon guardians are reduced [in rank]; those who are able to attain one enemy's head, their rank is to be restored.[16]

* * *

19.5: In attacking a besieged fortress, [an army] that is able to cut off eight thousand heads and more has fulfilled the quota. In a battle in an open field, [an army] that is able to cut off two thousand heads and more has fulfilled the quota.[17] As for the personnel[18] from the rank of *cao* and *xiao* and higher: the generalissimo rewards all the personnel from the army ranks.[19] Those whose rank was *gongshi* (first rank) become *shangzao* (second rank); those whose rank was *shangzao* become *zanniao* (third rank); {those whose rank was *zanniao*}[20] become *bugeng* (fourth rank). Those whose rank was {*bugeng* become}[21] *dafu* (fifth rank). Those who rank as officers and act as commandants of a county are granted six prisoners as their slaves and 5,600 in cash.[22]

Those who rank as *dafu* and are employed by the state[23] become *guan dafu* (sixth rank).[24] {Those whose rank was *guan dafu*}[25] become *gong dafu* (seventh rank). Those whose rank was *gong dafu* become *gong sheng* (eighth rank). {Those whose rank was *gong sheng*}[26] become *wu dafu* (ninth rank) and can then utilize taxes from the settlements of three hundred families. Those whose rank was *wu dafu* {become left and right *shuzhang* (tenth and eleventh rank).[27] Those who were left and right *shuzhang* become left *geng* (twelfth rank); those who were one of the three *geng* (twelfth to fourteenth rank)[28] become great *liangzao* (fifteenth rank)};[29] each of these is granted settlements of three hundred families and taxes from three hundred families.[30] Those who rank *wu dafu* [?] enjoy taxes from six hundred families and can raise retainers.[31] The generalissimo, his charioteer, and the third member of the chariot team are granted three ranks' promotion. Those who were guest-minister chancellors become regular ministers if the quota is fulfilled.[32]

* * *

19.6: After the battle, when [severed] heads are exposed,[33] they are checked for three days; if the general has no doubts, he delivers ranks of merit to soldiers and officers.[34] {As for delivering ranks of merit: if this was not done after [the heads] were hung for three days,} the four subcommandants of the county[35] {should be dismissed,}[36] and the county's assistant magistrate and commandant should be fined. He who is able to attain one head of an armored soldier should be promoted one rank; his field should be increased by one *qing*;[37] his house plot should be increased by nine *mu*. For every rank, he is granted the right to appoint one retainer, and then he is allowed to become a military or civilian official.

* * *

19.7: The rules for litigation among them [the rank holders]: a holder of higher rank investigates holders of lower ranks. When a person has his high rank abolished, he [still] should not be given as a slave or servant for a ranked person. From the second rank upward, if they [the rank holders] have committed a punishable crime, their [rank] should be decreased; for the holders of the first rank and below, if they have committed a punishable crime, their rank should be abolished.

* * *

19.8: When an unranked inferior dies, or when it happens to everyone up to the *dafu* rank, for each rank they should be allowed to plant one tree on their tomb.

* * *

19.9: When a fortress is attacked or a settlement is encircled, the State Minister of Works examines the breadth and the width of the wall; the State Commandant divides *xiao* and *tu* soldiers for every square foot and orders [them] to attack. He fixes the time and says: "Those who are the first to succeed will be considered the best of the vanguard; those who are the last will be censured as the worst of the rear; those who are twice censured will be dismissed."

They dig tunnels [beneath the walls] and pile firewood; when firewood is piled, it is burned. At every side of the wall, eighteen sappers should be placed. The sappers fight valiantly but are not permitted to cut off heads; if five members of the team succeed in penetrating [the fortress], then every sapper is rewarded one rank;[38] if he dies, it [his rank] is transferred to one of his heirs. If [the sappers] are afraid of death, a thousand people gather around them; they are admonished[39] and then punished beneath the walls by tattooing and the cutting off of their noses.

The State Commandant divides areas [for attack] and assaults them with the troops of the central army. The general creates a wooden platform[40] and observes the operation together with the Chief Supervisor and General (or Royal?)[41] Inspector. Those who are the first to break into [the fortress] are designated the best of the vanguard; those who are the last to enter are designated the worst of the rear. As for the sappers, their ranks are fully filled by volunteers;[42] if there are not enough volunteers, they are supplemented by those who want promotions.

21

PROTECTING FROM ROBBERS (禦盜)

This chapter was lost more than five hundred years ago.

22

EXTERNAL AND INTERNAL (外内)

The short chapter 22 reiterates the major message of the book: the state's primary goal is to turn its population into soldiers abroad and farmers at home. The external task—that is, territorial expansion—can be achieved through the proper utilization of rewards and punishments, with the former given a stronger emphasis (22.1). The internal task—filling in the granaries—should be achieved primarily through an economic assault on the merchants: by raising taxes and levies on them and by pushing up food prices, the ruler will diminish the merchants' profits and increase the farmers' income. "Then the people will have to cast away [the occupations of] merchants and peddlers and crafty and tricky people and engage in profiting from the soil" (22.2). The result will be the enrichment and empowerment of the state en route to turning the ruler into the new True Monarch (22.3).

* * *

22.1: Among the people's external tasks, nothing is more difficult than war; hence, he who takes law lightly cannot cause them [to engage in] it. What is called "taking law lightly"? It means that rewards are few, awe is meager, and excessive ways are not blocked. What are called "excessive ways"? It means that the argumentative and clever are esteemed, itinerant servants are employed, men of letters and those who have privately established a name are deemed illustrious.[1] When these three are not blocked, the people do not engage in war, and undertakings end in defeat. Thus, when rewards are few, those who heed [orders] do not benefit; when awe is meager, those who violate [orders] are not harmed. Hence, to attract [subjects] by opening excessive ways and to let them wage war while taking law lightly are like making a cat bait for a rat: Is it not too much?

Hence, he who wants to enable his people to wage war must take laws seriously. His rewards must be abundant, [his] awe must be severe; excessive ways must be blocked: the argumentative and clever should not be esteemed, itinerant servants should not be employed, men of letters and those who have privately established a name should not be illustrious. When rewards are abundant and awe is severe, the people see that he who [excels] at war is abundantly rewarded, and they forget about death; they see that those who do not fight are degraded and then regard life with bitterness. When rewards cause them to forget about death, while awe causes them to regard life with bitterness, and, moreover, excessive ways are blocked: to face the enemy in this situation is like shooting at a floating leaf with a hundred-*shi*-capacity crossbow—How can it not be pierced[2] through?

* * *

22.2: Among the people's internal tasks, nothing is more bitter than farming; hence, he who takes orderly rule lightly would never cause the people to engage in it. What is called "taking orderly rule lightly"? It means that one's farmers are poor whereas merchants are rich: hence, as food is cheap, money is valuable. When food is cheap, farmers are poor; when money is valuable, merchants are rich. When branch occupations are not forbidden, then crafty and tricky people benefit, and "peripatetic eaters"[3] multiply. In this case, farmers who use their force in the bitterest way still cannot compare with merchants and peddlers or crafty and tricky people.

If you can cause merchants and peddlers and crafty and tricky people not to prosper, then even if you do not want to enrich the state, you will not but attain that. Hence, it is said: "He who wants the farmers to enrich his state makes food within the borders expensive. He must impose multiple taxes on those who do not farm and heavy levies on profits from the markets." Then the people will have to work in the fields. Those who do not work in the fields will have to exchange [their products] for food; when food is expensive, those who work in the fields benefit.[4] When working in the fields brings benefit, then those who engage in it are many. When food is expensive, and purchasing it is not profitable, and in addition [it] is heavily taxed, then the people will have to cast away [the occupations of] merchants and peddlers and crafty and tricky people and engage in profiting from the soil. Thus, the people's strength is fully committed to the soil alone.

$$* * *$$

22.3: Therefore, he who rules the state lets benefits at the boundaries come exclusively from the military and benefits at the markets come exclusively from farming. He whose benefits at the boundaries come exclusively from the military is strong; he whose benefits at the markets come exclusively from farming is rich. Thus, when externally you are strong when waging war, and internally you are rich when [the army] is at rest, you shall become the [True] Monarch.

23

RULER AND MINISTERS (君臣)

C hapter 23 is another short chapter that again reminds the
reader of the need to maintain rewards and promotions in
a way that benefits tillers and soldiers and prevents the
rest from ascending the social ladder. When "those who stare angrily,
clench their fists, and speak about bravery," "those in freely falling
robes who debate doctrines," and "those who spend day after day
expending their labor at private gates" (23.3) are blocked from attaining ranks and emoluments, the people will turn to agriculture and
warfare.

This chapter is the third in the book that narrates the emergence of
the state, but the narrative here differs considerably from that of chapters 7 and 18 and resembles the more simplistic stories seen, for example, in the *Mozi* (II.11:109–110 ["Shang tong shang" 尚同上]) and the
Guanzi (XI.23:568 ["Jun chen xia" 君臣下]). Namely, the stateless society was "in turmoil and disordered" (23.1), and it is only through the
blessed intervention of the sages that it attained political and social
order. In distinction from other invocations of prestate society in the
Book of Lord Shang, the narrative in chapter 23 does not emphasize the
magnitude of changes in the past (or mutatis mutandis in the present)
but rather uses the story of state formation to validate mechanisms of
control, such as "duties of ruler and ministers, superiors and inferiors";
"allocation of the five offices"; "prohibitions of laws and regulations"

(23.1). These mechanisms are essential for the state's survival: they are not to be modified but rather to be properly maintained.

* * *

23.1: In the past, when there still were neither ruler and ministers nor superiors and inferiors, the people were in turmoil and disordered. Therefore, the sages arrayed the noble and the base, regulated ranks and positions, established titles and designations so as to distinguish the duties of the ruler and the ministers, superiors and inferiors. As the land was vast, the people numerous, and the myriad things plentiful, they allocated five offices to preserve them. As the people multiplied and villainy and wickedness were born, [the sages] established laws and regulations, made measures and weights to prohibit [transgressions].

Therefore, one must be cautious about the duties of ruler and ministers, superiors and inferiors, about the allocation of the five offices, and about the prohibitions of laws and regulations. If you occupy the ruler's position but your orders are not implemented, you are endangered; if the five offices are allocated but there are no constant [rules to govern them], there is turmoil; if laws and regulations are established but private goodness is put forth, the people are not in awe of punishments. When the ruler is respected, his orders are implemented; when offices are regulated, they have constant tasks; when laws and regulations are clear, the people are in awe of punishments. If laws and regulations are not clear, one cannot expect the people to implement orders. If the people do not follow orders, yet you expect the ruler to be revered, then even if you are as perceptive as Yao and Shun, you will not be able to govern well.

* * *

23.2: When the clear-sighted monarch rules All-under-Heaven, he relies on law to bring about orderly rule [and] bestows rewards according to merit. In general, the people are vigorous at war and do not shun death because they seek ranks and emoluments. When the clear-sighted ruler governs his state, those of his soldiers who have the merit of cutting off [the enemy's] heads and capturing prisoners will surely have a rank that is sufficiently honored and emoluments that suffice to live on. When farmers do not leave their plots, they should have enough to nourish both parents and to provide for military affairs. Hence, soldiers brave death for the sake of norms, and farmers are not indolent.

* * *

23.3: Yet the rulers of our age do not act thus. They cast away laws and rely on knowledge; they turn [their] back on merits and [advance their subjects] according to reputation. Hence, soldiers do not fight, and farmers drift around. I, your minister, have heard: the gate of directing the people is through what the ruler promotes. Thus, the people can be induced to till and fight, can be induced to become itinerant servants, and can be induced to study: it all depends on how superiors[1] grant them [ranks and emoluments]. If superiors grant these in exchange for merit and toil, the people go to war; if they grant them for [studying] *Poems* and *Documents*, the people study. The people follow after benefit as water flows downward: it has no preference among the four directions.[2] The people do only whatever brings them benefit, and the benefit is granted by superiors.

When [ranks and emoluments] are attained by those who stare angrily, clench their fists, and speak about bravery; when they are attained by those in freely falling robes who debate doctrines; when they are attained by those who spend day after day expending their labor at private gates[3]—if respect is granted to these three, then all those who have no merits can attain [ranks and emoluments]. [In that case,] the people abandon agriculture and warfare, and engage in these [activities]: some engage in debates and disputations to ask for [promotion]; some engage in flattery to ask for it; some contend for it through their bravery. Therefore, those who are engaged in agriculture and warfare decrease daily, whereas "peripatetic eaters" multiply daily: the state is in turmoil, its territory is dismembered, the soldiers are weak, and the ruler is debased. All this is because laws are cast away, while one's name and reputation are relied upon.

* * *

23.4: Therefore, the clear-sighted sovereign is attentive to laws and regulations. He does not heed words that do not conform to the law; he does not esteem behavior that does not conform to the law; he does not undertake a task that does not conform to the law. If words conform to the law, they are heeded; if behavior conforms to the law, it is esteemed; if a task conforms to the law, it is undertaken. Hence, the state is ordered, its lands expand, the army is strong, and the sovereign is revered. This is the utmost of orderly rule; the ruler of men must investigate this.

24

INTERDICTING AND ENCOURAGING
(禁使)

Chapter 24 is often considered to belong to a later layer of the *Book of Lord Shang*: it differs from the rest of the text both in its style—for example, its frequent use of metaphors—and in its content. The chapter is concerned exclusively with the maintenance of officials; the common topoi of governing the people, directing them to agriculture and warfare, and properly maintaining rewards and punishments are absent from it. Some scholars consider it as reflecting the impact of Shen Dao and Shen Buhai because of the primacy in it of the terms *shi* 勢 (power of authority), associated with the former, and *shu* 數 (methods), associated with the latter. The centrality of both terms in this chapter indeed distinguishes it from the rest of the *Book of Lord Shang*. Whether the chapter reflects the influence of Shen Dao and Shen Buhai is less obvious, though. For instance, the usage of the term *shi* is not identical to its use in the remaining fragments of Shen Dao's writings: at times, it refers to the power of the sovereign (which is indeed close to the use by Shen Dao), but at times it refers to the power of officials, which should be curbed (24.2); the latter usage is not attested in the *Shènzi* 慎子 (Shen Dao's) fragments. As for *shu*, its association with Shen Buhai is dubious because the term is never elaborated in the extant *Shēnzi* 申子 (Shen Buhai's) fragments (Yang Soon-Ja 2010). It would be more accurate to say that chapter 24 reflects an advanced stage of development of administrative thought in the *Book of Lord Shang* rather than the direct influence of either Shen Dao or Shen Buhai: a stage in which both terms, *shi* and *shu*, had became more prominent than they were previously.

Chapter 24 is surprisingly frank in exposing the intrinsic difficulty of maintaining the bureaucratic apparatus. The ruler's physical limitations prevent him from fully investigating multiple reports from remote provinces of his realm (24.3),[1] and he must always be aware of the possibility of officials conniving with each other to conceal their wrongdoing (24.2). Yet assistants and supervisors, established to monitor the officials' misconduct, are just as eager to pursue private interests as other officeholders, so they are unreliable. The suggested solution—as elsewhere in the *Book of Lord Shang*—is to rely exclusively on the impersonal "power of authority" and to employ proper "methods" of rule. The text does not explain, however, how these methods will solve the perennial problem of "Quis custodiet ipsos custodes?" (Who will guard the guardians?). Perhaps the only clear recommendation is to prevent officials' connivance by encouraging them—as well as the rest of the populace—to denounce each other's wrongdoing (24.3). Yet the text stops short of explaining how this goal will be achieved. There is also a hint that supervision from below would prevent the officials' machinations, but possible corruption of this section of the text (24.3) prevents us from assessing the topic in full.

* * *

24.1: The means by which the sovereign interdicts and encourages are rewards and punishments. Rewards follow merits; punishments follow crimes: hence, one cannot but be cautious in discussing merits and investigating crimes. Hence, if rewards elevate and punishments degrade, but the superiors have no certain knowledge of their way, this is like having no way at all.

* * *

24.2: All those who understand the Way [rely on] power [of authority] and methods. Hence, former kings did not rely on strength but relied on power [of authority]; they did not rely on trustworthiness but relied on methods. Now, when a seed of fleabane meets a whirlwind and is carried for thousands of miles, it is because it took advantage of the wind's power. When the measurer of abysses is able to know the depth of a thousand *ren*,[2] it is because he employed the method of hanging a rope. Hence, he who relies on power will arrive even at a distant location; he who keeps his methods will measure even the deepest [abyss].

Now, in the darkness of night, however huge mountains may be, even Li Lou[3] could not see them, yet in the brightness of daylight he will distinguish flying birds above and an autumn hair below. Thus, the eye's ability to see relies on the power of the sun. He who attained the utmost power [of authority] does not impeach[4] officials, yet they are clean; he arrays the methods, and every matter is [performed] appropriately. Nowadays, [the ruler] relies on many officials and numerous clerks; to monitor them he establishes assistants and supervisors. Assistants are installed and supervisors are established to prohibit [officials] from pursuing [personal] profit; yet assistants and supervisors also seek profit, so how will they be able to prohibit each other? Hence, orderly rule that is attained through relying on assistants and supervisors is orderly rule that barely survives. He who comprehends methods acts differently. He separates their [the officials'] powers and makes their ways difficult. Hence, it is said: "If power makes concealing difficult, even [Robber] Zhi will do no wrong."[5] Therefore, the former kings esteemed power.

* * *

24.3: Some say: "The sovereign should respond [to things] by employing emptiness and staying behind.[6] Then things will be duly examined; when they are examined, the vicious will be apprehended." I, your minister, consider this wrong. After all, officials monopolize authority and decide on affairs a thousand *li* away; and in the twelfth month they prepare a report to be approved [in the capital]. The affairs of the whole year are to be separately checked, but the sovereign listens to them only once; even when he sees something suspicious, he cannot render a decision if he lacks appropriate evidence.[7]

After all, when things approach, an eye cannot but see them; when words are compelling, an ear cannot but hear them. Therefore, the regulations of the ordered states are such that the people cannot escape punishment, just as whatever the eye has seen cannot escape one's mind. Yet nowadays in disordered states this is not so: they rely on manifold officials and numerous clerks. Yet though the clerks are numerous, their essence[8] is the same: and those whose essence is the same cannot [supervise] each other. Therefore, the former kings safeguarded themselves by making [the officials'] benefits different and disadvantages unequal. Thus, under the utmost orderly rule, husband and wife, friends and associates cannot disregard each other's evil and conceal each other's wrongdoing, yet the relatives do not consider this harmful: it is because the people cannot cover up for each other.[9]

The superiors and their underlings[10] deal with the same matter, but their benefits differ. Now, should the overseer of horses and the game warden supervise each other, it will be impermissible because they deal with the same matter, yet their benefits are identical.[11] {Sixteen to twenty-eight characters missing here.}[12] Yet were horses and birds able to speak, then the overseer of horses and the game warden would not be able to escape [the consequences of] their wrongdoing: this is because their benefits are different [from those of horses and birds].[13]

When the benefits are the same and the disadvantages are identical, the father will not be able to interrogate his son; the ruler will not be able to interrogate his subject. Officials and other officials: their benefits are the same, and their disadvantages are identical. Thus, letting those who deal with the same matter have different benefits is the starting point of the former kings. [Then even if] the people cover up things from their sovereign, he is not harmed by the concealment. The worthies cannot add to this, the unworthy cannot detract from this. Hence, to abandon worthiness and discard knowledge are the method of orderly rule.

25

ATTENTION TO LAW (慎法)

C hapter 25 reiterates the major message of the book: through the proper handling of rewards and punishments, the ruler should be able to direct the people to the singularly important tasks of agriculture and warfare. The emphasis here is on positive incentives: the avenues of social and economic advancement should be open exclusively to tillers and soldiers rather than to talkative intellectuals. The authors are particularly dissatisfied with the habitual "elevation of worthies": without an adequate means of determining his worth, an official is promoted or demoted exclusively due to the good reputation for him created by his partisans (25.1). This practice is doubly dangerous: first, because it encourages the formation of cliques (*dang* 黨) among the officials, which impairs the sovereign's power, and, second, because it distracts the people from agriculture and warfare by offering alternative, "private" avenues of individual advancement (25.2) (see also the warning against "privately established" reputation in section 22.1).

The authors' solution reiterates the message of many previous chapters, especially chapter 14: a strict reliance on law, meaning primarily impersonal norms of promotion and demotion, will ensure fairness and transparency and will let "those among the people who seek benefits to gain them nowhere else but in tilling and those who want to avoid harm to escape nowhere but to war" (25.5). The final phrase, which promises that the ruler who heeds the authors' advice will become

"Hegemon and Monarch" (*ba wang* 霸王), may well be considered the summarizing motto of the entire book.

* * *

25.1: In general, in our age everyone [seeks] orderly rule through [the ways that generate] turmoil. Hence, small-scale orderly rule generates small-scale turmoil; large-scale orderly rule generates large-scale turmoil; from generation to generation sovereigns are unable to order their people, and every state is in turmoil. What does it mean "[to seek] orderly rule through [the ways that generate] turmoil?" Elevation of the worthy and the able is what the world calls "orderly rule": that is why orderly rule is in turmoil. What the world calls a "worthy" is one who is defined as upright, but those who define him as good and upright are his clique. When you hear his words, you consider him able; when you ask his partisans, they approve it. Hence, one is ennobled before one has any merits; one is punished before one has committed a crime. This [configuration of] power plainly allows depraved officials to obtain resources to accomplish their maliciousness and allows petty men to obtain resources to implement their deceitfulness. To begin by lending officials and the people the roots of vice and deceitfulness and then to ask them to be upright and sincere: in this manner even Yu would not be able to rule just ten men.[1] So how can an ordinary ruler be able in this manner to control the people of a single state?

* * *

25.2: These men who form cliques do not wait for you[2] to accomplish their affairs. When the ruler promotes one of their associates, the people turn [their] back on the sovereign and incline toward private connections.[3] If the people turn [their] back on the sovereign and incline toward private connections, then the ruler is weak, whereas the ministers are powerful. If the ruler does not understand this, he will either be attacked by regional lords or pressed by the hundred clans.

The power of talkers is such that ignorant and clever alike learn from them. When the men-of-service learn from talkers, the people abandon substantial tasks and recite empty words. When the people abandon substantial tasks and recite empty words, [the state] has little strength and much wrongdoing. If the ruler does not understand this, then in battle he will lose his commander, and, when on the defensive, his walled city will be sold out [to the enemy].

* * *

25.3: Hence, when clear-sighted rulers and loyal ministers arise in our generation and are willing to command their states, they cannot forget the law for a single moment. Destroy and smash cliques and glibness, restrict and eradicate [empty] talk, rely on law, and [attain] orderly rule. Let the officials preserve nothing but the law; then even the crafty will not be able to behave villainously. Let the people be rewarded for their abilities nowhere but in warfare; then even when endangered they will not dare act deceitfully. So when the people are ruled by law and promoted according to [proper] methods, then those who praise them will be unable to add anything to their [reputation], and the slanderers will be unable to do them any harm. When the people observe that mutual praise adds nothing, they will become accustomed to loving without flattery;[4] and when they observe that slander does no harm, they will become accustomed to hating without causing harm. When loving does not lead to flattering and hating does not lead to harming, then both love and hatred have been rectified: this is the acme of orderly rule. Hence I, your minister, say: rely on law, and the state will be ordered.

* * *

25.4: When a one-thousand-chariot state is able to preserve itself in defense and a ten-thousand-chariot state is able to reinforce itself in war, then even if the sovereign is [as bad as] Jie,[5] he will not be able to bend an inch to surrender to the enemy. If [the state] is unable to wage war abroad and is unable to protect itself at home, then even if the sovereign is [as good as] Yao, he will not be able but to subdue to a state that is no match to his. From this we can observe that what makes the state powerful and the ruler respectable is force. These two [the state's power and the ruler's power] are rooted in force, yet the sovereigns of our age are unable to attain maximum force: Why is that? It is because they allow the people who are embittered to avoid tilling and those who imperiled to avoid fighting.[6] These two [tilling and fighting] are something that a filial son would find hard to do for his parents and a loyal minister would find hard to do for his ruler. Now if you want to encourage the multitudes to do whatever filial sons and loyal ministers find difficult, then I, your minister, think that it is impossible unless you coerce them with penalties and encourage them with rewards.

Yet nowadays all the vulgar proponents of orderly rule discard laws and measures and rely on argumentativeness and cleverness; they relinquish merits and force and advance benevolence and righteousness. Hence, the people are not committed to tilling and fighting. If the people do not concentrate their force on tilling, then at home provisions will be depleted; if they do not commit their spirit to fighting, then abroad the army will be weak. When internally provisions are depleted while externally the army is weak, then even if you have ten thousand *li* of territory and one million armed soldiers, it is the same as standing alone amid the plain.

* * *

25.5: Moreover: former kings were able to cause their people to walk on bare swords and suffer arrows and stones. Did their people want to do this? No! They were eager to learn this so as to escape harm. Hence, my teaching causes those among the people who seek benefits to gain them nowhere else but in tilling and those who want to avoid harm to escape nowhere but to war. Within the borders, everyone among the people first devotes himself to tilling and warfare and only then obtains whatever pleases him. Hence, though the territory is small, grain is plenty, and though the people are few, the army is powerful. He who is able to implement these two within the borders will accomplish the way of Hegemon and Monarch.

26

FIXING DIVISIONS (定分)

C hapter 26 is probably the latest chapter in the *Book of Lord Shang*. It differs from the rest in its terminology, such as the persistent invocation of "names and divisions" (*ming fen* 名分) as the essentials of orderly rule;[1] in its bureaucratic vocabulary, which includes nomenclature from the late Warring States or Imperial Qin periods; in its preoccupation with All-under-Heaven rather than with a single state; and in its usage of "Son of Heaven" (*tianzi* 天子) as the supreme ruler's appellation.[2] In terms of its content as well, this chapter stands apart from the rest of the book. Its focus is on how to maintain laws in a large territorial realm. It discusses in great detail such topics as the promulgation and dissemination of laws, the legal education of the populace, and the functioning of law officials (*fa guan* 法官), who are considered central actors in the administrative system. The dissemination of law will benefit all: not only will it prevent transgressions and bring about the blessed "eradication of punishments through punishments," but, more importantly, it will also protect the people from the officials' abuse (26.4). To successfully implement their regulatory function, laws must be fully understandable (26.6) and be elucidated by law officials, without whom the wording of the law may be less comprehensible (26.5). Clear understanding of the laws also prevents unwanted discussions of their content among the populace: such discussions by the very fact of their existence undermine proper sociopolitical order (26.5).

Much of the information contained in this chapter is commensu-
rate with what we know about late preimperial and Imperial Qin
practices (see, e.g., Sanft 2014a, 140–142) and with the administrative
and political realities of that period (Tong Weimin 2013, 220–223). It is
highly likely that the chapter was produced on the eve of the imperial unification: before the adoption of the new imperial title by King
Zheng 政 of Qin (the would-be First Emperor, r. 221–210 B.C.E.) but
well into the period of Qin's unequivocal dominance over other
polities.

The chapter might have been deliberately devised as the final part
of the *Book of Lord Shang*. In what appears to be a conscious imitation of
chapter 1—and in distinction from the rest of the book—it is constructed as a dialogue between Lord Xiao of Qin and Gongsun Yang
(Shang Yang). Yet whereas the first chapter focuses on revising (*geng* 更)
the laws, the last emphasizes their "fixation" (*ding* 定). This shift creates a full cycle from change to stability, from a small and highly
aspiring territorial state to an empire in the making. The goal stipulated in the last sentence of this chapter, "All-under-Heaven will be
greatly ordered" (26.6), appears to be imminent.

* * *

26.1: The lord[3] asked Gongsun Yang: "Today I have established the laws;
tomorrow I want to let the officials and the people understand them
clearly and use them as one, without private [interpretations]: How
can it be done?"

* * *

26.2: Gongsun Yang said: "For laws and ordinances, establish officials
and clerks, seek[4] those of them with sufficient understanding of the
contents of laws and ordinances, and make them regulators of All-
under-Heaven. Then let them present memorials to the Son of Heaven.
The Son of Heaven will thereupon order[5] each of them to be in charge
of laws and ordinances. They all will descend [from the throne hall],
receive the mandate, and proceed to their offices. For each official[6] in
charge of laws and ordinances who dares to forget an item of the laws

and ordinances that he oversees, let him be punished according to the item that he forgot.

If an official in charge of laws and ordinances has to be transferred or dies in office, then let a student read the content of laws and ordinances and fix them as a standard [to be memorized]. Allow him a few days to learn the content of laws and ordinances; if he misses the standard, punish him in accordance with laws and ordinances. If anyone dares to emend[7] laws and ordinances, if he erases or adds more than one character, he should be condemned to death without pardon. If officials or the people have questions about the contents of laws and ordinances from officials in charge of laws and ordinances, let them clearly report what they want to inquire about. Prepare a table of one *chi* and six *cun* length,[8] record clearly the year, month, day, and hour of the query about an item in laws and ordinances, and publicize this to officials and to the people.[9] If an official in charge of laws and ordinances does not publicize the matter, and a crime is committed violating the content of the laws and ordinances about which he was queried, let him be punished according to the punishment specified in the laws and ordinances about which he was queried. Give the left side of the document to an official or a commoner who queries the laws and ordinances, and the official in charge of laws and ordinances will carefully preserve the right side in a wooden box. Keep it in a chamber, and seal it with the seal of the chief official in charge of laws and ordinances. If later the official dies, matters should be maintained according to the right side of the document.

* * *

26.3: All laws and ordinances should be copied. One copy should be kept in the palace of the Son of Heaven. Make a forbidden chamber for laws and ordinances, which should be locked and sealed, and entrance prohibited. Inside the forbidden chamber, a copy of each law and ordinance will be preserved and sealed with an interdictory seal. If someone opens the seals of the forbidden chamber without permission and enters the forbidden chamber to examine the laws and ordinances kept there or emends a single character or more of these texts, he should be condemned to death without pardon. Once a year, transmit laws and ordinances from the forbidden chamber [to all the officials].[10]

* * *

26.4: The Son of Heaven establishes three law officials. In the palace, one law official is established. The chief prosecutor[11] establishes one law official and one clerk. The prime minister establishes one law official.[12] All regional lords and heads of commanderies and counties establish one law official and one clerk.[13] All these should provide for one law official. Heads of commanderies and counties and regional lords, once they receive the laws and ordinances dispatched to them, should study their content. If officials and the people want[14] to understand laws and ordinances, they should ask the law official. Henceforth among the people and officials under Heaven, all will understand the laws. When the officials clearly know that the people understand the laws and ordinances, they dare not treat the people but in accord with the law, and the people will dare not violate the law and disobey the law officials.[15] If [the officials] in treating the people do not do so in accord with the law, [the people] will ask the law official; the law official will tell them about the punishment according to the law, and the people will tell his words to the officials. When everyone understands [laws] like that, the officials will dare not treat the people but in accord with the law, and the people will dare not violate the law. In this case, among officials and the people under Heaven, even if there are worthy, good, argumentative, and clever, they will dare not use a single word to twist the law; even if someone possesses a thousand pieces of gold, he will not be able to use a single coin [to bribe his way]. Hence, the knowledgeable and the deceitful, the worthy and the good, all will focus on good deeds; all will devote themselves to self-regulating and to endorsing the common [rules]. {{When the people are ignorant, it is easy to rule them.}}[16] All this originates from the fact the laws are clear, are easily understandable, and are inescapably applied.

* * *

26.5: Laws and ordinances are the matter of life or death for the people, the basis of orderly rule; they are what safeguards the people. They are what the knowledgeable cannot trespass and the ignorant cannot fall short of [grasping].[17] Not to fix names and divisions but to desire orderly rule under Heaven is like being the one who wants to escape starvation but discards food, who wants to escape cold but discards clothes, who wants to arrive eastward but turns westward: it is clear how hopeless it is.

When one rabbit is running and one hundred people pursue it, it is not because they want to divide the rabbit into one hundred pieces, but because names are still not fixed.[18] Alternatively, when the whole market is full of rabbit sellers, yet the thief dares not take them, it is because names and divisions are already fixed. Hence, when names and divisions are not fixed, even Yao, Shun, Yu, and Tang will rush to pursue the rabbit; when names and divisions are already fixed, even a greedy thief will not take it.[19] Now, if laws and regulations are not clear, and their names (= items) are not fixed, the people under Heaven will be able to debate them. In their debates, the people differ, and [principles] cannot be fixed. When the sovereign makes laws above, but the lowly people debate them below, it means that laws and ordinances are not fixed, and inferiors become superiors. This is what is referred to as "names and divisions not being fixed." So if names and divisions are not fixed, even Yao and Shun will all behave crookedly and steal things:[20] Then what can be expected from the multitudes? This means to cause vice and evil to grow greatly. This is the way for the ruler to be stripped of his awe and power of authority, the way of losing the state and having the altars of soil and grain eliminated.

Now, the former sages created books and transmitted them to later generations, and there should be teachers to transmit them: only then can we understand the names (terms) [in these books].[21] If they are not transmitted by teachers, and everyone discusses them according to his own mind, then until the end of his life he will not comprehend the names and the meaning of these books. Hence, the sages must establish officials for the laws and establish clerks, making them the teachers of All-under-Heaven.[22] Names and divisions will thereby be fixed. When names and divisions are fixed, then great deceivers become trustworthy, great thieves become cautious and sincere, and each governs himself. Therefore, when names and divisions are fixed, this is the way of positioning oneself in orderly rule; when names and divisions are not fixed, this is the way of positioning oneself in turmoil. Thus, he who positions himself in orderly rule cannot be directed into turmoil; he who positions himself in turmoil cannot be directed into orderly rule. It is because when one positions himself in turmoil and tries to attain orderly rule, he only multiplies turmoil, whereas when one positions himself in orderly rule and tries to attain orderly rule, then he attains orderly rule. Therefore, sage kings established orderly rule from orderly rule; they did not establish orderly rule from turmoil.

* * *

26.6: The subtle and mysterious words that should be pondered over are difficult to grasp even by a man of superior knowledge. Only one in a myriad will be able to rectify everything without resorting to laws and ordinances, rules and regulations. Hence, the sages rule All-under-Heaven as appropriate to the myriad [and not to a single person]. Thus, if only a knowledgeable [man] can understand something, it cannot become law because not all the people are knowledgeable. If only a worthy can understand something, it cannot become law because not all the people are worthy. Therefore, when the sage makes a law, he must make it clear and easily understandable. When the names are correct, both the ignorant and the knowledgeable can understand them. Law officials and clerks in charge of laws are established as teachers of All-under-Heaven to let the people avoid sinking into a perilous situation.

Hence, when the sages are established in All-under-Heaven, and nobody suffers capital punishment, it is not because they have abolished capital punishment. Rather, the laws are clear and easily understandable, and law officials and clerks are established as teachers to direct [the people] to understand [the law]. The myriad people all understand what should be avoided and what should be pursued. They should avoid disaster and pursue good fortune: all will thereby govern themselves. Thus, the clear-sighted ruler relies on orderly rule and at the end attains orderly rule: hence, All-under-Heaven will be greatly ordered.

FRAGMENT OF "SIX LAWS" (六法)

The fragment of the chapter "Six Laws" is cited in the early Tang collection *Essentials of Orderly Rule from Multiple Books* (*Qunshu zhiyao* 群書治要), compiled in 631 by Wei Zheng 魏徵 (580–643). The short fragment reiterates the importance of changing with the times and liberating oneself from precedents and public opinion.

* * *

The former kings established laws as appropriate to the times; they measured tasks and then regulated undertakings. When laws are appropriate to their times, there is orderly rule; when undertakings correspond to tasks, there is success. Now the times have changed, but the laws have not yet been altered. When one strives to change but continues to maintain affairs according to the past, this means that laws contradict the times, and one's undertakings differ from one's tasks. Hence, although the laws are established, turmoil increases; although one performs the tasks, one's undertakings deteriorate.

Hence, when the sages ordered their states, they neither imitated antiquity nor conformed to current [customs]. They did what was appropriate to the times and therefore succeeded; or, when facing difficulties, they were able to escape. Nowadays the people's customs can be altered,[1] but the laws have not been changed; the conditions of the state have brought about change in its power, but it still commits itself to past tasks. Yet, after all, the law means to rule the people well; the task is [to focus on] useful [aspects] of undertakings. Hence, it has never happened that he whose law is inappropriate for the times and whose tasks are not suitable for utilization was not imperiled.

NOTES

PART I: INTRODUCTION

1. For the problems of the label "Legalist School," see Goldin 2011b; for my view of this term as heuristically convenient nonetheless, see Pines 2014b.

2. Shang 商 was a fief granted to Gongsun Yang in 340 B.C.E., just two years before his downfall and execution. The precise translation of the title *Shangjunshu* 商君書 should be *Book of Shang's Lord* or *Book of the Lord of Shang* (or even *Documents of the Lord of Shang*), but because the title *Book of Lord Shang* became ubiquitous in English studies, I prefer to retain it.

3. See, for example, Schwartz 1985, 330–335; Graham 1989, 267–292; and Lewis 2007, 46–50 (for Lewis's early treatment of Shang Yang, see also Lewis 1990, 61–64, and 1999a, 612–615). Naturally, Shang Yang is discussed in any major study of Legalist thought (Vandermeersch 1965; Ames 1994; Fu Zhengyuan 1996), but even in these publications he is overshadowed by a later and, in the eyes of many scholars, more sophisticated Legalist thinker, Han Fei 韓非 (d. 233 B.C.E.). For engaging discussion of aspects of the thought in the *Book of Lord Shang*, see Puett 2001, 114–117. Shang Yang's ideas are sometimes glossed over altogether: see Nivison 1999.

4. For collections of translations, see Li Yu-ning 1977b; Pines and Defoort 2016a. In looking for Shang Yang–focused articles in English in an indispensable bibliographical tool by Paul R. Goldin (2018), I have discovered only a few: Handelman 1995; Boesche 2008; M. Fischer 2012; Sanft 2014b; King 2018; in addition to my own publications, Pines 2012a, 2013b, 2016a, 2016b, 2016c, forthcoming A. To these one may add a new Ph.D. dissertation (King 2015). Note the marked increase in Shang Yang–related publications in recent years.

5. Leonard S. Perelomov's translation and study of the *Book of Lord Shang*, first published in 1968 and republished with a new afterword in 1993, was one of the finest productions of Soviet Sinology. It probably spurred interest in this text by a dissident Soviet scholar, Vitaly Rubin, whose major study of Chinese political philosophy, one-quarter of which was dedicated to Shang Yang, was published outside the Soviet Union (Rubin 1976, esp. 55–88; republished in Russian in Rubin 1999, 8–76). The *Book of Lord Shang* merited a monograph and partial translation into German (Kroker 1953; Kandel 1985) as well as an introductory-level translation into French (Lévi 1981, 2005). Most recently the full German translation cum study was published by Kai Vogelsang (2017). To translations, one may add two in Japanese (Moriya 1995, completely overshadowed by Yoshinami 1992) and numerous translations into colloquial Chinese, the best of which are those by Gao Heng (1974) and Zhang Jue (1993).

6. For Western scholars' habitual dislike of focusing on too practical and "this-worldly" aspects of early Chinese philosophy, see Pines 2015.

7. *Dongpo quanji* 105:14. All translations are mine unless otherwise noted.

1. SHANG YANG AND HIS TIMES

1. For the interstate dynamics of the Springs-and-Autumns period, see Pines 2002a, 105–135.

2. For the system of hereditary officeholding and hereditary allotments, see Qian Zongfan 1989; for the nature of hereditary allotments, see Lü Wenyu 2006; for the intellectual background of ministerial empowerment, see Pines 2002a, 136–163.

3. For the reforms of the Warring States period, see Yang Kuan 1998, 188–212; Zhao Boxiong 1990; Lewis 1999a. For the rise of *shi*, see Pines 2009, 115–135.

4. For the "iron revolution" and its impact, see Wagner 1993 and compare Yang Kuan 1998, 42–57; for agromanagerial functions of contemporaneous polities, see the example of Qin discussed in Pines with others 2014, 21–25.

5. See more in Lewis 1990, 53–96, and 1999a, 620–630; Yates 1999, 25–30.

6. See more in Pines 2000b (for the idea of unity); 2009, 13–111 (for the ideology of monarchism) and 187–218 (for the views of the lower strata); and 2013a (for meritocracy).

7. The precise nature of Shang Yang's economic reforms and their impact on landowning patterns in the state of Qin has been subject to many controversies ever since Zhu Xi 朱熹 (1130–1200) proposed a revisionist understanding of the phrase "opened up the one-thousand-pace and one-hundred-pace ridges among the fields" in "Kai qianmo bian" 開阡陌辨 (*Huian ji* 72:4–7).

For recent studies, see Moriya Mitsuo [1968] 2010, 52–81; Yuan Lin 2000, 215–257.

8. This inscription is recorded on a measuring vessel, Shang Yang-*fang sheng* 商鞅方升, currently in the possession of the Shanghai Museum (for details, see Wang Hui 1990, 54; Tong Weimin 2013, 312 n. 3).

9. For the introduction to this system of ranks of merit in English, see Loewe 1960; the discussion is updated in Loewe 2010. For systematic discussions in other languages, see Zhu Shaohou 2008; Korolkov 2010, 101–112. For the most detailed attempt to apprehend the impact of Shang Yang's reforms on Qin's social structure, see Du Zhengsheng 1985. Many insightful observations about the system's functioning are scattered throughout Barbieri-Low and Yates 2015; see especially pp. 872–876 and pp. 437–438n130 for further references to relevant secondary studies.

10. Qin allowed rank holders to remit mutilating punishments by performing forced labor for the state's needs. This redemption (hinted at in section 19.7 [as in the translation given here] of the *Book of Lord Shang*) may have been a particularly important incentive for getting a higher rank, given the notorious harshness of Qin law (see Pines with others 2014, 26–27).

11. In the Han dynasty, Shang Yang's name was mentioned along with the great masters of military thought: Sun Wu 孫武 (fl. ca. 500 B.C.E.), Wu Qi 吳起 (d. 381 B.C.E.), and Sun Bin 孫臏 (fl. ca. 350 B.C.E.) (*Hanshu* 23:1085). A text attributed to Shang Yang (possibly a version of the *Book of Lord Shang*) was included in the "military strategists" section of the Han imperial catalog (*Hanshu* 30:1757; see further in chapter 2, part I, and note 8 there). Earlier, Xunzi 荀子 (ca. 310–230 B.C.E.) also mentioned Shang Yang among the most renowned military leaders of the recent past (*Xunzi* X.15: 274 ["Yi bing" 議兵]).

12. According to the information in the *Records of the Historian*, this defeat prompted the state of Wei to relocate its capital to Daliang 大梁 (modern Kaifeng 開封). This is a mistake, however: as other data suggest, the relocation occurred around 361 B.C.E.—that is, before and not after this defeat (Yang Kuan 1998, 280 n. 1).

13. In the state of Chu, it was habitual to date years by the most important event that occurred during the year (see more in Shaughnessy 2014).

14. *Lüshi chunqiu* 22.2:1491–1492 ("Wu yi" 無義); compare *Zhanguo ce* 5.18:204 ("Qin ce 秦策 3").

15. All citations from the *Book of Lord Shang* refer to chapter and section number in the current translation.

16. The *Bamboo Annals* entry is cited in the *Suoyin* gloss on the *Shiji* 68:2233 n. 2.

17. Shang Yang's major settlement, Shang, was recently excavated (Shang Yang fenyi 2006). The archaeologists discovered many remains associated with the

Chu inhabitants of the site before it was occupied by Qin settlers. It is not incidental that Qin's first incursion into Chu came immediately after Shang Yang's enfeoffment (*Shiji* 40:1720).

18. For this interpretation of the title *da liangzao shuliang*, see Tong Weimin 2013, 314–319.

19. *Zhanguo ce* 3.1:71 ("Qin ce 1"). For the popularity of the abdication idea in the middle Warring States period, see Pines 2005b and Allan 2016 and 2015.

20. *Zhanguo ce* 3.1:72 ("Qin ce 1").

21. Shi Jiao is believed to be the author of the *Shizi* 尸子, classified in the Han imperial catalog as belonging to the "miscellaneous school" (*za jia* 雜家). His biographic data are provided by Ban Gu 班固 (32–92 C.E.) (*Hanshu* 30:1741). For aspects of the ideology of the *Shizi*, see Defoort 2001 and P. Fischer 2012.

2. THE TEXT: HISTORY, DATING, STYLE

1. *Han Feizi* V.18:120 ("Nan mian" 南面). This chapter of *Han Feizi* suffers from textual corruption; the original was possibly accompanied by detailed quotations of Shang Yang and of other personalities mentioned thereafter.

2. *Han Feizi* IX.30:225 ("Nei chu shuo shang. Qi shu" 内儲說上七術).

3. *Han Feizi* XIX.49:451 ("Wu du" 五蠹).

4. *Guanzi* is a heterogeneous collection produced between the fourth and the second century B.C.E., attributed to a Qi statesman Guan Zhong 管仲 (d. 645 B.C.E.).

5. Students of Shang Yang's teachings include such eminent personalities as Chao Cuo 晁錯 (d. 154 B.C.E.) and Dongfang Shuo 東方朔 (fl. 130s B.C.E.) (*Hanshu* 49:2276, 65:2864). The influence of *The Book of Lord Shang* on Chao Cuo is observable from Chao's memorials (Schwermann forthcoming); it is also possible (albeit less certain) that some of the book's ideas influenced the early Han Confucian Lu Jia 陸賈 (ca. 240–170 B.C.E.) (Li Cunshan 1998). For the government side's endorsement of Shang Yang during the Salt and Iron Debates in 81 B.C.E., see chapter 4, part I.

6. See *Shiji* 68:2237; *Huainanzi* 20:833.

7. Recall that well into the Han period Shang Yang's military renown rivaled his fame as a leading reformer.

8. See *Hanshu* 30:1757. Among the books eliminated by Ban Gu from the military section, one finds texts associated with *Guanzi* 管子, *Xunzi* 荀子 (named *Sun Qingzi* 孫卿子), *He Guanzi* 鶡冠子, and the like, all of whom are listed separately in the "Masters" section. Wang Shirun's views are given in Zhang Jue 2012, 331.

9. See *Suishu* 34:1003; *Jiu Tangshu* 47:2031.

10. See, for instance, *Tong dian* 1:7, which refers to chapter 15 of the *Book of Lord Shang*.

11. See *Tong zhi* 68:1; *Jun zhai dushu zhi* 30:20–21.

12. For the twenty-five-chapter version, see the comment by Chen Zhensun 陳振孫 (ca. 1183–1262) in *Zhizhai shulu jieti* 10:1; the twenty-four-chapter Yuan recension (lacking chapters 16 and 21) was the one utilized by Yan Wanli 嚴萬里 (1762–1843) for his collation.

13. The twenty-five-chapter recension was in the possession of Song Lian 宋濂 (1310–1381), as recorded in his *Wenxian ji* 文憲集 27:66.

14. The titles of chapters 16 and 21 are preserved in most recensions: they are "Essentials of Punishments" ("Xing yue" 刑約) and "Protecting from Robbers" ("Yu dao" 禦盜). The fragment preserved by Wei Zheng belongs to the chapter "Six Laws" ("Liu fa" 六法), which, judging from its placement in Wei Zheng's collection, was among the first chapters in the Tang dynasty version of the *Book of Lord Shang*.

15. The old glosses of an unidentified author survived in the 1626 republication of Feng Qin's 馮覲 edition of 1559; they were incorporated into Zhang Jue's critical edition (for the difficulty of verifying their authorship, see Zhang Jue 2012, 307–308).

16. The discussion of various currently available recensions is based on Zhang Jue 2012, 305–351.

17. Yan Kejun's most famous project was a compilation of the surviving texts from the pre-Tang period, resulting in his magnum opus, *Complete Texts of High Antiquity, Qin, Han, the Three Kingdoms, and the Six Dynasties* 全上古三代秦漢三國六朝文 (published posthumously in 1893). For the identity of Yan Wanli as Yan Kejun, see Cao Hongjun 1996; Tong Weimin 2013, 7–8 n. 27.

18. For the list of printing errors in Yan's recension and in the Zhejiang recension, see Zhang Jue 2012, 321–323.

19. It is interesting to note parallels between revival of the interest in the *Book of Lord Shang* and revival of interest in the *Mozi*. However, it seems that the impact of the late Qing literati on shaping attitudes toward the *Mozi* (see Defoort 2015) was much greater than their impact on subsequent studies of the *Book of Lord Shang*.

20. All pre-1949 editions of the *Book of Lord Shang* and a great variety of related studies were republished in 2015 in the *Shangjunshu* (*Book of Lord Shang*) section of the *Masters' Compendium* (*Zi zang* 子藏) (Fang Yong 2015).

21. The discussion in this section is largely paralleled in Pines 2016a.

22. Quoted in *Wenxian tongkao* (212:7) by Ma Duanlin 馬端臨 (1254–1332). Zhou is identified in Ma Duanlin's compendium only as "Mr. Zhou"; his identity was tentatively restored by Tong Weimin (2007).

23. See Ma Su, *Yi shi* 115:27; Wang Zhong is cited in Zhang Jue 2012, 399.

24. See, for instance, *Shangzi tiyao* [1778] n.d.

25. For the Republican period insistence on the belatedness of the *Book of Lord Shang* in its entirety and its subsequent rejection as a source for Shang Yang's activities and thought, see, for example, Hu Shi [1919] 1996: 322–323, Liang Qichao [1919] 1996, 80; Luo Genze [1935] 2001; Qian Mu [1935] 2001, 266–267; Guo Moruo [1945] 2008, 236; Qi Sihe [1947] 2001. In contrast to the somewhat cavalier approach adopted in many of these studies, Jan Duyvendak made an earnest, even if by now outdated, attempt to distinguish different temporal layers in the *Book of Lord Shang* ([1928] 1963, 75–87).

26. See Qian Mu [1935] 2001, 266–267; Fu Sinian 2012, 58–59. For a detailed analysis of these two chapter's interrelatedness, see Zheng Liangshu 1989, 82–103.

27. See, for example, Graham 1989, 267–292. Angus Graham's views of the *Book of Lord Shang* (and treatment of the text as secondary to *Han Feizi* in analyzing "Legalist" thought) clearly echo Chinese Republican period studies. David Nivison's (1999) lack of interest in Shang Yang's thought may also be related to this trend. For minuscule interest in the *Book of Lord Shang* in the West, see note 3 in the introduction to part I.

28. Among Western scholars, the concept of accretion is discussed briefly in Lewis 1999b, 58, and Boltz 2005. It is employed most consistently in Brooks and Brooks 1998. Alas, the overtly speculative nature of the Brooks and Brooks study (see Schaberg 2001b) made it difficult to treat the idea of accretion with due seriousness. Paul Fischer recently proposed an alternative "polymorphous texts" paradigm. He considers the masters' texts as "fluid entities variously constructed from related but disparate pericopes circulating independently or in diverse editions," and he dismisses the "accretion" paradigm as one that implies "that once a part of the received text has been 'established,' it can only be added to and not removed" (2009, 39–40 n. 107). I think this statement misrepresents the accretion theory; in fact, there is no major contradiction between views of, say, Mark Lewis and William Boltz and those proposed by Fischer in his "polymorphous text" paradigm. See also Matthias L. Richter's perceptive distinction between *additive* and *transformative* accretion (i.e., one in which new textual segments are added without influencing the original wording and one that does influence earlier parts of the text) (2013, 157–170).

29. This may be the reason why Sima Qian and the *Huainanzi* authors often cite titles of individual chapters when referring to a master's oeuvres. For a different explanation, see Kern 2015, 340–342.

30. In his study of "authentication" debates, Paul Fischer conveniently summarizes various criteria used to determine the text's authenticity and elucidates approaches employed by earlier scholars from the Han to the

Republican period. He considers anachronism as "extrinsic" argument because "a part or the whole of a text is judged anachronistic with regard to other, contemporary writings" (2009, 4). I prefer to call the arguments based on the text's content "internal" (Fischer's "intrinsic") rather than "extrinsic."

31. Zheng Liangshu 1989. Note that my scenario of individual chapters' dating and of intellectual evolution of "Shang Yang's school" differs considerably from Zheng's.

32. The introduction of cavalry into China proper is commonly associated with reforms instituted by King Wuling of Zhao 趙武靈王 (r. 325–299 B.C.E.) in 307 B.C.E. The story of King Wuling's reforms may be spurious, but there is no mention of the usage of cavalry in Chinese armies before around 300 B.C.E. (Yates 2003: 36–57), In the *Book of Lord Shang*, it is mentioned only in chapter 15, which was composed no earlier than 256 B.C.E.

33. It may be noted that no early text—such as the *Lunyu*, the core chapters of the *Mozi* (i.e., chapters 8–37, the earliest section of the book [see Wu Yujiang 1994, 1027–1028]), or the *Laozi*—identifies its opponents by their name. In distinction, naming opponents either individually or collectively (e.g., Ru 儒 [Confucians] and Mo 墨 [Mohists]) is common in texts from the second half of the Warring States period. The earliest text that clearly names the authors' rivals is the *Mengzi*, which was probably composed a generation or so after the bulk of the *Book of Lord Shang* was written.

34. The length of the *Book of Lord Shang* is slightly less than twenty-five thousand words, in comparison to the more than thirty-eight thousand words in the *Mengzi*. For counting the frequency of use of different particles in both texts, I relied on Miao Ruosu and Wu Shiqi 1998 for the *Book of Lord Shang* and on annotator Yang Bojun's appendix to *Mengzi yizhu* for the *Mengzi*.

35. In *Mengzi*, Yang Bojun counts one hundred instances of *gu* and almost four hundred instances of *ze*.

3. THE IDEOLOGY OF THE TOTAL STATE

1. In this chapter, I use the phrase "Shang Yang's thought" for heuristic convenience only. In light of the discussion in chapter 2, part I, one may speak only on the "thought of the *Book of Lord Shang*" rather than of Shang Yang as a person.

2. Fuxi 伏羲, Shennong 神農, the Yellow Thearch 黃帝, Yao 堯, and Shun 舜 were legendary primordial thearchs; Kings Wen 周文王 (d. ca. 1047 B.C.E.) and Wu 周武王 (d. ca. 1043 B.C.E.) are the founders of the Zhou dynasty.

3. *Zhuangzi* 29:778 ("Dao Zhi" 盗跖), 9:246–247 ("Ma ti' 馬蹄); see also the discussion in Pines and Shelach 2005, 140–142.

4. But compare with chapter 23, "Ruler and Minister," which postulates that prior to the formation of the state "the people were in turmoil and disordered" (23.1).

5. It is the most complex of evolutionary models of state formation. For a less-sophisticated but roughly similar model, see *Han Feizi* XIX.49:442–443 ("Wu du" 五蠹). For comparing distinct models of state formation in preimperial texts, see Pines and Shelach 2005 and Pines 2013b.

6. For a general discussion of *gong* and *si* in early Chinese thought, see Liu Zehua 2003, 332–375. For the inapplicability of the translation "public" for the term *gong*, see Goldin 2005, 58–65. For the identification between the ruler and the common interests in the *Book of Lord Shang*, see the discussion in the chapter text.

7. The combination *li zhi fa* 禮之法 (standard of ritual) is peculiar to the *Book of Lord Shang*; it implies here the essential norms of behavior embedded in the broader concept of ritual. For different meanings of the term *li* (禮, ritual) in preimperial discourse, see Pines 2000b.

8. The phrase *xing zhi chang* 性之常, "constant of one's nature," refers here to the fear of death. In seeking repute (and the potential elevation of their status, even if posthumously), the people are ready to sacrifice their lives.

9. The lion's share of modern studies concerned with early Chinese views of human nature focus overwhelmingly on Mengzi and Xunzi. Even when scholars expand the list of texts consulted (e.g., Graham 1967), they commonly ignore Shang Yang's important contribution to these debates. For laudable exceptions, see Xiao Yang 2006; Sato Masayuki 2013a, 155–157, and 2013b, 249–250.

10. Recall that King Wu led the rebellious forces that overthrew the Shang dynasty around 1046 B.C.E. In the aftermath of rebellion, he became the legitimate ruler of All-under-Heaven.

11. Xia 夏 is a semilegendary dynasty that allegedly succeeded the rule of the sage Thearch Shun 舜, whose surname was Yu 虞 (not to be confused with the Great Yu 禹, the legendary founder of the Xia). Tang 湯, the founder of the Shang dynasty, much like King Wu of Zhou, had forcibly seized power from his legitimate predecessor, the Xia king. "Above" refers to higher antiquity, "below" to events of the more immediate past.

12. *Shang* 上, "superiors," may refer here to the ruler alone.

13. For a survey of paleographic materials from preimperial and imperial Qin, see Pines with others 2014, 8–11. One should be cautious in dealing with these materials, which overwhelmingly reflect the viewpoint of Qin administrators; yet it is important to notice that from the currently available materials we have no evidence for the existence of independent elites or even of lineages as notable social units.

14. The size of the armies and their composition (i.e., the preponderance of infantry) are reflected in a series of speeches in the *Stratagems of the Warring*

15. *States* that survey military forces of major contemporaneous states. See a convenient summary in Yang Kuan 1998, 310.

15. One *qing* 頃 equals one hundred *mu* 畝 or 4.6 hectares (Hulsewé 1985, 19).

16. A canton (*xiang* 鄉) is a subcounty unit. For its administration, see Bu Xian-qun 2006.

17. See *Liye Qin jian (yi)* 2012, slip 8–1112 (Chen Wei 2012, 279); see also in Yates 2012–2013 the discussion of this slip and another broken slip (8–420) that may refer to a purchase of rank.

18. The suggestion to increase the price of grain so as to benefit the peasants makes sense, but the text never elaborates how this increase will be achieved. Compare this suggestion with the sophisticated economic policies advocated in the *Guanzi*, especially in the chapters called "Light and Heavy" ("Qing-zhong" 輕重) (Goldin forthcoming).

19. Recall that during Shang Yang's time Qin was still lagging behind most eastern states in its commercial development. It was not until 378 B.C.E. that markets were instituted in its cities, and coins were introduced only in 337 B.C.E. (i.e., after Shang Yang's death) (*Shiji* 6:289; the relative belatedness of monetarization of the Qin economy is reflected in archaeological data provided in Chen Longwen 2006, 222–244; note that Chen himself does not analyze this belatedness). Conceivably, full-fledged agromanagerial economy evolved in Qin only gradually in the aftermath of Shang Yang's reforms, and it is not reflected in the *Book of Lord Shang*.

20. See Creel 1974, 147–149; Goldin 2011b; and "Notes on Translation" in part II of this book.

21. It is not clear which utensils are referred to here. Duyvendak considers the term *qi* 器 (utensils or vessels) to be a substitute for the term *law* ([1928] 1963, 213 n. 1), but I am not convinced by his examples.

22. If my analysis of Shang Yang's legal thought is correct, the idea of a "mass line" developed by Mao Zedong in the 1930s bears a curious resemblance to it: first, the party should absorb "unsystematic and scattered ideas" of the masses; second, it should rework them; and third, it should bring the reworked ideas back to the masses "until the masses embrace them as their own" (Schram 1989, 46). For a similar interpretation of Shang Yang's ideas from the perspective of the modern philosophy of the "rule of law," see Wu Baoping and Lin Cunguang 2015.

23. For the early imperial period requirement of passports and transit documents for allowing movement among different counties, see Barbieri-Low and Yates 2015, 1115–1117. Conceivably, this requirement was a by-product of the system of total registration of the populace initiated by Shang Yang.

24. The phrase "those who obtain emoluments by talking" probably refers to scholars; "beneficial people" are probably farmers.

25. For Qin population registers discovered at the site of Liye, see, for example, Hsing 2014 and Sanft 2015, q.v. for further references. For keeping records of

oxen, horses, hay, and straw, see Qin statutes unearthed from Tomb 11, Shui-hudi (Hulsewé 1985, 100, B28–29, and 38, A20). See also Yates 2012–2013 and Yates 2013 for the degree of administrative control of the localities in the Qin Empire.

26. Gideon Shelach was the first to apply Scott's analysis to understanding the mechanisms of the state of Qin (2014, 134–135).

27. The first text that pairs Shang Yang and Shen Buhai is *Han Feizi* XVII.43:397–00 ("Ding fa" 定法). Pairing Shen Buhai and Shang Yang and adding Han Fei himself became common from the early Han dynasty (see, e.g., *Huainanzi* 6:230, 11:423, 20:833). Sima Qian identified these three thinkers as adherents of the teaching of "performance and title" (*xing ming* 刑名) (*Shiji* 62:2146, 68:2227; translation borrowed from Goldin 2013, 8). This term is synonymous to the later term *fa jia* (i.e., Legalists) (Creel 1974, 140).

28. I normally translate *shi* 士 as "men-of-service," but here the term may more broadly mean all the males of elite and subelite status.

29. See, for example, *Guanzi* XV.46:916 ("Ming fa" 明法); *Han Feizi* II.6:31–33 ("You du" 有度), II.7:41–42 ("Er bing" 二柄), *et saepe.*

30. For the importance of this topic in Warring States–period texts, see Pines 2009, 82–107.

31. This concept of an impersonal system that would accommodate even a mediocre ruler became fully developed in the *Han Feizi* (see, for instance, *Han Feizi*, XVII.40:392 ["Nan shi" 難勢]). This said, Han Fei was also aware of the potential damage that an inept ruler may cause to his state (see Graziani 2015).

32. Referring to the legend of Yao's 堯 abdication in favor of Shun 舜 and Shun's abdication in favor of Yu 禹, acts that violated the abdicators' obligations toward their progeny. See more in Allan 2015, 2016; Pines 2005b.

33. Referring to the distribution of territorial power among the relatives of the ruling house; this pattern of rule employed by the Western Zhou 西周 (ca. 1046–771 B.C.E.) is associated here also with the preceding Xia and Shang dynasties.

34. "Peripatetic eaters" (*youshizhe* 游食者) refers to all those who could make their living by moving from one place to another—that is, primarily scholars but also merchants and artisans (see a detailed discussion of them in section 6.6). These people who "treat their dwellings lightly" (3.7) are contrasted with peasants, who make their living from tilling the soil and therefore are not prone to move.

35. Laozi 3, quoted from *Boshu Laozi*, 237.

36. In the short text of the *Laozi*, statements in favor of the people's simplicity (*pu* 樸) recur thrice (paragraphs 19, 33, 57). In the *Book of Lord Shang*, the term *pu* is used no less than seventeen times to depict the desirable condition of the people. In other texts, the usage of this term in a positive context of

depicting the people's conditions is very limited: I discovered two references each in *Guanzi*, *Han Feizi*, *Lüshi chunqiu*, and *Xunzi*; notably, in the latter this term refers specifically to the condition of the Qin people in the aftermath of Shang Yang's reforms (*Xunzi* XI.16: 303 ["Qiang guo" 彊國]).

37.   Of course, the term *jiao* was employed in different contexts by thinkers unrelated to Confucius and his followers, but the predominant usage of it in political discourse is clearly "Confucian oriented."

38.   The text refers to "transformation" of customs in section 8.1 and to unification of popular customs in section 17.1. These topics became increasingly important for the state of Qin on the eve of the imperial unification and in its aftermath, as can be judged from such texts as the *Speech Document* (*Yu shu* 語書) from Tomb 11, Shuihudi (*Shuihudi* [1990] 2001, 13; Lin Shaoping 2015), and from the Qin imperial stele inscriptions (especially the Kuaiji 會稽 stele [*Shiji* 6:262; see also Lewis 2006, 192–212]). In the *Book of Lord Shang*, however, the unification of customs never becomes an important topic.

39.   For Graham's views, see Graham 1989, 267–285. The issue of the role of morality (or the lack thereof) in Shang Yang's thought is often debated in Chinese studies; for a recent comprehensive discussion, see Xu Jianliang 2012, 196–280, which also supplies further references.

40.   See, for example, *Mengzi* 1.6:12–13 ("Liang Hui Wang shang" 梁惠王上).

41.   Interestingly, Mao Zedong's earliest surviving essay was dedicated precisely to Shang Yang! See Schram 1992–2004, 1:5–6.

42.   Compare this speech to Mao's speech "On the Ten Major Relationships" (April 25, 1956), in which he proclaimed the ultimate expectation that "one day we will be able to do away with the Communist Party and the dictatorship of the proletariat. Our task is to hasten their extinction." Dialectically, though, hastening this day meant strengthening "the dictatorship of the proletariat" in the short term (https://www.marxists.org/reference/archive /mao/selected-works/volume-5/mswv5_51.htm).

43.   For the Qin stele inscriptions, see Kern 2000; for an analysis of the First Emperor's propaganda as realization of the messianic expectations of preimperial thinkers, see Pines 2014c.

44.   *Dongpo quanji*, 105:14.

4. THE TEXT'S RECEPTION AND IMPACT

1.   The best account heretofore on the changing views of Shang Yang prior to Mao Zedong's death (1976) is by Li Yu-ning (1977a, xiii–cxx); for the next decades, see Pines and Defoort 2016a. For a shorter and analytically less-sophisticated discussion, see Zeng Zhenyu 2003.

2.　　This placement of Shang Yang in the pantheon of victimized loyal servants is most vivid in *Zhanguo ce* 5.18:204–205 ("Qin ce 秦策 3") and in *Han Feizi* IV.13:97 ("He shi" 和氏).

3.　　Zhang Binglin 1900, 35.695.

4.　　Even Han Fei did not hesitate at times to expose weaknesses of Shang Yang's views (and perhaps even to exaggerate them a little bit). See *Han Feizi* XVII.43: 397–400 ("Ding fa" 定法).

5.　　*Zhanguo ce* 3.1:71–72 ("Qin ce 秦策 1").

6.　　Xunzi's views of Qin are present in *Xunzi* XI.16:303–304 ("Qiang guo" 強國). Although the text does not directly mention Shang Yang, it clearly attributes the Qin's strengthening during the past "four generations" to this reformer. Jia Yi's positive assessment of Shang Yang's reforms appears in his critical essay about the rule of Qin, "On Faulting Qin" ("Guo Qin lun" 過秦論), for which see *Xinshu* 1:1 and *Shiji* 6:278–279 (see also Sabattini 2017). Jia Yi's general attitude toward Shang Yang is somewhat controversial: Jia Yi is identified in the *Shiji* (130:3319) as an expounder of the ideas of Shang Yang and Shen Buhai, but the *Hanshu* (48:2244) alternatively cites him as Shang Yang's vehement critic. See also criticism of Shang Yang in Jia Yi's *Xinshu* 3:97–98 ("Shi bian" 時變). For Sima Qian's laudations of Shang Yang's practical achievements, see *Shiji* 68:2231.

7.　　*Mengzi* 7.14: 175 ("Li Lou shang" 離婁上).

8.　　*Lüshi chunqiu* 22.2:1491–1492 ("Wu yi"). The *Lüshi chunqiu* mentions elsewhere the pre-Qin stage of Shang Yang's career (11.5:605–606 ["Chang jian" 長見]).

9.　　For the nature of the *Lüshi chunqiu*, see Knoblock and Riegel 2000, 1–59; compare Sellmann 2002. For reading the text as a self-promotion campaign by men-of-service, see Pines 2009, 133–135.

10.　　For negative references to Shang Yang in the *Huainanzi*, see, for example, *Huainanzi* 6:230, 11:423, 20:833.

11.　　For changing views of the Qin dynasty, see Pines 2014a. For parallel changes in the views of Shang Yang, see, for example, Zeng Zhenyu 2003, 116–118. For a more detailed analysis of changing views of Shang Yang under the Han dynasty, see Wang Zijin 2012, 202–208.

12.　　*Yantielun* II.7:93–97 ("Fei Yang" 非鞅). As Leonard Perelomov notes, frequent references to Shang Yang throughout the *Salt and Iron Debates* indicate the great importance of this thinker's legacy during Emperor Wu's reign and immediately thereafter (1993, 129).

13.　　Michael Loewe's (1974, 1986) treatment of the first-century B.C.E. history is still the best introduction to the events of this age; for some important correctives, see also Lewis 1999b, 337–362, and Cai Liang 2014.

14.　　This accusation against Shang Yang was voiced by the major Confucian thinker Dong Zhongshu 董仲舒 (c. 195–115 B.C.E.), who claimed that Shang

Yang destroyed the ideal "well-field" (*jing tian* 井田) system of the past, allowing the land to be bought and sold and causing the pauperization of the peasants (*Hanshu* 24A:1137). This assertion is demonstrably wrong: the possibility of buying or selling land emerged only under the Imperial Qin (Yuan Lin 2000); it is not related at all to Shang Yang's reforms.

15. The text under discussion is quoted in Pei Yin's 裴駰 (fifth century) commentary on the *Records of the Historian* (*Shiji* 68:2238). Pei Yin claims that it is part of the *New Arrangement* (*Xinxu* 新序), a collection normally attributed to Liu Xiang (see more in Sanft 2011, 132); but a later commentary by Sima Zhen 司馬貞 (eighth century) identifies the author as Liu Xin. The cited section is not included in the current version of the *New Arrangement*.

16. Note the double use of the "internal/inside" (*nei* 內) and "external/outside" (*wai* 外) juxtaposition: in the first sentence it refers to domestic (economic) affairs versus foreign (war) affairs; in the second it refers to activities inside the court and outside it, in society at large.

17. Referring to "Hong fan" 洪範, one of the ideological centerpieces of the *Canon of Documents* (*Shangshu* 12:190b; for "Hong fan," see also Nylan 1992).

18. Referring to the poem "Great East" ("Da dong" 大東) of the *Canon of Poems* (*Mao shi* 13:460b).

19. *Sima Methods [of War]* (*Sima fa* 司馬法) is one of the major military classics of the Warring States period (see Sawyer 1993, 107–144). Houji 后稷 (Lord Millet), a legendary progenitor of the Zhou dynasty, is frequently viewed as the inventor of agriculture. On the evolving views of Houji, see Tomita Michie 2010.

20. See *Xunzi* XI.16:303–304 ("Qiang guo" 強國).

21. Both the knife and the saw were used for mutilating punishments.

22. Reading *lun* 論 (to make a legal decision) as *lun* 淪 (to drown).

23. The author ends with the assessment that Shang Yang could be employed effectively should King Huiwen "moderate his laws, add clemency, and extend this with trustworthiness" (*Shiji* 68:2238).

24. For Wang Anshi's poem and its place in his legacy, see Yang Xiaoshan 2007, 77. For Sima Guang's praise of Shang Yang's trustworthiness in dealing with the Qin people, see *Zizhi tongjian* 2:48–49. For the antagonism between Wang Anshi and Sima Guang, see Bol 1993.

25. Zhang Jue conveniently assembles multiple citations regarding Shang Yang and the *Book of Lord Shang* from the Warring States period to the Republican period (2012, 352–415). Although inevitably incomplete, this assemblage allows us to assess major trends in Shang Yang–related discussions through the ages.

26. I am grateful to Harry Miller for confirming my observation that extant Zhang Juzheng's materials lack direct references to Shang Yang. Wei

Qingyuan mentions similarities between Zhang's thought and the ideas of Shang Yang (1999, 8, 306, 314) but fails to notice the significant silence of Zhang with regard to Shang Yang persona.

27. Note that the term *zhengzhijia* in Zhang's writings differs from its current usage to mean "politician."

28. See Zhang Binglin 1900, 35.695–699. For Zhang Binglin's career and thought, see, for example, Laitinen 1990; Shimada Kenji 1990; Wong 2010.

29. For Kang Youwei's ideology, see, for example, Chang Hao 1987; compare Zarrow 2012, 24–88; for his intellectual rivalry with Zhang Binglin, see Wong 2010. Li Yu-ning briefly considers Shang Yang's possible influence on Kang's thought (1977a, l–li), but all of the examples she gives come from Kang's favorite book, *Gongyang zhuan* 公羊傳, and its commentaries.

30. See Mai Menghua [n.d.] 1986; Li Yu-ning 1977a, lv–lxiv.

31. See Liang Qichao [1906] 2003, esp. 342–345 and Liang Qichao [1911] 2014.

32. For instance, Wang Shirun (whose study was published in 1915), was a graduate of the School of Law at Hōsei University 法政大學, Tokyo, and made a legal career arriving at the position of a judge in China's supreme criminal court (1933). Jian Shu (whose edition was published in 1931) was a member of the Central Committee of the Guomindang (Kuomintang, Party of the Nation), and a head of secretariat of the ninth field army during the Northern Expedition of 1926–1928. Chen Qitian, who authored a major study of the *Book of Lord Shang* in 1935, was a leader of China's Youth Party (one of the "Third Way" parties that tried to navigate between the GMD and the Communist Party of China [CPC]).

33. See for instance the prefaces to the editions by Wang Shirun (1915) and Zhu Shizhe (1921) (cited from Zhang Jue 2012, 329–334, 338–342).

34. For Chen's political views, see Fung 1991. For his position as the representative of "New Legalists," see Yu Zhong 2016, 184.

35. For the book burning in Qin and resultant controversies, see Petersen 1995; Kern 2000, 183–196; Pines 2009, 180–183, and 2014a.

36. For a very good summary of pre–Cultural Revolution views of Shang Yang in the People's Republic of China, see Li Yu-ning 1977a, lxxx–lxxxxvi.

37. For the anti-Confucian campaign (more precisely, the "criticize Lin [Biao 林彪, 1907–1971], criticize Confucius [pi Lin pi Kong 批林批孔]" campaign), see Louie 1980, 97–136, and Perelomov 1993, 372–386. For the political background for the campaign, see MacFarquhar and Schoenhals 2006, 366–373.

38. The classical endorsement of Shang Yang is an article by Liang Xiao 梁效, which is translated in Li Yu-ning 1977b, 180–195. The name "Liang Xiao" stands for "Two Schools" (*liang xiao* 兩校). It was a penname used by the Great Criticism Group of Peking University and Tsinghua University (Macfarquhar and Schoenhals 2006, 368).

39. For summaries of recent research trends regarding the *Book of Lord Shang*, see Zhao Yuzhuo 2010; Tong Weimin 2013, 11–16; Pines and Defoort 2016b.
40. This common-ground approach is fully visible in the studies by Liu Zehua (1991, 1996, 2000).
41. For a further assault on Shang Yang by Zhang Linxiang, see his monograph dedicated to the *Book of Lord Shang* (Zhang Linxiang 2008, 212–242).
42. See, for example, Wang Shilong 2012; Cheng Bu 2013; Zhu Yongjia 2013, to mention only a few recent publications that strongly and unequivocally endorse Shang Yang. Of somewhat higher scholarly value is yet another recent pro–Shang Yang publication, Zhao Ming 2013.
43. See the blog entry "Nothing Blacker Than the *Book of Lord Shang*: What Did This Restricted Book Speak About?" 最黑不過《商君書》, 這本禁書都講了些 什麼? (December 22, 2015, http://toutiao.com/i6230964693549187585/). The term *restricted* implies that the book served emperors only and was not supposed to be seen by the masses. Compare Wu Xiaobo's 吳曉波 blog entry "Beware of the Ghost of Shang Yang-ism" 警惕商鞅主義的幽靈 (July 29, 2010, http://www.ftchinese.com/story/001033813?full=y). Expressing the opposite view is the blog "How We Misread Shang Yang?" 我們對商鞅還存在哪些誤讀? (January 18, 2016, http://www.bjd.com.cn/10llzk/201601/18/t20160118 _10794896.html).
44. For that speech, see http://cpc.people.com.cn/n/2014/0522/c64387-25048530 .html (accessed February 11, 2016).
45. Glossing "strong" as referring to the "strong people" rather than to "a strong army" not only is "politically correct" but also apparently dissociates the slogan from the *Book of Lord Shang* with its insistence on "weakening the people" (as given in the title of chapter 20). However, the view that Shang Yang promulgated the goal of "a rich state and a strong people" is not new: it was advocated by one of Shang Yang's admirers, Sang Hongyang, during the Salt and Iron Debates of 81 B.C.E. (*Yantielun* II.7:93 ["Fei Yang" 非鞅]).
46. Bryan Van Norden's analysis of a "real" option (in which case "going over" new ideas is recommendable) and a "notional" one (which can at most provide "some inspiration for thoughts about elements missing from modern life") (1996, 226) is borrowed from Williams 1985.

PART II: NOTES ON TRANSLATION

1. For readers interested in the original texts by these commentators: all are collected in volumes 6–8 of the *Shangjunshu* (*Book of Lord Shang*) section of the *Masters' Compendium* (*Zi zang* 子藏) (Fang Yong 2015) and are listed in terms of their historical sequence here. See Yu Yue [1885] 2015; Sun Yirang

[1894] 2015; Tao Hongqing [n.d.] 2015; Yu Chang [n.d.] 2015; Wang Shirun [1915] 2015; Yin Tongyang [1923] 2015; Jian Shu [1931] 2015; and Zhu Shizhe [1948] 2015.

1. REVISING THE LAWS

1.   See Burton Watson's translation (1993, 91–92).
2.   Nothing is known about Shang Yang's two opponents, Gan Long and Du Zhi, but based on their surnames it appears they were descendants of aristocratic lineages from the Zhou domain who served at the court of Qin. The Du lineage was prominent already during the Western Zhou 西周 (ca. 1046–771 B.C.E.); its members later served the state of Qin, which inherited the lands of the Zhou domain (for instance, a Qin officer named Du Hui 杜回 is mentioned in the *Zuo zhuan* [Xuan 15.5:764]). The Gan lineage came from the Eastern Zhou royal domain, descendants of King Xiang of Zhou 周襄王 (r. 651–619 B.C.E.).
3.   "Altars of soil and grain" (*sheji* 社稷) is a referent to the collective entity of the state's inhabitants in texts from the Springs-and-Autumns period on (Masubuchi Tatsuo 1963, 139–163).
4.   "The hundred clans" (*bai xing* 百姓) is a referent for the entire populace in Warring States period texts.
5.   Guo Yan 郭偃 is a seventh-century B.C.E. diviner (*bu* 卜) from the state of Jin. In the Warring States period, his name became associated with exceptional political wisdom. A text attributed to him, *Guo Yan lun shi* 郭偃論士 (Guo Yan discusses men-of-service), was discovered in 1972 in Tomb 1, Yinqueshan, Linyi 臨沂銀雀山 (Shandong) (*Yinqueshan 2* 2010, 181–182; Yates 2004, 355–358). The term *fa* 法 in the title of the text attributed to Guo Yan apparently refers to "methods" rather than to "laws."
6.   The Three Dynasties are (the semilegendary) Xia 夏, Shang 商 (ca. 1600–1046), and Zhou; the list of the Five Hegemons varies from one source to another, but it invariably includes Lord Huan of Qi 齊桓公 (r. 685–643 B.C.E.) and Lord Wen of Jin 晉文公 (r. 636–628 B.C.E.), in addition to three other powerful overlords of the Springs-and-Autumns period.
7.   Following Gao Heng (1974, 213), I emend *nu* 怒 (to display anger) with *nu* 孥 (to execute the wife and children of a convicted criminal). The latter preserves the idea of the escalation of violence as times passes, which fits well the overall perceptions in the *Book of Lord Shang*. However, the original reading as *nu* 怒 is equally acceptable.
8.   Fuxi 伏羲, Shennong 神農, the Yellow Thearch 黄帝, Yao 堯, and Shun 舜 were legendary thearchs; Kings Wen 周文王 (d. ca. 1047 B.C.E.) and Wu 周武王 (d. ca. 1043 B.C.E.) are the founders of the Zhou dynasty.

9. "Orders to Cultivate Wastelands" is the title of the second chapter of the *Book of Lord Shang*, although it is not at all clear that the chapter's contents are related to the order supposedly issued by Lord Xiao.

2. ORDERS TO CULTIVATE WASTELANDS

1. Wang Shirun suggests doubling the phrase 百官之情不相稽, which means that the hundred officials' speedy performance is the reason the peasants will have extra time. Following Zhang Jue (2012, 18 n. 4), I do not find this emendation necessary. "Extra time" presumably means more time to invest in agricultural activities.

2. Most commentators agree that *shang yi* 上壹 refers to the uniformity of the taxation system, with *shang* acting as a verb (to pay taxes upward). *Ping* 平 refers here, pace Duyvendak ([1928] 1963, 176), not to "peace" but to equality: the annual adjustment of tax rates according to the yields will ensure that nobody becomes excessively rich or impoverished (for the actual functioning of the Qin system of taxation, see Korolkov 2010, 142–169).

3. Following the parallel sentence two sentences later, and following the general context, it appears reasonable to emend 臣 (ministers) here to 官 (officials).

4. Following Gao Heng (1974, 20 n. 6), I emend *xia* 下 with *shang* 上 and read them as a hierarchy of importance (first, attitude toward the rulers; second, attitude toward the officials). Alternatively, the meaning would be "the inferiors do not reject superiors, and in the middle they are not embittered toward the officials." None of the proposed reconstructions of this sentence (see Zhang Jue 2012, 18–19 n. 6) is entirely satisfactory.

5. During the Warring States period, the boundaries between foreign and domestic affairs were not strictly delineated; from contemporaneous anecdotes, we know of ministers who gained their position through the support of a neighboring state and even of some ministers who served several competing polities simultaneously (see Lewis 1999a, 633–634, for the latter). The dislike of foreign meddling in one's domestic affairs is expressed several times in the *Book of Lord Shang* (see, e.g., sections 3.2 and 3.3; cf. *Han Feizi* XIX.49:453 ["Wu du" 五蠹]). It is not clear here how the esteem of learning and foreign meddling in domestic appointments are connected; the connection presumably has something to do with traveling "persuaders" (*shui ke* 說客), who relied on their rhetorical skills to enhance their position in the interstate market of talent.

6. From the context, it seems that those "who rely on their mouths" are the retainers of officers and nobles, whose bountiful emoluments allowed them to sustain many dependents.

7.   Following Gao Heng (1974, 21 n. 11), I read *shi* 使 as "to conscript" for public works. Imposing heavy levies on household members not engaged in agricultural production served the goal of reducing the attractiveness of non-agricultural pursuits; see section 2.13 in the text.

8.   This passage is paralleled in the chapter "Ruling the State" ("Zhi guo" 治國) of the *Guanzi* (XV.48:924; Rickett 1998, 177).

9.   The logic behind this statement is obscure. Wang Shirun (cited in Zhang Jue 2012, 21 n. 1) argued that "sell" and "buy" should be reversed: when the peasants know that grain cannot be bought elsewhere, they will have to work hard to produce it. Ma Zongshen refutes this commonly accepted interpretation: he considers the clause "If peasants cannot sell grain, then indolent peasants will strenuously exert themselves" in the context of Shang Yang's efforts to suppress commerce and encourage the peasants to deliver extra grain to the state granaries and not to private merchants (1985, 5 n. 26). Because peasants will be rewarded for extra contribution of grain (see, e.g., sections 20.3 and 22.2), they will "strenuously exert themselves" in the fields.

10. In the years of good harvests, the merchants are presumably overjoyed because they can buy extra grain and sell it, with copious profits, in the years of famine.

11. From the context, it is evident that hired labor was not used in agriculture but in other works maintained by the nobles. It is not at all clear, though, how the usage of hired labor would affect the "favored sons" (*ai zi* 愛子); it is not even clear whether the indolent favored sons come from noble families (How would they benefit from hiring the laborers?) or from the peasantry, who might have sent favored sons to work for the nobles because this work was probably less demanding than tilling and sowing.

12. It is not clear whether only the hirelings will have to shift to agricultural activities or also "favored sons and indolent people."

13. Establishing state control over forestry, hunting, fishing, and possibly mining ("unify[ing] [control over] mountains and marshes") is yet another step aimed at limiting the profitability of nonagricultural exploits.

14. Reading *pu* 樸 here as referring to the original cost of production.

15. Yu Yue proposed reading *zhu* 誅 as a loan for *zhu* 朱 or *zhu* 侏, synonymous with *yu* 愚, meaning "ignorant." Gao Heng (1974, 25 n. 44) follows him. This explanation has the advantage of avoiding a meaningless reading of *zhu* as "punishment" because, according to the chapter's authors, the ignorant are not supposed to be punished. However, it is also not clear why the binome *zhuyu* 誅愚 appears first in a negative context (these people are not supposed to find sustenance) and then as a positive synonym of "tranquil peasants." Zhang Jue tries to resolve the contradiction by parsing the sentences differently: "Do not let the people shift locations on their own initiative: then they

will be ignorant" (2012, 27 n. 2). The problem with this solution is a very awk-ward parsing that is at odds with the style of the chapter.

16. Following Gao Heng (1974, 25 n. 44) I accept earlier suggestions by Sun Yirang and Yu Chang, reading the second character *nong* 農 as redundant and replac-ing it with *zhi* 之 (so that 亂農農民 becomes 亂農之民)

17. "Minor sons," *yuzi* 餘子, are all those sons (from the second down) who did not have the right to inherit their father's position. Here the term presum-ably refers to the sons of the old hereditary nobility, who, although techni-cally ineligible for the father's noble status, were still protected by him from labor obligations and might have also enjoyed preferential access to offices. By eliminating these two rights, Shang Yang was effectively undermining aristocratic lineages.

18. Gao Heng reads *shi* 世 as *shi* 使 (1974, 26 n. 47). Otherwise, the minor sons are supposed to be conscripted on a hereditary basis, which does not make sense.

19. In the translation of this sentence, I relied heavily on Zhang Jue's gloss (2012, 29–30 n. 4).

20. From the *Zuo zhuan*, we know many examples of nobles' minor sons who served as stewards in other noble lineages, perhaps enjoying a network of mutual assistance and protection. Some of them could eventually be appointed to higher positions. Shang Yang suggests abolishing this possibility.

21. Here, *guo* 國 is juxtaposed to *bai xian* 百縣, "the hundred counties," which suggests that it refers to the capital and not to the entire state.

22. "Drifting and settling" refers to the peripatetic mode of life of many officials of the Warring States period, who crossed borders in search of better employ-ment opportunities, drifting from one state to another until settling in one of them. Ironically, Shang Yang personally was a beneficiary of this mode of life: a native of the state of Wei 衛, he first was employed in Wei 魏 and then shifted his allegiance to Qin.

23. For *bian* 變 as "extraordinary things," see Gao Heng's gloss (1974, 26 n. 51). *Fang* 方 (methods) may refer to the expertise of so-called technical special-ists or magicians (*fangshi* 方士).

24. For the army markets in the Warring States period, see Tong Weimin 2013, 94–96.

25. Gao Heng suggests omitting a few characters in this sentence (1974, 27 nn. 58–59) and reconstructs it as follows: "those who steal the grain will have no place to sell it; those who transport the grain will not hoard it privately."

26. My interpretation of this passage differs from that of other commentators. I think that it defines for the first time the issue of one's responsibility for one's nominees and the existence of dossiers of each official's personal career (for an example of such a dossier, see document 8-269 from Liye [*Liye* 2012,

26; Dai Weihong 2014]). The idea is to establish firm control over one's decisions when in office so as to prevent the unauthorized employment of junior
administrative staff. Doing so will assumedly reduce sinecures and direct
more of the population toward agricultural work.

27. Following Wang Shirun's reading of *ao* 敖 (haughty) as *ao* 遨 (drifting) (Zhang
Jue 2012, 33 n. 6). Otherwise, the sentence would say, "the people are not
haughty." Both readings are unsatisfactory because the connection between
the people's "drifting" or "haughtiness" and the officials' morality is not self-
evident, but I failed to find a better alternative.

28. In all likelihood, the merchants' private dependents were relieved of labor
obligations to the state, which might have encouraged some peasants to seek
the merchants' patronage (this situation of screening one's dependants from
corvée obligations recurred many times later in Chinese history, most notably at the end of the Han dynasty and for centuries thereafter). By naming
these servants as eligible for corvée service, Shang Yang both undermined
the merchants' social power and created a negative incentive for peasants
to seek the merchants' patronage.

29. That is, the merchants will have no spare time to travel throughout the country in search of profit.

30. "Embellishments" probably refers to the rites performed when the merchants travel across the country. Once they stop traveling, no rites will be
performed as well.

31. The authors are apparently pointing to the danger that malevolent clerks
might become patrons of the criminals.

3. AGRICULTURE AND WARFARE

1. "Exhausting" (*lao* 勞) here means that the people are engaged in agriculture and warfare but do not benefit from these pursuits (Zhang Jue 2012,
40 n. 3).

2. The addition in figure brackets follows Gao Heng's suggestion (1974, 32 n. 5).

3. Reading *kong* 空 as equivalent to *kong* 孔; see Zhang Jue 2012, 41 n. 5. Compare a similar recommendation in *Guanzi* XXII.73:1262 ("Guo xu" 國蓄) (Rickett 1998, 378). Yet in *Guanzi* the "single opening" refers to the ruler's focus
on a single item of price manipulation, whereas in the *Book of Lord Shang* it
refers to agriculture and warfare. See the gloss by Ma Yuancai 馬元材 (a.k.a.
Ma Feibai 馬非百, 1896–1984) in *Guanzi*, 1262. For the importance of maintaining "a single opening" for benefits, see also *Book of Lord Shang* 20.6, 5.8, 13.5.

4. "Foreign powers" evidently refers to foreign states, which often meddled in
the domestic affairs of their rivals by fostering ties with powerful statesmen.
See section 2.3 and note 5 for that chapter.

5. Zhang Jue (2012, 42 n. 13) notices that the word *jiao* 教 (teaching) should be understood here as standing for the related term *xiao* 效 (to emulate): if the people emulate the behavior of elites and subelites and disengage from agriculture and warfare, the state will be dismembered. The same meaning applies to the word *jiao* at the end of section 3.3.

6. "Peddling influence to underlings" refers to promoting lower officials as a private favor and not according to the constant norms advocated by the author(s).

7. Following Zhang Jue 2012, 44 n. 10, I read *mo* 末 as a dialectic variant meaning "to seek."

8. Reading *guan* 官 as a verb: "to appoint officials" (Zhang Jue 2012, 46 n. 1). This usage recurs throughout the chapter.

9. Reading *zhuan* 搏 here and throughout the *Book of Lord Shang* as standing for *zhuan* 專: "concentrate," "focus," "consolidate," "unify."

10. When the ruler is fond of "words" and promotions are whimsical, without regard to constant norms, this behavior allows the people alternative ways of enrichment and social advancement aside from agriculture and warfare.

11. The Monarch (*wang* 王) or the True Monarch (*wang zhe* 王者) here and throughout the text stands for an ideal ruler, the unifier of All-under-Heaven, the apex of the authors' expectations. For this figure, see more in Pines 2009.

12. Emending *zuo* 作 (make) with *fei* 非 (not), following Gao Heng (1974, 35 n. 28).

13. Compare to sections 4.3 and 13.4.

14. "Peripatetic eaters" (*youshizhe* 游食者) is a referent in the *Book of Lord Shang* to all those who can make their living by moving from one place to another—that is, primarily scholars but also merchants and artisans (see a detailed discussion of them in section 6.6). These people who "treat their dwellings lightly" (3.7) are contrasted with peasants, who make their living from tilling the soil and, therefore, are not prone to moving from one place to another.

15. *Xiang* 鄉 (canton) in Imperial Qin was a subcounty unit of sizable proportions (as judged from Liye materials). In this context, it perhaps refers to a smaller rural unit of a few hamlets (hence, one bundle of *Poems* and *Documents* in every *xiang* means that these texts proliferated widely).

16. Note that here and elsewhere *zhan* 戰, "fighting," in the *Book of Lord Shang* refers exclusively to *offensive* warfare; hence, it is often juxtaposed with *shou* 守, "defense."

17. That is, they can wage war.

18. This promise (which is repeated verbatim in section 4.5) is somewhat discouraging because it implies a huge delay in unifying All-under-Heaven (the precondition for the ruler to become the True Monarch). It is possible that the passage came from an early stage of Shang Yang's reforms, when ultimate victory over all enemies still appeared somewhat unrealistic. Compare Mengzi's estimate that military unification of All-under-Heaven is

unattainable: it is like "looking for a fish by climbing a tree" (*Mengzi* 1.7:16 ["Liang Hui Wang 梁惠王 shang"]).

19.   This is an odd digression from the book's constant insistence on rewards and punishments as the essential means to rule the people; the passage possibly hints at the ideal future situation in which the people have already internalized the law, so there is no need for either rewards or punishments. Compare sections 17.1–17.3.

4. ELIMINATING THE STRONG, WITH 20. WEAKENING THE PEOPLE AND 5. EXPLAINING THE PEOPLE

1.   The existence of an internal exegesis is not peculiar to the *Book of Lord Shang*; the same thing can be found, for instance, in the *Wu xing* 五行 text discovered in both Tomb 1, Guodian 郭店 (Hubei), and Tomb 3, Mawangdui 馬王堆 (Hunan); the second provided exegesis to the first (Pang Pu 2000). For more parallels, see, for example, the chapters "Ban fa" 版法 and "Ban fa jie" 版法解 or "Xing shi" 形勢 and "Xing shi jie" 形勢解 of the *Guanzi*.

2.   In making this rearrangement, I was inspired by W. Allyn Rickett's (2001) similar treatment of parallel cases in the *Guanzi*.

3.   As explained in section 4.2 and in the exegetical passage 20.1, the first "strong" refers to powerful and not submissive people; the second refers to the politics of strengthening, rather than weakening, the people. A more accurate translation would then be "one who eliminates the strong by strengthening [them] will be weak," but I prefer to retain the enigmatic language of the original in my translation. See also section 20.10.

4.   This phrase presumably recommends preserving constant standards (or laws, *fa* 法) on the state level, while preserving high flexibility in their implementation by the sovereign. See the exegesis in 20.5.

5.   In the current recensions, the sentence says: "When the state has a lot of things, it will be dismembered; when the sovereign has a few things, he will be strong." My emendation follows Wang Shirun, who based it on the exegesis in 20.6. See the discussions in Gao Heng 1974, 43 n. 7, and Zhang Jue 2012, 58–59 n. 11.

6.   That is, a medium-size state. If this is a reference to Qin, then it surely reflects its relative weakness at the time of the chapter's composition. In the Warring States period, a large state was usually referred to as a "ten-thousand-chariot state" (Pines 2002b, 698–699).

7.   This sentence is not commented upon directly in section 20.6, and its content is not clear. Gao Heng (1974, 43 n. 8) proposes to emend it as follows:

"When a thousand-chariot state preserves ten thousand things, it is strong; when it preserves one thousand things, it will be dismembered."

8. This reconstruction follows Gao Heng's suggestions (1974, 155 n. 1). The current text states simply: "When the people are weak, the state is strong; when the state is strong, the people are weak," which does not make much sense. Other commentators whom I consulted ignore the problem.

9. The addition in figure brackets follows Jian Shu's suggestion (Zhang Jue 2012, 239 n. 4).

10. Emending "weak" to "simple" following Jian Shu's suggestion (Zhang Jue 2012, 239 n. 4).

11. The phrase is not clear; Jian Shu proposes the following reconstruction: "when they are regulated, they can be employed, when they overstep [regulations], they are disordered" (Zhang Jue 2012, 239 n. 4).

12. Zhang Jue suggests (following chapter 5) that the text speaks of "being close to one's relatives" (2012, 239 n. 1). This suggestion would solve the apparent contradiction between the positive usage of the word *shan* 善 at the beginning of this section and the negative usage at its end, but there are no clear indicators to support his amendment.

13. In reading *kui* 匱 as meaning "fully dedicate oneself," I follow Zhang Jue (2012, 239 nn. 3–4). The usual meaning of this character (exhausted, depleted) does not make sense here; a few commentators suggest that it should be preceded by "not," reading the sentence to say, "if they are harmonious, they are *not* exhausted."

14. The word *ranks* is added following Wang Shirun (Zhang Jue 2012, 240 nn. 3–4).

15. In chapter 4, the sentence sounds different: "When a rich state is ruled as if poor, it is called multiplying riches; he who multiplies riches is strong." The difference derives primarily from a single character: *pin* 貧 (poor) in chapter 4 is replaced by *min* 民 (people) in chapter 20 (also, section 20.3 slightly abridges the sentence from section 4.1). For the "six parasites," see section 4.2.

16. "Few rewards" probably means that rewards are granted only in exchange for military success and there are no alternative avenues to attain them, as is frequently discussed throughout the text.

17. One cannot avoid the feeling that the exegesis in this section is highly skewed to avoid the unequivocal original recommendation to perform in military affairs whatever the enemy is ashamed of.

18. The term *an* 安, "peace," apparently refers to domestic stability—that is, "minimal changes" in the state—not to avoidance of war.

19. For an explanation of this point, see section 3.2: "If the people see that above the benefits come from a single opening, they will engage in the One"—that is, focus on agriculture and warfare.

20. The wording here differs from the current version in section 4.1, which, after Wang Shirun's emendation (see note 5 for this chapter) says: "When the state has few things, it will be dismembered; when the state has many things, it will be strong."

21. This is only an indirect restatement of the sentence in section 4.1, unlike much closer quotations throughout most of chapter 20.

22. Following Gao Heng (1974, 223), I read *pu* 樸 as "root."

23. Namely, the ruler is personally responsible for the proliferation of "parasitic affairs."

24. Following a common view among the commentators that proposes the inversion of *zhifa* 治法 and *zhizheng* 治政 to *fazhi* 法治 and *zheng zhi* 政治, respectively (Zhang Jue 2012, 61 n. 7).

25. Reading *chang guan* 常官 as "officials who rule according to constant [patterns]," following the common usage of *chang* in the *Book of Lord Shang* as meaning "standards," "norms," and "regulations" (Zhang Jue 2012, 61 n. 8). Also reading *qian* 遷 as referring to promotions, following Gao Heng (1974, 44 n. 17). See section 3.3 for both usages.

26. Following section 20.9, "large" means focusing on multiple matters and employing many routes to attain orderly rule; "small" refers to exclusive reliance on laws.

27. In section 20.10, the word *zheng* 政, "to govern," is employed instead of *gong* 攻, "to attack." This sentence explains the opening phrase of section 4.1.

28. This subsection is not commented on in either of the exegetical chapters. Note that here the term *guan* 官 (officials) at the beginning of the section is replaced with *guiren* 貴人 (nobles).

29. "Multiplication" 眾 here stands apparently for employing multiple norms of rule instead of uniform standards; it probably refers to the "talks" by traveling persuaders. A good government should be "moderate" (*xing* 省)—that is, apply a singular set of norms.

30. This sentence appears confusing because the same word, *qiang* 強, may refer to both a negative phenomenon of "strong people" and a positive phenomenon of "strong state." For an alternative reconstruction by Tao Hongqing, see Zhang Jue 2012, 247 n. 11.

31. The original in section 4.2 uses *gong* 攻, "to attack," rather than *zheng* 政, "to govern." The bottom line of this passage (and of other passages that play with the words *strong* and *weak* in chapter 4 and 20) is that the people should be weakened: only then will they heed orders, as a result of which the army will be strong and so will the state. The idea is that the state should deter the people by doing whatever they detest (i.e., inflicting heavy punishments) and avoid doing whatever pleases the people is reiterated in section 7.4 in a much clearer way.

32. This is an example of a very rare attack on family values in traditional Chinese thought. Chen Li 陳澧 (1810–1882) was appalled: "One should not talk

about rites, music, *Poems, Documents*, benevolence and righteousness; but as for filiality and fraternal duties, they were admired by everyone since the beginning of humankind. Yet Shang Yang considers them parasites that will [lead the state] to certain dismemberment and collapse. [For] [o]ne who is neither owl nor leopard [two supposedly parent-devouring animals] but still says these words . . . even being dismembered by chariots is not enough to erase his crime!" (*Dongshu dushu ji* 12:247). Even Zhang Binglin 章炳麟 (1869–1936), who effusively hailed Shang Yang's political theories, felt it necessary to note that "the reason that I censure Shang Yang is that he destroyed filial piety and fraternal obligations, spoiling thereby heavenly endowed human nature" ([1900] 1996–2002, 35.698).

33. Most of this passage repeats, almost verbatim, a passage from section 3.5; see also section 13.4.

34. Two recensions of the text have *ren ju* 任舉 (appointing and elevating) instead of *ren yu* 任譽 (appointment based on reputation).

35. Jiang Lihong, following Zhu Shizhe, reads *shu* 鼠 (rat) as *chu* 處 (dwelling) (1996, 35), but I think he is wrong: the fact that the "rat" causes villainy to become unstoppable suggests that the original meaning is correct.

36. Inversing the order of "easy" and "difficult" here and in the previous sentence (Gao Heng 1974, 54 n. 11).

37. For adding "superiors" (or the ruler) as an object of the people's fear or love, see Zhang Jue 2012, 65 n. 4.

38. Yan Wanli (a.k.a. Yan Kejun) omitted this sentence from his collated text because he considered it redundant, but most scholars tend to view it as an essential part of the text in light of the exegesis in section 5.4 and in light of the parallels in section 13.5. The only questionable part is 輕其重者 (to punish heavy crimes lightly). I tend to accept Jiang Lihong's view (1996, 30–31), according to which these four characters are redundant, so I placed them in double figure brackets.

39. This sentence, which is ignored by the exegesis in both chapter 5 and 20 and which artificially cuts off the discussion of proper implementation of the punishments and rewards, may be a later addition or a misplaced slip.

40. It is not clear how the punishments will enrich the poor; they presumably will encourage the poor to dedicate more effort to agriculture. "Impoverishing the rich with rewards" refers to selling ranks to them (see, e.g., section 13.1).

41. It is likely that the correct sequence should be: "When penalties are heavy, punishments inspire awe; when rewards are light, ranks are respected."

42. My translation follows Zhang Jue (2012, 78–79 n. 7). Wang Shirun and other scholars suggest adding "not" before "ordered," making the sentence simple: "when the people are disordered, then there is turmoil."

43. For reading *sha* 殺 as "to eradicate," see Zhang Jue 2012, 80 n. 1.

44. Most commentators debate the place of the word *guo* 國 in this sentence (see, e.g., Zhang Jue's suggestion: "when the people are poor, they weaken the state" [2012, 80–81 n. 1]). I think, however, that the character *guo* either is redundant or should be placed at the end of the sentence: "when there are parasitic [affairs], [the state] is weak."

45. For the "three functions," see section 4.2.

46. This sentence repeats a sentence in section 4.8, with the substitution of *de* 德, "virtue," for *hui* 惠, "kindness."

47. The text does not specify what either the "six excesses," *liu yin* 六淫, or the "four difficulties," *si nan* 四難, are. My guess is that the "six excesses" are related to the "six parasitic affairs" discussed in section 4.2 and elsewhere, and the "four difficulties" may be related to "disgrace, humiliation, toil, and bitterness," which are identified in section 6.9 as "what the people detest." Otherwise, the "four difficulties" are related to farming and fighting.

48. This passage repeats verbatim the one in section 3.7.

49. This sentence is left without exegesis.

50. According to the exegesis in section 5.8, *shai* 殺 should be read not as "to kill" but as "to diminish" or "to decrease" (i.e., decrease the people's force by utilizing it for the sake of the state). See also section 8.2 for "spending" the people's force.

51. The sentence is not clear; I read *guan* 官 as referring to "[parasitic] affairs," as in section 4.2 (Gao Heng 1974, 47 n. 29). "Attacking force" (*gong li* 攻力) may refer to "reducing" it, as in section 5.8—that is, when the people are powerful, their force should be reduced through engagement in external expansion.

52. The last two sentences of this paragraph are left without exegesis.

53. Following Tao Hongqing, I read *yao* 要 (essentials) as a substitute for *wu* 惡 (to detest); things that the people detest are agriculture and warfare, without which, however, one's desires for riches and glory are unattainable (Zhang Jue 2012, 83 n. 10).

54. I believe that a negation should come here: their aspirations are *not* exhausted; hence, they still have private interests. Ditto for the next sentence.

55. The last two sentences of this paragraph are probably commenting on the now lost segment of chapter 4. The state does not need to store up human and material resources (force and grain) because these resources are readily available.

56. Most commentators tend to emend "ninth" with "fifth," following section 5.9.

57. It is not clear which utensils are meant here. Duyvendak considers "utensils" as a substitute for "law" ([1928] 1963, 213 n. 1), and Lian Shaoming echoes him, suggesting "regulations" (2001, 21–22), but I am not convinced by their examples.

58. Most commentators suggest "abscond from paying taxes in grain" (Gao Heng 1974, 48 n. 34; Zhang Jue 2012, 68 n. 3).

59. This sentence is repeated in section 5.7.

60. The sentence points to a fundamental contradiction between commercial and agricultural pursuits.

61. "Basic commodities" refers to grain; "deceitful [undertakings]" refers to commerce. The desire to keep grain prices high so as to make agriculture more attractive is reiterated in section 22.2.

62. *Liang* (ounce) is estimated as 15.84 grams; a *shi* (picul) is 30,480 gram (see Hulsewé 1985, 19, where there is a typo: the last zero in *shi* is omitted).

63. The state that promotes commerce rather than agriculture will have to buy grain abroad, which means that the state will be depleted of both gold (used to buy foreign grain) and grain (which will not be produced sufficiently at home).

64. Reading *kou* 口 as referring to the general number of the populace; see Zhang Jue 2012, 72 n. 1.

65. The phrase "those who obtain emolument by talking" probably refers to scholars; "beneficial people" are probably farmers.

66. These two sentences recur almost verbatim in section 9.5; see that chapter and my comments in notes 9 and 10, p. 271.

67. Wan 宛 is located in modern Nanyang 南陽, southwestern Henan Province.

68. All the rivers mentioned here (except for the Yangzi) as well as the Deng Forest mark the northern and northwestern boundaries of the state of Chu. The precise identification of Fangcheng 方城 is disputed: it is likely that the name referred first to mountain ranges and hills going from Funiu Mountain 伏牛山 eastward, and then southward toward the Tongbai Mountains 桐柏山. These crescent-like ranges and hills served as a natural boundary of Nanyang 南陽 Basin, which was the major gate to Chu's heartland to the east of the Han River. By the fifth century B.C.E., a series of fortifications, including a long protective wall were built in the area (Li Yipi 2014).

69. The discussion of Chu history in this section echoes that in *Xunzi* X.15:281–283 ("Yi bing" 議兵), where, however, the narrative is more accurate from a chronological point of view. According to the *Records of the Historian*, Tang Mie 唐蔑 was killed during Chu's campaign against the joint forces of Qin, Qi, Han, and Wei in 301 B.C.E. Qin's assault on Yan 鄢 (Chu's major stronghold in the middle Han River valley) and on the Chu capital Ying 郢 (near modern Jingzhou, Hubei) was conducted in 279–278 B.C.E. Xunzi clearly distinguishes between the two campaigns, but the *Book of Lord Shang* does not, which may indicate a much later date of composition of the passage in the latter. The data on Zhuang Qiao 莊蹻 are confusing: he presumably was a Chu general who fought against Qin but later rebelled against the king of Chu; according to several accounts, he established a separate kingdom in Yunnan, in the

territories once conquered by Chu (see also Yang Kuan 1998, 405–407). Zhuang Qiao's rebellion and subsequent fragmentation of Chu into "three to four" (*Xunzi*) or "five" (*Book of Lord Shang*) parts are not narrated in the *Records of the Historian*.

70. Wang Shirun considers the last sentence a misplaced slip from chapter 14.2 (Zhang Jue 2012, 251 n. 26).

6. CALCULATING THE LAND

1. The sentence 開則行倍 may be incomplete: in terms of the parallelism in this section, it should be followed by another sentence that would focus on "attracting" the populace (*lai* 徠). Alternatively, as Gao Heng has proposed (1974, 62 n. 4), the word *lai* should have followed *kai* 開, in which case the sentence would read, "By opening up [the lands] and attracting [immigrants], [lands and populace] can be multiplied."

2. The characters in figure brackets are missing in the text and are taken from the parallel passage in section 15.1, following Yu Yue's suggestion.

3. In reading *shǔ* 數 as "calculating proportions," I follow Li Ling (1991, 24), yet I think he is wrong with regard to the next use of *shu*, which I translate literally as "numbers." Note that in section 6.3 the same term (pronounced as *shù* 數) refers to the methods of rule.

4. Li Ling explains that the small *mu* 畝 to which the text refers here comprised one hundred paces by one pace; one square *li* contained 900 *mu* (300 × 300 paces). One hundred *li* squared (i.e., 100 × 100 *li*) is then 9 million *mu*, of which, according to the proportions outlined in the text, six-tenths are agriculturally productive, which means 5.4 million *mu*. Following the proportion of one serviceman for every 500 *mu*, we get 10,800 soldiers, which is close to what the text says. Yet the apportionment of one serviceman per 500 *mu* and 10,000 soldiers per 100 *li* squared is still small for the authors, who consider it reflective of an insufficient level of agricultural productivity and of population density.

5. "Water" is added following Gao Heng's suggestion (1974, 62 n. 18) because the object of *xu* 畜 (read here as *xu* 蓄, "to accumulate") is missing.

6. The author's usage of the first-person pronoun *chen* 臣 (I, your subject [or your minister]) suggests that the text might have originated from a court memorial submitted by Shang Yang or one of his followers.

7. For "unifying rewards" as the primary means of encouraging soldiers, see especially section 17.2.

8. The combination *li zhi fa* 禮之法, "standard of ritual," is peculiar to the *Book of Lord Shang*; it implies here the essential norms of behavior embedded in

the broader concept of ritual. For different meanings of the term *li* 禮, "ritual," in preimperial discourse, see Pines 2000a.

9. *Xing zhi chang* 性之常, the "constant of one's nature," refers here to the fear of death. In seeking fame, the people are ready to sacrifice their lives.

10. Reading the binome as *chen zi* 臣子, following Yan Wanli's edition, which in turn adopted it from the now lost recension from the private library of Qin Silin 秦四麟 (fl. 1590). Other extant recensions have *tianzi* 天子 (Son of Heaven) here, which does not make sense because "above" and "below" clearly refer to social gradations, and responsibility toward the Son of Heaven cannot be marked as "below." Zhang Jue emends the binome *chen zi* to *chenmin* 臣民 (subjects) (2012, 94) but does not explain the reason for this amendment; maybe it is a typo.

11. All the commentators whom I consulted insist that merits and the name (fame, repute) are brought to the ruler, but I think that interpretation is wrong. The "method" of rule is to bring a good name (which may refer not just to repute but also elevation of one's social status) only to those who have real merits—literally to "bring together" merits and the name. For *zhi* 致 as "bringing together," see a gloss by Zheng Xuan 鄭玄 (127–200) on *Zhouli* 周禮 in *Guxun huizuan*, 3522 n. 44.

12. "Without moving" (literally "sitting," 坐) refers to a very common trope in the Warring States period discourse: the possibility of attaining positive results with minimal action (*wuwei* 無爲, usually translated as "nonaction" or, following Edward Slingerland [2003], "effortless action").

13. Legendary thearchs Yao and Shun stand here for ideal rulers who were able to attain power without violence; Kings Tang and Wu (founders of the Shang and Zhou dynasties, respectively, see note 19 for this chapter) stand for rulers who seized power by force but nonetheless achieved broad approval. See the references to these rulers in sections 1.4 and 15.6. Kings Tang and Wu are elsewhere (sections 6.7 and 7.2) contrasted with the primeval monarch Shennong (the Divine Husbandman), who epitomizes nonviolent and noncoercive rule.

14. Normally, I translate *shi* 士 as "men-of-service," but here the term may have a broader meaning, referring to all the males of elite and subelite status.

15. Reading *chong* 重 as "to accumulate" and *pian* 偏 here and later as a substitute for *bian* 遍 (everywhere) (Zhang Jue 2012, 98–99 nn. 20–21). Intellectuals, merchants, and artisans rely on their individual skills and hence can easily find employment abroad.

16. Following Wang Shirun, replacing *chen* 臣 (ministers) with *min* 民 (people) (Zhang Jue 2012, 99 n. 23).

17. A story of primeval sage rulers, such as Shennong 神農 (the Divine Husbandman), introducing essential knowledge to the people, is attested to in

several texts of the Warring States period, such as the *Xici Commentary* 繫辭傳 on the *Canon of Changes* (*Yijing* 易經) (Puett 2001, 86–90); see also section 7.2 and, for Shennong's rule, section 18.1.

18. If the designation "the country of one thousand chariots" (i.e. medium-ranked country) refers to Qin, it further suggests an early date of the chapter's composition, i.e., prior to Qin's expansion and its becoming a "ten thousand chariot" country.

19. Tang 湯, the founder of the Shang 商 dynasty (ca. 1600–1046 B.C.E.), and King Wu 武王, the de facto founder of the Zhou 周 dynasty (1046–256 B.C.E.), forcibly seized power from their predecessors, the rulers of the Xia 夏 and Shang dynasties, respectively.

20. Reading *neng* 能 (able) as *tai* 態 (pretentious) (Gao Heng 1974, 69 n. 52).

21. The word *cang* 藏 (accumulated) is absent from all the extant recensions, but Zhang Jue supplements it from Chen Shen's 陳深 1590 publication of collection from the Masters' texts (Zhang Jue 2012, 101).

22. It is unclear whether the term *shi* 勢 (the powerful) here stands for foreign powers (i.e., foreign states) or for domestic power holders, such as nobles or senior ministers. "Accomplishing a name" (*chengming* 成名) refers to building one's reputation.

23. Adding *luren* 戮人 (felons), following Wang Shirun's suggestion (Zhang Jue 2012, 104–105 n. 14).

24. Following Gao Heng's reading of *fa* 伐 as "being proud of" (1974, 71 n. 69). The petty men are proud of their depravity instead of being ashamed of it because they know that felons reap benefits and even attain office.

25. This is the only place in the *Book of Lord Shang* in which the term *junzi* 君子, a "noble man," the singularly valorized term in Confucian discourse, appears in a positive context as referring to model power holders. In section 6.10, this term is used to define elite members in general (a common usage outside Confucian ethical discourse). The term *junzi* does not recur elsewhere in the *Book of Lord Shang*.

7. OPENING THE BLOCKED

1. For *zheng* 征 as "seizing one's property," see Gao Heng's gloss (1974, 74 n. 3).

2. Translating *song* 訟 as quarrels, following Gao Heng (1974, 74 n. 5).

3. The word *li* 利, "benefit," is absent from Yan Wanli's recension (Zhang Jue 2012, 108).

4. The precise meaning of the term *xiang chu* 相出 in the text is disputed. Some suggest that it means "mutual support" or "mutual promotion" by the worthies (see, e.g., Zhang Jue 2012, 109 n. 16), but this reading contradicts the text's clear rejection of the worthies' behavior. I follow Gao Heng's gloss (1974, 74 n. 11).

5. "Rope" here stands for guiding principles; despite the difference between the ruler and the minister, the principles that should guide their action are the same.

6. This citation follows closely the statement in section 6.7, except that in the latter *wang* 王 (to become Monarch) is replaced with *sheng* 勝 (to overcome).

7. Reading *sheng* 生 (life) as *xing* 性 (nature), following Wang Shirun (Zhang Jue 2012, 111 n. 2).

8. For Shennong, see sections 6.7 and 18.1 as well as their accompanying notes.

9. For Kings Tang and Wu, see 6.7 and note 19 for chapter 6 (p. 268).

10. In most recensions, the word *zhi* 智 (knowledge) is replaced by *ai* 愛 (love, care); Zhang Jue follows Yan Kejun's suggestion, restoring *zhi* (2012, 110–111 n. 5).

11. "Not follow[ing] the present": he does not follow what is customary nowadays.

12. Xia 夏 is the semilegendary dynasty that allegedly succeeded the rule of the sage Thearch Shun 舜, whose surname was Yu 虞 (not to be confused with the Great Yu 禹, the legendary founder of the Xia).

13. As noted earlier, King Wu led the rebellious forces that overthrew the Shang dynasty (p. 268, note 19).

14. "Above" refers to higher antiquity, "below" to events of the more recent past.

15. In Yan Wanli's recension, *zhi* 治 (to order) is substituted with *xiao* 效 (to imitate).

16. That is, pace common opinion, true righteousness means doing what the people detest (i.e., employing punishments), as the authors explain in the text.

17. "What the people detest" here and throughout this passage refers to punishments.

18. Most recensions have *li* 利 (benefit) instead of *xing* 刑 (punishments); Zhang Jue follows Yan Wanli's amendment and restores *xing* (2012, 114 n. 8).

19. Yan Wanli proposed that a parallel sentence, 亂國賞多而刑少, be added here: "In a calamitous state, there are many rewards and few punishments" (Zhang Jue 2012, 116 n. 1).

20. This is the only place in the *Book of Lord Shang* where peace among competing polities is presented as a desirable state of affairs. It is not clear how the proper implementation of rewards and punishments within each of the two competing states would contribute to peace—even if temporary—between them.

8. SPEAKING OF THE ONE

1. Note that the chapter calls here to "transform" customs, while in section 8.3 the authors recommend establishing laws on the basis of current customs. This dialectic approach presumes that, on the one hand, laws should be based

on understanding the people's disposition (i.e., understanding their intrinsic quest for rewards and fear of punishments) and should accord with this disposition or "customs." Yet, on the other hand, laws should not slavishly follow what is customary but also transform the people's behavioral norms, primarily through causing them to become fully committed to agriculture and warfare. See more on this topic in section 11.1 (note 1, p. 272) and section 17.1 (note 1, p. 278).

2. The phrase "private gates" here and elsewhere refers to powerful courtiers using their influence to circumvent the uniform norms of promotion and demotion advocated by Shang Yang (see, e.g., section 3.3).

3. One can discern subtle irony in the text's usage of the respected term *shi* 士, "men-of-service," for those engaged in agriculture and war rather than for the elite, who as persuaders and traveling scholars are referred to either by lowly term *min* 民, "people," normally associated with the lower strata, or by the neutral term *ren* 人, "men."

4. "Root" and "branch" occupations are usually associated with agriculture and commerce, respectively, yet one should remember that both terms can refer to a variety of other essential versus nonessential matters as well (Sterckx 2015, 211 n. 2).

5. "To consolidate force" refers to focusing the population on agriculture and war; "to spend force" (literally, "to reduce," *shai* 殺) refers to investing the people's force and wealth in either war or the purchase of ranks of merit, which will prevent excessive wealth from accumulating in individual households.

6. It is not clear what *hua* 化, "transformation," refers to here; none of the commentaries I have consulted offer a convincing explanation.

7. This is the earliest known appearance of the stock phrase *fu guo qiang bing* 富國強兵 (rich state and strong army).

8. Following Tao Hongqing, I replace *duan* 短 with *zhi* 知 (knowledge); following Gao Heng (1974, 83 n. 10), I read *zhang* 長 as a verb, "to increase." "Opening" and "blocking" here apparently refer to different paths of socioeconomic advancement: if the state opens the way of agriculture cum warfare without blocking alternative routes, the people will be too sophisticated; but if the alternatives are blocked, the people will become simple.

9. Emending *ling* 令 to *jin* 今, following Yu Yue (Zhang Jue 2012, 125 n. 9). For 修今, "following the present," as referring to being committed to what is customary today without investigating its worth, see section 7.3. "Above" and "below" refer to the past (which is always "above") and the present, respectively.

10. Compare to sections 5.9 and 6.9 and the need to relate the laws to the people's customs and sentiments.

9. IMPLEMENTING LAWS

1. My understanding of the phrase "the materials forged themselves" differs from that of other commentators, who interpret it in the context of human materials. From the subsequent discussion in the chapter, I believe that the text hints at the economic sufficiency of the properly run state, and I read *lian* 練 as *lian* 煉, "to refine," "to forge." In this case, the three parts of the first sentence in this chapter nicely fit the three major fields of Shang Yang's concern: political order, economic affluence, and military strength.

2. I interpret *xiang wan* 相萬 as referring to the ancient paragons' huge superiority over current rulers. See Zhang Jue's gloss (2012, 129 n. 11). The Three Monarchs are the founders of the Three Dynasties (Xia, Shang, and Zhou); for the Five Hegemons, see section 1.3, note 6, p. 254.

3. This idealistic passage resembles the ideas in *Mengzi* (e.g., 1.5:10 ["Liang Hui Wang shang" 梁惠王上]) and *Xunzi* (e.g., IV.8:137 ["Ru xiao" 儒效]), but even in these two texts the minimal territory for future prosperity was defined as one hundred *li* squared. In the *Book of Lord Shang*, this passage is very odd.

4. The last sentence in the paragraph appears disconnected from the previous discussion.

5. Emending *renjun* 人君 (a ruler) to *rensheng* 人生 (human beings), following Tao Hongqing (Zhang Jue 2012, 132 n. 6).

6. Here and later in this chapter, *de* 德 refers primarily to "kindness" and not more broadly to "virtue," as given previously in the text.

7. I follow several commentators who read *jiaoliu* 教流 as *jiaohua* 教化 (for their views, see Zhang Jue 2012, 133 n. 7; Zhang interprets *liu* 流 as "implementation"). "Educational transformation" refers here, as elsewhere in the *Book of Lord Shang*, to the full internalization of laws and regulations.

8. This statement is at odds with the subsequent ones, which—like the rest of the *Book of Lord Shang*—emphasize that a ruler's individual qualities merit little in comparison to the overarching importance of laws and standards.

9. Li Zhu 離朱 is a legendary paragon of keen sight; he is also mentioned in sections 20.11 and 24.2, where he appears under his better-known name Li Lou 離婁.

10. Wu Huo 烏獲 (d. 306 B.C.E.) was renowned for his strength. This reference to him clearly indicates the relative lateness of the chapter's composition. A *jun* 鈞 is thirty *jin* 斤 (catties)—that is, approximately 7.620 kilograms.

11. The chapter returns here to one of the central points in the text: the ruler's personality, even if sagacious, matters little; what is truly important is the utilization of impersonal methods of rule: namely, the law.

10. METHODS OF WAR

1. The translation is based on the rearrangement 兵強弱敵 proposed by Tao Hongqing (Gao Heng 1974, 94 n. 12).
2. For the role of *miaosuan* 廟算 (calculations done in the ancestral temple) in early Chinese military thought, see McNeal 2012, 117–122; compare Galvany 2015, 154–156.
3. Following Sun Yirang's rearranging of 行是必久王 to 行是久必王 (Zhang Jue 2012, 139 n. 7).

11. ESTABLISHING THE ROOTS

1. Duplicating *su cheng* 俗成 (when they become customs), following Sun Yirang's suggestion (Zhang Jue 2012, 142 n. 4). The relation between laws and the people's customs is a recurrent topic in the *Book of Lord Shang*. In establishing the laws, the ruler is supposed to take the people's customs into account (6.9, 8.3), but laws are also supposed to transform these customs (8.1): after the laws are internalized, they change the people's mood, especially their attitude toward war (11.2, 17.4, 18.3). Here the text possibly hints at new customs of commitment to war and agriculture (as in 8.1): hence, when laws become customs, the equipment (or, more broadly, supplies) is ready.
2. In translating this sentence, I rely heavily on Jiang Lihong's understanding (1996, 71), based on parallels with section 18.4.
3. The sentence is clearly corrupt and is difficult to reconstruct; Jiang Lihong frankly comments, "The meaning is not clear" (1996, 72). Gao Heng correctly notices that the three parts of the sentence are related to the three essentials of successful war: orderly rule, internalization of military values (customs), and technical preparedness (1974, 97 n. 15). For *guo shi* 過勢 as "superior power," see Lian Shaoming 2001, 24.

12. MILITARY DEFENSE

1. Gao Heng interprets "going-to-die people" as referring to crack troops (1974, 100 n. 5), but the context suggests that it is a reference to defenders who have no choice but to die in defending their settlement. The latter reading fits the discussion in the next section well.
2. This is an odd claim. Perhaps the author is implying that some of the defenders will not have to fight the attackers.

3.   Once again this statement is odd and contradicts the one at the beginning of this section. It is not clear how to reconcile the two. Possibly, now, as the attacker is exhausted, his forces are those that face inevitable death, whereas the defenders, due to their resolute fight, have a chance to survive.

4.   This is a very tentative reconstruction of the sentence based primarily on Zhang Jue 2012, 147 n. 8.

5.   It is not clear what "these three" are. Jian Shu's hypothesis that this phrase refers to lost segments of the text seems to me the most convincing (Jiang Lihong 1996, 73).

6.   *Ruo* 弱, "infirm," may refer to people shorter than a fixed height; I am grateful to Robin D. S. Yates for this suggestion.

7.   According to Robin D. S. Yates, *fa liang* 發梁, "releasing the bridges," refers to "releasable bridges," the term employed in the military chapters of the *Mozi* (Yates 1994, 364–370). These bridges were constructed over a trench or ditch filled with sharp stakes. Yates explains, "The bridge had some kind of trigger mechanism, possibly related to that of a crossbow, or consisting of a simpler mechanism: underneath may have been a pole which was inserted into a hole at the defenders' end and held in position by a pin running through it at right angles. When the trigger or pin was pulled, the bridge rotated, depositing all who stood on it into the ditch, where they would be impaled by the stakes, and captured, or suffer a slow and painful death. The idea was to try to entice elements of the enemy onto the bridge by engaging them beyond, pretending to be defeated, and fleeing across the bridge. When the enemy pursued, the bridge was 'fired' or released, and the leaders unceremoniously revolved into the trench. Their fellows, horrified at the fate of their brave comrades, would abandon the siege in fright; or so the Mohists hoped" (1994, 364–365). I am indebted to Yates for pointing me to his explanation of this terminology.

13. MAKING ORDERS STRICT

1.   Compare to sections 4.3, 5.2, and 20.9.

2.   Compare to sections 4.6 and 5.9.

3.   My reading of this sentence is based on the reconstruction by Gao Heng (1974, 104 n. 4). He identifies the "eminent people" (*xian min* 顯民) as members of the elite, who under the unified system of laws and regulations will have to abandon the plans to advance socially by means of crooked ways. Once they abandon these plans, there will be no need to punish the "eminent people." I am not entirely sure whether this interpretation is correct or not, particularly because the binome *xian min* never recurs in the *Book of Lord Shang*, but I have found no alternative explanation that is more convincing.

4.   This is yet another difficult sentence. I accept Zhu Shizhe's reading of *gui qi* 貴齊 as standing for *guizu* 貴族, "nobles," and *qimin* 齊民, "commoners" (Zhang Jue 2012, 155 n. 7), although this combination never recurs elsewhere in the texts, at least as far as I am aware. I also accept Gao Heng's reading of *fa* 伐 as synonymous with *gong* 功 (merit) (1974, 104 n. 6), but, again, such a usage is very odd. The reconstruction of this sentence is tentative at best.

5.   For *du* 都 as "regional capital" rather than "national capital," see Tong Weimin 2013, 163.

6.   Compare to section 4.2.

7.   Compare to section 20.9.

8.   "Ten" probably refers to divergent ways of social and economic advancement; "one" is the way of agriculture cum warfare. Compare to sections 3.2 and 20.6.

9.   Reading *chi* 恥 (to be ashamed of) as a mistake for *qu* 取 (to obtain), following Gao Heng (1974, 106 n. 19).

10. Commentators debate the meaning of *bei* 備 here without proposing any convincing solution. In my eyes, *bei* in this case stands for "occupying an official position" (see, for example, the phrase 身備漢相, "one who personally occupies a position of the prime minister of the Han," in *Hanshu* 84:3417). Attaining positions due to support from foreign powers was a common problem at the courts of the Warring States, and it is repeatedly criticized in the *Book of Lord Shang* (e.g., in sections 2.3, 3.2, 3.3).

11. The commentators are perplexed why the six parasites become nine items (separated by a comma in my translation and by *yue* 曰, "what is named," in the original) and why the number "twelve" is then given. There is no convincing answer to these questions; see the different comments assembled in Zhang Jue 2012, 159–160 n. 1.

12. For *pu* 樸 as "root," see section 4.2 and note 22 for that chapter (p. 262).

13. Compare to sections 3.5 and 4.3.

14. Commentators are perplexed by this sentence; I generally follow Zhang Jue's elaboration of Yin Tongyang's approach (2012, 160 n. 5), except I am not sure what "few" and "many" refer to; I tentatively accept that their referent is "attainments," but this does not seem entirely logical to me: Why should those who have plenty of attainments be "derided" (*sun* 損)?

15. Compare to sections 4.3 and 5.3.

16. Compare to sections 4.4 and 5.4.

17. Compare to sections 3.2, 20.6, and 5.8. This phrase is also paralleled in the chapter "The State's Store of Grain" ("Guo xu" 國蓄) of the *Guanzi* (XXII.73:1262; Rickett 1998, 378); see also note 3 in chapter 3 (p. 258).

18. Compare to section 4.4.

19. The last sentence appears to be corrupt and so is possibly the end of the previous one. I accept Jiang Lihong's punctuation and his substitution of *yi fu*

壹輔 with *fu yi* 輔壹 (1996, 82). (Jiang suggests adding the word *jiao* 教 [teaching], as in section 3.8, but I am not convinced; Shang Yang frequently employs *yi* 壹 as a noun, "the One," and not as an adjective; the One refers to agriculture and warfare.) For 仁者, 心之續也, I accept Gao Heng's substitute of *xu* 續 with *yu* 裕 (1974, 109 n. 31), but I also strongly suspect that this sentence is an old gloss that was inadvertently incorporated into the main text.

14. CULTIVATION OF AUTHORITY

1.   Here and throughout the chapter I translate *fa* 法 intermittently as "standards" (when the term refers to impersonal standards of rule) or "law" (when the term is more specific), but it should be remembered that in the original the single term *fa* is used.

2.   Divisions (or distinctions, *fen* 分) became an important category of social and political discourse of the late Warring States period, closely related to upholding ritual hierarchy and fixing each person's allotment. See more on this topic in Sato Masayuki 2000, 27–31.

3.   The idea of the ruler's exclusive decision making (*du duan* 獨斷; for this term, see Giele 2006, 21–23) became an important topic in other so-called Legalist texts; see, for example, Shen Buhai's statement (Creel 1974, 389, fragment 19); *Guanzi* XVII.52:998–999 ("Qi chen Qi zhu" 七臣七主); *Han Feizi* II.6:36–37 ("You du" 有度) and II.7:39–43 ("Er bing" 二柄); and so forth. In the *Book of Lord Shang*, however, this statement is exceptional.

4.   Reading *yue* 約 as *yao* 要, following Gao Heng (1974, 111 n. 8). In the context of this sentence, *fa* is more specific and should be translated as "law." This sentence is the only place in the *Book of Lord Shang* to refer to the pair *wen* 文 (civilian) and *wu* 武 (military, martial) as complementary aspects of policy making. (But see also sections 15.4 and 17.2, in which this pair is hinted at.)

5.   The idea that the ruler is established for the sake of the common good (for the people) permeates texts of different ideological affiliations and may be considered a common conviction among the political ideologues of the Warring States period. See, for example, *Mozi jiaozhu* III.12:119–120 ("Shang tong zhong" 尚同中); *Shenzi*, 16 ("Wei de" 威德); *Xunzi* XIX.27:504 ("Da lue" 大略); and *Lüshi chunqiu* 20.1:1321–1322 ("Shi jun" 恃君). Compare *Zuozhuan*, Xiang 14:1016, and *Mengzi* 14.14:328 ("Jin xin xia" 盡心下).

6.   Referring to the legend of Yao's abdication in favor of Shun and Shun's abdication in favor of Yu 禹, acts that violated the abdicators' obligations toward their progeny. See more in Allan 2016 and 2015; Pines 2005b.

7.   Referring to the distribution of territorial power to the relatives of the ruling house. This pattern of rule employed by the Western Zhou 西周 (ca.

1046–771 B.C.E.) is associated here also with the preceding Xia 夏 and Shang 商 (ca. 1600–1046 B.C.E.) dynasties.

8. The text apparently refers to the same practice criticized in section 3.3: selling the ruler's power to the bidders from below, who sought positions and promotions.

9. I understand *zhiguan* 秩官 as high-ranking officials and *li* 吏 as their underlings, the clerks who covet the people's wealth under the protection of powerful masters. It is possible that these clerks were the major beneficiaries of the office selling practiced by high officials, mentioned in the previous sentence in the text.

15. ATTRACTING THE PEOPLE

1. For both projects and their impact, see *Shiji* 29:1407–1408. For Sichuan's becoming a major attraction for immigrants in the aftermath of Qin's development efforts, see Sage 1992, 132–134.

2. For a perceptive, even if at times speculative, comparison between chapters 6 and 15 of the *Book of Lord Shang*, see Yoshinami Takashi 1985. For this chapter's importance as a first indicator of Qin's potential retreat from the ideal of universal military service, see Pines 2016b.

3. The land arrangement cited here repeats the one mentioned in section 6.2. Yet in the latter the number of the occupants was "ten thousand soldiers" (*zu* 卒) or servicemen (*yi* 役)—that is, ten thousand households or around fifty thousand people. Section 15.1, in distinction, speaks of fifty thousand laborers (*zuo fu* 作夫). Clearly, the laborers are not equal to "servicemen" (it would be impossible to expect a fivefold increase in the occupants of a hundred *li* squared from the time chapter 6 was written to the time chapter 15 was composed). Rather, it is likely that the term *zuo fu* refers to every able-bodied man or woman (ages fifteen to sixty), who constituted 60 to 70 percent of household members. In this case, we can speak of seventy to eighty thousand expected inhabitants of a unit one hundred *li* squared: a 40 to 60 percent increase in population in the wake of increased agricultural productivity in the second half of the Warring States period.

4. Li Ling considers the number "one million" as referring to the soldiers who should be supported by the tillers (1991, 26); this is indeed roughly the size of Qin's standing army by the late Warring States period. But I believe the number refers to square *li* of arable lands, which are two-tenths of Qin's territory. This reference fits nicely the estimate of the territory of Qin as five times one thousand *li* squared—that is, five million square *li* ($5 \times 1,000 \times 1,000$) or approximately eight hundred thousand square kilometers, which is close to historical truth.

5. "Three Jin" is a common reference to Jin's 晉 three successor states: Han, Wei, and Zhao. By the time of the composition of chapter 15, the state of Zhao had been badly defeated at Changping (see the introduction to this chapter) and was no longer a real threat to Qin. Han and Wei remained Qin's major rivals to the east.

6. That is, in the overpopulated and unproductive lands of Han and Wei, the people can hope neither for social advancement (a good name) nor for economic prosperity (fields and houses).

7. Reading *fu* 復 as "穴 + 復" (a cave). *Yin-yang* 陰陽 refers here to the sunny and shady banks of the river (Zhang Jue 2012, 177 n. 10).

8. That is, the people of Jin do not migrate westward toward Qin.

9. Following Gao Heng (1974, 118 n. 19) and other scholars (e.g., Zhang Jue 2012, 177–178 n. 16), I consider *ruo* 弱 (weak), in front of *bu duo* 不奪 (inability to seize), as redundant, possibly mistakenly transposed from the next sentence.

10. The count of "four generations" is not clear. Gao Heng thinks it refers to the Qin rulers, Lord Xiao 孝公 (r. 361–338 B.C.E.), King Huiwen 惠文王 (r. 337–311 B.C.E.), King Wu 武王 (r. 310–307 B.C.E.), and King Zhaoxiang, 昭襄王 (r. 306–251 B.C.E.) (1974, 118 n. 23). The problem with this count is that the next sentence places King Xiang of Wei 魏襄王 (r. 318–296 B.C.E.) as the first in the list of Qin's incessant victories; if so, one should count four generations of the kings of Wei rather than of Qin, coming to the reign of King Jingmin 魏景湣王 (r. 242–229 B.C.E.). This would push the chapter to a later stage of history than what appears from its depiction of Qin campaigns in section 15.5. Tong Weimin (2008) convincingly argues in support of Gao Heng's interpretation.

11. "Submitting to justice" (*gui yi* 歸義) is a *terminus technicus* for surrendering to a legitimate authority.

12. "East of the Mountain" (*shan dong* 山東) refers to all the countries to the east of Qin. The mountain referred to is either Mount Yao 殽山 (in western Henan) or Mount Hua 華山 (in eastern Shaanxi).

13. There is much uncertainty about the correct meaning of 且直言之謂也, 不然. Among multiple amendments proposed by commentators from Yan Wanli (Yan Kejun) on, I have followed Gao Heng, who considers *zhi* 直 as miswritten for *qi* 其 (1974, 121 n. 33), which refers to the words of the Qin officials, against whom the author polemicizes. For other attempts to make sense of this phrase, see the glosses in Zhang Jue 2012, 181 nn. 12–15.

14. Most current recensions have "three generations" rather than "four" here; for the difficulty in determining which is right, see note 10 for this chapter.

15. "Old Qin people" are the natives of Qin; the "new people" are immigrants from elsewhere.

16. This is the only reference to cavalry in the entire *Book of Lord Shang*.

17. This appears to be a direct quotation from the chapter "Da wu" 大武 ("The Great Martial") of *Yi Zhou shu* 逸周書 (Lost documents of Zhou) (*Yi Zhou shu* 2.8:122); the translation of this quotation follows McNeal 2012, 113.

18. "Great Martial" is the chapter of the *Yi Zhou shu* cited in note 17; it is likely that "Broad Civilian" refers to another text that is currently lost.

19. Reading *yi min* 異民 as referring to migrants. The text implies that all the migrants will flock to Qin alone. See Yu Chang's gloss, cited in Zhang Jue 2012, 183 n. 12.

20. Referring to the victory of Qin armies under General Bai Qi over the coalition of Han, Wei, and Eastern Zhou principality forces in 294 B.C.E. (Yang Kuan 1998, 379–380).

21. The battle of Huayang 華陽, in which Qin armies defeated Zhao and Wei forces, occurred in 273 B.C.E. (Yang Kuan 1998, 407–408).

22. For the Changping victory, see the introduction to this chapter. The degree of Qin's losses can be deduced from a special order conscripting everybody older than fifteen issued by King Zhaoxiang of Qin 秦昭襄王 (r. 306–251 B.C.E.) at the final stage of the Changping campaign (*Shiji* 73:2334).

23. Reading *ke* 客 as referring to an army that acts outside its native territory.

24. For these rulers, see sections 6.6, 6.7, and 7.2 as well as notes 13 and 19 for chapter 6 (pp. 267–268).

25. Most commentators think that this should say "four kings" instead of "three kings."

26. This is an exceptional instance of the author's self-identification as a sage. The sentence itself may have suffered from textual corruption; for a variety of other reconstructions, see Zhang Jue 2012, 188 n. 15.

17. REWARDS AND PUNISHMENTS

1. A derisive attitude toward popular customs (*su* 俗) and the desire to unify them became a common point of the thinkers of the late Warring States period (see, e.g., Lewis 2006, 192–201; cf. Pines 2005a, 181–187). The dictum to unify divergent customs is clearly pronounced both in Qin bureaucratic documents, such as the *Speech Document* (*Yu shu* 語書) of 227 B.C.E., unearthed from Tomb 11, Shuihudi (Hubei) (*Shuihudi* [1990] 2001, 13–16; Lin Shaoping 2015), as well as in slightly later pronouncements of the First Emperor (*Shiji* 6:243, 261; Kern 2000, 29, 48).

2. The combination "no rewards," "no punishments," and "no teaching" is yet another hint of a utopian situation in which the people will internalize regulations and attain self-rule so that the state's intervention in their lives is no longer needed. For similar pronouncements, see, for example, sections 7.5, 7.6, and 13.6. For a (somewhat speculative) attempt to interpret these utopian

undertones in the *Book of Lord Shang* in terms of the modern philosophy of the rule of law, see Wu Baoping and Lin Cunguang 2015.

3.   Reading *bin* 賓 as synonymous with *fu* 服, "to subdue," "to subjugate," but also implying that the rivals will arrive at one's court (cf. Gao Heng 1974, 128 n. 11; Zhang Jue 2012, 193 n. 7).

4.   The precise location of the early power base of Tang 湯, the founder of the Shang dynasty, is debated (see Jiang Lihong 1996, 97–98). Qizhou 岐周 (which Maria Khayutina translates as "Zhou-under-Qi" [2008, 25]) was located under Mount Qi 岐 in the central Wei 渭 River basin. The notion of a small territory of one hundred *li* squared (roughly 1,600 square kilometers) being the springboard of the future dynastic founders of the Shang and the Zhou is a commonplace in Warring States texts. See, for example, *Mengzi* 3.1:57 and 3.3:74 ("Gongsun Chou shang" 公孫丑上); *Xunzi*, VII.11:204 ("Wang ba" 王霸).

5.   Mingtiao 鳴條, located in southern Shanxi, is the location of a decisive battle between Tang and the last king of the Xia dynasty, Jie 桀. Mu Fields 牧野, in northeastern Henan, is the location of the decisive battle around 1046 B.C.E. between the forces of King Wu of Zhou and the last Shang ruler, Zhòu 紂 (d. ca. 1046 B.C.E.).

6.   A *she* 社 was a hamlet of twenty-five households; that a *she* was registered under a soldier's name means that the soldiers received these hamlets as their hereditary holding.

7.   For reading Nongze 農澤 as referring to the marshes at Hongnong 弘農 in western Henan, see Zhang Jue 2012, 194 n. 18. For King Wu's release of war horses and oxen after the victory over the Shang, see *Liji* XXXVIII.19:1026 ("Yue ji" 樂記).

8.   One *sheng* 升 is approximately two hundred cubic centimeters.

9.   The three degrees of family members (*san zu* 三族) are parents, children, and siblings of the criminal (Barbieri-Low and Yates 2015, 188).

10. This anecdote may have been adapted from the *Zuo zhuan*, Xi 28.3:453–455, where, however, the sequence of events and their internal logic differ considerably. Lord Wen of Jin 晉文公 (r. 636–628 B.C.E.) is the most illustrious of the Springs-and-Autumns period hegemons, under whose rule the state of Jin became the leader of the Zhou world.

11. The character *li* 吏 (officer) does not appear in most current recensions; it is supplemented from the citation in the *Taiping yulan* 太平御覽 collection (Zhang Jue 2012, 197 n. 8).

12. Dian Jie 顛頡 was one of the five retainers of the future Lord Wen of Jin when the latter, still the fugitive Prince Chong'er 公子重耳, lived in exile after he fled from domestic troubles.

13. Jin's invasions of the state of Cao 曹 and of the town Wulu 五鹿 (a Wei 衛 territory) occurred in 632 B.C.E. For 反鄭之埤 as meaning "to overrun the

walls of Zheng" (i.e., Jin's assault on Zheng 鄭 in the same year), see Zhang Jue 2012, 200 n. 23.

14. Following Sun Yirang, I read *zheng* 徵 as miswritten for Wei 衛 (Zhang Jue 2012, 200 n. 24). Arranging field divisions eastward would facilitate the future movement of Jin armies through the fields of Wei. Compare to *Zuo zhuan* Cheng 2.3:797–798. The victory of the Jin armies over those of Chu at Chengpu 城濮 in 632 B.C.E. was the culmination of Lord Wen of Jin's success as the new hegemon of the Zhou world.

15. According to the commonly accepted narrative, the Duke of Zhou 周公 (d. ca. 1035 B.C.E.) punished his brothers Guanshu 管叔 and Huoshu 霍叔 (as well as Caishu 蔡叔) because they joined the rebellion of the loyalists of the ousted Shang dynasty around 1042 B.C.E.

16. Both the knife and the saw were used for mutilating punishments.

17. For reading *qingzhuo* 清濁 (clean and dirty) as *qing ye* 請謁 (request an audience), see Jiang Lihong 1996, 104. In the Warring States period, not a few high officials were appointed only after a personal audience with the ruler, a practice to which the authors of the *Book of Lord Shang* were vehemently opposed (see, e.g., section 9.4). Ironically, according to the *Shiji* (68:2228), this was precisely the way that Shang Yang's career in Qin began.

18. This phrase may contain an allusion to the *Laozi* 4 and 56 (*Boshu Laozi*, pp. 241 and 98, respectively), although the similarity may be accidental. See also *Guanzi* VI.16:295 ("Fa fa" 法法).

19. For translating *hetong zhe* 合同者 as "colleagues," I follow Gao Heng (1974, 133 n. 60).

20. "The One" in the *Book of Lord Shang* normally refers to agriculture cum warfare, but in this context it apparently stands for unification of rewards, punishments, and teaching.

18. CHARTING THE POLICIES

1. Current recensions have "the Yellow Thearch" (Huangdi 黃帝) here. Jiang Lihong points out that the opening lines of section 18.1 are cited almost verbatim in *juan* 9 of *The Great History* (*Lu shi* 路史) by Luo Bi 羅泌 (1131–1189), where, however, the name "Yellow Thearch" is replaced by "Human Thearch" (Rendi 人帝) (Jiang Lihong 1996, 106–107). The latter is undoubtedly the correct version because the Yellow Thearch appears in the text of section 18.1 at a later stage of the historical sequence. Jiang Lihong further infers from the text of *The Great Commentary on Venerated Documents* (*Shangshu dazhuan* 尚書大傳, second century B.C.E.), cited in *Fengsu tongyi* 1:3, that the Human Thearch is Fuxi 伏羲. The sequence of thearchs, then, resembles the one in

section 1.4, which mentions Fuxi, Shennong, and the Yellow Thearch (but not the primordial ruler, Hao Ying).

2. For Shennong's rule, see also sections 6.7 and 7.2.

3. The Yellow Thearch is normally viewed as the founder of Chinese civilization and the state.

4. Both the knife and the saw were used for mutilating punishments.

5. The addition in figure brackets follows Yu Yue's suggestion (Zhang Jue 2012, 212 n. 1).

6. A canton (*xiang* 鄉) is a subcounty unit. For its administration, see Bu Xianqun 2006.

7. *Qianxi* 遷徙 here clearly refers to migrants who will never find a refuge elsewhere because they are registered under the canton's jurisdiction. This means that escaping from the army's ranks is not a viable option for a soldier eager to avoid punishment.

8. This phrase encapsulates the problem of any legal system: the laws themselves matter little unless one is able to make them universally enforceable. The modern relevance of this phrase is buttressed by its usage by the would-be general secretary of the Communist Party of China, Xi Jinping 習近平 (b. 1953), in a speech in 2007 (see http://cpc.people.com.cn/n/2014/0522/c64387-25048530.html, accessed February 11, 2016).

9. When laws are not strict enough, then even the inevitability of being apprehended does not deter criminals, and, as a result, lawbreakers multiply, as do punishments. Recall that Shang Yang's goal is to "to eradicate punishments with punishments," not to pile them up.

10. This statement is at odds with the rest of the *Book of Lord Shang*, which advocates granting rewards to meritorious soldiers and tillers. It seems that this chapter's authors understood the issue of rewards differently than most other chapters' authors.

11. Robber Zhi 盜跖 is an epitome of villainy; Boyi 伯夷 is a paragon of moral purity.

12. I tentatively translate *ke* 可 as "management" following Gao Heng (1974, 141).

13. This unequivocal emphasis on the importance of worthy ministers stands in sharp contrast with several other chapters of the *Book of Lord Shang* that warn against excessive trust in the discourse of "worthiness," which is prone to manipulations by unscrupulous ministers (see, e.g., sections 24.3 and 25.1).

14. The sentence appears to be corrupt; the translation is tentative.

15. I read here the first-person pronoun *wu* 吾 as the second-person "you" following Harbsmeier 1997. Compare with section 25.2 for a similar usage.

16. Replacing *yu* 欲 (desires) with *su* 俗 (customs); see Gao Heng 1974, 142 n. 43, and Zhang Jue 2012, 217 n. 9.

17. The promise that under an ideal political system the ruler will be at rest while All-under-Heaven will be properly ruled is a common trope in the texts of the Warring States period (Pines 2009, 82–107). In the *Book of Lord Shang*, though, this promise is a rarity.

18. That is, he is able to let others serve him.

19. In translating this phrase, I relied on Zhang Jue's gloss (2012, 219 n. 4).

20. According to Zhang Jue's explanation, the desires of the strong ruler are to unify All-under-Heaven; hence, he reads *yi* 益 as "to assist," "to help" (2012, 219 n. 7). It is not at all clear, nonetheless, why the people of All-under-Heaven would be "fond of" the ruler even if his desires are not satisfied.

21. The last sentence of the paragraph is unmistakably reminiscent of the *Laozi* 33: 勝人者有力, 自勝者強: "He who overcomes others is strong, he who overcomes himself is powerful" (*Boshu Laozi*, 403).

22. This sentence may be an implicit polemic against the *Mengzi*, which postulates: "If others do not respond to your love with love, look into your own benevolence" (*Mengzi* 7.4:167 ["Li Lou shang" 離婁上]).

19. WITHIN THE BORDERS

1. The earliest detailed testimony to the Qin rank system is from the early Han text "Household Ordinances" ("Hu lü" 戶律) unearthed at Tomb 247, Zhangjiashan (*Zhangjiashan Hanmu*, 175–176, slips 310–316; Barbieri-Low and Yates 2015, 790–793). Anthony Barbieri-Low and Robin D. S. Yates provide a translation of all the ranks (2015, xxii), but I prefer to transliterate throughout this chapter.

2. Li Ling suggests that *qi* 乞 (request) should be replaced with *xi* 餼 (to support, to provide for) (1991, 26). The suggestion makes perfect sense but is not supported by any gloss known to me.

3. *Shuzi* 庶子 is rendered as "retainer" here. Literally, *shuzi* means "minor son" (i.e., a son from a secondary wife or concubine). Li Ling avers that this term is a vestige of the aristocratic age (1991, 26). The practice of having retainers accompany and serve the soldiers during a campaign remained intact into the early imperial age.

4. I follow Li Ling (1991, 26) in translating *dafu* 大夫 neither as "nobles" nor as a referent to specific ranks, but as an antonym of *xiaofu* 小夫, used later in the text: *dafu* is a common designation of ranked men, whereas *xiaofu* designates the unranked.

5. In translating *yang* 養 as "to provide for their needs," I follow Jiang Lihong's gloss (1996, 114); Li Ling notes a similar usage in the Han period bamboo slips from Juyan 居延 (1991, 26–27).

6. In translating this sentence, I follow Li Ling (1991, 27), who in turn adopts Zhu Shizhe's suggestion. Many alternative explanations were proposed by scholars from Yu Yue on, who read *chu* 出 as a mistake for *shi* 士; but none of the manifold explanations makes better sense of the sentence than Li Ling's. The exact position of *xiao* 校, *tu* 徒, and *cao* 操 is not verifiable, but it is likely that they were infantrymen (for a view that they were minor officers, see Tong Weimin 2012). It is not clear why the lowest rank, *gongshi* 公士, is not mentioned here, but it is probably because the text focuses on the lowest military ranks only, and these lowest ranks existed below the system of "common" (*gong* 公) ranks of merit.

7. Li Ling suggests that, judging from the original meaning of the rank titles, the soldiers of ranks 2–4 were not pure infantrymen but auxiliaries of chariot fighters (1991, 27).

8. I follow Gao Heng (1974, 237–238), in reading *yu* 羽 as miswritten *zhao* 兆, which stands for *tao* 逃 (fleeing). However, I reject the common interpretation of *qing* 輕 as standing for *jing* 剄 (execution by cutting the throat). I follow Zhang Jue, who argues that the squad members whose fellow fled should be punished not by execution but by reduction of their rank (2012, 226 n. 6); alternatively, *qing* may refer to another form of punishment, but surely not execution. Zhang is correct that if *qing* refers to execution, it would be impossible to understand how the punishment is "revoked" in the case of the successful capture of an enemy's head. See also section 19.4 and note 16 for this chapter.

9. Gao Heng parses the sentence differently, reversing the order of the last two characters. He reads the sentence then as 不得首, 斬; that is, if the commanders failed to get enemy's heads, they should be executed (1974, 238, unnumbered note). I reject this parsing because it is highly unreasonable that all centurions and platoon leaders would be executed in cases of military failure. For the regulation that medium-rank nobles (ranks 5–9, presumably the rank of centurions and platoon leaders mentioned in the text) should not be allowed to cut off the enemy's heads, see a document from the *Miscellaneous Excerpts from Qin Law*, excavated from Tomb 11, Shuihudi (Hulsewé 1985, 105, C5); see also Yates 2009, 32.

10. Most scholars read "five hundred" as referring to the number of soldiers under the given commander; I follow Li Ling's amendment based on the Han military documents from Shangsunjiazhai, Datong County 大通上孫家寨 (Qinghai); he identifies "five hundred" as a commander's rank (referring to the commander's salary in bushels of grain, as was common in Qin) (1991, 27–28).

11. Short combat weapons: daggers and short spears.

12. Note how easily the text shifts from military personnel (*jiang* 將, "general") to civilian officeholders (*ling* 令, "magistrate").

13. Commentators debate whether the word 封, "enfeoffed," is redundant here. Some commentators tend to identify it with the "state commandant" spoken about later in the chapter's text. Yet Zhang Jue may be right in assessing that this commandant may have been a commandery-level commandant (i.e., in charge of military forces of the largest administrative unit); this will explain why his rank is lower than that of the generalissimo (Zhang Jue 2012, 228–229 n. 4). For the possibility that the adjective *guo* 國 before the commandant's title refers not to the central government but to a commandery, see also Yang Zhenhong 2015, 3–13. In any case, *wei* 尉 (commandant) in this sentence refers to a senior official in charge of military affairs rather than to a field commander.

14. Following Gao Heng (1974, 148 n. 21), I read *jiang* 將 as an abbreviation of *da jiang* 大將 (generalissimo).

15. Emending *li* 吏 for *shi* 事 (occasion, event), following Sun Yirang's suggestion (Zhang Jue 2012, 229 n. 6).

16. Scholars disagree about the meaning of *qing* 輕 here; I read it as referring to rank reduction, just as in section 19.3, note 9.

17. The difference between the two numbers strongly suggests that the army, after occupying the fortress, was supposed to massacre all of its defenders.

18. The term *li* 吏 normally should refer to officers, but in this case it may refer to most soldiers as well because it includes the lowest ranks. Or maybe it stands here as a loan for *shi* 士?

19. I follow Jiang Lihong's parsing of the sentence (1996, 116).

20. Adding four characters 故爵簪褭, following Yu Yue's suggestion (Zhang Jue 2012, 229 n. 14).

21. Adding three characters 不更就, following Yu Yue's suggestion (Zhang Jue 2012, 229 n. 6) (Gao Heng, 1974 n. 150).

22. The sentence is not entirely clear; Gao Heng assumes that it speaks of promoting petty officers to county commandants (*xian wei* 縣尉) (1974, 238). I think he is wrong: it clearly would be impossible to create many new commandant offices. Rather, the text speaks of a special reward for an officer who holds the position of a county commandant. (Alternatively, the term *wei* 尉 may refer to a lower degree of power holders—that is, constable; see note 35 for this chapter). In interpreting the otherwise inexplicable term *jia* 加 as referring to a cash reward, I follow Gao Heng (1974, 238). Because we do not know the dating of the chapter, it is impossible to assert the value of 5,600 coins at the time of its composition, but, judging from the Imperial Qin documents from Liye and from the Yuelu Academy 岳麓書院 hoard, it was a considerable sum: an adult male slave was worth 4,300 in cash (*Liye* 2012, 66, board 8-1282; Chen Wei 2012, 306–307), and one set of armor (in which fines were calculated) was worth 1,344 in cash (Yu Zhenbo 2010).

23. In translating this sentence, I rely on Zhang Jue (2012, 230 n. 17).

24. Adding *guan* 官, following Zhu Shizhe's suggestion here and in the next section.

25. Adding five characters 故爵公大夫, following Yu Yue's suggestion (Zhang Jue 2012, 230 n. 22).

26. Adding four characters 故爵公乘, following Yu Yue's suggestion (Zhang Jue 2012, 230 n. 22).

27. For reading *da* 大 as a mistake for *zuo you* 左右 (left and right), see Gao Heng's gloss (1974, 148 n. 38).

28. In the text: four *geng* 更, but Gao Heng avers that this is a mistake for three *geng* (left, central, and right *geng*) (1974, 148 n. 38).

29. The twenty-two characters of the text surrounded by figure brackets (就為大庶長; 故大庶長, 就為左更; 故四更也, 就為大良造, probably the length of one slip), were misplaced to the end of the current section; Yu Yue proposed the restoration given here. *Da liangzao* 大良造 was probably the highest rank attainable through military merits. In the Qin hierarchy formed in the aftermath of Shang Yang's reform, six more ranks were added above the three *geng*; then instead of *da liangzao* we have *shao shangzao* 少上造 (fifteenth rank) and *da shangzao* 大上造 (sixteenth rank).

30. Granting settlements is different from granting tax income derived from them; settlements become the owner's fief. This vestige of the aristocratic system was not abolished under Shang Yang, but much later; we have a document of enfeoffment from Shang Yang's time ("Clay Document" [*washu* 瓦書]; see Yuan Zhongyi 1993).

31. Gao Heng correctly points out that the text is wrong (1974, 150 n. 40): *wu dafu* is a lower rank that can enjoy the tax collected from only three hundred families; the tax from six hundred families belongs to the upper ranks, two *shuzhang*, three *geng*, and grand *liangzao* (ranks 10–15), who, as is clear from the text, were allotted three hundred families as a fief in addition to the income from the taxes of an additional three hundred families. Raising retainers (literally "guests" 客) was a common practice among the highest nobility of the Warring States period (see Shen Gang 2003).

32. "Guest-minister" chancellors (*keqing* 客卿) were top appointees in the Qin government apparatus who were not Qin natives; they were of great importance after Shang Yang's era (see Huang Liuzhu 2002, 41–50; cf. Moriya Kazuki 2001). However, it seems that at the time of this chapter's composition, these ministers still ranked below regular ministers (*zheng qing* 正卿).

33. Following Jiang Lihong (1996, 119), I believe that the character *san* 三 after "heads" is redundant.

34. *Shi dafu* 士大夫 here refers to holders of the lowest four ranks (equivalent to *shi*, the lower segment of traditional nobility) and of the next six ranks (equivalent to *dafu*—that is, midlevel nobles).

35.   Qin counties normally had one commandant (*wei* 尉), who is duly mentioned in the next sentence, so clearly the four *wei* here are his subordinates. One of the military chapters of the *Mozi* mentions a *wei* as a low-level military-cum-police official akin to what was later known as "constable" (*tingzhang* 亭長) (*Mozi chengshou* 52.47:19 ["Bei cheng men" 備城門]), but in this case the number four is inexplicable (there were surely more than four constables in a county). I prefer to render "four *wei*" as "four subcommandants."

36.   Following Sun Yirang, the seventeen characters of the text inside the figure brackets (夫勞爵，其縣過三日，有不致士大夫勞爵，能 [= 罷]) are transferred here from their misplaced location in the third section of this chapter. For reading *neng* 能 as *ba* 罷 (dismiss, abolish) here and in section 19.7, I follow Sun Yirang (Zhang Jue 2012, 227 n. 8).

37.   One *qing* 頃 equals one hundred *mu* 畝 or 4.6 hectares (Hulsewé 1985, 19).

38.   I follow Duyvendak's suggestions here, identifying *xiandui* 陷隊 as sappers and not as crack troops, as Zhu Shizhe and Zhang Jue advocate (Gao Heng 1974, 153 n. 62; Zhang Jue 2012, 236 n. 7). The only substitution of a character, then, is *ru* 入 (penetrate) for *ren* 人. The small number of the unit's members suggests that they are not crack troops but indeed sappers.

39.   The term *guijian* 規諫, "admonition," is normally used in reference to reproving one's superiors, but here it evidently refers to the public admonition of the sappers before punishments are carried out.

40.   For reading *yi* 壹 as *tai* 臺 (platform), I follow Tao Hongqing (Zhang Jue 2012, 237 n. 16).

41.   Most recensions have *wang* 王 (royal) here, but Yan Wanli has *zheng* 正 (general, chief). Both terms are acceptable, but the choice has far-reaching implications for the text's dating (see the introduction to this chapter).

42.   Gao Heng reads *ji* 幾 as *qi* 祈, meaning "to request, to volunteer" (1974, 239). Zhang Jue suggests *ji* 冀 (to aspire), which preserves the same meaning (2012, 237 n. 20).

22. EXTERNAL AND INTERNAL

1.   In section 25.1, see more on the dangers of a privately established reputation as the road to social advancement.

2.   Reading 陷 as "to pierce through," following Yin Tongyang (Zhang Jue 2012, 254 n. 10) and Gao Heng (1974, 166 n. 9). "Hundred-*shi*-capacity crossbow" is glossed as an exceptionally powerful crossbow, equal in its power to a bow that can be shot only by someone able to lift a weight greater than five hundred kilograms (Gao Heng 1974, 166 n. 7).

3. For *you shi zhe* 游食者, "peripatetic eaters," as a referent for all those who can make their living by moving from one place to another—scholars, merchants, and artisans—see section 3.6.

4. The suggestion to increase the price of grain so as to benefit the peasants makes sense, but the text never elaborates how this will be achieved. Compare this suggestion with sophisticated economic policies advocated in the *Guanzi*, especially in the "Light and Heavy" ("Qingzhong" 輕重) chapters (Goldin forthcoming).

23. RULER AND MINISTERS

1. "Superiors" (*shang* 上) may refer here to the ruler alone.
2. See *Guanzi* XX.64:1175 ("Xing shi jie" 形勢解).
3. For "private gates" (i.e., seeking promotions through private patronage), see section 8.1.

24. INTERDICTING AND ENCOURAGING

1. This point is prominent in *Han Feizi*, arguably the most ruler-oriented text in the entire corpus of preimperial writings (see, e.g., *Han Feizi* II.6:36 ["You du" 有度]). For the resultant tension between Han Fei's overt monarchism and his perceptive understanding of the individual ruler's limitations, see Graziani 2015.

2. *Ren* 仞 is a measure of depth equal to the distance between two outstretched arms.

3. Li Lou 離婁 is a legendary paragon of keen sight (in section 9.5 he is referred to as Li Zhu 離朱).

4. Most commentators and translators read *can* 參 in this context as "establishing manifold officials," deducing this reading primarily from the subsequent discussion in the text. In distinction, I read *can* as in the compound *canhe* 參劾, "to impeach." In an ideal state of affairs, the officials are so fearful of the ruler that even without the employment of punitive means against them, they do not transgress; this is yet another illustration of "eradicating punishments through punishments."

5. The word *shi* 勢, "power," shifts in the last two instances here from depicting the ruler's supreme power of authority to the power of a single office. This usage is confusing and leaves the bottom line vague: What was the power valued by former kings? Was it reliance on their own power of authority or just the power to put limitations on their underlings' power?

6.   This saying is clearly reminiscent of the *Laozi*'s valorization of "emptiness" (e.g., *Laozi* 5; *Boshu Laozi*, p. 144) and "staying behind" (*Laozi* 67; *Boshu Laozi*, pp. 160–162). Interestingly, the ruler's "emptiness" is recommended in *Han Feizi* (e.g., I.5:26 ["Zhu Dao" 主道]). Here is a rare example of an overt disagreement between the authors of the *Book of Lord Shang* and the authors of the *Han Feizi*.

7.   Most commentators assume that in this sentence *bi* 蔽 refers to making a decision, whereas *yun* 員 stands for material evidence. This reading is not entirely satisfactory, though, because *bi* 蔽 is used later in the same passage in its regular meaning of "being deceived" or "matters being covered up." This sentence is possibly corrupt.

8.   Literally, their body (*ti* 體) is the same, referring to the fundamental unity of interests among the officials.

9.   This is the clearest exposition of the principle of collective responsibility in the *Book of Lord Shang* (see also section 18.3).

10. Reading *li* 吏 as clerks or the officials' underlings. An alternative reading would be "the ruler and his officials." The term *li* 吏 can refer in different contexts to the officials as a whole or to lower officials or just to clerks. See, for example, Liu Min 2014, 167.

11. Following Yu Yue, I emend *yi* 異, "different," to *tong* 同, "identical."

12. The number of missing characters is different from one recension to another; see Zhang Jue 2012, 267 n. 7.

13. Following earlier commentators, I read *yan* 焉 as a noun: "yellow bird." The overseer of horses and the game warden would be able to benefit at the expense of horses and birds under their control only because they cannot be denounced by those horses and birds. Note that the argument deviates from the previous discussion of mutual control of officials and refers to their control from below by the populace (whose complaints may moderate the officials' wrongdoing). The topic is not developed elsewhere in the chapter but is hinted at again in chapter 26.

25. ATTENTION TO LAW

1.   Yu 禹 is the legendary founder of the Xia dynasty.

2.   Again, following Harbsmeir 1997, I read the first-person pronoun *wu* 吾 as "you." Compare with section 18.6 for a similar usage.

3.   This saying brings to mind the chapter "Ming fa" 明法 of the *Guanzi* (XV.46:916). The *Han Feizi* also repeatedly warns the ruler about following the ministerial advice in promoting officials because it will encourage formation of cabals and subsequent loss of the ruler's authority. See, for example, the chapters "You du" 有度 (II.6:31–33) and "Er bing" 二柄 (II.7:41–42), among others.

4.   The four characters 相管附惡 make no sense here; I follow Wang Shirun's replacement of them with 習愛人不阿 based on the parallels in the next sentence (Zhang Jue 2012, 275 n. 8).

5.   Jie 桀 was the paradigmatic bad last ruler of the semilegendary Xia dynasty.

6.   Most commentators and translators consider the latter phrase hortatory (the state should let the people find it bitter not to till and find it dangerous not to fight) and try to explain that 無 here does not mean negation of tilling and fighting. I think this reading is wrong: the sentence clearly answers the previous question, Why do rulers fail to strengthen their states? The answer is that the populace is still able to avoid tilling and waging war: a condition that should be changed.

26. FIXING DIVISIONS

1.   The concept of "names" (*ming* 名) is one of the most multifaceted ones in early Chinese thought (see, e.g., Makeham 1994). In the context of administrative thought, *ming* may refer to "title," as in the *Han Feizi* (Goldin 2013, 8–10; see also Makeham 1990–1991). In the *Book of Lord Shang*, it normally refers to one's repute and social status (e.g., sections 6.4, 6.5, and 8.1, among others). In chapter 26, it occasionally refers to the items of legal codes (26.5) but mostly to something akin to a proper bureaucratic nomenclature. This chapter usually connects *ming* with *fen* 分, another important term of philosophical and administrative discourse that refers to social divisions, distinctions, individual allotment, and the like (Sato Masayuki 2000, 27–31). The compound *mingfen*, which in chapter 26 refers to the essence of legal and administrative practices, is very rarely used in preimperial and early imperial texts (the only exception being a possibly spurious text, *Yin Wenzi* 尹文子, for which see Gao Liushui 1996, 85–100).

2.   Among many other linguistic peculiarities of this chapter is its frequent invocation of the compound *limin* 吏民, which here means "officials and the people." As Liu Min notes, this compound proliferated after the late Warring States period; at times, it could point to two separate entities (officials and the people, as in this chapter); at other times, it could point to a special social stratum of commoners and petty officials or clerks (most of whom were originally commoners), in distinction from high officials (2014, 14–138).

3.   The unnamed lord is Lord Xiao of Qin.

4.   For emending *pu* 撲 to *fu* 柎, which can be glossed as "to request" or "to seek," see Gao Heng 1974, 243.

5.   Following Gao Heng (1974, 186 n. 5), I have added *ling* 令, "to order," here.

6.   Following Zhu Shizhe, I emend *min* 民 to *ren* 人, referring here to officials only (Zhang Jue 2012, 280 n. 7).

7.   Literally "to cut" (*duo* 剟) and "to revise" (reading *ding* 定 as *ding* 訂).

8.   One *chi* 尺 is approximately twenty-three centimeters; one *cun* 寸 is one-tenth of a *chi*.

9.   Meticulous recording of the date and hour of the arrival and dispatching of official documents is stipulated in the Qin administrative regulations from Tomb 11, Shuihudi (*Shuihudi* 2001, 61, slips 184–185; Hulsewé 1985, 86, A96), and is amply demonstrated by the Liye documents. The Shuihudi Tomb 11 documents contain a section titled "Answers to Questions Concerning Qin Statutes" ("Qin lü dawen" 秦律答問), which indicates that the promulgation of legal knowledge among officials (even if not among the people in general) was indeed essential for Qin administrators.

10.   This section is perhaps the earliest systematic depiction of archive keeping in early China (see a brief discussion in Wu Jie 1992).

11.   The office of *yushi* 御史 (overseer, inspector) existed in Qin (and other Warring States) from a relatively early stage of the Warring States period, but on the eve of the imperial unification the Qin *yushi* was charged with supervising regional administration, which made his office equivalent to that of "chief prosecutor" (Tong Weimin 2013, 219).

12.   The office of "prime minister" (*chengxiang* 丞相) was established in Qin in 309 B.C.E.

13.   The coexistence of "regional lords" (*zhuhou* 諸侯) with heads of commanderies and counties (*junxian* 郡縣) caused many scholars to propose an early Han dating for this chapter because it was then that the empire's territory was divided between the areas under direct imperial control (commanderies and counties) and the areas under autonomous regional lords. Yet a similar situation existed on the eve of the unification as well. Although Qin did maintain centralized control over its territories through the commanderies and counties system, it treated some of the neighboring polities ruled by regional lords as its dependencies, whose leaders had a status similar to that of the governors of Qin commanderies (see details in Ōkushi Atsuhiro 1999).

14.   Adding *yu* 欲 (to want), following Wang Shirun (Zhang Jue 2012, 285 n. 8).

15.   For the commoners' legal knowledge under the Qin and early Han Empires, see Korolkov 2011.

16.   Duyvendak ([1928] 1963, 331 n. 1) and Perelomov (1993, 318 n. 15) consider this phrase an interpolation; therefore, I place it in double figure brackets.

17.   This sentence is restored here on the basis of a citation in the *Qunshu zhiyao* 群書治要 compilation (Zhang Jue 2012, 286).

18.   Here "names" refers to one's property rights to the rabbit.

19.   This rabbit parable is told in the *Lüshi chunqiu* (17.6:1109–1110 ["Shen shi" 慎勢]), where it is attributed to Shènzi 慎子 (Shen Dao).

20.   Reading *xi* 析 as "behaving crookedly" and *jian* 姦 as "stealing," following glosses by Zhu Shizhe and Zhang Jue (Zhang Jue 2012, 287 n. 8).

21. This is an interesting indication of the parallel oral-cum-written transmission of ancient texts by the end of the Warring States period.

22. The idea of turning officials into teachers appears in *Han Feizi* XIX.49:452 ("Wu du" 五蠹) and is echoed in the 213 B.C.E. memorial by Li Si 李斯 (d. 208 B.C.E.), who initiated the infamous book burning (*Shiji* 87:2546).

FRAGMENT OF "SIX LAWS"

1. On the importance of altering the people's customs in the *Book of Lord Shang*, see section 17.1 and note 1 for that chapter (p. 278).

BIBLIOGRAPHY

Allan, Sarah. 2015. *Buried Ideas: Legends of Abdication and Ideal Government in Recently Discovered Early Chinese Bamboo-Slip Manuscripts.* Albany: State University of New York Press.

——. 2016. *The Heir and the Sage: Dynastic Legend in Early China.* Rev. ed. San Francisco: Chinese Materials Center.

Ames, Roger T. 1994. *The Art of Rulership: A Study of Ancient Chinese Political Thought.* Albany: State University of New York Press.

Barbieri-Low, Anthony J. 2007. *Artisans in Early Imperial China.* Seattle: University of Washington Press.

Barbieri-Low, Anthony J. and Robin D. S. Yates. 2015. *Law, State, and Society in Early Imperial China: A Study with Critical Edition and Translation of the Legal Texts from Zhangjiashan Tomb No. 247.* Leiden: Brill.

Baxter, William H. 1998. "Situating the Language of the *Lao-tzu*: The Probable Date of the *Tao-te-ching*." In *Lao-tzu and the* Tao-te-ching, ed. Livia Kohn and Michael LaFargue, 231–253. Albany: State University of New York Press.

Boesche, Roger. 2008. "Kautilya's *Arthashastra* and the Legalism of Lord Shang." *Journal of Asian History* 42, no. 1: 64–90.

Bol, Peter K. 1993. "Government, Society, and State: On the Political Visions of Ssuma Kuang and Wang An-shih." In *Ordering the World: Approaches to State and Society in Sung Dynasty China*, ed. Robert R. Hymes and Conrad Schirokauer, 128–192. Berkeley: University of California Press.

Boltz, William G. 2005. "The Composite Nature of Early Chinese Texts." In *Text and Ritual in Early China*, ed. Martin Kern, 50–78. Seattle: University of Washington Press.

Boshu Laozi jiaozhu 帛書老子校注. 1996. Compiled and annotated by Gao Ming 高明. Beijing: Zhonghua shuju.

Brooks, E. Bruce and A. Taeko Brooks. 1998. *The Original Analects: Sayings of Confucius and His Successors*. New York: Columbia University Press.

Bu Xianqun 卜憲群. 2006. "Qin Han zhi ji xiangli liyuan zakao: yi Liye Qin jian wei zhongxin de tantao" 秦漢之際鄉里吏員雜考——以里耶秦簡為中心的探討. *Nandu xuetan* 南都學壇 1:1–6.

Cai, Liang. 2014. *Witchcraft and the Rise of the First Confucian Empire*. Albany: State University of New York Press.

Cao Hongjun 曹紅軍. 1996. "'Yan Kejun' 'Yan Wanli' bian" "嚴可均"、"嚴萬里" 辨. *Wenjiao ziliao* 文教資料 6:105–108.

Chang Hao. 1987. *Chinese Intellectuals in Crisis: Search for Order and Meaning (1890–1911)*. Berkeley: University of California Press.

Chen Hongtai 陳紅太. 2013. *Zhongguo zhengzhi jingshen de yanjiu: cong Kongzi dao Sun Zhongshan* 中國政治精神的演進——從孔子到孫中山. Jilin: Renmin chubanshe.

Chen Li 陳力. 2009. "Cong kaogu ziliao kan *Shangjunshu* 'Lai min' de zhenshixing: Jian tan Zhanguo wanqi Qin Xianyang fujin yimin fenbu de tedian" 從考古資料看《商君書 · 徠民》的真實性：兼談戰國晚期秦咸陽附近移民分佈的特點. *Bianjiang minzu kaogu yu minzu kaoguxue jikan* 邊疆民族考古與民族考古學集刊 1:312–321.

Chen Longwen 陳隆文. 2006. *Chunqiu Zhanguo huobi dili yanjiu* 春秋戰國貨幣地理研究. Beijing: Renmin chubanshe.

Chen Qitian 陳啓天. 1935. *Shang Yang pingzhuan* 商鞅評傳. Shanghai: Shangwu.

Chen Wei 陳偉, ed. 2012. *Liye Qin jiandu jiaoshi (di yi juan)* 里耶秦簡牘校釋 (第一卷). Wuhan: Wuhan daxue chubanshe.

Cheng Bu 程步. 2013. *Zhen Shang Yang* 真商鞅. Qingdao: Qingdao chubanshe.

Cheng Liaoyuan 程燎原. 2011. "Xian Qin 'fazhi' gainian zai shi" 先秦 "法治" 概念再釋. *Zhengfa luntan* 政法論壇 29, no. 2: 3–13.

Chunqiu Zuozhuan zhu 春秋左傳注. 1990. Annotated by Yang Bojun 楊伯峻. Beijing: Zhonghua shuju.

Creel, Herrlee G. 1953. *Chinese Thought from Confucius to Mao Tse-tung*. Chicago: University of Chicago Press.

——. 1974. *Shen Pu-hai: A Chinese Political Philosopher of the Fourth Century B.C.* Chicago: University of Chicago Press.

Dai Weihong 戴衛紅. 2014. "Hunan Liye Qinjian suo jian 'fayue' wenshu" 湖南里耶秦簡所見 "伐閱" 文書. *Jianbo yanjiu* 簡帛研究 2013:82–92.

Defoort, Carine. 2001. "Ruling the World with Words: The Idea of *Zhengming* in the *Shizi*." *Bulletin of the Museum of Far Eastern Antiquities* 73:217–242.

——. 2015. "The Modern Formation of Early Mohism: Sun Yirang's *Exposing and Correcting the Mozi*." *Toung Pao* 101, nos. 1–3: 208–238.

Deng Guoguang 鄧國光. 2011. *Jingxue yi li* 經學義理. Shanghai: Shanghai guji chubanshe.

Dongpo quanji 東坡全集. n.d. By Su Shi 蘇軾 (1036–1101). E-*Siku quanshu* edition.

Dongshu dushu ji 東塾讀書記. [n.d.] 2008. By Chen Li 陳澧 (1810–1882). Reprinted in *Chen Li ji* 陳澧集, 6 vols., compiled by Huang Guosheng 黃國聲, 2:1–352. Shanghai: Shanghai guiji chubanshe.

Du Zhengsheng 杜正勝. 1985. "Cong juezhi lun Shang Yang bianfa suo xingcheng de shehui" 從爵制論商鞅變法所形成的社會. *Zhongyang yanjiuyuan lishi yuyan yanjiusuo jikan* 中央研究院歷史語言研究所集刊 56, no. 3: 485–544.

Duyvendak, Jan J.-L., trans. [1928] 1963. *The Book of Lord Shang: A Classic of the Chinese School of Law.* Reprint. Chicago: University of Chicago Press.

Fang Yong 方勇, ed. 2015. *Zizang: Fajia bu: Shangjunshu juan* 子藏·法家部·商君書卷. 9 vols. Beijing: Guojia tushuguan chubanshe.

Fengsu tongyi jiaozhu 風俗通義校注. 2010. By Ying Shao 應劭 (140–206). Annotated by Wang Liqi 王利器. Beijing: Zhonghua shuju.

Fischer, Markus. 2012. "*The Book of Lord Shang* Compared with Machiavelli and Hobbes." *Dao* 11, no. 2: 201–221.

Fischer, Paul. 2009. "Authentication Studies (辨偽學) Methodology and the Polymorphous Text Paradigm." *Early China* 32:1–43.

——, trans. 2012. *Shizi: China's First Syncretist.* New York: Columbia University Press.

Fu Sinian 傅斯年 (1896–1950). 2012. *Zhanguo zijia xulun* 戰國子家敘論. Shanghai: Shanghai guji chubanshe.

Fu Zhengyuan. 1996. *China's Legalists: The Earliest Totalitarians and Their Art of Ruling.* Armonk, N.Y.: M. E. Sharpe.

Fung, Edmund S. K. 1991. "The Alternative of Loyal Opposition: The Chinese Youth Party and Chinese Democracy, 1937–1949," *Modern China* 17.2: 260–289.

Galvany, Albert. 2015. "Signs, Clues, and Traces: Anticipation in Ancient Chinese Political and Military Texts." *Early China* 38:151–193.

Gao Heng 高亨. 1974. *Shangjunshu zhu yi* 商君書注譯. Beijing: Zhonghua shuju.

Gao Liushui 高流水, trans. and annotator. 1996. *Yinwenzi quanyi* 尹文子全譯. In Gao Liushui and Lin Hengsen 林恒森, *Shenzi, Yinwenzi, Gongsun Longzi quanyi* 慎子、尹文子、公孫龍子全譯, 83–167. Guiyang: Guizhou renmin chubanshe.

Gentz, Joachim. 2015. "Defining Boundaries and Relations Between Textual Units: Examples from the Literary Tool-Kit of Early Chinese Argumentation." In *Literary Forms of Argument in Early China*, ed. Joachim Gentz and Dirk Meyer, 112–157. Leiden: Brill.

Gentz, Joachim and Dirk Meyer. 2015. "Introduction: Literary Forms of Argument in Early China." In *Literary Forms of Argument in Early China*, ed. Joachim Gentz and Dirk Meyer, 1–36. Leiden: Brill.

Giele, Enno. 2006. *Imperial Decision-Making and Communication in Early China: A Study of Cai Yong's Duduan.* Opera Sinologica no. 20. Wiesbaden: Harrasowitz.

Goldin, Paul R. 2005. *After Confucius: Studies in Early Chinese Philosophy.* Honolulu: University of Hawai'i Press.

——. 2011a. *Confucianism.* Durham, N.C.: Acumen.

——. 2011b. "Persistent Misconceptions About Chinese 'Legalism.'" *Journal of Chinese Philosophy* 38, no. 1: 88–104.

——. 2013. "Han Fei and the *Han Feizi*." In *Dao Companion to the Philosophy of Han Fei*, ed. Paul R. Goldin, 1–21. Dordrecht: Springer.

——, comp. 2018. "Ancient Chinese Civilization: Bibliography of Materials in Western Languages." September 23 version. file:///C:/Users/Owner/Downloads/Ancient _Chinese_Civilization_Bibliograph.pdf.

——. Forthcoming. "Economic Cycles and Price Theory in Early Chinese Texts." In *Between Command and Market: Economic Thought and Practice in Early China*, ed. Elisa Sabattini and Christian Schwermann. Leiden: Brill.

Graham, Angus C. 1967. "The Background of the Mencian Theory of Human Nature." *Tsing Hua Journal of Chinese Studies* 6:215–274.

——. 1989. *Disputers of the Tao: Philosophical Argument in Ancient China*. La Salle, Ill.: Open Court.

Graziani, Romain. 2015. "Monarch and Minister: The Problematic Partnership in the Building of Absolute Monarchy in the *Han Feizi* 韓非子." In *Ideology of Power and Power of Ideology in Early China*, ed. Yuri Pines, Paul R. Goldin, and Martin Kern, 155–180. Leiden: Brill.

——. Forthcoming. "What's in a Slogan? The Political Rationale and the Economic Debates Behind 'Enrich the State' (*Fuguo* 富國) in Early China." In *Keywords in Chinese Thought and Literature*, ed. Li Wai-yee and Yuri Pines. Hong Kong: The Chinese University Press.

Guanzi jiaozhu 管子校注. 2004. Compiled by Li Xiangfeng 黎翔鳳. Beijing: Zhonghua shuju.

Guo Moruo 郭沫若. [1945] 2008. "Qianqi fajia de pipan" 前期法家的批判. Reprinted in Guo Moruo, *Shi pipan shu* 十批判書, 227–249. Beijing: Zhongguo huaqiao chubanshe.

Guxun huizuan 故訓匯纂. 2007. Compiled by Zong Fubang 宗福邦, Chen Shinao 陳世鐃, and Xiao Haibo 蕭海波. Beijing: Shangwu.

Han Feizi jijie 韓非子集解. 1998. Compiled by Wang Xianshen 王先慎 (1859–1922). Collated by Zhong Zhe 鍾哲. Beijing: Zhonghua shuju.

Handelman, Don. 1995. "Cultural Taxonomy and Bureaucracy in Ancient China: The Book of Lord Shang." *International Journal of Politics, Culture, and Society* 9, no. 2: 263–294.

Hanshu 漢書. 1997. By Ban Gu 班固 (32–92) et al. Annotated by Yan Shigu 顏師古 (581–645). Beijing: Zhonghua shuju.

Harbsmeier, Christoph. 1997. "Xunzi and the Problem of Impersonal First Person Pronouns." *Early China* 22: 181–220.

Hou Hanshu 後漢書. 1997. By Fan Ye 范曄 (398–445) et al. Annotated by Li Xian 李賢 et al. Beijing: Zhonghua shuju.

Hsing I-t'ien 邢義田. 2014. "Qin-Han Census and Tax and Corvée Administration: Notes on Newly Discovered Materials." In *Birth of an Empire: The State of Qin*

Revisited, ed. Yuri Pines, Lothar von Falkenhausen, Gideon Shelach, and Robin D. S. Yates, 155–186. Berkeley: University of California Press.

Hu Hanmin 胡漢民. [1931] 1975. "*Shangjunshu* jian xu" 商君書箋序. Reprinted in *Shangjunshu jianzheng* 商君書箋正, ed. Jian Shu 簡書, 1–7. Taibei: Guangwen shuju.

Hu Shi 胡適. [1919] 1996. *Zhongguo zhexue shi dagang* 中國哲學史大綱. Reprint. Beijing: Dongfang chubanshe.

———. [1930] 1998. *Zhongguo zhonggu sixiang shi changpian* 中國中古思想史長篇. Reprinted in *Hu Shi wenji* 胡適文集, 6 vols., ed. Ouyang Zhesheng 歐陽哲生, 6:423–668. Beijing: Beijing daxue chubanshe.

The Huainanzi: A Guide to the Theory and Practice of Government in Early China. 2010. Trans. and ed. John S. Major, Sarah A. Queen, Andrew Seth Meyer, and Harold D. Roth. New York: Columbia University Press.

Huang Liuzhu 黃留珠. 2002. *Qin Han lishi wenhua lungao* 秦漢歷史文化論稿. Xi'an: San Qin chubanshe.

Huang Shaomei 黃紹梅. 2010. *Shang Yang fan renwenguan yanjiu* 商鞅反人文觀研究. Taibei: Hua Mulan chubanshe.

Huangshi richao 黃氏日抄. n.d. By Huang Zhen 黃震 (1213–1280). E-*Siku quanshu* edition.

Hubei Sheng Jingzhou diqu bowuguan 湖北省荊州地區博物館. 1982. "Jiangling Tianxingguan 1 hao Chu mu" 江陵天星觀1號楚墓. *Kaogu xuebao* 考古學報 1:71–118.

Huian ji 晦菴集. n.d. By Zhu Xi 朱熹 (1130–1200). E-*Siku quanshu* edition.

Hulsewé, A. F. P. 1985. *Remnants of Ch'in Law: An Annotated Translation of the Ch'in Legal and Administrative Rules of the 3rd Century B.C. Discovered in Yün-meng Prefecture, Hu-pei Province, in 1975*. Leiden: Brill.

Jian Shu 簡書, annotator. [1931] 1975. *Shangjunshu jianzheng* 商君書箋正. Taibei: Guangwen shuju.

———, annotator. [1931] 2015. *Shangjunshu jianzheng* 商君書箋正. Reprinted in *Zizang: Fajia bu: Shangjunshu juan* 子藏 · 法家部 · 商君書卷, 9 vols., ed. Fang Yong 方勇, 7:313–525. Beijing: Guojia tushuguan chubanshe.

Jiang Lihong 蔣禮鴻, annotator. 1996. *Shangjunshu zhuizhi* 商君書錐指. Beijing: Zhonghua shuju.

Jiu Tangshu 舊唐書. 1997. By Liu Xu 劉昫 (888–947) et al. Beijing: Zhonghua shuju.

Jun zhai dushu zhi 郡齋讀書志. n.d. Compiled by Chao Gongwu 晁公武 (1105–1180). E-*Siku quanshu* edition.

Kandel, Jochen. 1985. "Das Buch des Fürsten Shang und die Einführung der Monodoxie: Eine annotierte Übersetzung der Kapitel III und VIII des *Shang-chün shu*." In *Religion und Philosophie in Ostasien: Festschrift für Hans Steininger zum 65 Geburtstag*, ed. Gert Naudorf, Karl-Heinz Pohl, and Hans-Hermann Schmidt, 445–458. Würzburg: Königshausen + Neumann.

Kern, Martin. 2000. *The Stele Inscriptions of Ch'in Shih-huang: Text and Ritual in Early Chinese Imperial Representation.* New Haven, Conn.: American Oriental Society.

——. 2015. "The Masters in the *Shiji.*" *T'oung Pao* 101, nos. 4–5: 335–362.

Khayutina Maria. 2008. "Western 'Capitals' of the Western Zhou Dynasty (1046/5–771 B.C.): Historical Reality and Its Reflections Until the Time of Sima Qian." *Oriens Extremus* 47:25–65.

King, Brandon R. 2015. "Adapting with the Times: Fajia Law and State Development." Ph.D. diss., The Chinese University of Hong Kong.

——. 2018. "The [Not So] Hidden Curriculum of the Legalist State in the *Book of Lord Shang* and the *Han-Fei-Zi.*" *Comparative Philosophy* 9.2: 69–92.

Knoblock, John and Jeffrey Riegel, trans. 2000. *The Annals of Lü Buwei: A Complete Translation and Study.* Stanford: Stanford University Press.

Korolkov, Maxim. 2010. "Zemel'noe zakonodatel'stvo I kontrol' gosudarstva nad zemlej v epokhu Chzhan'go i v nachale ranneimperskoj epokhi (po dannym vnov' obnaruzhennykh zakonodatel'nykh tekstov." Ph.D. diss., Russian Academy of Sciences, Institute of Oriental Studies.

——. 2011. "Arguing About Law: Interrogation Procedure Under the Qin and Former Han Dynasties." *Études Chinoises* 30:37–71.

Kroker, Eduard Josef. 1953. *Der Gedanke der Macht im Shang-kün-shu: Betrachtungen eines alten chinesischen Philosophen.* St. Gabrieler Studien 12. Vienna: St. Gabriel.

Laitinen, Kauko. 1990. *Chinese Nationalism in the Late Qing Dynasty: Zhang Binglin as an Anti-Manchu Propagandist.* London: Curzon.

Laozi. See *Boshu Laozi jiaozhu.*

Lévi, Jean, trans. 1981. *Le livre du prince Shang.* Paris: Flammarion.

——, trans. 2005. *Le livre du prince Shang.* 2nd ed., with an updated introduction. Paris: Flammarion.

Lewis, Mark E. 1990. *Sanctioned Violence in Early China.* Albany: State University of New York Press.

——. 1999a. "Warring States: Political History." In *The Cambridge History of Ancient China: From the Origins of Civilization to 221 B.C.,* ed. Michael Loewe and Edward L. Shaughnessy, 587–650. Cambridge: Cambridge University Press.

——. 1999b. *Writing and Authority in Early China.* Albany: State University of New York Press.

——. 2000. "The Han Abolition of Universal Military Service." In *Warfare in Chinese History,* ed. Hans Van de Ven, 33–76. Leiden: Brill.

——. 2006. *The Construction of Space in Early China.* Albany: State University of New York Press.

——. 2007. *The Early Chinese Empires: Qin and Han.* Cambridge, Mass.: Harvard University Press.

Li Cunshan 李存山. 1998. "*Shangjunshu* yu Handai zun Ru: Jianlun Shang Yang jiqi xuepai yu Ruxue de chongtu" 商君書與漢代尊儒——兼論商鞅及其學派與儒學

的衝突. *Zhongguo shehui kexueyuan yanjiusheng xuebao* 中國社會科學院研究生學報1:35–40. (English translation in *Contemporary Chinese Thought* 47.2 [2016]: 112–124.)

Li Ling 李零. 1991. "*Shangjunshu* zhong de tudi renkou zhengce yu juezhi" 《商君書》中的土地人口政策與爵制. *Guji zhengli yu yanjiu* 古籍整理與研究 6:23–30.

Li Yipi 李一丕. 2014. "Henan Chu changcheng fenbu ji fangyu tixi yanjiu" 河南楚長城分佈及防禦體系研究. *Zhongyuan wenwu* 中原文物 5: 44–50, 74.

Li Yu-ning. 1977a. "Introduction." In *Shang Yang's Reforms and State Control in China*, ed. Li Yu-ning, xiii–cxx. White Plains, N.Y.: M. E. Sharpe.

——, ed. 1977b. *Shang Yang's Reforms and State Control in China*. White Plains, N.Y.: M. E. Sharpe.

Lian Shaoming 連劭名. 2001. "*Shangjunshu* xin zheng" 《商君書》新證. *Wenxian* 文獻 4:18–33, 125.

Liang Qichao 梁啟超. [1919] 1996. *Xian Qin zhengzhi sixiang shi* 先秦政治思想史. Reprint. Beijing: Dongfang.

——. [1906] 2003. "Zhongguo falixue fada shi lun" 中國法理學發達史論. Reprinted in Liang Qichao, *Yin bing shi wenji dianjiao* 飲冰室文集點校, 6 vols., collated by Wu Song 吳松, Lu Yunkun 盧雲崐, Wang Wenguang 王文光, and Duan Bingchang 段炳昌, 1:340–375. Kunming: Yunnan jiaoyu chubanshe.

——. [1911] 2014. *Zhongguo liu da zhengzhijia* 中國六大政治家. Rpt. Beijing: Zhonghua shuju.

Liji jijie 禮記集解. 1995. Compiled by Sun Xidan 孫希旦. Ed. Shen Xiaohuan 沈嘯寰 and Wang Xingxian 王星賢. Beijing: Zhonghua shuju.

Lin Shaoping 林少平. 2015. "Lun *Yu shu* yu Shang Yang sixiang yuanyuan" 論《語書》與商鞅的思想淵源. http://www.bsm.org.cn/show_article.php?id=2182.

Liu Min 劉敏. 2014. *Qin-Han bianhu qimin wenti yanjiu: yi yu limin, juezhi, huangquan guanxi wei zhongdian* 秦漢編戶齊民問題研究——以與吏民、爵制、皇權關係為重點. Beijing: Zhonghua shuju.

Liu Zehua 劉澤華. 1991. *Zhongguo chuantong zhengzhi siwei* 中國傳統政治思維. Changchun: Jilin jiaoyu chubanshe.

——, ed. 1996. *Zhongguo zhengzhi sixiang shi* 中國政治思想史. 3 vols. Hangzhou: Zhejiang renmin chubanshe.

——. 2000. *Zhongguo de Wangquanzhuyi* 中國的王權主義. Shanghai: Renmin chubanshe.

——. 2003. *Xi er zhai wengao* 洗耳齋文稿. Beijing: Zhonghua shuju.

——. 2012. "'Wenge' zhong de jingen, cuowei yu zhu yishi de mengsheng—Yantao lishi de sixiang zishu zhi er" "文革" 中的緊跟、錯位與自主意識的萌生——研討歷史的思想自述之二. *Shixue yuekan* 史學月刊 11:97–101.

Liye Qin jian (yi) 里耶秦簡 (壹). 2012. Published by Hunan sheng wenwu kaogu yanjiusuo 湖南省文物考古研究所. Beijing: Wenwu chubanshe.

Loewe, Michael. 1960. "The Orders of Aristocratic Rank of Han China." *T'oung Pao* 48, nos. 1–3: 97–174.

——. 1974. *Crisis and Conflict in Han China*. Chatham, U.K.: Mackay.

——. 1986. "The Former Han Dynasty." In *The Cambridge History of China*, vol. 1: *The Ch'in and Han Empires, 221 B.C.–AD 220*, ed. Denis C. Twitchett and John K. Fairbank, 103–222. Cambridge: Cambridge University Press.

——. 2010. "Social Distinctions, Groups, and Privileges." In *China's Early Empires: A Reappraisal*, ed. Michael Nylan and Michael Loewe, 296–307. Cambridge: Cambridge University Press.

Louie, Kam. 1980. *Critiques of Confucius in Contemporary China*. New York: St. Martin's Press.

Lü Wenyu 呂文鬱. 2006. *Zhoudai caiyi zhidu* 周代的采邑制度. Beijing: Shehui kexue wenxian chubanshe.

Luo Genze 羅根澤. [1935] 2001. "*Shangjunshu* tanyuan" 《商君書》探源. Reprinted in *Luo Genze shuo zhuzi* 羅根澤說諸子, compiled by Zhou Xunchu 周勛初, 369–380. Shanghai: Shanghai guji chubanshe.

Lüshi chunqiu jiaoshi 呂氏春秋校釋. 1995. Compiled and annotated by Chen Qiyou 陳奇猷. Shanghai: Shanghai guji chubanshe.

Ma Zongshen 馬宗申. 1985. *Shangjunshu lun nongzheng si pian zhushi* 商君書論農政四篇注釋. Beijing: Nongye chubanshe and Shaanxi kexue jishu chubanshe.

MacFarquhar, Roderick and Michael Schoenhals. 2006. *Mao's Last Revolution*. Cambridge, Mass.: Belknap Press of Harvard University Press.

Mai Menghua 麥孟華. [n.d.] 1986. *Shang jun pingzhuan* 商君評傳. Reprinted in *Zhuzi jicheng* 諸子集成, 8 vols., 5:paginated separately. Shanghai: Shanghai shudian.

Makeham, John. 1990–1991. "The Legalist Concept of *Hsing-ming*: An Example of the Contribution of Archeological Evidence to the Re-interpretation of Transmitted Texts." *Monumenta Serica* 39:87–114.

——. 1994. *Name and Actuality in Early Chinese Thought*. Albany: State University of New York Press.

Mao shi zhengyi 毛詩正義. [1815] 1991. Annotated by Zheng Xuan 鄭玄 (127–200) and Kong Yingda 孔穎達 (574–648). Reprinted in *Shisan jing zhushu fu jiaokanji* 十三經注疏附校勘記, 2 vols., compiled by Ruan Yuan 阮元 (1764–1849), 1:259–629. Beijing: Zhonghua shuju.

Mao Zedong. 1975. *Selected Works of Mao Tse-Tung* [*Mao Zedong*]. 4 vols. Peking [Beijing]: Foreign Languages Press.

Masubuchi Tatsuo 增淵龍夫. 1963. *Chūgoku kodai no shakai to kokka* 中國古代の社會と國家. Tokyo: Kōbun.

McNeal, Robin. 2012. *Conquer and Govern: Early Chinese Military Texts from the* Yi Zhou shu. Honolulu: University of Hawai'i Press.

Meng Jifu 蒙季甫. 1942. "*Shangjunshu* 'Shuo min' 'Ruo min' pian wei jieshuo 'Qu qiang' pian kanzheng ji" 商君書說民弱民篇為解說去強篇刊正記. *Tushu jikan* 圖書集刊 1:51–57.

Mengzi yizhu 孟子譯注. 1992. Annotated by Yang Bojun 楊伯峻. Beijing: Zhonghua shuju.

Miao Ruosu 苗若素 and Wu Shiqi 吳世琪. 1998. *Shangjunshu cidian* 商君書詞典. In *Xian Qin yaoji cidian (Liezi, Shang jun shu, Chunqiu Gongyang zhuan)* 先秦要籍詞典 (列子·商君書·春秋公羊傳), ed. Wang Shishun 王世舜, 65-96. Beijing: Xueyuan chubanshe.

Miller, Harry. 2009. *State Versus Gentry in Late Ming Dynasty China, 1572-1644*. New York: Palgrave Macmillan.

Miyake Kiyoshi 宮宅潔. 2015. "Qinguo zhanyi shi yu yuanzhengjun de goucheng" 秦國戰役史與遠征軍的構成. *Jianbo* 簡帛 11:153-170.

Moriya Hiroshi 守屋洋, trans. 1995. *Shōkun sho: Chūgoku ryū tōchi no gaku* 商君書: 中国流統治の学. Tokyo: Tokuma shoten.

Moriya Kazuki 森谷一樹. 2001. "Senkoku Shin no sōhō ni tsuite" 戰國秦の相邦について. *Tōyōshi kenkyū* 東洋史研究 60, no. 1: 1-29.

Moriya Mitsuo 守屋美都雄. 2010. *Zhongguo gudai de jiazu yu guojia* 中國古代的家族與國家. Trans. Qian Hang 錢杭 and Yang Xiaofen 楊曉芬. Shanghai: Shanghai guji chubanshe [originally published in 1968].

Mozawa Michinao 茂澤方尚. 1991. "*Kanpishi* 'Chokurei' hen to *Shōkunsho* 'Kinrei' hen' ryōhen no zengo kankei ni tsuite" 『韓非子』「飭令」篇と『商君書』「靳令」篇——両篇の前後関係について. *Komazawa shigaku* 駒澤史學 43:1-23.

Mozi chengshou gepian jianzhu 墨子城守各篇簡注. 2005. Compiled by Cen Zhongmian 岑仲勉 (1886-1961). Beijing: Zhonghua shuju.

Mozi jiaozhu 墨子校注. 1994. Compiled and annotated by Wu Yujiang 吳毓江 (1898-1977). Beijing: Zhonghua shuju.

Nivison, David S. 1999. "The Classical Philosophical Writings." In *The Cambridge History of Ancient China*, ed. Michael Loewe and Edward L. Shaughnessy, 745-812. Cambridge: Cambridge University Press.

Nylan, Michael. 1992. *The Shifting Center: The Original "Great Plan" and Later Readings*. Monumenta Serica Monograph Series 24. Nettetal, Germany: Steyler.

Ōchi Shigeaki 越智重明. 1993. *Sengoku Shin Kan shi kenkyū* 戰國秦漢史研究. Vol. 2. Fukuoka: Chūgoku Shoten.

Ōkushi Atsuhiro 大櫛敦弘. 1999. "Shin hō—Unmei Suikochi Shin kan yori mita toitsu zenya" 秦邦—雲夢睡虎地秦簡よち見た「統一前夜」. In *Ronshū: Chūgoku kodai no moji to bunka* 論集: 中國古代の文字と文化, 319-332. Tokyo: Kyūko shoin.

Pang Pu. 2000. "A Comparison of the Bamboo Slip and the Silk Manuscript *Wu Xing*." *Contemporary Chinese Thought* 32, no. 1: 50-57.

Perelomov, Leonard S. 1968. *Kniga Pravitelia Oblasti Shan (Shang jun shu)*. Moscow: Nauka.

——. 1993. *Kniga Pravitelia Oblasti Shan (Shang jun shu)*. With a new afterword. Moscow: Ladomir.

Petersen, Jens Østergård. 1995. "Which Books Did the First Emperor of Ch'in Burn? On the Meaning of *Pai Chia* in Early Chinese Sources." *Monumenta Serica* 43:1-52.

Pines, Yuri. 2000a. "Disputers of the Li: Breakthroughs in the Concept of Ritual in Pre-imperial China." *Asia Major*, Third Series, 13, no. 1: 1–41.

——. 2000b. " 'The One That Pervades the All' in Ancient Chinese Political Thought: The Origins of 'the Great Unity' Paradigm." *T'oung Pao* 86, nos. 4–5: 280–324.

——. 2002a. *Foundations of Confucian Thought: Intellectual Life in the Chunqiu Period, 722–453 B.C.E.* Honolulu: University of Hawai'i Press.

——. 2002b. "Lexical Changes in Zhanguo Texts." *Journal of the American Oriental Society* 122, no. 4: 691–705.

——. 2005a. "Bodies, Lineages, Citizens, and Regions: A Review of Mark Edward Lewis' *The Construction of Space in Early China*." *Early China* 30:155–188.

——. 2005b. "Disputers of Abdication: Zhanguo Egalitarianism and the Sovereign's Power." *T'oung Pao* 91, nos. 4–5: 243–300.

——. 2009. *Envisioning Eternal Empire: Chinese Political Thought of the Warring States Era.* Honolulu: University of Hawai'i Press.

——. 2012a. "Alienating Rhetoric in the *Book of Lord Shang* and Its Moderation." *Extrême-Orient, Extrême-Occident* 34:79–110.

——. 2012b. *The Everlasting Empire: Traditional Chinese Political Culture and Its Enduring Legacy.* Princeton: Princeton University Press.

——. 2013a. "Between Merit and Pedigree: Evolution of the Concept of 'Elevating the Worthy' in Pre-imperial China." In *The Idea of Political Meritocracy: Confucian Politics in Contemporary Context*, ed. Daniel Bell and Li Chenyang, 161–202. Cambridge: Cambridge University Press.

——. 2013b. "From Historical Evolution to the End of History: Past, Present, and Future from Shang Yang to the First Emperor." In *Dao Companion to the Philosophy of Han Fei*, ed. Paul Goldin, 25–46. Dordrecht: Springer.

——. 2014a. "Introduction to Part III: The First Emperor and His Image." In *Birth of an Empire: The State of Qin Revisited*, ed. Yuri Pines, Lothar von Falkenhausen, Gideon Shelach, and Robin D. S. Yates, 227–238. Berkeley: University of California Press.

——. 2014b. "Legalism in Chinese Philosophy." In *Stanford Encyclopedia of Philosophy*, ed. Edward N. Zalta et al. Stanford: Stanford University. http://plato.stanford .edu/entries/chinese-legalism/.

——. 2014c. "The Messianic Emperor: A New Look at Qin's Place in China's History." In *Birth of an Empire: The State of Qin Revisited*, ed. Yuri Pines, Lothar von Falkenhausen, Gideon Shelach, and Robin D. S. Yates, 258–279. Berkeley: University of California Press.

——. 2015. "Introduction: Ideology and Power in Early China." In *Ideology of Power and Power of Ideology in Early China*, ed. Yuri Pines, Paul R. Goldin, and Martin Kern, 1–28. Leiden: Brill.

——. 2016a. "Dating a Pre-imperial Text: The Case Study of the *Book of Lord Shang*." *Early China* 39:145–184.

——. 2016b. "A 'Total War?' Rethinking Military Ideology in the *Book of Lord Shang*." *Journal of Chinese Military History* 5, no. 2:97–134.

——. 2016c. "Social Engineering in Early China: The Ideology of the *Shangjunshu* (*Book of Lord Shang*) Revisited." *Oriens Extremus* 55 (2016): 1–37.

——. Forthcoming A. "Agriculturalism and Beyond: Economic Thought of the *Book of Lord Shang*." In *Between Command and Market: Economic Thought and Practice in Early China*, ed. Elisa Sabattini and Christian Schwermann. Leiden: Brill.

——. Forthcoming B. "'To Die for the Sanctity of the Name:' Name (*ming* 名) as Prime-Mover of Political Action in Early China." In *Keywords in Chinese Thought and Literature*, ed. Li Wai-yee and Yuri Pines. Hong Kong: The Chinese University Press.

Pines, Yuri and Gideon Shelach. 2005. "'Using the Past to Serve the Present:' Comparative Perspectives on Chinese and Western Theories of the Origins of the State." In *Genesis and Regeneration: Essays on Conceptions of Origins*, ed. Shaul Shaked, 127–163. Jerusalem: Israel Academy of Science and Humanities.

Pines, Yuri, with Lothar von Falkenhausen, Gideon Shelach, and Robin D. S. Yates. 2014. "General Introduction: Qin History Revisited." In *Birth of an Empire: The State of Qin Revisited*, ed. Yuri Pines, Lothar von Falkenhausen, Gideon Shelach, and Robin D.S. Yates, 1–36. Berkeley: University of California Press.

Pines, Yuri, and Carine Defoort, eds. 2016a. *Chinese Academic Views on Shang Yang Since the Open-up-and-Reform Era*. Published as a special issue of *Contemporary Chinese Thought*, 47, no. 2.

——. 2016b. "Chinese Academic Views on Shang Yang Since the Open-up-and-Reform Era." *Contemporary Chinese Thought* 47, no. 2: 59–68.

Puett, Michael J. 2001. *The Ambivalence of Creation: Debates Concerning Innovation and Artifice in Early China*. Stanford: Stanford University Press.

Qi Sihe 齊思和. [1947] 2001. "*Shang Yang bianfa kao*" 商鞅變法考. Reprinted in Qi Sihe, *Zhongguo shi tanyan* 中國史探研, 247–278. Shijiazhuang: Hebei jiaoyu chubanshe.

Qian Mu 錢穆. [1935] 2001. *Xian Qin zhuzi xi nian* 先秦諸子繫年. Reprint. Beijing: Shangwu yinshuaguan.

Qian Zongfan 錢宗範. 1989. "Xizhou Chunqiu shidai de shilu shiguan zhidu ji qi pohuai" 西周春秋時代的世祿世官制度及其破壞. *Zhongguoshi yanjiu* 中國史研究 3:20–30.

Qunshu zhiyao 群書治要. [631] 1996–2002. Compiled by Wei Zheng 魏徵 (580–643). Reprinted as vol. 1187 of *Xuxiu Siku quanshu* 續修四庫全書. Shanghai: Shanghai guji chubanshe.

Richter, Matthias L. 2013. *The Embodied Text: Establishing Textual Identity in Early Chinese Manuscripts*. Leiden: Brill.

Rickett, W. Allyn, trans. 1998. *Guanzi: Political, Economic, and Philosophical Essays from Early China*. Vol. 2. Princeton: Princeton University Press.

——, trans. 2001. *Guanzi: Political, Economic, and Philosophical Essays from Early China.* Vol. 1. Rev. ed. Boston: Cheng and Tsui.

Rong Zhaozu 容肇祖. 1937. *"Shangjunshu kaozheng"* 商君書考證. *Yanjing xuebao* 燕京學報 21:61–118.

Rubin, Vitaly. 1976. *Individual and State in Ancient China.* New York: Columbia University Press.

——. 1999. *Lichnost' i vlast' v drevnem Kitae: Sobranie Trudov.* Moscow: "Vostochnaia literatura" RAN.

Sabattini, Elisa Levi. 2017. "How to Surpass the Qin: On Jia Yi's Intentions in the *Guo Qin lun." Monumenta Serica* 65, no. 2: 263–284.

Sage, Steven F. 1992. *Ancient Sichuan and the Unification of China.* Albany: State University of New York Press.

Sanft, Charles. 2011. "The Moment of Dying: Representations in Liu Xiang's Anthologies *Xin xu* and *Shuo yuan." Asia Major,* Third Series, 24, no. 1: 127–158.

——. 2014a. *Communication and Cooperation in Early Imperial China.* Albany: State University of New York Press.

——. 2014b. "Shang Yang Was a Cooperator: Applying Axelrod's Analysis of Cooperation in Early China." *Philosophy East and West* 64, no. 1: 174–191.

——. 2015. "Population Records from Liye: Ideology in Practice." In *Ideology of Power and Power of Ideology in Early China,* ed. Yuri Pines, Paul R. Goldin, and Martin Kern, 249–269. Leiden: Brill.

——. 2017. "Concepts of Law in the *Shangshu."* In *The* Classic of Documents *and the Origins of Chinese Political Philosophy,* ed. Martin Kern and Dirk Meyer, 446–474. Leiden: Brill.

Sanguo zhi 三國志. 1997. By Chen Shou 陳壽 (233–297). Annotated by Pei Songzhi 裴松之. Beijing: Zhonghua shuju.

Sato Masayuki. 2000. "The Development of Pre-Qin Conceptual Terms and Their Incorporation Into Xunzi's Thought." In *Linked Faiths: Essays on Chinese Religions and Traditional Culture in Honor of Kristofer Schipper,* ed. Jan A. M. de Meyer and Peter M. Engelfriet, 18–40. Leiden: Brill.

——. 2003. *The Confucian Quest for Order: The Origin and Formation of the Political Thought of Xun Zi.* Leiden: Brill.

——. 2013a. "Did Xunzi's Theory of Human Nature Provide the Foundation for the Political Thought of Han Fei?" In *Dao Companion to the Philosophy of Han Fei,* ed. Paul R. Goldin, 147–165. Dordrecht: Springer.

—— 佐藤將之. 2013b. *Xunzi lizhi sixiang de yuanyuan yu Zhanguo zhuzi zhi yanjiu* 荀子禮治思想的淵源與戰國諸子之研究. Taida zhexue congshu 8. Taibei: Taida chuban zhongxin.

Sawyer, Ralph D., trans. 1993. *The Seven Military Classics of Ancient China.* Boulder: Westview.

Schaberg, David. 2001a. *A Patterned Past: Form and Thought in Early Chinese Historiography.* Cambridge, Mass.: Harvard University Asia Center.

——. 2001b. "'Sell It! Sell It!:' Recent Translations of *Lunyu*." *Chinese Literature: Essays, Articles, Reviews (CLEAR)* 23:115–139.

——. 2011. "Chinese History and Philosophy." In *The Oxford History of Historical Writing*, vol. 1: *Beginnings to AD 600*, ed. Andrew Feldherr and Grant Hardy, 394–414. Oxford: Oxford University Press.

Schram, Stuart R. 1989. *The Thought of Mao Tse-Tung*. Cambridge: Cambridge University Press.

——, ed. 1992–2004. *Mao's Road to Power: Revolutionary Writings 1912-1949*. 7 vols. Armonk, N.Y.: M. E. Sharpe.

Schwartz, Benjamin I. 1985. *The World of Thought in Ancient China*. Cambridge, Mass.: Harvard University Press.

Schwermann, Christian. Forthcoming. "From Theory to Practice? Putting Chao Cuo's Memorials on Economics and Finance Into Historical Perspective." In *Between Command and Market: Economic Thought and Practice in Early China*, ed. Elisa Sabattini and Christian Schwermann. Leiden: Brill.

Scott, James. C. 1998. *Seeing Like a State: How Certain Schemes to Improve the Human Condition Have Failed*. New Haven: Yale University Press.

Sellmann, James D. 2002. *Timing and Rulership in Master Lü's* Spring and Autumn Annals (Lüshi chunqiu). Albany: State University of New York Press.

Shang Yang fenyi kaogudui. 2006. "Shaanxi Danfeng Xian Qin Shangyi yizhi" 陝西丹鳳縣秦商邑遺址. *Kaogu* 考古 3:32–38.

Shangshu zhengyi 尚書正義. [1815] 1991. Annotated by Kong Yingda 孔穎達 (574–648). Reprinted in *Shisan jing zhushu fu jiaokanji* 十三經注疏附校勘記, 2 vols., compiled by Ruan Yuan 阮元 (1764–1849), 1:109–258. Beijing: Zhonghua shuju.

Shangzi tiyao 商子提要. [1778] n.d. By Ji Yun 紀昀 (1724–1805) et al. E-*Siku quanshu* edition.

Shaughnessy, Edward L. 2014. "The Qin *Biannian ji* 編年記 and the Beginnings of Historical Writing in China." In *Beyond the First Emperor's Mausoleum: New Perspectives on Qin Art*, ed. Liu Yang, 115–136. Minneapolis: Minneapolis Institute of Arts.

Shelach, Gideon. 2014. "Collapse or Transformation? Anthropological and Archaeological Perspectives on the Fall of Qin." In *Birth of an Empire: The State of Qin Revisited*, ed. Yuri Pines, Lothar von Falkenhausen, Gideon Shelach, and Robin D. S. Yates, 113–140. Berkeley: University of California Press.

Shelach, Gideon and Yuri Pines. 2006. "Secondary State Formation and the Development of Local Identity: Change and Continuity in the State of Qin (770–221 B.C.)." In *Archaeology of Asia*, ed. Miriam T. Stark, 202–230. Malden, Mass.: Blackwell.

Shen Gang 沈剛. 2003. *Qin Han shiqi de ke jieceng yanjiu* 秦漢時期的客階層研究. Changchun: Jilin wenshi chubanshe.

Shenzi jijiao jizhu 慎子集校集注. 2013. Collated by Xu Fuhong 許富宏. Beijing: Zhonghua shuju.

Shiji 史記. 1997. By Sima Qian 司馬遷 (ca. 145–90 B.C.E.) et al. Annotated by Zhang Shoujie 張守節, Sima Zhen 司馬貞, and Pei Yin 裴駰. Beijing: Zhonghua shuju.

Shimada Kenji. 1990. *Pioneer of the Chinese Revolution: Zhang Binglin and Confucianism*. Stanford: Stanford University Press.

Shuihudi Qinmu zhujian 睡虎地秦墓竹簡. [1990] 2001. Ed. Shuihudi Qinmu zhujian zhengli xiaozu 睡虎地秦墓竹簡整理小組. Reprint. Beijing: Wenwu chubanshe.

Slingerland, Edward. 2003. *Effortless Action: Wu-wei as Conceptual Metaphor and Spiritual Ideal in Early China*. Oxford: Oxford University Press.

Smith, Kidder. 2003. "Sima Tan and the Invention of Daoism, 'Legalism,' *et Cetera*." *Journal of Asian Studies* 62, no. 1: 129–156.

Sterckx, Roel. 2015. "Ideologies of the Peasant and Merchant in Warring States China." In *Ideology of Power and Power of Ideology in Early China*, ed. Yuri Pines, Paul R. Goldin, and Martin Kern, 211–248. Leiden: Brill.

Suishu 隋書. 1997. By Wei Zheng 魏徵 (580–643) et al. Beijing: Zhonghua shuju.

Sun Yirang 孫詒讓, annotator. [1894] 2015. *Shangzi zhayi* 商子札迻. Reprinted in *Zizang: Fajia bu: Shangjunshu juan* 子藏·法家部·商君書卷, 9 vols., ed. Fang Yong 方勇, 6:45–58. Beijing: Guojia tushuguan chubanshe.

Tao Hongqing 陶鴻慶, annotator. [n.d.] 2015. *Du Shangjunshu zhaji* 讀商君書札記. Reprinted in *Zizang: Fajia bu: Shangjunshu juan* 子藏·法家部·商君書卷, 9 vols., ed. Fang Yong 方勇, 7:1–16. Beijing: Guojia tushuguan chubanshe.

Teng Mingyu 滕銘予. 2003. *Qin wenhua: cong fengguo dao diguo de kaoguxue guancha* 秦文化: 從封國到帝國的考古學觀察. Beijing: Xueyuan chubanshe.

——. 2014. "From Vassal State to Empire: An Archaeological Examination of Qin Culture." Trans. Susanna Lam. In *The Birth of Empire: The State of Qin Revisited*, ed. Yuri Pines, Lothar von Falkenhausen, Gideon Shelach, and Robin D. S. Yates, 71–112. Berkeley: University of California Press.

Tomita Michie 富田美智江. 2010. "Sengoku jidai no Kōshoku zō—ken ron Shōhaku So kan Kōshoku" 戰國時代の后稷像—兼論上博楚簡后稷. *Chūgoku shutsudo shiryō kenkyū* 中國出土資料研究 14:34–58.

Tong dian 通典. n.d. Compiled by Du You 杜佑 (735–812). E-*Siku quanshu* edition.

Tong Weimin 仝衛敏. 2007. "Zhou Shi 'She bi' kao" 周氏〈涉筆〉考. *Guji zhengli yanjiu xuekan* 古籍整理研究學刊 1:89–93.

——. 2008. "*Shang jun shu*, 'Laimin pian' chengshu xintan" 《商君書·徠民篇》成書新探. *Shixue shi yanjiu* 史學史研究 3: 79–85. (English translation in *Contemporary Chinese Thought* 47.2 [2016]: 138–151.)

——. 2012. "Cong Shuihudi Qin jian kan '*xiao, tu, cao*' de shenfen" 從睡虎地秦簡看 "校、徒、操" 的身份. *Zhongguo guojia bowuguan guankan* 中國國家博物館館刊 12:68–72.

——. 2013. *Chutu wenxian yu Shangjunshu zonghe yanjiu* 出土文獻與《商君書》綜合研究. Vols. 16–17 of *Gudian wenxian yanjiu jikan* 古典文獻研究輯刊, ed. Pan Meiyue 潘美月 and Du Jiexiang 杜潔祥. Taibei: Hua Mulan chubanshe.

Tong zhi 通志. n.d. Compiled by Zheng Qiao 鄭樵 (1104–1162). E-*Siku quanshu* edition.

Vandermeersch, Léon. 1965. *La formation du légisme*. Paris: École Française d'Extrême Orient.

Van Els, Paul and Sarah A. Queen, eds. 2017. *Between Philosophy and History: Rhetorical Uses of Anecdotes in Early China*. Albany: State University of New York Press.

Vankeerberghen, Griet. 2001. *The Huainanzi and Liu An's Claim to Moral Authority*. Albany: State University of New York Press.

Van Norden, Bryan W. 1996. "What Should Western Philosophy Learn from Chinese Philosophy?" In *Chinese Language, Thought, and Culture: Nivison and His Critics*, ed. Philip J. Ivanhoe, 224–249. La Salle, Ill.: Open Court.

Vogelsang, Kai, trans. 2017. *Shangjun shu: Schriften des Fürsten von Shang*. Stuttgart: Alfred Kröner.

Wagner, Donald B. 1993. *Iron and Steel in Ancient China*. Leiden: Brill.

Wang Hui 王輝. 1990. *Qin chutu wenxian biannian* 秦出土文獻編年. Taibei: Xinfeng.

Wang Shilong 王世龍. 2012. *Diguo jiansheshi—Shang Yang* 帝國建設師——商鞅. Beijing: Zhongguo gongren chubanshe.

Wang Shirun 王時潤, annotator. [1915] 2015. *Shangjunshu jiaoquan* 商君書斠詮. Reprinted in *Zizang: Fajia bu: Shangjunshu juan* 子藏·法家部·商君書卷, 9 vols., ed. Fang Yong 方勇, 7:49–223. Beijing: Guojia tushuguan chubanshe.

Wang Zijin 王子今. 2012. *Qin Han shehui yishi yanjiu*. 秦漢社會意識研究. Beijing: Shangwu.

Watson, Burton, trans. 1993. *Records of the Grand Historian*. Vol. 3: *Qin Dynasty*. Hong Kong: Chinese University of Hong Kong.

Wei Qingyuan 韋慶遠. 1999. *Zhang Juzheng he Mingdai zhonghouqi zhengju* 張居正和明代中後期政局. Guangzhou: Guangdong gaodeng jiaoyu chubanshe.

Wenxian ji 文憲集. n.d. By Song Lian 宋濂 (1310–1381). E-*Siku quanshu* edition.

Wenxian tongkao 文獻通考. n.d. By Ma Duanlin 馬端臨 (1254–1332). E-*Siku quanshu* edition.

Williams, Bernard. 1985. *Ethics and the Limits of Philosophy*. Cambridge, Mass.: Harvard University Press.

Wittfogel, Karl A. 1957. *Oriental Despotism: A Comparative Study of Total Power*. New Haven: Yale University Press.

Wong, Young-tsu. 2010. *Beyond Confucian China: The Rival Discourses of Kang Youwei and Zhang Binglin*. London and New York: Routledge.

Wu Baoping 吳保平 and Lin Cunguang 林存光. 2015. "Shang Yang zhi 'fa' de zhengzhi zhexue fansi: Jianlun fazhi de gongneng, jiazhi he jingshen" 商鞅之 "法" 的政治哲學反思——兼論法治的功能、價值和精神. *Wuhan daxue xuebao (zhexue, shehuikexue ban)* 武漢大學學報 (哲學社會科學版) 68, no. 3: 86–91. (English translation in *Contemporary Chinese Thought* 47.2 [2016]: 125–137.)

Wu Jie 吳傑. 1992. "*Shangjunshu* yu dang'an guanli"《商君書》與檔案管理. *Zheji-ang dang'an* 浙江檔案 2:39.

Wu Yujiang 吳毓江. 1994. "*Mozi gepian zhenwei kao*" 墨子各篇真偽考. In *Mozi jiaozhu* 墨子校注, compiled and annotated by Wu Yujiang, 1025–55. Beijing: Zhonghua shuju.

Xiao Yang. 2006. "When Political Philosophy Meets Moral Psychology: Expressiv-ism in the *Mencius*." *Dao* 5, no. 2: 257–71.

Xinshu jiaozhu 新書校注. 2000. By Jia Yi 賈誼 (201–168 B.C.E.). Ed. Yan Zhenyi 閻振益 and Zhong Xia 鍾夏. Beijing: Zhonghua shuju.

Xu Jianliang 許建良. 2012. *Xian Qin fajia de daode shijie* 先秦法家的道德世界. Beijing: Renmin chubanshe.

Xunzi jijie 荀子集解. 1992. Annotated by Wang Xianqian 王先謙 (1842–1917). Ed. Shen Xiaohuan 沈嘯寰 and Wang Xingxian 王星賢. Beijing: Zhonghua shuju.

Yang Kuan 楊寬. 1998. *Zhanguo shi* 戰國史. Rev. ed. Shanghai: Renmin chubanshe.

Yang, Soon-Ja. 2010. "The Secular Foundation of Rulership: The Political Thought of Han Feizi (ca. 280–233 B.C.) and His Predecessors." Ph.D. diss., University of Pennsylvania.

Yang Xiaoshan. 2007. "Wang Anshi's 'Mingfei qu' and the Poetics of Disagreement." *Chinese Literature: Essays, Articles, Reviews (CLEAR)* 29:55–84.

Yang Zhenhong 楊振紅. 2015. *Chutu jiandu yu Qin Han shehui (xubian)* 出土簡牘與秦漢社會（續編）. Guilin: Guangxi Shifan Daxue chubanshe.

Yantielun jiaozhu 鹽鐵論校注. 1996. Compiled by Huan Kuan 桓寬 (first century B.C.E.). Annotated by Wang Liqi 王利器. Beijing: Zhonghua shuju.

Yates, Robin D. S. 1979. "The Mohists on Warfare: Technology, Technique, and Jus-tification." In "Studies in Classical Chinese Thought," ed. Henry Rosemont Jr. and Benjamin I. Schwartz, thematic issue of *Journal of the American Academy of Religion* 47, no. 3: 549–603.

——. 1987. "Social Status in the Ch'in: Evidence from the Yün-meng Legal Docu-ments. Part One: Commoners." *Harvard Journal of Asiatic Studies* 47, no. 1: 197–236.

——. 1994. "Early Poliorcetics: The Mohists to the Sung." In *The Science and Civilisation in China*, vol. 5, pt. 6: *Military Technology: Missiles, and Sieges*, ed. Joseph Needham and Robin D. S. Yates, with the collaboration of Krzysztof Gawlikowski, Edward McEwen, and Wang Ling, 241–485. Cambridge: Cambridge University Press.

——. 1999. "Early China." In *War and Society in the Ancient and Medieval Worlds: Asia, the Mediterranean, Europe, and Mesoamerica*, ed. Kurt Raaflaub and Nathan Rosen-stein, 7–45. Washington, D.C.: Center for Hellenic Studies, Trustees for Har-vard University and Harvard University Press.

——. 2002. "Slavery in Early China: A Socio-cultural Perspective." *Journal of East Asian Archaeology* 3, nos. 1–2: 283–331.

——. 2003. "The Horse in Early Chinese Military History." In *Junshi zuzhi yu zhan-zheng* 軍事組織與戰爭 (Papers from the Third International Conference on

Sinology, History Section), ed. Huang Kewu 黃克武, 1–78. Taibei: Institute of Modern History Academia Sinica.

——. 2004. "Texts on the Military and Government from Yinqueshan: Introductions and Preliminary Transcriptions." In *Xin chu jianbo yanjiu* 新出簡帛研究, ed. Sarah Allan (Ailan 艾蘭) and Xing Wen 邢文, 334–387. Beijing: Wenwu.

——. 2009. "Law and the Military in Early China." In *Military Culture in Imperial China*, ed. Nicola Di Cosmo, 23–44; 341–343. Cambridge, MA: Harvard University Press.

——. 2012–2013. "The Qin Slips and Boards from Well No. 1, Liye, Hunan: A Brief Introduction to the Qin Qianling County Archives." *Early China* 35–36:291–330.

—— [Ye Shan 葉山]. 2013. "Jiedu Liye Qinjian—Qindai difang xingzheng zhidu" 解讀里耶秦簡—秦代地方行政制度. *Jianbo* 8:89–138.

Yi shi 繹史. n.d. By Ma Su 馬驌 (1621–1673). E-*Siku quanshu* edition.

Yi Zhou shu huijiao jizhu 逸周書匯校集注. 1995. Compiled by Huang Huaixin 黃懷信 et al. Shanghai: Shanghai guji chubanshe.

Yin Tongyang 尹桐陽, annotator. [1923] 2015. *Shangjunshu xin shi* 商君書新釋. Reprinted in *Zizang: Fajia bu: Shangjunshu juan* 子藏·法家部·商君書卷, 9 vols., ed. Fang Yong 方勇, 8:5–126. Beijing: Guojia tushuguan chubanshe.

Yinqueshan 銀雀山. 2010. *2 Yinqueshan Hanmu zhujian (er)* 銀雀山漢墓竹簡 (貳). Ed. Yinqueshan Hanmu zhujian zhengli xiaozu 銀雀山漢墓竹簡整理小組. Beijing: Wenwu.

Yoshimoto Michimasa 吉本道雅. 2000. "Shō Kun henhō kenkyū josetsu" 商君變法研究序說. *Shirin* 史林 83–84:1–29.

Yoshinami Takashi 好并隆司. 1985. "Shōkunsho Raimin, Sanchi ryōhen yori mita Shinchō kenryōku no keisei katei" 商君書徠民、算地兩篇よりみた秦朝權力の形成過程. *Tōyōshi kenkyū* 44, no. 1: 1–22.

——. 1992. *Shōkunsho kenkyū* 商君書研究. Hiroshima: Keisuisha.

Yu Chang 于鬯, annotator. [n.d.] 2015. *Shangjunshu jiaoshu* 商君書校書. Reprinted in *Zizang: Fajia bu: Shangjunshu juan* 子藏·法家部·商君書卷, 9 vols., ed. Fang Yong 方勇, 6:59–94 (a handwritten draft), 6:95–114 (a reprint of the 1963 Zhonghua shuju version). Beijing: Guojia tushuguan chubanshe.

Yu Yue 俞樾, annotator. [1885] 2015. *Shangzi pingyi* 商子平議. Reprinted in *Zizang: Fajia bu: Shangjunshu juan* 子藏·法家部·商君書卷, 9 vols., ed. Fang Yong 方勇, 6:1–44. Beijing: Guojia tushuguan chubanshe.

Yu Zhenbo 于振波. 2010. "Qin lü zhong de jiadun bijia ji xiangguan wenti" 秦律中的甲盾比價及相關問題. *Shixue jikan* 史學集刊 5:36–38.

Yu Zhong 喻中. 2016. "Fajia sanqi lun" 法家三期論. *Faxue pinglun* 法學評論 3: 173–184.

Yuan Lin 袁林. 2000. *Liang Zhou tudi zhidu xin lun* 兩周土地制度新論. Changchun: Dongbei shifan daxue.

Yuan Zhongyi 袁仲一. 1993. "Du Qin Huiwen wang si nian wa shu" 讀秦惠文王四年瓦書. *Qin wenhua luncong* 秦文化論叢 1:275–285.

Zarrow, Peter. 2012. *After Empire: The Conceptual Transformation of the Chinese State, 1885-1924*. Stanford: Stanford University Press.

Zeng Zhenyu 曾振宇. 2003. "Lishi de Shang Yang yu fuhaohua de Shang Yang" 歷史的商鞅與符號化的商鞅. *Qilu xuekan* 齊魯學刊 6:115–120. (English translation in *Contemporary Chinese Thought* 47, no. 2 [2016]: 69–89.)

Zhang Binglin 章炳麟. [1900] 1996-2002. *Qiu shu* 訄書. Reprinted in *Xuxiu Siku quanshu* 續修四庫全書, 953:549–784. Shanghai: Shanghai guji chubanshe.

Zhang Jue 張覺, annotator. 1993. *Shangjunshu quanyi* 商君書全譯. Guiyang: Guizhou renmin chubanshe.

——, annotator. 2006. *Shangjunshu jiaozhu* 商君書校注. Changsha: Yuelu shushe.

——, comp. and annotator. 2012. *Shangjunshu jiaoshu* 商君書校疏. Beijing: Zhishi chanquan chubanshe.

Zhang Linxiang 張林祥. 2006. "Jinbuguan haishi bianyiguan: *Shangjunshu* lishiguan zai renshi" 進步觀還是變異觀——《商君書》歷史觀再認識. *Xibei Shida xuebao (shehuikexue ban)* 西北師大學報 (社會科學版) 43, no. 3: 82–89. (English translation in *Contemporary Chinese Thought* 47.2 [2016]: 90–111.)

——. 2008. "*Shang jun shu*" *de chengshu yu sixiang yanjiu* 《商君書》的成書與思想研究. Beijing: Renmin chubanshe.

Zhangjiashan Hanmu zhujian (er si qi hao mu) 張家山漢墓竹簡 (二四七號墓). 2001. Published by Zhangjiashan Hanmu zhujian zhengli xiaozu 張家山漢墓竹簡整理小組. Beijing: Wenwu chubanshe.

Zhanguo ce zhushi 戰國策注釋. 1991. Annotated by He Jianzhang 何建章. Beijing: Zhonghua shuju.

Zhao Boxiong 趙伯雄. 1990. *Zhoudai guojia xingtai yanjiu* 周代國家形態研究. Changsha: Hunan jiaoyu.

Zhao Ming 趙明. 2013. *Da biange shidai de lifazhe—Shang Yang de zhengzhi rensheng* 大變革時代的立法者——商鞅的政治人生. Beijing: Beijing daxue chubanshe.

Zhao Yuzhuo 趙玉卓. 2010. "Gaige kaifang yilai *Shang jun shu* yanjiu zongshu" 改革開放以來《商君書》研究綜述. *Taiyuan chengshi zhiye jishu xueyuan xuebao* 太原城市職業技術學院學報 1:52–53.

Zheng Liangshu 鄭良樹. 1989. *Shang Yang ji qi xuepai* 商鞅及其學派. Shanghai: Shanghai guji chubanshe.

Zhizhai shulu jieti 直齋書錄解題. n.d. By Chen Zhensun 陳振孫 (ca. 1183–1262). E*Siku quanshu* edition.

Zhu Shaohou 朱紹侯. 2008. *Jungong juezhi kaolun* 軍功爵制考論. Beijing: Shangwu yinshuguan.

Zhu Shizhe 朱師轍, annotator. [1948] 1956. *Shangjunshu jiegu dingben* 商君書解詁定本. Reprint. Beijing: Guji chubanshe.

——, annotator. [1948] 2015. *Shangjunshu jiegu dingben* 商君書解詁定本. Reprinted in *Zizang: Fajia bu: Shangjunshu juan* 子藏·法家部·商君書卷, 9 vols., ed. Fang Yong 方勇, 7:483–641. Beijing: Guojia tushuguan chubanshe.

Zhu Yongjia 朱永嘉. 2013. *Shang Yang bianfa yu Wang Mang gaizhi* 商鞅變法與王莽改制. Beijing: Zhongguo chang'an chubanshe.

Zhuangzi jinzhu jinyi 莊子今注今譯. 1994. Annotated by Chen Guying 陳鼓應. Beijing: Zhonghua shuju.

Zizhi tongjian 資治通鑒. 1992. By Sima Guang 司馬光 (1019–1086). Annotated by Hu Sanxing 胡三省 (1230–1302). Beijing: Zhonghua shuju.

Zuo zhuan. See *Chunqiu Zuozhuan zhu.*

INDEX

Cold Mountain: 100 Poems by the T'ang Poet Han-shan, tr. Burton Watson. Also in paperback ed. 1970

Twenty Plays of the Nō Theatre, ed. Donald Keene. Also in paperback ed. 1970

Chūshingura: The Treasury of Loyal Retainers, tr. Donald Keene. Also in paperback ed. 1971; rev. ed. 1997

The Zen Master Hakuin: Selected Writings, tr. Philip B. Yampolsky 1971

Chinese Rhyme-Prose: Poems in the Fu Form from the Han and Six Dynasties Periods, tr. Burton Watson. Also in paperback ed. 1971

Kūkai: Major Works, tr. Yoshito S. Hakeda. Also in paperback ed. 1972

The Old Man Who Does as He Pleases: Selections from the Poetry and Prose of Lu Yu, tr. Burton Watson 1973

The Lion's Roar of Queen Śrīmālā, tr. Alex and Hideko Wayman 1974

Courtier and Commoner in Ancient China: Selections from the History of the Former Han by Pan Ku, tr. Burton Watson. Also in paperback ed. 1974

Japanese Literature in Chinese, vol. 1: Poetry and Prose in Chinese by Japanese Writers of the Early Period, tr. Burton Watson 1975

Japanese Literature in Chinese, vol. 2: Poetry and Prose in Chinese by Japanese Writers of the Later Period, tr. Burton Watson 1976

Love Song of the Dark Lord: Jayadeva's Gītagovinda, tr. Barbara Stoler Miller. Also in paperback ed. Cloth ed. includes critical text of the Sanskrit. 1977; rev. ed. 1997

Ryōkan: Zen Monk-Poet of Japan, tr. Burton Watson 1977

Calming the Mind and Discerning the Real: From the Lam rim chen mo of Tsoṇkha-pa, tr. Alex Wayman 1978

The Hermit and the Love-Thief: Sanskrit Poems of Bhartrihari and Bilhaṇa, tr. Barbara Stoler Miller 1978

The Lute: Kao Ming's P'i-p'a chi, tr. Jean Mulligan. Also in paperback ed. 1980

A Chronicle of Gods and Sovereigns: Jinnō Shōtōki of Kitabatake Chikafusa, tr. H. Paul Varley 1980

Among the Flowers: The Hua-chien chi, tr. Lois Fusek 1982

Grass Hill: Poems and Prose by the Japanese Monk Gensei, tr. Burton Watson 1983

Doctors, Diviners, and Magicians of Ancient China: Biographies of Fang-shih, tr. Kenneth J. DeWoskin. Also in paperback ed. 1983

Theater of Memory: The Plays of Kālidāsa, ed. Barbara Stoler Miller. Also in paperback ed. 1984

The Columbia Book of Chinese Poetry: From Early Times to the Thirteenth Century, ed. and tr. Burton Watson. Also in paperback ed. 1984

Poems of Love and War: From the Eight Anthologies and the Ten Long Poems of Classical Tamil, tr. A. K. Ramanujan. Also in paperback ed. 1985

The Bhagavad Gita: Krishna's Counsel in Time of War, tr. Barbara Stoler Miller 1986

The Columbia Book of Later Chinese Poetry, ed. and tr. Jonathan Chaves. Also in paperback ed. 1986

The Tso Chuan: Selections from China's Oldest Narrative History, tr. Burton Watson 1989

Waiting for the Wind: Thirty-six Poets of Japan's Late Medieval Age, tr. Steven Carter 1989

Selected Writings of Nichiren, ed. Philip B. Yampolsky 1990

Saigyō, Poems of a Mountain Home, tr. Burton Watson 1990

The Book of Lieh Tzu: A Classic of the Tao, tr. A. C. Graham. Morningside ed. 1990

The Tale of an Anklet: An Epic of South India—The Cilappatikāram of Iḷaṅkō Aṭikaḷ, tr. R. Parthasarathy 1993

Waiting for the Dawn: A Plan for the Prince, tr. with introduction by Wm. Theodore de Bary 1993

Yoshitsune and the Thousand Cherry Trees: A Masterpiece of the Eighteenth-Century Japanese Puppet Theater, tr., annotated, and with introduction by Stanleigh H. Jones Jr. 1993

The Lotus Sutra, tr. Burton Watson. Also in paperback ed. 1993

The Classic of Changes: A New Translation of the I Ching as Interpreted by Wang Bi, tr. Richard John Lynn 1994

Beyond Spring: Tz'u Poems of the Sung Dynasty, tr. Julie Landau 1994

The Columbia Anthology of Traditional Chinese Literature, ed. Victor H. Mair 1994

Scenes for Mandarins: The Elite Theater of the Ming, tr. Cyril Birch 1995

Letters of Nichiren, ed. Philip B. Yampolsky; tr. Burton Watson et al. 1996

Unforgotten Dreams: Poems by the Zen Monk Shōtetsu, tr. Steven D. Carter 1997

The Vimalakirti Sutra, tr. Burton Watson 1997

Japanese and Chinese Poems to Sing: The Wakan rōei shū, tr. J. Thomas Rimer and Jonathan Chaves 1997

Breeze Through Bamboo: Kanshi of Ema Saikō, tr. Hiroaki Sato 1998

A Tower for the Summer Heat, by Li Yu, tr. Patrick Hanan 1998

Traditional Japanese Theater: An Anthology of Plays, by Karen Brazell 1998

The Original Analects: Sayings of Confucius and His Successors (0479–0249), by E. Bruce Brooks and A. Taeko Brooks 1998

The Classic of the Way and Virtue: A New Translation of the Tao-te ching of Laozi as Interpreted by Wang Bi, tr. Richard John Lynn 1999

The Four Hundred Songs of War and Wisdom: An Anthology of Poems from Classical Tamil, The Puṟanāṉūṟu, ed. and tr. George L. Hart and Hank Heifetz 1999

Original Tao: Inward Training (Nei-yeh) *and the Foundations of Taoist Mysticism*, by Harold D. Roth 1999

Po Chü-i: Selected Poems, tr. Burton Watson 2000

Lao Tzu's Tao Te Ching: A Translation of the Startling New Documents Found at Guodian, by Robert G. Henricks 2000

The Shorter Columbia Anthology of Traditional Chinese Literature, ed. Victor H. Mair 2000

Mistress and Maid (Jiaohongji), by Meng Chengshun, tr. Cyril Birch 2001

Chikamatsu: Five Late Plays, tr. and ed. C. Andrew Gerstle 2001

The Essential Lotus: Selections from the Lotus Sutra, tr. Burton Watson 2002

Early Modern Japanese Literature: An Anthology, 1600–1900, ed. Haruo Shirane 2002; abridged 2008

The Columbia Anthology of Traditional Korean Poetry, ed. Peter H. Lee 2002

The Sound of the Kiss, or The Story That Must Never Be Told: Pingali Suranna's Kalapurnodayamu, tr. Vecheru Narayana Rao and David Shulman 2003

The Selected Poems of Du Fu, tr. Burton Watson 2003

Far Beyond the Field: Haiku by Japanese Women, tr. Makoto Ueda 2003

Just Living: Poems and Prose by the Japanese Monk Tonna, ed. and tr. Steven D. Carter 2003

Han Feizi: Basic Writings, tr. Burton Watson 2003

Mozi: Basic Writings, tr. Burton Watson 2003

Xunzi: Basic Writings, tr. Burton Watson 2003

Zhuangzi: Basic Writings, tr. Burton Watson 2003

The Awakening of Faith, Attributed to Aśvaghosha, tr. Yoshito S. Hakeda, introduction by Ryuichi Abe 2005

The Tales of the Heike, tr. Burton Watson, ed. Haruo Shirane 2006

Tales of Moonlight and Rain, by Ueda Akinari, tr. with introduction by Anthony H. Chambers 2007

Traditional Japanese Literature: An Anthology, Beginnings to 1600, ed. Haruo Shirane 2007

The Philosophy of Qi, by Kaibara Ekken, tr. Mary Evelyn Tucker 2007

The Analects of Confucius, tr. Burton Watson 2007

The Art of War: Sun Zi's Military Methods, tr. Victor Mair 2007

One Hundred Poets, One Poem Each: A Translation of the Ogura Hyakunin Isshu, tr. Peter McMillan 2008

Zeami: Performance Notes, tr. Tom Hare 2008

Zongmi on Chan, tr. Jeffrey Lyle Broughton 2009

Scripture of the Lotus Blossom of the Fine Dharma, rev. ed., tr. Leon Hurvitz, preface and introduction by Stephen R. Teiser 2009

Mencius, tr. Irene Bloom, ed. with an introduction by Philip J. Ivanhoe 2009

Clouds Thick, Whereabouts Unknown: Poems by Zen Monks of China, Charles Egan 2010

The Mozi: A Complete Translation, tr. Ian Johnston 2010

The Huainanzi: A Guide to the Theory and Practice of Government in Early Han China, by Liu An, tr. and ed. John S. Major, Sarah A. Queen, Andrew Seth Meyer, and Harold D. Roth, with Michael Puett and Judson Murray 2010

The Demon at Agi Bridge and Other Japanese Tales, tr. Burton Watson, ed. with introduction by Haruo Shirane 2011

Haiku Before Haiku: From the Renga Masters to Bashō, tr. with introduction by Steven D. Carter 2011

The Columbia Anthology of Chinese Folk and Popular Literature, ed. Victor H. Mair and Mark Bender 2011

Tamil Love Poetry: The Five Hundred Short Poems of the Aiṅkuṟunūṟu, tr. and ed. Martha Ann Selby 2011

The Teachings of Master Wuzhu: Zen and Religion of No-Religion, by Wendi L. Adamek 2011

The Essential Huainanzi, by Liu An, tr. and ed. John S. Major, Sarah A. Queen, Andrew Seth Meyer, and Harold D. Roth 2012

The Dao of the Military: Liu An's Art of War, tr. Andrew Seth Meyer 2012

Unearthing the Changes: Recently Discovered Manuscripts of the Yi Jing (I Ching) and Related Texts, Edward L. Shaughnessy 2013

Record of Miraculous Events in Japan: The Nihon ryōiki, tr. Burton Watson 2013

The Complete Works of Zhuangzi, tr. Burton Watson 2013

Lust, Commerce, and Corruption: An Account of What I Have Seen and Heard, by an Edo Samurai, tr. and ed. Mark Teeuwen and Kate Wildman Nakai with Miyazaki Fumiko, Anne Walthall, and John Breen 2014

Exemplary Women of Early China: The Lienü zhuan of Liu Xiang, tr. Anne Behnke Kinney 2014

The Columbia Anthology of Yuan Drama, ed. C. T. Hsia, Wai-yee Li, and George Kao 2014

The Resurrected Skeleton: From Zhuangzi to Lu Xun, by Wilt L. Idema 2014

The Sarashina Diary: *A Woman's Life in Eleventh-Century Japan*, by Sugawara no Takasue no Musume, tr. with introduction by Sonja Arntzen and Itō Moriyuki 2014

The Kojiki: *An Account of Ancient Matters*, by Ō no Yasumaro, tr. Gustav Heldt 2014

The Orphan of Zhao *and Other Yuan Plays: The Earliest Known Versions*, tr. and introduced by Stephen H. West and Wilt L. Idema 2014

Luxuriant Gems of the Spring and Autumn, attributed to Dong Zhongshu, ed. and tr. Sarah A. Queen and John S. Major 2016

A Book to Burn and a Book to Keep (Hidden): Selected Writings, by Li Zhi, ed. and tr. Rivi Handler-Spitz, Pauline Lee, and Haun Saussy 2016

The Shenzi Fragments: *A Philosophical Analysis and Translation*, Eirik Lang Harris 2016

A Record of Daily Knowledge and *Poems and Essays*: Selections, by Gu Yanwu, tr. and ed. Ian Johnston 2017

The Book of Lord Shang: Apologetics of State Power in Early China, by Shang Yang, ed. and tr. Yuri Pines 2017

The Songs of Chu: An Ancient Anthology of Works by Qu Yuan and Others, ed. and trans. Gopal Sukhu 2017

Ghalib: Selected Poems and Letters, by Mirza Asadullah Khan Ghalib, tr. Frances W. Pritchett and Owen T. A. Cornwall 2017

Quelling the Demons' Revolt: A Novel from Ming China, attributed to Luo Guanzhong, tr. Patrick Hanan 2017

Erotic Poems from the Sanskrit: A New Translation, R. Parthasarathy 2017

The Book of Swindles: Selections from a Late Ming Collection, by Zhang Yingyu, tr. Christopher G. Rea and Bruce Rusk 2017

Monsters, Animals, and Other Worlds: A Collection of Short Medieval Japanese Tales, ed. R. Keller Kimbrough and Haruo Shirane 2018

Hidden and Visible Realms: Early Medieval Chinese Tales of the Supernatural and the Fantastic, compiled by Liu Yiqing, ed. and tr. Zhenjun Zhang 2018